RESPECT, PLURALISM, AND JUSTICE

Respect, Pluralism, and Justice

Kantian Perspectives

THOMAS E. HILL, JR.

OXFORD
UNIVERSITY PRESS

OXFORD

UNIVERSITY PRESS

Great Clarendon Street, Oxford OX2 6DP

Oxford University Press is a department of the University of Oxford.

It furthers the University's objective of excellence in research, scholarship,
and education by publishing worldwide in

Oxford New York

Athens Auckland Bangkok Bogotá Buenos Aires Calcutta
Cape Town Chennai Dar es Salaam Delhi Florence Hong Kong Istanbul
Karachi Kuala Lumpur Madrid Melbourne Mexico City Mumbai
Nairobi Paris São Paulo Singapore Taipei Tokyo Toronto Warsaw

and associated companies in Berlin Ibadan

Oxford is a registered trade mark of Oxford University Press
in the UK and certain other countries

Published in the United States
by Oxford University Press Inc., New York

British Library Cataloguing in Publication Data

Data available

Library of Congress Cataloging in Publication Data
Hill, Thomas E.
Respect, pluralism, and justice : Kantian perspectives / Thomas E. Hill, Jr.
Includes bibliographical references and index.
1. Kant, Immanuel, 1724–1804—Ethics. 2. Ethics—History—18th century. 3. Respect for persons.
4. Pluralism. 5. Justice. I. Title.
B2799.E8 H555 2000 170'.92—dc21 99–088980
ISBN 0–19–823835–5
ISBN 0–19–823834–7 (Pbk.)

1 3 5 7 9 10 8 6 4 2

Typeset by Best-set Typesetter Ltd., Hong Kong
Printed in Great Britain
on acid-free paper by
T. J. International Ltd
Padstow, Cornwall

SOURCES AND
ACKNOWLEDGEMENTS

I thank the following for permission to reprint the essays in this collection.

'Kantian Pluralism' originally appeared in *Ethics*, 102 (1992), 743–62, © 1992 by the University of Chicago. All rights reserved. It is reprinted here with the permission of the University of Chicago Press.

'A Kantian Perspective on Moral Rules' appeared in James Tomberlin (ed.), *Philosophical Perspectives, 6: Ethics, 1992*. Reprinted by permission of Ridgeview Publishing Company.

'Basic Respect and Cultural Diversity' and 'Must Respect be Earned?' were originally published as 'Respect for Humanity' in Grethe B. Peterson (ed.), *The Tanner Lectures on Human Values*, xviii (Salt Lake City: University of Utah Press, 1997), 1–76. Reprinted courtesy of the University of Utah Press and the Trustees of the Tanner Lectures on Human Values.

'Donagan's Kant' originally appeared in *Ethics*, 104 (1993), 22–52, © 1993 by the University of Chicago. All rights reserved. It is reprinted here by permission of the University of Chicago Press.

'Kant on Responsibility for Consequences' originally appeared in *Jahrbuch fur Recht und Ethik*, 2 (1994), 159–76.

'Kant on Punishment: A Coherent Mix of Deterrence and Retribution?' originally appeared in *Jahrbuch fur Recht und Ethik*, 5 (1997), 291–314.

'A Kantian Perspective on Political Violence' originally appeared in *The Journal of Ethics*, 1 (1997), 105–40. Reprinted with the kind permission of Kluwer Academic Publishers.

'The Problem of Stability in *Political Liberalism*' originally appeared in *Pacific Philosophical Quarterly*, 75 (1994), 333–52. Reprinted by permission of Blackwell Publishers.

'Conscience and Authority' was delivered to the US Air Force Academy on 5 November 1996 as the Joseph A. Reich, Sr. Distinguished Lecture on War, Morality and the Military Profession.

The essays reprinted here, with only minor revisions, no doubt remain deficient in many ways, and for this I take full responsibility. I gratefully acknowledge, however, that while working on these essays I received help from many people. Some of these are acknowledged in my notes to individual chapters, but my debts are more extensive than these notes indicate. For financial support, I am grateful to the University of North Carolina at Chapel Hill, especially for a Z. Smith Reynolds Faculty Research Leave in 1992 and an Institute of Arts and Humanities Fellowship in 1997. My colleagues in the philosophy department have been philosophically stimulating, encouraging, and helpful in many ways. In particular, I have benefited from discussions about issues in moral theory with colleagues Bernard and Jan Boxill, Geoffrey Sayre McCord, Gerald Postema, Simon Blackburn, Douglas Long, Roderick Long, Jay Rosenberg, and the late David Falk. I have been fortunate also to have had long conversations, at various times, with many former graduate students and scholars from other universities about Kantian perspectives on topics discussed in this volume. Prominent among these were Samuel Bruton, Richard Dean, Jeffrey Downard, Barbara Herman, Sarah Holtman, Robert Johnson, Jeffrie Murphy, Andrews Reath, Cynthia Stark, Karen Stohr, and Valerie Tiberius. For several years now a few graduate students have joined me, outside of classes, in weekly sessions devoted to close, detailed re-examination of some of Kant's ethical writings. I appreciate the contributions of this group, which included Bruton, Dean, and Stohr, as well as Andrew Johnson, Sean McKeever, and Wendy Nankas.

A very special thanks is due to Samuel Bruton and Richard Dean for their excellent work as research assistants at different periods. Most recently, Richard Dean was extremely thorough, efficient, and judicious in editing the essays, suggesting revisions, and preparing the manuscript for publication. I owe much to both Dean and Bruton for stimulating conversations about Kant as well as their help on more mundane tasks.

As always, I am grateful to my father for his encouragement and for being a model of dedication to philosophical inquiry. My sons, Kenneth and Tom, have been supportive by taking an interest in my philosophical reflections even though their professional lives are more practically oriented. My debt to Robin is both too large and too private to convey adequately here. Her constant support and help have been indispensable, and I am very grateful. In her work as a social worker and manager at a hospice facility, the requirements of justice and respect regardless of a person's background and condition are immediate and vividly real. In this, as in other relations, she exemplifies the sort of respect for humanity that, more abstractly, I have tried to describe.

CONTENTS

ABBREVIATIONS FOR KANT'S WORKS

A   *Anthropology from a Pragmatic Point of View*, tr. Mary Gregor (The Hague: Martinus Nijhoff, 1974). Translated from *Anthropologie in pragmatischer Hinsicht abgefasst*, in *Kants gesammelte Schriften*, ed. under the auspices of the Königliche Preussische Akademie der Wissenschaften (Berlin: Walter de Gruyter, 1908–13), vii. 117–333.

C2   *Critique of Practical Reason*, 3rd edn., tr. Lewis White Beck (New York: Macmillan Publishing Co., 1993). Translated from *Kritik der Praktischen Vernunft*, in *Kants gesammelte Schriften*, v. 1–164.

C3   *Critique of Judgment*, tr. Werner S. Pluhar (Indianapolis: Hackett Publishing Co., 1987). Translated from *Kritik der Urtheilskraft*, in *Kants gesammelte Schriften*, v. 167–485.

G   *Groundwork of the Metaphysics of Morals*, tr. H. J. Paton (New York: Harper and Row, 1964). Translated from *Grundlegung zur Metaphysik der Sitten*, in *Kants gesammelte Schriften*, iv. 387–463.

LE   *Lectures on Ethics*, tr. Louis Infield (New York: Harper and Row, 1963). Translated from *Eine Vorlesung Kants über Ethik*, ed. Paul Menzer (Berlin: im Auftrage der Kantsgesellschaft, 1924).

MM   *The Metaphysics of Morals*, tr. Mary Gregor (Cambridge: Cambridge University Press, 1996). Translated from *Die Metaphysik der Sitten*, in *Kants gesammelte Schriften*, vi. 203–491.

R   *Religion within the Limits of Reason Alone*, tr. Theodore M. Green and Hoyt H. Hudson (New York: Harper and Row, 1960). Translated from *Die Religion innerhalb der Grenzen der blossen Vernunft*, in *Kants gesammelte Schriften*, vi. 1–202.

Numbers in square brackets refer to the relevant page of *Kants gesam-melte Schriften*. This edition of Kant's work is commonly called the Akademie (or Academy) edition. When works of Kant other than those abbreviated above are cited, a full reference will be given in a footnote.

Introduction

In the past thirty years or so there has been a remarkable revival of interest in Kant's moral philosophy. At the same time philosophers have become increasingly willing to address substantive social and moral problems. Whether or not these trends are causally connected, their intersection, I believe, has been fruitful and can be even more so. Trying seriously to work out the implications of Kant's moral theory for practical issues helps to reveal both its strengths and its weaknesses. Also, if we move beyond old stereotypes of Kant, rethinking those practical issues from a Kantian perspective can open up new ways of understanding them. John Rawls's work in political philosophy is an especially prominent example of how interests in Kantian theory and practical problems can be mutually enriching, but there are many other examples. Few, if any, philosophers who work in a Kantian tradition today accept all of Kant's doctrines, and among them there is a considerable diversity in both their interpretations of Kant and their preferred ways of developing Kantian theory. The essays in this volume represent my attempts to contribute to this process of developing aspects of a Kantian moral theory, in large part by considering possible Kantian responses to substantive moral issues. Perhaps even more than my fellow-workers in this field, I am sceptical about many of Kant's particular ideas; and my proposals for developing moral theory in a broadly Kantian way are significantly different from those of others, notably Barbara Herman, Christine Korsgaard, and Onora O'Neill. We share, however, a common conviction that further effort to refine and extend some of Kant's basic insights is potentially rewarding, both for moral theory in general and for dealing with substantive moral problems.

My primary concern in these essays, then, is not with narrow questions of historical scholarship but with how one might develop a plausible Kantian type of moral theory and what this would say about practical problems. Nevertheless, I also try to point out, when I can, places at which Kant's texts have been misunderstood. Often, though not always, initial objections can be deflected simply by more careful reading. I share the traditional ideal of historical scholarship, which is to make good sense of an author's ideas while remaining completely faithful to the letter of the text; but with Kant, and perhaps all great philosophers, this is sometimes impossible. Then the best one can do is to note the problem and try to convey the spirit of what the author seemed to be saying. At various points, however, it seems that no amount of effort to read carefully and find merit in the spirit of a text can prevent a reflective reader from concluding that the author's position is indefensible, or even repugnant. People will differ, of course, about how many of these points are in Kant's ethical writings and how central they are, but my general aim has been simply to call these as I see them and then to consider how a Kantian type of moral theory could be developed without the untenable point. Some of my essays are more focused than others on explaining Kant's position or reconstructing his arguments. Some essays are more explicitly critical than others while some move immediately to the project of working out a modified Kantian perspective. These differences, I trust, will be clear in context.

The general project that I have just described has been my guiding thought in developing all of the essays presented here, as well as some others to be published later, but the specific focus of various papers was partly in response to invitations to philosophical conferences on various topics. This was the case, for example, with the essays on pluralism, responsibility for consequences, political violence, conscience and authority, and Alan Donagan's version of Kantian ethics. In each of these cases an invitation to discuss a broad topic encouraged me to reflect more seriously than I otherwise would have about what a plausible Kantian ethics should say about the matter in question. I found that the challenge posed by the invitations, rather than leading to pat 'applications' of familiar Kantian principles, actually led me to think about Kantian theory in a fresh way. In any case, proceeding in this way was well suited to my preferred way of initially approaching philosophical problems, which, for better or worse, is to explore possibilities, offer interpretative hypotheses, and make tentative suggestions rather than to attempt to give definitive arguments. The diversity of audiences for the essays also explains some of the variation in their scope and mode of presentation. 'Basic Respect and Cultural Diversity', for example, was meant for a more general audience than most of the other essays, and 'Conscience and Authority' was written for undergraduates at a military academy. The context of writing also resulted in occasional overlap in content between some essays, notably 'A Kantian

Perspective on Moral Rules' and 'A Kantian Perspective on Political Violence'. In this case, the later essay expanded ideas briefly summarized in the earlier one in order to apply them to a specific practical problem.

Readers will note common themes running through the essays. In particular, they express the same evaluative attitude towards certain aspects of Kant's moral philosophy. For example, on the negative side, the essays are quite uniformly hostile to Kant's strict rigourism with regard to certain moral principles. That is, they accept the common criticism that Kant was mistaken to hold that substantive principles such as 'Do not lie' and 'Uphold the law of the land' are absolutely binding in all circumstances. Such unconditional prohibitions, I maintain, do not follow from Kant's basic moral theory, despite what he himself thought, and some of Kant's particular moral opinions, taken literally, are quite repugnant (e.g. that women should not be allowed to vote and castration should be the punishment for sodomy). Again, I do not try to defend Kant's transcendental idealism, with its idea of noumenal wills independent of space and time. My working hypothesis is that much of Kant's normative moral theory can be separated from this background or at least that a modified Kantian ethics can do without it. Also, although Kant had good reason to think that his normative and analytical claims are not amenable to proof by empirical means, he sometimes goes too far in denying the relevance of empirical information to ethical disputes. For example, Kant too readily dismisses the evidence of a criminal's background as irrelevant to the punishment due; and he leans too readily on faith, rather than evidence, in maintaining that every competent adult has a Kantian conscience, that perpetual peace is possible, and that corrupt rulers will listen to moral arguments. Kant's arguments often seem to prove less than they proclaim, and at various points Kant offers little or no argument at all. Even those most sympathetic to Kant's ethics, I think, typically concede most of these points.

On the positive side, however, the essays presented here highlight and express admiration for several aspects of Kant's moral philosophy. I take these to be themes at the core of any plausible development of ethical theory that we should recognize as (broadly) Kantian. Among these themes, for example, is the importance of human dignity, with its implication that we must respect all persons. Another important, related theme is that the Categorical Imperative, in its various forms taken together, expresses relatively formal features of a framework for moral deliberation and respectful dialogue through which more substantive issues can be appropriately addressed. Also significant is Kant's rejection of consequentialist modes of thinking. Here Kant does not merely express the now familiar complaint that consequentialism is counter-intuitive at points but presents an alternative framework that challenges the foundations of consequentialism. Like the modern liberals he has influenced, he argues that reasonable persons with quite different personal projects and values can acknowledge their common grounds for principles of justice that provide a fair and secure framework within which they may pursue their ends. Moreover, the principles, in theory, affirm the freedom and equality of all persons, and, contrary to Hobbes, place limits of justice on rulers as well as citizens. Despite the indefensibility of Kant's extreme stands on punishment and revolution, revisiting his thinking even about these can be instructive. Regarding punishment, properly understood, Kant arguably does not support the deplorable deep retributivism often attributed to him; and, regarding revolution, Kant's basic moral theory arguably provides the resources to correct his intolerably extreme position.

The essays in this volume are meant to be complementary, but each is more or less self-contained and can be read independently of the others. Since reading them in any particular order is not crucial, the following preview, or series of brief abstracts, may be useful. The essays cluster in three groups according to the main focus of the discussions: first, basic features of a Kantian framework for moral deliberation and dialogue; second, respect for persons grounded in human dignity; and third, the requirements of justice and the appropriate responses to moral and legal wrongdoing.

I. *Elements of a Kantian Perspective.* The initial pair of essays contrasts Kant's moral theory with other types of moral theory and sketches a Kantian perspective for moral deliberation about rules.

1. 'Kantian Pluralism' characterizes the type of ethical theory that Kant developed, comparing it with contemporary theories along several dimensions. The essay distinguishes several senses in which an ethical theory might be regarded as *pluralistic* and argues that, perhaps surprisingly, many of the practical concerns commonly advocated under the label *pluralism* are addressed in Kantian ethics.

2. 'A Kantian Perspective on Moral Rules' sets the stage for subsequent discussion by sketching a deliberative framework drawn from a combination of Kant's formulations of the Categorical Imperative. Several problems in using this sort of heuristic framework are identified, and brief suggestions are made regarding ways that Kantian theory

might be developed to meet them. The Kantian perspective, I maintain, has structural similarities to rule-utilitarianism and Rawls's theory of justice, but it differs from them in important ways.

II. *Respect for Humanity.* The next set of three essays focuses on respect for humanity. The first two were given as Tanner Lectures at Stanford University, and the third was written as a memorial appreciation of Alan Donagan's contributions to Kantian moral theory.

3. 'Basic Respect and Cultural Diversity' explores the implications of respect for humanity when interpreted as appropriately valuing persons *as valuers*. After briefly reviewing other historical views that contrast with Kant's, the essay proposes ways of supplementing Kant's ethics by a richer account of how we actually value various things—that is, an account which is sensitive to the fact that we are not merely 'free and rational' but also social and historically embedded persons. The essay then explores the significance of this expanded perspective for dealing with problems raised by cultural diversity, concluding with comments on whether the 'canon' of college and university literature should be replaced with more culturally diverse readings.

4. 'Must Respect be Earned?' addresses the questions '*Why* should we respect humanity in all persons?' and '*Why not* regard extremely immoral persons as having *forfeited* all respect?' It sketches some Kantian grounds for presuming that all human beings ought to be respected, and then addresses several objections. The Kantian perspective sketched earlier suggests reasons for a strong presumption against treating respect for humanity as forfeitable; and, arguably, neither self-protection, criminal punishment, nor vehement moral censure require that we set aside this presumption.

5. 'Donagan's Kant' respectfully criticizes Alan Donagan's attempt to derive a list of strict substantive moral rules from the imperative to respect humanity. The essay argues for interpreting Kant's idea that rational nature is an end in itself as a 'thinner', more formal moral requirement than Donagan's. So interpreted, I suggest, the idea makes the Kantian basic moral framework better able to serve as a guide for conflict resolution and conscientious judgement in a world of diverse values, disagreement, and uncertainty.

III. *Justice and Responses to Wrongdoing.* This final set of essays addresses more specific problems of justice. The first two focus on appropriate responses to moral and legal wrongdoing of private individuals: punishment and holding offenders morally liable for the consequences of their deeds. The third considers revolution as a response to the injustices committed by public officials. Shifting attention to a contemporary Kantian account of justice, the fourth essay concerns the Kantian grounds for John Rawls's movement from a comprehensive moral theory of justice to a more limited political conception. Finally, I have included, as the fifth essay of this set, a brief and more elementary lecture on conscientious resistance to authority, presented to the cadets at the United States Air Force Academy.

6. 'Responsibility for Consequences' moves beyond time-worn debates on whether we can determine what we ought to do independently of the predicted consequences. Rather, the pertinent questions concern moral blame and liability for the bad consequences of our deeds after we have acted. The essay attempts to explain and assess objections to the answers suggested by Kant's brief remarks about imputability in *The Metaphysics of Morals*. Although some initial objections miss the mark, I argue that, if Kant's principles are construed as moral (rather than legal) guidelines, they are not adequately sensitive to differences in contexts.

7. The next essay, 'Kant on Punishment: A Coherent Mix of Deterrence and Retribution?', concerns Kant's controversial ideas about the proper judicial response to crime. Although Kant is often regarded as an extreme retributivist, the need to deter crime also plays a significant role in his theory of criminal law. Kant's combination of deterrent and retributive elements, however, must be distinguished from others that are less plausible. Kant thought that criminal punishments should be designed to match the victim's empirically discernible losses in degree and kind, except when this would be impossible or degrading; for courts cannot measure the ultimate moral desert of criminals. Kant's justification, contrary to common opinion, is not deeply retributive. 'Punishment', however, is also not a mere disincentive in a 'price' system of social control; it has an inherent expressive function, conveying a public message of moral disapproval of the criminal conduct in question. This helps to explain his (qualified) acceptance of the law of retribution and his condemnation of the making of exceptions for pragmatic reasons. It also accounts for the retributive 'tone' of Kant's remarks, despite his insistence that public courts deal only with 'external actions', not with overall moral worth or character assessment.

8. 'A Kantian Perspective on Political Violence' critically discusses Kant's strict opposition to political violence even against corrupt rulers. Kant's arguments seem inadequate to support his extreme conclusion. To develop a more reasonable Kant*ian* position, then, the essay develops the moral framework for deliberation suggested in earlier papers.

This combines core ideas from each of Kant's formulations of the Categorical Imperative. Though only a perspective for deliberation, not a decision procedure, this arguably rules out the most extreme positions, prohibitive and permissive, on political violence. Despite Kant's hopes, the values implicit in his fundamental principle fail to support easy, inflexible solutions; but they establish strong presumptions against lawless coercion and killing, undermining social order, treating persons as dispensable, underestimating options, arrogant faith in one's own judgement, and reckless simplicity in political thinking.

9. 'The Problem of Stability in *Political Liberalism*' concerns the relation between two of the most influential Kantian works in political philosophy in this century, John Rawls's *A Theory of Justice* and *Political Liberalism*. The rationale for Rawls's shift in position from the earlier book to the later, it is argued, is a recognized need to satisfy a deeply Kantian requirement on the legitimate exercise of state coercive power. In a pluralistic world where reasonable people differ about the truth of religion and morality, the requirement can be met only by showing the possibility of an overlapping consensus on shared political principles. Contrary to what Rawls at times suggests, the main reason for his move from a 'comprehensive moral theory' to a 'political conception' of justice was not a (doubtful) expectation that consensus on his principles would be a significant stabilizing force. Rather, the primary reason was his recognition of a need to provide reasons for his political principles that are respectful of the diversity of moral and religious opinions among reasonable people.

10. 'Conscience and Authority' raises the question whether we should resist state authorities when their orders conflict with our conscience. In terms intended for an audience without knowledge of Kant and ethical theory, the essay sketches three distinct ways of conceiving of conscience. It then argues that none of these gives us reason to suppose that conscience guarantees morally justifiable decisions about when to resist authoritative orders. In Kant's view, conscience can at best signal that our practices are at odds with our moral beliefs or that we have failed to scrutinize these beliefs sufficiently. Kant holds that conscience cannot err, but its role, in effect, is limited to warning us and punishing us for doing less than our best to live by our considered moral judgements. Conscience is no easy, or even difficult, way to gain access to moral truth or objective justifiability. For that, there can be no substitute for reasonable moral deliberation and discussion. From a Kantian perspective, as I conceive it, we must still regard our conclusions as fallible even though we cannot do better. This essay

draws from a more thorough paper on conscience, not included here, and deliberately sacrifices complexity of scholarship for suitability to a general audience.

A final note. Readers may notice that my style is often more exploratory than argumentative. Kant's texts guide and constrain my interpretations, but my proposals are often interpretative hypotheses or suggestions for reconstruction rather than attempts to establish a definitive reading. In some essays I simply present my understanding of a Kantian perspective on a topic in order to focus on its practical implications rather than to defend it. My proceeding in these ways does not stem from any post-modern aversion to examining texts closely to discern what an author most likely meant. To the contrary, I think that we need more of that scholarly discipline in the history of philosophy, and I respect and learn from those who make historical accuracy their primary aim. Also, an exploratory style need not reflect timidity or impatience with details. Philosophy, as a cooperative discipline, can learn from more than one way of treating historical classics. The ideal is to be clear and open about when we are interpreting a text in the narrowest sense, when we are trying to reconstruct it with due sensitivity to the context, and when we are deliberately deviating from the text to develop views only inspired by it. Respecting these distinctions has been my ideal, even though no doubt I have not always succeeded. Among the reasons for being some-what tentative in commenting on Kant's ethics is, of course, the evident complexity and difficulty of the texts, which have led distinguished scholars to radically different readings. A tentative attitude not only respects other scholars but respects readers who have only begun to think through the texts for themselves. It can be productive simply to invite others to think with us along alternative lines even though we are not yet completely certain where these lines lead or how firmly they are grounded. An attack-and-defend ethos in philosophy can stifle poten-tially valuable exploratory thinking by encouraging the attitude that one must construct impregnable defensive walls before going public with a potentially controversial idea. That attitude among professional philosophers seems to be diminishing to some extent, and, if so, we should welcome the change.

PART I

Elements of a Kantian Perspective

Kantian Pluralism

'Pluralism' can mean many different things, and Kant's ethics can be read in quite different ways. Thus the title 'Kantian Pluralism' may seem quite natural to some, an oxymoron to others, and perfectly clear to no one. I use the label not to refer to a particular thesis but only to suggest a range of questions to be considered. In fact my first aim here is simply to sort out several different controversies that might pass under the heading 'pluralism' in ethical theory and to note some of the problems that each type of pluralism raises. These distinctions form the framework for a second aim, namely, to make some suggestions about the senses in which Kant's ethics, suitably reconstructed, can be regarded as pluralistic. My discussion will be wide ranging, and so my proposals must be tentative and incomplete. My primary purpose is just to further discussion, using ideas of pluralism to raise new questions about Kantian ethics. If, in addition, my remarks help to undermine some familiar stereotypes of Kantian ethics, that would also be a welcome result.

ISSUES CONCERNING PLURALISM AND KANTIAN ETHICS

Plurality of Basic Moral Principles

Though today no doubt the term 'pluralism' suggests something different, ethical theories have been classified as monistic or pluralistic depending on whether they accept one or many basic ethical principles. Some main advantages and liabilities of each type are by now quite familiar, but may be worth reviewing briefly.

The paradigm of a monistic theory, of course, is act-utilitarianism.[1]

This essay was written for presentation to a conference on 'Pluralism in Ethical Theory' at Hollins College, sponsored by the Hollins Institute for Ethics and Public Policy, in June 1991. I am grateful to the participants at that conference, and especially to Larry Becker, for thoughtful comments.

[1] Definitions vary, but widely familiar accounts of act- and rule-utilitarianism are given in William K. Frankena, *Ethics* (Englewood Cliffs, NJ: Prentice-Hall, 1973), ch. 3;

This holds that there is one and only one fundamental ethical principle. All other so-called moral principles are merely convenient 'rules of thumb' to save the time and effort of calculating utilities in each separate case; or else, as some maintain, they are rules which the unsophisticated may usefully be taught to regard as strict standards but which are actually derivative and only approximately accurate. The basic moral principle, on this view, resolves all apparent conflicts of duty, at least theoretically.

A paradigm of pluralism is the intuitionism of W. D. Ross, who held that there are many self-evident, basic, and independent principles of prima facie duty.[2] Ross's list, which was not meant to be complete, included fidelity, gratitude, justice, reparation, non-injury, self-improvement, and beneficence. Ross held that these principles give moral reasons for acting but have a weight that is not derived from general utility and is sometimes in conflict with it. To hold such specific moral principles rigidly as without exception, Ross realized, would regularly lead to conflicts of duty, and so Ross qualified all of his basic principles, adding in effect an 'other things equal' clause to each.[3]

Both of these paradigms face familiar objections. Act-utilitarianism seems to accept conflicts with common sense for the sake of theoretical neatness. Rossian pluralism buys intuitive plausibility and security against conflicts of (actual) duty, but it pays a heavy price by abandoning some traditional aims of ethical theory, namely, to illuminate the grounds of moral convictions and to aid reflective judgement regarding difficult cases.

Various mixed theories fall between these two extreme paradigms. Rule-utilitarianism, for example, distinguishes two levels of moral deliberation: review of principles and everyday decisions.[4] At the higher level principles are to be endorsed, qualified, or rejected on grounds of the utility of their general acceptance, and decisions regarding particular cases are to be made as directed by the resulting set of principles. Such

Richard Brandt, *Ethical Theory* (Englewood Cliffs, NJ: Prentice-Hall, 1959), ch. 15; and David Lyons, *Forms and Limits of Utilitarianism* (Oxford: Clarendon Press, 1965).

[2] W. D. Ross, *The Right and the Good* (Oxford: Clarendon Press, 1930), ch. 2.

[3] Actually Ross's idea of prima facie duty is somewhat more complex than what is commonly expressed by 'other things equal', for even if overridden by a more stringent moral consideration, a prima facie duty (e.g. to keep one's promises) may leave a moral residue (e.g. a need to apologize).

[4] See, e.g., Richard Brandt, 'Toward a Credible Form of Utilitarianism', in Hector-Neri Castañeda and George Nakhnikian (eds.), *Morality and the Language of Conduct* (Detroit: Wayne State University Press, 1965), 107–43, and *A Theory of the Good and the Right* (Oxford: Clarendon Press, 1979); also R. M. Hare, *Moral Thinking* (Oxford: Clarendon Press, 1981).

theories, it is usually conceded, offer more hope of matching ordinary considered judgements than act-utilitarianism does; and yet, unlike Ross's intuitionism, mixed theories like rule-utilitarianism offer a procedure for resolving apparent conflicts between specific principles (fidelity, gratitude, non-injury, etc.). Any apparent conflicts of duty that arise on the lower level (action/decision) are supposed to be resolvable, at least in theory, at the higher level (review of principles).

Each mixed theory has its own problems, of course, and the two-level approach itself has also been criticized. Some, for example, argue that there is something odd, dubious, or even 'schizophrenic' about a theory which advocates a fundamental principle of ethics that good people cannot keep in mind and use as they go through daily life. Virtuous people, they suggest, will be moved to help their friends and to be loyal to their families from particular concerns, not because general utility, impartially considered, favours moral codes with rules prescribing such behaviour, or anything like this.[5]

Such objections are overstated, I think, if they deny that there can be a distinction between what a virtuous person has in mind in acting and what two-level moral theorists (at their best) are trying to articulate, namely, a general comprehensive account of the deep presuppositions and grounds of the moral judgements we make about such actions. None the less, the objection raises a reasonable worry about two-level theories, though one that may apply to some two-level theories more than to others. That is, a plausible ethical theory, it seems, must ground its more specific prescriptions in the sort of attitudes that people can admirably maintain and act from in daily life, even if a virtuous person need not (and should not) always focus his or her attention explicitly on such prescriptions and the general grounds for them.

When we reflect on Kant's ethics in the context of the controversies just reviewed, the natural questions that arise are these: was Kant a monist, a pluralist, or a mixed theorist with regard to fundamental moral principles, and how does he fare with regard to the common objections to theories of his type?

Incommensurable Values

The pure theorist's yearning to make all moral questions resolvable in principle naturally leads to the wish to combine a monistic ethical theory, such as act-utilitarianism, with a value theory that makes all

---

[5] See Michael Stocker, 'The Schizophrenia of Modern Moral Theories', *Journal of Philosophy*, 73 (1976), 453–66.

values commensurable. Ideally, it is supposed, the values would be empirically determinable, measurable quantities of something that permits objective cross-person comparative judgements. Bentham's hedonistic calculus, for all its faults, represents this understandable though misdirected wish.[6] G. E. Moore also held that one's duty is determined by the intrinsic value produced by the various actions open to one.[7] He acknowledged that the non-natural property of intrinsic goodness could not be measured, but his theory still interpreted moral judgements as estimates of relative *amounts* of one 'simple' property. More sophisticated versions of utilitarianism rest content with ordinal rankings of the 'preferences' of individuals and a procedure for taking into account the preference structures of all persons. Here the fiction of quantitative measurement of value is given up, but none the less what is right is regarded as a function of what is valuable to individuals and this in turn is usually determined by just one sort of value, namely, preference (e.g. as revealed in patterns of choice).

A common pattern of complaint against all such theories is that they fail to see that our deepest values are irreducibly diverse, incommensurable, incalculable, fragmented, and in conflict. Though there are distinguishable objections here, the worry is obviously not merely that we lack practical means to measure quantities of value of a single kind. The suspicion, rather, is that the pure theorist's hope of reducing apparently diverse types of value to a common denominator is in danger of purchasing theoretical elegance at the cost of abandoning the common-sense (and sensible) judgements that initially gave rise to philosophical reflection on morals. Here we see the same sort of objection as that expressed by 'pluralists' in the first sense against attempts by 'monists' to reduce diverse moral considerations to one simple principle.

Unfortunately, the alternative to introducing the fiction of commensurable values into philosophical theories of ethics may seem equally unpromising. If we admit incommensurable values, it may seem that we must simply accept that we inevitably live with a fragmented set of values that pull us in opposing directions and impose moral dilemmas (or conflicts) that are tragic but utterly unresolvable. This would leave us with urgent moral questions without answers or, worse, with

---

[6] Jeremy Bentham, *'A Fragment on Government' and 'An Introduction to the Principles of Morals and Legislation'*, ed. Wilfrid Harrison (Oxford: Blackwell, 1960), esp. pp. 151–4 of the latter work.
[7] G. E. Moore, *Principia Ethica* (Cambridge: Cambridge University Press, 1903), and *Ethics* (Oxford: Oxford University Press, 1912).

unequivocal opposing moral demands that are impossible to satisfy. Some philosophers espouse these implications with pessimistic resignation while others seem to affirm them joyfully as a part of the wonderful paradoxes of the human condition. But, in any case, in admitting incommensurable values, we must acknowledge at least the possibility of unresolvable moral conflicts or unanswerable moral questions. Accepting these is at least the default position: what we face if all reasonable strategies for resolving conflicts fail.

Practically, of course, a monistic theory with commensurable values (e.g. hedonistic act-utilitarianism) may leave us with as many, or more, undecidable moral questions as pluralistic theories with incommensurable values.[8] In so far as practical concerns motivate the worry about moral conflicts and gaps resulting from a theory, theorists who accept incommensurable values may adopt a strategy that serves as well as, or better than, inserting a paper guarantee against such problems into their theories. This strategy would be first to grant that any theory acknowledging incommensurable values may leave some questions unanswerable but then to develop within the theory reasonable ways to arbitrate as far as possible the most urgent and persistent clashes of pre-theoretical moral judgements. Any theory must simplify and strain against common opinion to some degree, but theories adopting the strategy just mentioned would respect the familiar idea that some values are incommensurable as well as respecting important common assumptions about morality and reason. These assumptions, sometimes challenged but still widely shared, are that moral reflection and debate are concerned to find reasons for acting, that the reasons in question are meant somehow to harmonize interests and to mediate among diverse judgements, and that reason cannot demand both that we do something and that we not do it.

Ethical theories that acknowledge incommensurable values may be said to be more 'pluralistic', in a sense, than those that do not. In this sense a theory would be pluralistic if it held that there are fundamentally different kinds of value, some of which are not amenable to measurement, calculation, or ranking; and this would be so even if the theory also held that there is an ideal procedure of rational reflection

---

[8] This, of course, is because of the familiar facts that we cannot measure and compare pleasures and pains, or predict consequences, with certainty or precision. I do not mean to press the old idea that these limitations constitute decisive objections to utilitarianism. My point is simply that, because of these limitations, utilitarians face practical quandaries, moral issues one cannot decide with confidence, just as other moral theorists do.

and dialogue that we should employ to resolve, as far as possible, practically important conflicts among and within individuals. Later I will suggest that Kantian ethics is best understood as a pluralistic theory of just this sort, but first I need to identify some further questions about 'pluralism' and sketch the sort of Kantian ethical theory I have in mind.

The Right Independent of the Good

As theories are often classified, a theory of value is regarded as distinguishable from a theory of right conduct. Roughly, the first concerns what sort of life, experiences, and achievements are good and worth pursuing for their own sakes, and the second concerns what one's moral duties are, what justice demands, and the like. When we divide matters this way, the question arises whether the theory of right is independent of the theory of value or whether one depends upon the other. Classic utilitarians, for example, have a hedonistic theory of value and a consequentialist theory of right, combined in a way that makes what is right depend on what is valuable. Rawls's theory of justice has been characterized as making rightness independent of goodness, though closer examination reveals complexities that defy such a simple characterization. Theories that make judgements of value dependent on prior judgements of right are possible but not so common. The question of how 'the right' and 'the good' are related is the background for another idea of 'pluralism' and another controversy within which to locate Kantian ethics.

'Pluralists' are often thought of, most generally and vaguely, as those who tolerate, accept, endorse, or glorify the diversity of values in different cultures and individuals. Applying this idea to the present issue, we may think of ethical theories as pluralistic, in a third sense, if they maintain that we can determine the fundamental principles of right conduct without relying on independent judgements about what sorts of lives, experiences, and achievements are intrinsically valuable. Some such theories may be sceptical or agnostic about whether there can be objective judgements about intrinsic value, but this is not necessary for the theories to be pluralistic in the sense intended here. A theory would be pluralistic even if it held that some ways of life are known to be intrinsically better than others, provided it also maintained that the basic principles of duty constitute a prior framework constraining the individual pursuit of what is intrinsically valuable and justified without appeal to claims about intrinsic value. Moderately pluralistic theories might admit that the theory of right needs to assume some minimal and relatively uncontroversial judgements of intrinsic value but maintain that basic principles of right can be determined without resolving the questions about the intrinsic worth of different 'life-styles' that are at the centre of real practical disputes.

The idea of a pluralistic ethical theory here is obviously drawn from the analogous idea of liberal pluralism with regard to political issues. Such theories attempt to define and defend rights and/or justice while remaining (more or less) neutral with regard to evaluations of personal ends and preferences. Many complain that such theories are not really neutral or that the neutrality within the theory is motivated by, or unintentionally reflects, controversial 'liberal' values that are assumed without question all along. Sometimes this complaint may be just an ad hominem, used to excuse unrestrained reliance on unliberal values, saying in effect, 'Since you liberals, despite your declarations of neutrality, simply take your values for granted, then we non-liberals cannot be faulted for pressing our value preferences in political theory and practice.'

There is, however, a more serious concern apart from this, which applies at least as, if not more, forcefully to *ethical* pluralism in my third sense. This is the thought that, though people can disagree about what is intrinsically valuable and the concept itself is philosophically puzzling, most of us apparently do judge some experiences, activities, or qualities of life to be better in themselves than others, and it is natural to suppose that these judgements should affect our views about what it is right to do. Unless there are strong reasons to resist these common practices, it seems, they can reasonably be reflected in our moral theories. The fact that some utilitarians mistakenly made the right nothing but a function of intrinsic value is not an adequate reason to insist on complete independence. Moreover, many of the reasons for trying to keep questions of political justice isolated from controversies about intrinsic values do not apply to ethical theories intended as guides to individual judgement rather than as blueprints for coercive institutions.

Permissive, Undogmatic, and Non-judgemental Attitudes

The general idea that pluralism expresses a favourable attitude toward diversity of values suggests other dimensions of moral theories along which they may be classified as more or less pluralistic. Since my main interest lies elsewhere, I include together several distinctions in this section. The common thread is the idea that morality should not be *stifling* in various possible ways. Pluralist theories, it may be supposed, affirm a less stifling morality in so far as they oppose *unnecessary restrictions* on liberty, *dogmatic assertions* of moral truth, and *moralistic judgements* about other cultures and the life-styles chosen by other individuals. The ideas here are distinct even though they are often conflated or presumed to be inseparable.

Theories are more or less permissive (or liberty-oriented) depending on how much and how severely they hold individual and group choices to be morally constrained. Quite permissive theories, however, could be extremely dogmatic in the way they present both their minimal moral constraints and their insistence on liberty. And the reverse is possible: one could advocate modestly and undogmatically a vision of morality that is, in theory, an all-encompassing guide, classifying virtually all possible acts as either wrong or obligatory. Dogmatism is a way of presenting a theory and its supposed applications, and this has no necessary connection with how much room the theory allows for morally permissible choice.

Dogmatism and severe constraint of liberty are both distinct from an attitude of judgemental moralism. What I have in mind here is the readiness to preach self-righteously and to blame and condemn others, prejudging their values and conduct and presuming without warrant that one is in a position to see and enforce the truth about what others should be doing. Some moral theories may explicitly condemn such attitudes, a few may openly encourage them, and others may remain neutral or vary their endorsement according to the particulars of each situation.

Theories can be called (loosely) 'pluralistic' in a fourth sense, then, if they would rate as unusually far along these various dimensions toward the limits of the permissive, the undogmatic, and the anti-judgemental. Where one should be along these dimensions is, of course, a matter of controversy.

In my rough sorting-out of types of pluralism, I have deliberately omitted several other dimensions along which theories can be rated as more or less 'relativistic'. Perhaps, after all, some who advocate 'pluralism', and some who deplore it, may have in mind these other distinctions. They might suppose, for example, that a real pluralist could not speak of 'moral truth' or even 'rational moral principles'. But as I have enough distinctions on my plate for my present purposes, I shall set these further matters aside.[9]

---

[9] Richard Brandt usefully distinguishes types of ethical relativism in *Ethical Theory*, ch. 11; see also David B. Wong's *Moral Relativity* (Berkeley: University of California Press, 1984), which has an extensive bibliography.

PLURALISTIC ASPECTS OF KANT'S ETHICS

Many theories, as diverse as those of Rawls and Nozick, are considered both 'pluralistic' and 'Kantian' in some relevant senses, and so it is perhaps not as surprising now as it might once have been to speak of 'Kantian pluralism'. But it is still worth recalling that Kant's ethics has often been caricatured as a paradigm of a stiflingly restrictive, dogmatic, judgemental, one-dimensional theory that generates conflicts of duty and fails to take account of the diversity of individuals and cultural settings. Though one cannot fail to notice features of Kant's writings that might prompt this distorted picture, any careful and extended reading would reveal that the caricature is inaccurate and unfair. More important for my purposes, many of the features of Kant's writings that suggest this picture are separable from the main lines of his thinking about the more fundamental questions of ethics. So considering the ways that Kant's basic theory is pluralistic may be useful, not just to keep the historical record straight, but also to assess the prospects of developing ethical theory along Kantian lines.

How is Kant's ethics pluralistic? Let me count the ways. Or better, since there are unresolved tensions in Kant's ethical writings, what I really want to note are the pluralistic features of a Kantian ethics as this is most plausibly reconstructed (in my opinion). Here, unfortunately, I cannot avoid drawing from work on Kant's theory (others' and my own) that would take too long to summarize fully. To some extent, too, the reconstructed Kantian ethics that I refer to is a project in progress rather than finished work. But I shall proceed none the less.

First, some general remarks on my strategy for interpreting and reconstructing Kant's ethics may help to put my subsequent remarks in perspective.

1. We should take seriously Kant's distinction between practical and theoretical philosophy. The *Groundwork* and *The Metaphysics of Morals* are primarily concerned with the question. 'What ought I to do?', sincerely raised from a first-person deliberative standpoint by more or less mature and rational moral agents faced with significant moral questions. The main point is not to persuade sceptics or to instil in readers a motivation to be moral; nor is it to resolve intuitively 'hard cases' or to give us criteria for blame and enable us to sort the wicked from the virtuous. Even more, the aim is not to explain, empirically or metaphysically, how moral agency works or even to conjecture how we

can 'comprehend' or picture rational deliberation and choice. Kant does not, of course, directly address particular first-order moral questions (What should I do now?) but seeks to articulate at various levels of abstraction certain practical presuppositions of these questions. What seems at first obscure metaphysics contrary to Kant's own critical standards can sometimes be read as expressing a practical idea that is arguably independent of that. To suppose so, at least, is a potentially fruitful interpretive strategy.

2. Contrary to the usual assumptions of many textbooks on ethics, Kant's discussion of the Categorical Imperative in the *Groundwork* was not mainly for the purpose of providing a handy decision guide for particular moral problems. Kant's instincts were right, I think, when he implied that examples were not quite appropriate in the highly condensed and abstract argument of the *Groundwork*, for his main focus was on other matters. He jumps too quickly from the highest levels of theory to the complexities of real moral issues, supposing (as those who live mostly at that elevated level naturally would) that 'applications' are rather obvious and straightforward. The forms of the Categorical Imperative articulate various general and abstract presuppositions of moral agency, and—a point of which Kant seemed to be more aware in *The Metaphysics of Morals*—particular conclusions do not simply fall out apart from further background and reflection.

3. As we all know, Kant had not only abstract ideas about moral agency but also some very strong and definite moral opinions. Though the latter can give useful clues for interpreting the former, the two do not always hang together.[10] Many of Kant's more specific convictions seem now to be based on cultural prejudices of the time, as his arguments often reveal. Perhaps Kant can be faulted for so readily accepting views that to us seem quite harsh and sometimes even outrageous, but criticism of this sort should not close our minds to the possibility that Kant has better things to offer on a more theoretical level.

4. Some ethical theories make virtues primary, others give priority to what is desirable to promote, and still others treat demands and constraints on action as more basic. Kant, I suggest, does none of the above. Contrary to his image and despite his stern tone regarding duty, Kant's

---

[10] Though initially I intended no pun on 'hanging together', the idea is that objections deemed decisive or 'fatal' to Kant's particular moral beliefs (e.g. about lying to potential murderers, or punishing sodomy with castration) do not necessarily condemn his main theory. Kant, like other philosophers, may be mistaken in his beliefs about what particular judgements follow from his theory.

ethics might be more aptly called an ethics of attitude.[11] That is, though Kant has much to say about what duty requires and forbids, these matters, I take it, are in a sense derivative from the idea that to be a moral agent is to be a person (with a 'will') committed to regarding oneself and others in certain ways (reflected in versions of the Categorical Imperative). Deliberating rationally with such commitments we find that we must acknowledge duties and rights regarding actions of various kinds, but ethics cannot begin with these duties and rights, and exactly what in particular they are needs to be worked out.

Now let us consider how Kant stands with regard to the types of pluralism I distinguished earlier.

One Principle or Many?

It seems strange that after so many years of attention to Kant's work it should remain a question how many basic moral principles there are in Kant's ethical theory. But there is, none the less, a question. The case for *one* basic principle is that Kant says, more than once, that there is only one Categorical Imperative, and he refers to his later formulas as versions of the same principle.[12] (There is, incidentally, remarkable controversy even about how many versions there are.[13]) The case for *many* basic principles is primarily that the various formulations of the Categorical Imperative seem to many upon examination to be independent and not equivalent. Also the Categorical Imperative, some argue, is not itself a moral principle in the same sense as more specific principles of duty.[14] As a 'formal' characterization of the demands of morality or practical reason, it cannot function as the first line in practical syllogisms yielding particular moral prescriptions as their outcome. If so, it might seem that Kant's 'basic moral principles' must be the various first principles of right and virtue presented in *The Metaphysics of Morals*, making Kant a 'pluralist' after all.

Setting aside nice points of scholarly controversy, a reasonable reconstruction of Kant's ethics, I think, would so far as possible combine the main ideas of the various formulations of the Categorical Imperative into one basic principle. This can be regarded in the theory both as a

[11] Rawls once referred to Kant's ethics as an ethics of self-esteem, and this fits with the view I am suggesting.

[12] See, e.g., G, 88 [421], 103 [436].

[13] T. C. Williams summarizes some of this controversy in *The Concept of the Categorical Imperative* (Oxford: Clarendon Press, 1968), 22–3.

[14] See, e.g., ibid.; and A. R. C. Duncan, *Practical Reason and Morality* (Edinburgh: Nelson, 1957).

higher-order moral principle and as a general characterization of the rational commitments presupposed in moral agents. Kant suggests at one point that the idea of a 'kingdom/realm of ends' characterizes the moral constraints on maxims more completely than previous forms of the Categorical Imperative.[15] This, I think, is a proposal worth developing, even though Kant himself did not do so. The central idea is that a moral agent is fundamentally committed to abiding by whatever 'laws' he/she would make, along with other rational agents, as a legislator in a possible kingdom of ends. The image recalls Rousseau's political theory and foreshadows Rawls's theory of justice; but there are important differences.

To summarize briefly suggestions I have made elsewhere,[16] the main features of the Kantian legislative point of view include these. The members are rational and have autonomy, in certain senses. They 'abstract from personal differences'. They make only 'universal laws'. They are 'ends in themselves' and recognize each other as such. Setting aside the special case of God, each member is both 'author' and 'subject' of the laws and morally bound (ultimately) only by these. Their rationality must include more than 'means–end' reasoning, for as rational they view the 'humanity' of each as an 'end in itself', something with 'dignity', above 'price', and not subject to trade-offs. Autonomy implies not only independence from external moral authorities (God, the state, tradition, etc.) but also, in a sense considered later, freedom to choose one's personal ends as opposed to 'discovering' them in nature or social practices.[17] 'Abstracting from personal differences', like Rawls's 'veil of ignorance', asks us to set aside our particular values as members of this or that group (gender, race, country, family, etc.) when, at the highest level of deliberation, we reflect on what constraints on action and institutions should form the framework of any moral life.

The formula of the kingdom of ends, so construed, obviously includes central ideas from other versions of the Categorical Imperative. Like the formula of autonomy, it calls for us to recognize each person as, in a sense, an equal sovereign legislator of moral laws.[18] Like the formula of humanity, it requires us to attribute an unconditional and incompa-

---

[15] G, 103–4 [436].

[16] Thomas E. Hill, Jr., *Dignity and Practical Reason in Kant's Moral Theory* (Ithaca, NY: Cornell University Press, 1992), chs. 3, 10, 11, and 'A Kantian Perspective on Moral Rules', Ch. 2 of this volume.

[17] This idea is discussed in Hill, *Dignity and Practical Reason in Kant's Moral Theory*, chs. 5 and 7, and in my collection of essays, *Autonomy and Self-respect* (Cambridge: Cambridge University Press, 1991), ch. 12.   [18] G, 98 [431].

rable value to persons as rational/moral agents.[19] Like the first formula (most generally described), its content is (vaguely) 'conform to universal law'.[20] Moreover, it implies that our particular policies (or maxims) are subject to review by reflection on what rational agents, as legislators, *would will* as 'laws' for everyone. This, in turn, restricts particular choices to what one *can will*, qua rational, as permissible for anyone in one's own situation.[21]

Any 'laws' adopted from this legislative point of view would, of course, be quite general and not immediately applicable to particular moral questions. They would require interpretation and specification, in the light of further reflection on the context, which opens room (more room than Kant acknowledged) for reasonable differences of opinion. By hypothesis, however, to view an alleged principle as a 'moral law' is to regard it as representing an ideal convergence point in the appropriate reflections of rational agents. Thus moral principles, on this conception, cannot be strictly inconsistent with one another. So long as actual moral agents continue to disagree about moral principles, the theory implies that at least one of them must be mistaken. Again, if we assume (with Kant) that reason cannot unequivocally demand the impossible, then moral principles cannot yield moral dilemmas in the strict sense, that is, situations in which, without qualification, one must do A, must do B, and cannot do both.[22] If dilemmas seem to result from reflections from the legislative perspective, then we must rethink the matter, for, as Alan Donagan notes, theories that purport to express

---

[19] G, 96 [429].   [20] G, 88 [421].

[21] This background assumption here is that one cannot rationally will an act as permissible for anyone if it is forbidden by laws that the rational legislators would will. The assumption that actual rational choice is constrained by hypothetical rational choice (i.e. what we *can will now* by what we *would will if . . .*) has been frequently challenged in contemporary discussions of contract theory. To place Kant in this controversy it is important, I think, to note that Kant also holds that fully rational moral agents *do actually will* that they should conform to whatever laws they together *would legislate* in the kingdom of ends. There is, of course, no actual moral legislative assembly that votes on proposed moral principles, and people often violate the moral principles that they acknowledge and even then, in a sense, they exercise their own free will (*Willkür*). Despite all this, Kant held that as a rational moral agent one constantly acknowledges as one's own and holds oneself to the general standards expressed in the Categorical Imperative. That is, one 'wills', in another sense (*Wille*), for oneself as well as for others, the standard of conforming to the laws that would be made in the kingdom of ends. This willing is not a matter of exercising a choice 'option' but rather finding this general commitment inseparable from one's conception of oneself as a rational moral agent. This idea too can be challenged, but that is a different controversy.

[22] Alan Donagan argues that to be in a genuine moral dilemma would be to face strict duties impossible to fulfil and not resulting from one's own prior moral failures: 'Moral Dilemmas, Genuine and Spurious: A Comparative Anatomy,' *Ethics*, 104 (1993), 7–21.

demands of reason must be 'repaired or discarded' if they generate genuine moral dilemmas.[23] Though apparent conflicts of duty in Kant's theory *could* be grounds to revise or reject it, given the distance between the highest abstractions of theory and the complexities of particular situations, the first step should be to re-examine whether the allegedly unresolvable dilemma was derived as rigorously and definitively as initially supposed.

A theory might still leave one with unresolvable moral questions ('moral gaps'), with very strong moral considerations pulling in opposite directions, even if its principles were strictly consistent and it yielded no conflicting particular demands that were both absolute and impossible to meet ('moral dilemmas'). The Kantian legislative perspective could not rule this out but at best would provide a perspective from which to rethink the problem (so far as it results from disagreements of principle rather than of perception and fact).

To summarize, Kantian ethics would be monistic (in my first sense) and, moreover, a theory with at least two levels of reflection. Though importantly different from rule-utilitarianism, it would be similar to such two-level theories in submitting apparent conflicts of first-order duties for resolution at a higher level of reflection. Strict inconsistency and dilemmas would not be tolerated, but the elimination of moral gaps and the attainment of rational solutions to 'hard cases' would be at best a project under the theory, not something assured in advance.

Incommensurable Values?

Unlike some monistic theories, Kant's ethics denies that there is a single dimension of value that would make moral judgements, in principle, a matter of calculation. Some 'ends' are rationally necessary and 'objective'; others are contingent and 'relative'. The former have dignity; the latter only price. Dignity is a kind of value 'above all price', so dignity may not be violated no matter what (merely) relative ends must be sacrificed for it.[24] More radically, dignity 'admits of no equivalents', and

---

[23] 'Moral Dilemmas, Genuine and Spurious: A Comparative Anatomy,' *Ethics*, 12–13.
[24] G, 95–103 [427–36], esp. 102 [434–5]; see also Hill, *Dignity and Practical Reason in Kant's Moral Theory*, chs. 2, 10. In *The Metaphysics of Morals*, Kant identifies objective ends as ends that we have duties to adopt (namely, others' happiness and our own perfection), but in *Groundwork* the objective ends are persons, or rational beings, or humanity in persons. Kant attributes 'dignity' variously to persons (conceived as members of the kingdom of ends), humanity, 'every rational nature', lawgiving, a morally

so one cannot justifiably trade off dignity here for dignity there. To ascribe dignity to rational agents, then, is to assign them 'value' of a kind not admitting of quantitative comparison. Somehow the ascription must be understood in another way.

Some aspects of the idea seem clear enough. Dignity is an 'unconditional' value and so the favourable attitude we must take toward persons, whatever else it is, is not dependent on their being useful to us, liked by us, belonging to the same communities as us, and so on. It is not even dependent on their moral record and so is not something that one earns or can forfeit. As I have argued elsewhere, Kant's use of the idea in *The Metaphysics of Morals* suggests that what the attitude calls for is 'preserving, developing, exercising, and honoring' those aspects of human beings that are distinctive to them as rational free agents (i.e. their 'humanity').[25]

The idea of dignity, I would now add, should also be interpreted in terms of the political metaphors that seem so pervasive in Kant's ethics. To view persons as free rational agents is to see them as jointly legislating the moral principles that constitute the basic framework within which they are 'free to set ends' of their own. To acknowledge their dignity is to take the attitude that they are, in a sense, 'sovereigns' both in constituting general moral principles and in determining the non-moral good for themselves. Unlike Hare's 'decisions of principle', moral principles are not seen as products of individual 'voluntary' choice; but, also unlike traditions, divine commands, and natural facts, they are viewed as deep, internally motivating commitments of any rational agent. Within the limits of these principles, the good life for individuals is determined not by existing 'intrinsic values' but by the individuals' free choice of particular ends.

In attributing an inviolable dignity to each rational agent Kant seems fundamentally committed to incommensurable values. Dignity is a value that is above price, always to be respected, and admits no trade-offs. This seems at once to invite moral dilemmas and paradoxes. Sometimes in treating one person as priceless and irreplaceable, we naturally

---

good disposition, and persons who fulfil their duties. Most commentators, including myself, have supposed that Kant's dominant view was that persons have dignity even if they lack a good will, provided they have a capacity for a good will, a minimal rational nature, or a power to set ends. But this assumption does not square well with all of Kant's texts. See Richard Dean, 'What Should We Treat as an End in Itself?', *Pacific Philosophical Quarterly*, 77 (1996), 268–88.

[25] Hill, *Dignity and Practical Reason in Kant's Moral Theory*, ch. 2. See also Christine Korsgaard, 'Kant's Formula of Humanity', in *Creating the Kingdom of Ends* (Cambridge: Cambridge University Press, 1996), 106–32.

suppose, we will inevitably be treating another person as something more expendable. If I am faced with the choice of saving either a hundred persons or one, then their incalculable value seems to imply that neither choice is morally preferable, which seems paradoxical, or else that I will be wrong whichever I do, which seems morally perverse.

The problem, however, is not so simple and may not be so troublesome as it seems at first. The idea that persons have dignity (or are 'ends in themselves') is best understood, I have suggested, not as a specific and directly applicable action principle but, rather, as an abstract expression of the basic attitude of Kantian moral legislators.[26] The point is not, for example, that contributing to the death of a person is always wrong or that it is morally indifferent whether we save the lives of one person or a million. Rather, when we reflect about what general social and personal guidelines we can reasonably affirm from a moral point of view, commitment to dignity reflects an attitude that places the highest priority on maintaining mutual respect, affirming practices that give each person a fair and equal chance for a life appropriate to a rational agent, and endorsing principles only when anyone's acting under them could reasonably be defended to anyone else who was willing to look at the matter from a moral point of view. Moreover, certain rationales for principles would be excluded. For example, we could not decide what principles to adopt simply by engaging in cost–benefit reasoning, such as 'Each person has dignity, two have twice as much as one, etc., and so we should go with the principles that maximize net benefit (lives, or whatever).' Reasoning one's way to particular moral principles and policy guides will not, on this view, be easy, rigorously deductive, or uncontroversial; but this, one might argue, is a fact of life, acknowledged by any reasonable ethical theory.

In affirming dignity as an incommensurable value, Kantian theory may well leave us with some unanswerable moral questions; but in principle, I take it, the theory could not acknowledge strict moral dilemmas. A central tenet of Kantian theory is that to judge that one has a strict duty is to acknowledge that one is under a categorical imperative, a practical demand of reason that is within one's power to fulfil. Thus when I face a situation in which it seems that I must do A, I must do B, and I cannot do both,[27] Kantian theory would have to say, 'Appear-

---

[26] Here I summarize a line of thought developed in *Dignity and Practical Reason in Kant's Moral Theory*, ch. 10.

[27] Donagan would add that in such a situation the impossibility is not due to my own prior violation of a moral principle. In the original version of this essay I suggested that

ances must be mistaken; either the argument to the dilemma must be wrong or your working conception of how to derive duties must be revised; so think again.'[28]

The Right Independent of the Good?

Given the way this issue is usually understood, Kant's ethics must be classified as a theory that places 'the right' prior to 'the good'. It does not start with the assumption that happiness, preference satisfaction, or any other substantive ends are intrinsically valuable, objective goods, or agent-neutral reasons to act. Rather, the principles of right and duty are determined by rational reflection from a point of view that counts each agent as equally authoritative regarding moral principles and equally free to set and pursue individual ends within the limits set by these principles.[29] The moral principles are not justified by the thought that they maximize, or even justly distribute, some independent good; and what they prescribe is not that one aim to produce a certain quantity or distribution of such goods.

The Kantian position suggested here is a mix of obvious and controversial claims, as may become clearer in the following example. Suppose I believe that I would get pleasure from seeing a certain film and I feel pulled toward going to see it. The Kantian idea that this expected pleasure and satisfaction of desire is not a fixed, objective value, independent of right, implies several claims: (1) As utilitarians agree, it may be wrong, all things considered, for me to indulge this enjoyment (e.g. if I have prior obligations, it is an exploitive film, etc.). (2) Contrary to classic utilitarians, the fact that I would enjoy it does not *by itself*

I might agree with Donagan, but in a later essay I suggest reasons for Kantians to reject Donagan's claim that moral dilemmas are possible if and only if agents generate their own dilemmas by their previous wrongdoing. See 'Moral Dilemmas, Gaps, and Residues', in H. E. Mason (ed.), *Moral Dilemmas and Moral Theory* (New York and Oxford: Oxford University Press, 1996), 167–98.

[28] If strict moral dilemmas are unmistakenly derivable from a particular interpretation, or reconstruction, of the Categorical Imperative procedure and so some aspect of the Kantian theory in question must be revised, it seems more in the spirit of Kant's dominant concerns to revise the Categorical Imperative procedure than to give up the idea that duties are rational demands within one's power to fulfil.

[29] When I say that persons are 'equally authoritative' with regard to moral principles, the sort of moral authority in question is supposed analogous to political authority as conceived, e.g., by Rousseau. That is, the idea is that the source of the moral force of principles is supposed to be the will of all persons, conceived as equals. My point is not the idea that everyone is equally 'expert', knowledgeable, clear-headed, and articulate about what the moral principles are (even though Kant was more optimistic about the latter than most of us).

constitute evidence weighing in support of the judgement that others morally ought to help me gain the enjoyment, for moral duty is not a function of value pluses and minuses assigned to possible outcomes. (3) As any theory of non-moral rational choice would acknowledge, the fact that I would enjoy the film does not in itself give me adequate (non-moral) reason, all things considered, to see the film, for I may have more pressing needs or interests. (4) Most radically, the fact that I would enjoy the film is not even something that in itself gives me a (non-moral) reason that I must weigh in favour of seeing the film, for, moral demands aside, nothing is in itself fixed as valuable for me independently of my endorsing it, as a rational agent, as among my personal ends.[30] The Kantian idea, then, is not merely the trivial and obvious claims 1 and 3; it includes the controversial moral thesis 2 and the radical non-moral thesis 4.

The Kantian position presented here is in some respects radical and controversial, but it will seem even more so, in fact quite mad, if confused with certain other claims. It is important, for example, not to construe the Kantian point as a denial of a duty of beneficence. Presumably Kantian legislators, even abstracting from the content of personal ends, would rationally will that everyone, within the constraints of stricter duties, make it a policy to promote the ends of others, though allowing some room for choice about when, where, and how much. Knowing that one would enjoy an available activity naturally inclines one to pursue it, and, if one sees no reason to the contrary, one commonly and reasonably chooses to make a place for the activity among one's ends. We can assume, then, that virtually all people include engaging in enjoyable activities among their ends, and so it is a reasonable presumption, in most cases, that helping to enable others to engage in enjoyable activities is a prime example of the sort of thing the moral principle of beneficence guides us to do. What beneficence directly requires that one promote (to some degree) is the realization of the permissible ends of others, whatever these chosen ends may be. Enjoyable activities and other more particular ends become morally important (when not excluded by other principles) because these are what people choose to go for, not because the activities, or the pleasant experiences they bring, have an objective 'intrinsic value'.

Beneficence merely illustrates how personal ends can have indirect moral significance as one attempts to work out specific applications of general moral principles. Once chosen, the ends of particular individ-

---

[30] This last theme is discussed in Hill, *Autonomy and Self-respect*, ch. 12.

uals, separately or in common pursuits, should also prove morally important under other moral principles. What friendship, gratitude, and even respect require on particular occasions depends, of course, on who the particular persons affected are, how they 'define themselves' (as some put it), and what their deepest commitments and aspirations are.

Another claim not to be conflated with the Kantian idea considered here is that 'the right' can be determined with complete neutrality regarding matters that are (broadly speaking) evaluative. The Kantian idea, I take it, is not that moral principles can be determined simply from 'naturalistic' definitions of terms, from psychological facts together with non-controversial principles of rationality, and so on. At the heart of Kantian theory are ideas of rational agency, duty, and freedom that are neither uncontroversial nor 'purely descriptive', 'normatively neutral', etc. To suppose that one might develop an adequate ethical theory on evaluatively non-committal foundations is, I think, a mistake, though it would also be foolish to conclude from this that any evaluative starting point is just as worthy of allegiance as any other.

Finally, the priority of the right over the good that I have in mind is not a denial of various claims that Kant makes about the unqualified *goodness* of a good will, the dignity or unconditioned and incomparable *worth* of rational/moral agents, and the fact that all imperatives represent acts as *good* to do (as means or in themselves).[31] These can all be understood, I think, as consistent with 'the right prior to the good', as this is generally meant. They should not be understood as affirming the existence of substantive intrinsic values independent of and prior to the processes of rational reflection from which the more basic principles of right are supposed to be drawn. The ideas of a good will and dignity are too inseparably bound up with the idea of the right and not sufficiently substantive to be the sort of goods at issue in debates about the relative priority of the right and the good.

Any development of Kantian theory along these lines must, of course, confront the now-familiar objections to contemporary theories that place the right prior to the good. For example, can one give a rationally persuasive account of the procedures determining the right that will actually yield substantive moral principles? Has the procedure illicitly presupposed particular value judgements about which it purports to be neutral? If a theory of right is developed in austere detachment from particular facts about the 'internal values' of actual social practices, will it be so indiscriminately permissive of diversity that it will undermine

---

[31] G, 61 [393], 102 [434], 81 [413].

culture and foster disharmony? To these standard objections another may be added. Do we really see what is non-morally good or valuable to a person as *chosen*? Is the radical idea that individuals determine their (non-moral) good by freely choosing their ends compatible with what seems to many an obvious fact, namely, that in a sense we *find* what we value as ends through experience and reflection and we even suppose at times that we *discover* what is valuable in itself?[32]

Permissive, Undogmatic, and Non-judgemental?

The terms of my last type of 'pluralism' are too indefinite to permit exact classifications of theories. But I want to close with a few comments on how Kant's theory fares in this category, because this category best matches the currently popular idea of pluralism as opposition to attitudes that stifle diversity of cultures and life-styles.

First, because Kantian ethics starts from the idea of rational agents abstracting as far as possible from particular cultural commitments and preferences, arguments from this idea should tend to support a relatively open society with liberties protected and diversity permitted. Cultural diversity would not be glorified as valuable for its own sake, but it would not be suppressed for the purpose of promoting the general happiness. This is, of course, what Rawls's development of a Kantian theory of justice leads us to expect, and it corresponds to Kant's ideas in the *Rechtslehre*, where the overarching concern is liberty of external action under universal laws.[33] But the Kantian perspective should also tend toward an analogous conclusion regarding non-enforceable ethical judgements. Even here liberty is the presumption, for no individual or group pursuits are forbidden unless a case can be made against them that is grounded in what all would agree to from the rational legislative perspective. As Kant suggests, respect for persons as those whose choices are the source of value would seem to require a positive attitude toward both the diverse (permissible) ends that people actually choose and their continuing capacity and opportunity to choose. Duty constrains individual choice not in order to promote a given vision of a valuable life but largely to grant others similar opportunity to pursue their own visions.

Would a Kantian ethical theory endorse, or invite, dogmatic moral-

---

[32] This question raises two further questions, which express doubts of different kinds. First, is the radical denial of objective intrinsic value judgements tenable? Second, does my account of 'Kantian theory' exaggerate or distort Kant's own view of the matter? Both questions, I think, merit more attention. The second question is discussed in ch. 3.

[33] *Rechtslehre* is pt. 1 of *The Metaphysics of Morals*.

izing? Readers of Kant know that in theory Kant himself insistently opposed dogmatism,[34] but they may also recall that in practice Kant sometimes asserted strict principles with such fervour and so little argument that one could be forgiven for suspecting Kant of having a dogmatic streak. But the issue is the theory, not the man—in fact the reconstructed basic theory, not the man's theory in every detail.

It would take a long time, and much detailed work, to argue that Kantian ethics, or some alternative, gave more convincing support than other theories to ideals opposing dogmatism: openness to criticism from all quarters; willingness to revise opinions when confronted with good reasons; civility and respect in argument; resolve to convince others rather than awe them with one's authority; commitment to guiding rather than goading; and so on. But the richness of the basic ideas of Kantian ethics for this purpose should be obvious. Requirements of respect are among the more obvious applications of the idea of dignity.[35] What one morally ought to do is supposed to be determined by reason and from a point of view that gives no special status to anyone. Moral truths, if there are any, are ideal convergence points of the best practical reasoning of everyone, not facts about a remote world of theological truth, Platonic forms, or Moorean non-natural facts, to which (one might suppose) experts have special access. Kant's conception of reason, unlike that of many philosophers, is not that of an intuitive power that enables the gifted to see hidden metaphysical facts that ordinary folk must take on authority. It is a reflective capacity that virtually all are supposed to have and are urged to use, and in ethics what it seeks is not an accurate description of the world but a way of life that mutually respectful human beings, committed to some formal constraints of reasonableness, can agree on. There are many problems with this view, but a special tendency to encourage dogmatism does not seem prominent among them.

Finally, does Kantian ethics endorse or encourage self-righteousness and judgemental blaming attitudes? Here, as before, a thorough answer would be long and complex, but some tendencies may be readily noted. On the one hand, Kant's remarks on punishment, unnatural sex, and common lies do not readily leave the impression of one who is perfectly self-disciplined in withholding moral blame from others.[36] Also, any

---

[34] See, e.g., Kant's essay 'What is Enlightenment?', in *Kant: Political Writings*, ed. Hans Reiss (Cambridge: Cambridge University Press, 1991), 54–60.

[35] See, e.g., MM, 209–13 [462–8].

[36] MM, 104–13 [331–42], 178–80 [424–5], 182–4 [429–30], and 'On a Supposed Right to Lie because of Philanthropic Concerns', in *Grounding of the Metaphysic of Morals*, tr. James Ellington, 3rd edn. (Indianapolis: Hackett Publishing Co., 1993), 63–7.

theory that advocates more stringent standards than another may tend to give the self-righteous more opportunities to judge and blame. And, of course, theories that affirm that individual choices can be morally wrong by reference to an objective standard other than the agent's own preferences, voluntary commitments, etc. cannot undermine the moralistic judge's authoritative tone quite as obviously as some relativistic theories can.

In surprisingly many ways, however, Kant's theoretical writing runs contrary to our moralistic tendencies.[37] Repeatedly Kant insists that we know far too little of human motivation, of others or our own, to make confident judgements about when, if ever, individuals are acting in morally worthy ways. Even those who have never done anything externally wrong may be, in their fundamental maxims, no better than the common criminal. Although each criminal must accept a fair and often severe punishment appropriate to the crime, this is ultimately to maintain the institutions needed to secure liberty, not because wickedness demands suffering.[38] The principle of respect is not qualified according to our judgements of others' moral worth. No matter how horrible a person's crimes, each person must be regarded with respect as a human being. Mockery and treating people with contempt are contrary to due respect, as are also many familiar forms of self-disparagement.[39] More important, the emphasis in Kant's theory is on the deliberative first-person question. 'What ought *I* to do?', not comparative (or even absolute) questions of moral status. Nothing is good without qualification but a good will; but, for deep reasons, you can and should be responsible for the goodness only of your own will, not the wills of others.[40]

See also Kant's correspondence with Maria von Herbert in *Kant's Philosophical Correspondence, 1759–99*, ed. and tr. Arnulf Zweig (Chicago: University of Chicago Press, 1967), 174–5, 188–90.

[37] This theme is developed in Hill, *Dignity and Practical Reason in Kant's Moral Theory*, ch. 9.

[38] This is contrary to the common view of Kant's remarks on punishment, but I give some reasons for this interpretation in ch. 7 of this volume.

[39] See MM, 186–7 [434–6], 212–13 [466–8].   [40] MM, 150–2 [385–8].

2

A Kantian Perspective on Moral Rules

Both Kantian and utilitarian theories are in need of further development, and in fact even their strongest advocates now tend to see the theories more as projects in progress than as finished products with every detail engraved in stone. My main concern in this paper is to develop some ideas within the Kantian tradition, without worrying about whether the views presented are orthodox or radically revisionary. More specifically, I sketch some features of a Kantian perspective for reflection on moral rules, contrast this with some other views, and briefly call attention to some problems and strategies for addressing them.

My discussion is meant to be suggestive rather than argumentative, for too many details need to be filled in before one can draw more than tentative conclusions about these matters. Such abstract and incomplete reflections are no substitute, of course, for more narrowly focused attention to theoretical and practical issues. But sometimes it is useful to step back from more detailed issues to ask what large projects in moral philosophy seem most worth developing. Since, as most proponents agree, current versions of both Kantian and rule-utilitarian theories need to be further refined, revised, and supplemented, one cannot decide between these approaches by first seeing exactly what they prescribe for particular cases and then comparing these outcomes with intuitive judgements. In this situation, other sorts of comparison become more important. We should consider, for example, *the sort of moral reflection* each theory recommends, independently of how (or whether) the theories may in the end lead to different judgements about specific cases. My concern here will be with a Kantian normative theory considered at this more abstract level. One should not suppose, however, that at this level moral judgement is unnecessary and we can evaluate competing theories by purely theoretical criteria, such as simplicity, comprehensiveness, and formal elegance. We have relevant moral convictions not only about what it is right to do but also about how we should decide what is right to do.

What are called 'ethical theories' are sets of ideas designed for various purposes, arising in different contexts, often addressing distinct problems. The perspective to be sketched here is not a comprehensive moral theory; nor is it an answer to the 'metaethical' issues that have recently returned to centre stage in moral philosophy. Rather, what I call 'the Kantian perspective' is meant to be considered as a way of framing and guiding the moral reflection of conscientious agents when they are deliberating about certain practical questions. The usual candidates for this role are other 'normative ethical theories', as often presented in ethics textbooks: for example, act-utilitarianism, rule-util-itarianism, Rossian pluralism, Rawlsian contractualism (as sometimes adapted for ethics), and Kant's 'universal law' and 'ends in themselves' formulations of the Categorical Imperative. With many variations and a few alternatives, these normative theories are often offered as candi-dates for acceptance to students presumed to be conscientious and morally sensitive about many familiar local matters but not yet reflec-tive and articulate about how to assess unfamiliar and troublesome cases. The context of discussion, typically, is not a metaphysical debate about the reality of moral properties, a chaplain's sermon to cynical or sociopathic criminals, or the project of a Cartesian moral philosopher who, doubting all his previous moral opinions, now seeks to build an entire moral system from sparse but indubitable premises. Theories are considered not as self-evident truths or even theorems to be proved but as possible frameworks to use in shaping one's moral reflections, and they are offered not as having morally neutral credentials but as ideas themselves subject to moral evaluation.

My remarks here presuppose a similar context. More specifically, I want to consider how certain aspects of Kant's ethics, or some reason-able adaptation of them, might serve us if we were sincerely trying as reasonable, conscientious persons to resolve some practical questions about how to conceive, specify, and apply certain moral rules and prin-ciples.[1] For these purposes an ethical theory is no use to us unless it can guide our decisions or help to structure our dialogue; and, even if choice-

---

[1] Throughout this paper I will repeatedly use the expression 'reasonable and consci-entious' to convey an ordinary, indefinite idea of sensible, well-intentioned people trying to decide well and act as they morally ought. This is the audience, at least in their best moments, that Kant thought he was addressing. The word 'rational' has acquired too many technical associations among philosophers to serve the same purpose. Also I should note that, though I mostly write of 'rules' rather than 'rules and principles' in this chapter, the longer phrase might serve as well or better. I mean to facilitate eventual comparison about publicly affirmed general moral norms with rule-utilitarian thinking about the same, and for this purpose the term 'rule' is apt. However, in Kant's philosophy the sort of norms in question are the intermediate 'principles' in *The Metaphysics of Morals*, not the Categorical Imperative itself, not specific local norms, and not merely personal 'prin-ciples' of individuals.

guiding, the theory will carry no authority for us unless it coheres with our basic outlook as reasonable, conscientious moral agents.

One further caveat. Though discussion here will focus on moral rules, we should acknowledge that rules are not applicable to all aspects of moral living. Even in situations that fall under moral rules, it is not always necessary, best, or even appropriate for an agent to be thinking primarily of rules. Also, though rules have a place in moral reflection, they generate problems that must be faced. For example, any system of rules raises worries about conflicts, gaps, alternative interpretations, and hard cases. Too often familiar moral generalizations ignore relevant differences among particular cases or are defended from a perspective alien to our outlook in daily life.

Assuming, then, the context of discussion as I have described it, my aim and plan is as follows. The main object is to sketch the elements and outlines of a way of thinking about moral rules that is drawn from one of Kant's less influential formulations of the Categorical Imperative, namely, the principle that one ought always to conform to the laws of a possible kingdom of ends. As liberally reconstructed here, this principle combines central ideas from Kant's· other formulations. The principle calls for a way of thinking analogous in structure to John Rawls's theory of justice, but the differences are important. Like rule-utilitarianism, the Kantian principle distinguishes moral reflection about rules from moral judgement on particular cases, and both theories require us to think about what would happen if various rules were generally adopted. But despite these similarities, the Kantian perspective on rules is fundamentally different from rule-utilitarian perspectives.

More specifically, in the first section I indicate how the elements, or construction materials, of the kingdom of ends are drawn from Kant's more familiar ideas of a good will and the previous formulations of the Categorical Imperative. No simple formula, I think, can meet the unreasonable demand for a precise and morally adequate decision procedure; and, as is well known, there are special difficulties in trying to use Kant's famous formulas of universal law and ends in themselves as comprehensive and decisive tests to determine in particular cases what one ought to do. None the less, as Kant suggests, these formulas, along with the ideas of a good will and the formula of autonomy, provide the basic ideas from which an idealized model of moral legislation can be built, and it may be that these ideas stand better together than they do alone.

Then, in the second section, I outline an ideal of moral legislation that results when these preliminary ideas are put together in a certain conception of the kingdom of ends. This ideal, both in Kant's work and as briefly sketched here, is obviously underdefined in important ways and needs to be refined and supplemented if it is to be of any practical use. But even in its somewhat indeterminate form the kingdom of ends, construed as a perspective for moral legislation, contrasts significantly with Rawls's idea of the original position, rule-utilitarianism, and Kant's other formulations of the Categorical Imperative.

In the final section I discuss briefly some problems which arise when we try to use the idealized Kantian perspective as a heuristic for thinking about real-world issues.

ELEMENTS OF THE KANTIAN
LEGISLATIVE PERSPECTIVE

The Kantian idea to be considered here is a reconstruction and modification of Kant's idea of a 'Reich der Zwecke', or 'kingdom of ends'.[2] It has obvious affinities with ideas of John Rawls and others, but my focus will be on its roots in Kant's ethics. Kant presents the ideal of a 'kingdom of ends' as in some way a combination of the ideas expressed in other formulations of the Categorical Imperative. It expresses a 'complete determination' of maxims, he says, in a way that helps to bring the abstract universal law formula 'nearer to intuition' and so better able to 'secure acceptance'.[3] In the *Groundwork* Kant does not give examples to illustrate the application of his kingdom of ends principle, and he even suggests that for guiding moral judgement the 'universal law' formula is better.[4] In Kant's later ethical writings the principle is largely passed over in favour of the more famous first two formulas. Thus in a scrupulously balanced interpretative account of Kant's ethics, the kingdom of ends principle would not play the central role that it will have in this discussion. Nevertheless, the idea is worth considering in its own right. Moreover, as Kant suggests, it brings together many of his other ideas, and these stand better united than they do alone.

In this section I want to review some basic features of a moral attitude that would, I think, be endorsed not only by Kant but also by most

---

[2] My discussion of the Kantian perspective here draws from and continues my discussions in the following essays: 'The Kingdom of Ends', 'Making Exceptions without Abandoning the Principle: or How a Kantian Might Think about Terrorism', and 'Kantian Constructivism in Ethics', in *Dignity and Practical Reason in Kant's Moral Theory* (Ithaca, NY: Cornell University Press, 1992).

[3] G, 100–7 [433–40], esp. 104 [437].   [4] G, 104 [437].

contemporary philosophers who count their theories as Kantian. Kant himself goes beyond these minimal points in various ways, but my aim here is to draw from these ideas, not to give an exact representation of Kant's position. The idea is to draw out some central elements of a moral attitude from Kant's discussion of a good will, the idea of duty, and three formulations of the Categorical Imperative (universal law, humanity as an end in itself, and autonomy). These are the building blocks for a reconstruction of the idea that we 'legislate' moral rules in a kingdom of ends.

1. Like other forms of the Categorical Imperative, the kingdom of ends principle is supposed to express basic commitments of reasonable, conscientious persons, that is, ourselves so far as we have 'good wills'. One of these commitments is implicit in Kant's initial idea that a good will is *good unconditionally* and *above all else*.[5] We begin with a thought experiment. Among the many things we find worth seeking and preserving, which do we count as good in all possible contexts, that is, as things that we cannot, on deep reflection, justify (to ourselves and others) sacrificing for anything else? Many things, such as money, fame, and power, we would find it reasonable to sacrifice under some imaginable circumstances. If the legendary Satan offered you continual 'happiness' in return for your basic commitment to live as a reasonable moral person, even then, Kant thought, you could not really justify the choice to yourself, though you might in fact be tempted to accept the bargain. Reasonable moral agents, in Kant's view, are deeply committed to trying to live as they should, not just 'as a rule' but always. Though of course not wanting to sacrifice other goods, they acknowledge that they should forgo any desired goods if the price were to be abandoning or violating their commitment to do what, in their best judgement, they find morally obligatory.

This leaves open, of course, the content of what each will judge to be morally required. It is misguided, or at least premature, to object that acknowledging the supreme value of a good will might require one to sacrifice even one's family for the impartial good of all; for the Kantian idea as construed here is formal and modest. That is, it says, 'Do what you must to maintain your good will,' which is to follow your best judgement as to what, all things considered, is morally and rationally required in the situation. If, as is likely, you judge the sacrifice of your family to be morally wrong, then you are committed to avoiding it, no matter what public or 'impartial' goods may thereby be lost.

---

[5] See G, 61–4 [393–6].

The commitment to the overriding value of a good will, for Kantians, is not a matter of pursuing any general end of the kinds philosophers have typically urged, such as personal happiness, self-realization, or the general welfare. Nor is it a commitment to the rules of external authorities, such as God, state, or community. Abstractly, it is a will to 'conform to universal law as such'.[6] One conceives of something as a 'universal law', in Kant's sense, if one sees it as a principle of conduct for everyone that is 'practically necessary', a principle the violation of which one could not justify to oneself or others. In sum, as reasonable, conscientious agents we are deeply committed to conforming to *whatever general principles* our reflections as such agents prescribe. The presumption at this point is that there will be principles of this sort; but that has yet to be seen.

2. Kant reaches a similar point from a different angle by analysing the idea of duty.[7] To acknowledge that one has moral duties, as any conscientious person does, is to accept that there is at least one general principle of conduct that is a 'categorical imperative', that is, a rational moral requirement for everyone not based or conditional on its serving one's contingent personal ends (and not merely saying 'take the means to your ends'). The only principle that could, strictly, fit this description, Kant says, is (once again) 'Conform to universal law as such.'[8] Thus, again, what we know of all reasonable, conscientious agents is that they are deeply and overridingly committed to constraining and guiding their conduct by whatever principles for everyone they find, upon appropriate reflection, supported by compelling reasons. The sort of reasoning in which we are to find the content of moral principles cannot be exclusively self-interested or instrumental reasoning, for that would yield not duties but only prudential and conditional requirements. These conceptual points are, of course, no proof that there are moral duties; they are only preliminary clues as to how to look for them.

3. Kant's first effort to give more content to the abstract idea of 'conforming to universal law' was to simply identify this requirement with his famous first formulation of the Categorical Imperative and then to give examples to illustrate how that formula could guide moral judgement. Kant makes this crucial move twice,[9] but critics find it baffling and even sympathetic interpreters can see a gap in the argument. If we assume for now my loose and informal reconstruction of Kant's thought

---

[6] See G, 70 [402].   [7] See G, 82–8 [414–21].
[8] G, 88 [420].   [9] G, 70 [402] and 88 [420–1].

up to the crucial step, the problem is this. Even though 'conform to universal law' is a commitment of conscientious agents, it is only a very minimal requirement, telling one very little about how to go about moral deliberation. Kant and his followers, however, find quite substantive procedures for moral judgement in the universal law formula: one ought never to act except in such a way that one can also will that one's maxim should become a universal law.[10] Interpretations of this vary, but on any account one must identify a maxim for proposed actions, try to 'conceive' that very maxim *as* a universal law in some sense, and (if successful) determine whether one 'can will' that universal law along with one's initial maxim. There are many ways of construing these several steps; but, whatever the way, if it yields substantive guidance in particular cases without borrowing from independent moral principles, it seems clearly to have gone beyond the minimal requirement 'conform to universal law', understood in the thin sense that makes the latter initially plausible.

Whether or not the universal law formula really follows from 'conform to universal law' in the initial sense, its content is meant to express something fundamental about a moral attitude. However one construes the details, it is supposed to be concerned with willingness to reciprocate, to avoid being a free-rider, and to check one's personal policies by reflecting about what would be reasonable from a broader perspective. This much seems rather uncontroversial as a partial characterization of the attitude of a conscientious person. The problems begin, however, when one tries to work out the details behind the hope (which Kant encouraged) that this simple formula, by itself, could serve as a direct test for determining right and wrong in particular cases. A massive literature has developed over many years as Kant's sympathizers have constructed ingenious devices to make the formula work as an action guide and Kant's critics have invented new counterexamples to undermine their attempts.[11]

[10] See G, 70 [402], 88 [421], 104 [436]. Most commentators, reasonably, distinguish the strict uninterpreted (or not yet 'typified') version of the formula from the interpreted versions that are applicable to cases. Thus, for example, 'Act only on that maxim through which you can at the same time will that it should become a universal law,' G, 88 [421], expresses the former, whereas 'Act as if the maxim of your action were to become a universal law of nature,' G, 89 [421], expresses the latter. See C2, 70–6 [68–73]. See also H. J. Paton, *The Categorical Imperative* (London: Hutchison and Co., 1958), 133–64, esp. 157–64.
[11] See, for example, Nelson T. Potter and Mark Timmons (eds.), *Morality and Universality: Essays on Ethical Universalizability* (Dordrecht: Reidel, 1985); M. G. Singer, *Generalization in Ethics* (New York: Atheneum, 1971); Onora (O'Neill) Nell, *Acting on Principle* (New York: Columbia University Press, 1975); and *Constructions of Reason*

It is not to my purpose to review or take sides in this debate, but it is worth noting one persistent problem and one constructive suggestion that have emerged from the controversy. The problem stems from the notorious difficulty of specifying the maxim of an action. The difficulty is not that we cannot easily tell what maxim a person has acted on in the past; for in Kant's theory the primary task is deliberating about prospective conduct and, surprisingly, assessment of the moral worth of past acts is of little importance for that task.[12] The problem is that it is difficult to find any way of characterizing the proper description of the maxim to be tested without relying upon one's antecedent sense of how the test should come out. But if that is so, we do not really have any sort of litmus test of the rightness or wrongness of particular acts; for our independent judgements regarding the latter are guiding our selection of inputs for the alleged test. The formula might still be acceptable as a framework within which to conceptualize the results of one's moral judgements, but not acceptable by itself as a guide to such judgements.

Admittedly some conditions on the description of maxims are implicit in Kant's theory, both in what he says about them and in the role they are supposed to play. For example, it is clear that my maxim cannot include features of a prospective act that I am not aware of in deliberation. For example, if Mary has no idea that her accepting a job will result in John's losing his, then her maxim could not include reference to that fact. Also, most details that are not salient for an agent seem not to belong in an honest statement of the agent's maxim. For example, if I am thinking of repeating a rumour, then it is unlikely to be relevant that the victim is 49 years old, dark-haired, left-handed, and English-speaking. It is tempting to say that factors unimportant to the agent should be excluded from the description of that agent's maxim, but this would raise problems. Suppose, for example, that I know that my repeating a rumour will severely damage another person, but I am indifferent to this fact. Testing a maxim that makes no reference to the damage seems likely to give a morally wrong result; and, quite apart from this, it seems bizarre to suppose that I could assess my proposed

(Cambridge: Cambridge University Press, 1989); Christine Korsgaard, 'Kant's Formula of Universal Law', in *Creating the Kingdom of Ends* (Cambridge: Cambridge University Press, 1996), 106–32; Thomas Pogge, 'The Categorical Imperative', in Paul Guyer (ed.), *Kant's Groundwork of the Metaphysics of Morals: Critical Essays* (Lanham, Md.: Rowman and Littlefield, 1998), 189–213; and Barbara Herman, *The Practice of Moral Judgment* (Cambridge, Mass.: Harvard University Press, 1993).

[12] This is a theme I develop in 'Kant's Anti-moralistic Strain', in *Dignity and Practical Reason in Kant's Moral Theory*, ch. 9.

act morally without reference to the pertinent fact that I would be knowingly harming another person.

Much has been said, and more can be, about what is relevant in constructing the maxim, but it seems that ultimately conditions of relevance must be guided by independent moral judgement. In fact one finds again and again that both sides in debates about Kant's formula tend to pick the maxim description that yields the results they want, relying on their prior sense of the morally appropriate conclusion in the case. For them, at least, the formula is not working as a test.

Struggling with another problem in applying the universal law formula leads to a more constructive suggestion. The problem is raised by the familiar example of a fanatic who is willing to accept everyone's living by maxims that most of us find morally repugnant. A fanatical Nazi, for example, might be willing to accept everyone's persecuting those who have, or whose immediate ancestors have, certain physical characteristics.[13] That is, we are to imagine that he would accept this even if he believed that he himself fit the description. (Imagine that if someone were to convince him, with real or forged papers, that he falls into the hated class, he would accept persecution and even ask to be destroyed.) Now there are various ways to approach the case, but one suggestion is this. What counts is not what the fanatic personally, with all his prejudices and idiosyncrasies, would be willing to accept for all to do. The relevant question is, 'What can he *rationally* will (or will *as a rational agent*)?' This seems to call for reflection from a broader perspective, where 'reasons' are not exclusively person-relative. In effect, maxims that one *can will qua rational* can be construed as simply those that one can personally adopt without conflict with whatever 'universal laws' one is committed to as a reasonable, conscientious agent.

This suggestion makes the universal law formula more similar to the abstract requirement from which it was supposed to follow, namely, 'conform to universal law as such'. Moreover, as will be evident, construing the formula this way points towards the sort of reflection that characterizes legislators in the kingdom of ends.[14] By requiring agents

---

[13] The example is from R. M. Hare, *Freedom and Reason* (Oxford: Oxford University Press, 1963), 158–85.

[14] There remains a significant difference, however, between the reconstructed universal law formula and the kingdom of ends principle to be discussed. The difference is that, even as modified, the universal law formula still requires one to identify a maxim for the proposed action and try to figure out what this very maxim would be 'as a universal law', where this can be understood in various ways, for example, a law of permission ('everyone may . . .'), or a psychological law ('everyone does . . .'), or a teleological law

to assess their 'maxims', the formula at least expresses the idea that moral deliberation requires one to evaluate not only the expected consequences of one's act but also, under other descriptions, what one sees oneself as doing, one's aims, and one's underlying policies and reasons. The formula represents the conscientious person as one who evaluates his or her own acts and policies, not merely in terms of their effectiveness towards desired goals, but as implicitly taking a stand on what others may reasonably do. But this is not to suggest, of course, that the universal law formula can function by itself as a moral litmus test, for no results emerge until we add some other basic ideas to supplement the formula and we do some substantive thinking as reasonable, conscientious agents with relevant empirical information.

4. Further elements of a Kantian conception of a basic moral attitude are suggested by the idea of humanity as an end in itself.[15] Familiar in general but controversial in detail, this expresses the thought that human beings have dignity, not mere price. Independently of talents, accomplishments, and social status, each person is to be regarded as having a special worth that conscientious agents must always take into account. This value is not derived from one's being useful or pleasing to others, and it takes precedence over values that are contingent in those ways. More controversially, dignity is not value that can be quantified but is 'without equivalent'.[16] One cannot, for example, justify disregarding or violating the dignity of a few persons with the thought that thereby one would promote more dignity in many other persons. One acknowledges the dignity of other rational agents by constraining one's pursuit of one's own ends, restricting oneself solely to means–ends activity that those affected by one's action could, on appropriate reflection, agree with. The ground of dignity, on Kant's view, is a person's rational and moral capacities, but to respect a person's dignity one must appropriately take into account the whole person. We must pay attention to the reasonable claims and conscientious opinions of others and give special weight to what preserves, promotes, and honours each person's capacity to live as a reasonable, conscientious agent. Since they are *human* beings, the only rational persons we must deal with have a full array of natural human needs as well as personal loves

('our natural end is to . . .'). The kingdom of ends principle, by contrast, allows one to assess one's proposed act, under any description, by the standards of the prescriptive 'laws' for everyone that one would endorse in morally appropriate reasonable reflection.

[15] See G, 95–8 [427–30].

[16] G, 102–3 [434–6]. My way of understanding these ideas is more fully developed in chs. 1 and 9 of *Dignity and Practical Reason in Kant's Moral Theory*.

and individual projects. One cannot treat them with dignity without giving due regard to their quite reasonable concern for these matters as well.

These ideas about human dignity add some substance to a Kantian conception of a basic moral attitude, but they do not encourage one to treat Kant's formula of humanity as an end in itself as a self-contained, definitive moral guide to be used on a case-by-case basis. The formula expresses in a general way an important conception of a moral attitude, but this does not translate immediately into simple action principles. The basic attitude leaves many unresolved questions for further dialogue and reflection. Any resolution, it seems, will require further moral judgement, and universal agreement is not guaranteed. While it is clear that one must not trade or sacrifice the dignity of anyone for 'more dignity' for others, this leaves it distressingly open how to decide notorious hard cases where it seems one cannot fully respect the dignity of all. What exactly one must do (and avoid) in order to respect dignity remains a matter of judgement, as does the question how much and in what ways one must promote others' ends. Others must be *able to agree* with one's choice of ends and means, as I said, 'on appropriate reflection'; but what sort of reflection is appropriate needs to be further specified.

5. Kant's formula of autonomy provides further material for characterizing a Kantian conception of a basic moral attitude.[17] The formula tells us that conscientious agents view every rational agent as, in a sense, legislating moral laws. The most general moral principles that characterize a basic moral attitude express, not divine, natural, or conventional requirements, but rather our 'wills' as conscientious, reasonable agents, what we find upon deep reflection to be pervasive and overriding commitments.[18] Less general moral rules, regarding lies, promises, mutual aid, and so on, are to be seen ideally as joint products of all moral agents deliberating with due regard to both the necessary and contingent values of each person. As in theological conceptions of morality, moral rules are legislated by (or expressive of) the will of an authority; but, as in Rousseau's ideal political society, the authority is not external but a 'general will' that includes, crucially, each person's own acknowledged commitments.

---

[17] See G, 98–100 [431–3]. There is further discussion of autonomy in chs. 5, 6, and 7 of *Dignity and Practical Reason in Kant's Moral Theory* and in Henry Allison's *Kant's Theory of Freedom* (Cambridge: Cambridge University Press, 1990), especially pt. 2.

[18] Admittedly Kant held that we should view moral duties as if they were commands of God and he implies that, along with all rational beings, God legislates moral laws in the kingdom of ends (though without being 'subject' to them). But Kant never maintains that divine command is the source of the authority of moral laws.

We are supposed to think of moral agents as having *autonomy* of the will and so as legislating, in some sense, independently of inclinations and contingent desires. This invokes a quasi-theological idea of the law-marker as standing, God-like, outside the world, devoid of both personal feelings and natural human preferences, and then declaring what is rational for human beings in utter disregard of their natural needs and individual concerns. Scholars disagree about whether Kant was in fact captivated by this sort of picture, but one can draw out some main points about the role of autonomy in moral judgement without invoking any metaphysical images of a quasi-noumenal world.[19]

At a minimum, when we deliberate morally we cannot count the fact that we are inclined to do something, or even that it will promote our happiness, as in itself a sufficient reason for choice. Similarly, one cannot determine what is reasonable to choose by relying uncritically on authorities, precedents, social demands, ties of friendship, or claims about natural human tendencies. All of these may figure in one's reasoning at some stage, but one should not assume prior to critical reflection that they give decisive reasons for choosing. The autonomy of moral agents, however, means more than these negative points.[20] More positively, agents with autonomy acknowledge reasons of another kind that may conflict with and override their personal desires. They presuppose that they can recognize, and on appropriate reflection would accept, such reasons as justifying. Though they feel 'bound' by them, they do not regard the obligation as externally imposed, because they deeply identify themselves as persons committed to acknowledging the force of such considerations.

Further, the ideal of deliberating with autonomy would mean trying, so far as one can, to identify one's preferences, hopes, and fears so that one can consider reflectively whether or not they are good reasons for action. Empirical states, as Kant acknowledged, must figure in the psychological explanation of what we do; but this does not mean that all judgement is blind or that every desire is a prima facie good reason for action. The ideal of autonomy prescribes trying to assess relevant facts and arguments squarely and non-evasively, taking into account ways in which judgements can be skewed by our impulsiveness, wishful thinking, and preference for what is close and familiar. Since, if honest, we realize how poorly we approximate the ideal by ourselves, it should

---

[19] I say 'quasi-noumenal' rather than 'noumenal' because Kant repeatedly insists that the latter term marks not only what is beyond empirical knowledge but also what cannot be pictured.   [20] See G, 114–15 [446–7] and the references in n. 16.

encourage us to submit our opinions and values to the challenge of others with divergent viewpoints.

The formula of autonomy, like the previous ones, raises many questions and obviously cannot function as a self-standing moral decision procedure. It proposes a way of conceiving of moral deliberation and its conclusions, but it is not an abstract rule-generator that can replace factual enquiries, hard thinking, and moral dialogue. Moral deliberation, so conceived, cannot ultimately rest with appeals to authority, the untested voice of individual conscience, or even universal (if uncritical) moral conviction. A sober, non-evasive, and comprehensive awareness of the relevant empirical realities of the world in which one lives is what any rational person seeks as the ideal *background* for particular judgements, but values and moral imperatives cannot simply be *inferred* from such facts.

The ideal of moral agents as jointly legislating moral laws, I suggested, urges us to curb our moral self-complacency by consulting others, listening to divergent views, and submitting our own convictions to criticism. But, unfortunately, we see ample evidence that, even among reasonable, conscientious people, real moral discussion often fails to produce the convergence of judgement that Kant expected among ideally rational legislators with autonomy. This is one reason, among others, that the principle that we should regard each person as a rational, autonomous legislator of moral laws cannot serve by itself as a determinate decision guide. The idea behind the principle, however, can still help to frame morally appropriate attitudes. In practice, we should not only deliberate appropriately but also seek dialogue with other reasonable moral agents, especially those whose lives we will most affect. When disagreements persist, we must often judge and decide how to act anyway; for to suspend judgement and remain passive is itself to take a moral stand. Then, having taken into account the reasoning of others and admitting our fallibility, as conscientious persons we must still act on our own best judgement. In this non-ideal (but typical) situation, we can perhaps still partially express the ideal of acknowledging others as moral legislators by restricting our conduct to what we ourselves can sincerely endorse *as justifiable to other moral deliberators*, even though we lack assurance of their agreement.[21]

---

[21] The metaphor must shift to accommodate deep disagreements. Rather than guiding ourselves by laws that we can see ourselves legislating together with all others by unanimous agreement, we must at least guide ourselves by 'bills' or proposed legislation that, in good conscience, we can stand up to defend before other legislators as worthy of their concurrence.

THE KINGDOM OF ENDS AS A
LEGISLATIVE PERSPECTIVE

The Kantian themes of the previous section can be combined in a conception of an ideal point of view for deliberation about moral rules. The conception is admittedly abstract, incomplete, and problematic. It has obvious structural similarities with Rawls's theory of justice, and this is no accident,[22] though the dissimilarities are also important. The key points can be summarized briefly, for my purpose here is only to show how the legislative ideal is a natural extension of the ideas sketched in the preceding section and to distinguish it from some views with which it might be confused.

The main idea is that one must always conform to the moral laws that would be legislated by oneself and others in a kingdom of ends. This principle itself is supposed to be a basic moral requirement that indicates how to think about more specific moral rules, for example, about deception, promises, mutual aid, imposing risks, killing and letting die. Since the legislators in the kingdom of ends are meant to represent abstractly basic features of a reasonable attitude regarding moral rules, the idea is that one *should* accept the norms that *would* be adopted by legislators in the kingdom. The judgements of the ideal legislators are expected to converge because they are conceived as having the same basic moral attitudes and as being uninfluenced by the many factors that commonly distort ordinary moral judgement. Assuming this ideal convergence of judgement, reasonable, conscientious persons could see the resulting moral rules as, in a sense, self-imposed, that is, not merely demands from others but as reasonable applications of their own deep commitments.

The defining elements of the legislative perspective are drawn from the ideas sketched in the previous section.[23] The members are *rational* in a robust sense, implying more than instrumental rationality. They will not make rules unless they judge that there is good reason to do so, and they are concerned with reasons that anyone falling under the rules could acknowledge. They have *autonomy* of the will, and as rational and autonomous legislators they will *universal laws*. They recognize one

[22] This is not accidental, of course, because Rawls draws from Kant and I draw from Rawls.

[23] See n. 1. Also I should add that my way of understanding how members 'make universal laws' (analogous to political legislation rather than 'universalizing one's maxims'), while supported in Kant's texts, is not the only, or perhaps even the most straightforward, reading of all the relevant passages.

another as *ends in themselves*, with dignity above price. Accordingly, they place a high value on preserving, developing, exercising, and respecting the rational and moral capacities of persons, and they unconditionally attribute a worth to persons that cannot be quantified and is not subject to trade-offs. Acknowledging that each valued member has personal ends of his or her own, they give weight to whatever enhances members' abilities and opportunities to pursue those ends successfully within the bounds of the moral rules they adopt.

In addition to these stipulations, Kant describes the legislators in his kingdom of ends as 'abstracting from personal differences'.[24] This condition reflects the idea that the appropriate attitude for deliberating about moral rules requires a kind of impartiality, a willingness to set aside irrelevant differences between oneself and others for whom the rules are intended. Any useful interpretation of the ideal, however, would need to specify this morally appropriate sense of impartiality. There are familiar problems with interpreting it as a 'veil of ignorance' as extensive as that which characterizes Rawls's 'original position', and even more serious problems with treating it as abstraction from everything empirical, leaving members to reflect about only what is essential to rational agency.

Requiring decisions to be made in ignorance of certain facts is a useful thought experiment or psychological device that can help decision-makers to discount irrelevant personal preferences and minimize other distorting influences on judgement. It serves this function, for example, both in Rawls's theory and in the practice of sequestering juries. But in many common contexts the 'impartiality' that is called for is not selective blindness to facts but rather being guided effectively by given standards, without being distracted by irrelevancies, when one has to judge or decide about cases understood in full detail. If one can make oneself judge by specified standards rather than by irrelevant concerns, then the better one understands the situation in question the wiser one's decision should be.

This suggests a way of interpreting 'abstracting from personal differences' that may be more useful, at least if the conception of a kingdom of ends is to serve any practical action-guiding purpose. The idea would be, not to exclude empirical information about the context for which legislators are to make rules, but only to insist that their decisions about rules be guided so far as possible by specified moral procedures, values, and criteria of relevance instead of by special preferences and

---

[24] G, 100–1 [433].

attachments they have as individuals that are morally irrelevant to the matter at hand. To be realistic, however, we cannot expect that all standards of moral relevance are already implicit in the abstract model, and so we must rely to some extent on our independent judgements about what is morally relevant in the context at hand. But a Kantian perspective is clearly incompatible with at least these two extreme ideas about moral relevance: first, the idea that a rule's being especially beneficial to a particular individual (e.g. oneself) rather than to others is a relevant reason in itself for a legislator to favour the rule, and, second, that all that counts is maximizing the satisfaction of preferences, no matter whose preferences or how they are to be satisfied.

For the kingdom of ends to be of practical use, many details would need to be supplied and some troublesome questions addressed. But already we can note some contrasts between the Kantian legislative ideal as sketched here and some more frequently discussed approaches to moral deliberation.

First, consider the contrast between the kingdom of ends principle and the universal law formulation of the Categorical Imperative. Many of the problems with using the latter as a moral guide stem from the fact that, on the usual readings, it requires us to settle on a particular description that we can identify as *the maxim* of a proposed action. The kingdom of ends formula, like rule-utilitarianism, asks us instead to work out a system of moral rules, which can then serve as a standard as we review our proposed action considered in detail, under many descriptions, without having to select a privileged description as expressing 'the maxim'. Furthermore, the universal law formula tells us to test particular acts by considering them in a possible world different from ours in one way (and whatever else that entails), namely, that everyone adopts our proposed maxim. But the kingdom of ends principle asks us to assess acts by considering them in a more radically and systematically changed world, that is, the world as we think it would be under an ideal system of moral rules. In shifting to the second perspective, we can acknowledge that different sets of interrelated rules shape forms of life in such a way that particular rules and acts typically cannot be assessed in isolation from their normative context. The universal law formula asks us to consider what *particular maxims* we *can will* as universal law, and the kingdom of ends principle invites us directly to consider what *general rules* we *would will* as universal laws. And the sense of 'willing as universal law' is not quite the same.

Second, the formula of humanity as an end in itself is also commonly taken to be a specific action guide that one can apply case by case without raising questions about the network of rules and social relations within which the initial problem arises. This approach leads too easily to conflicts of duty and simplistic moral judgements. What is needed to respect the dignity of one person often seems contrary to the dignity of another. To avoid moral paralysis it is necessary to try to adjudicate such problems at a higher level of deliberation, reflecting on what general rules and policies best reflect the dignity of all. Though some problems may be unresolvable, by incorporating the value of human dignity into the broader legislative perspective of the kingdom of ends we introduce constructive ways of thinking about the troublesome cases.[25] Rather than trying to determine in isolation whether Mary is now treating John as an end, we can try to work out what general moral rules we would reasonably urge for adoption if we had, constraining and shaping our other concerns, an overriding commitment to human dignity. Hard cases would still need to be addressed, but rather than considering them individually we would think about what broad policies are relevant and how, if at all, we can specify legitimate exceptions.

Third, the main idea here is obviously similar to Rawls's abstract model for reflecting on the principles of justice, but one should not overlook important dissimilarities. For example, Rawls's original position was designed for the specific purpose of resolving controversies about the principles of justice governing the basic structure of society, and the defining features of that deliberative position were selected for their suitability for this particular aim.[26] Another difference is that, though the original position is supposed to 'represent' some basic moral values, its members do not presuppose or make any moral judgements. They do not, for example, rely on their sense of what is morally relevant, and they select principles from prudent self-interest rather than by judgement as to what is just. The Kantian legislators are not mutually disinterested. They are overridingly committed to human dignity, which implies not only that they are constrained in their choice of means but also that they value to some extent the personal ends of each. Further, the Kantian legislators are not exclusively focused on the distribution of the 'primary goods' that Rawls considers most crucial when the focus is the justice of the basic economic and political institutions. The goods inherent in the idea of dignity, or humanity as an end in itself,

---

[25] I attempt to show how this might work in ch. 10 of *Dignity and Practical Reason in Kant's Moral Philosophy.*

[26] See John Rawls, *A Theory of Justice* (Cambridge, Mass.: Harvard University Press, 1971).

are overriding for Kantian legislators; and, in addition to considering these, in trying to use the ideal as a heuristic guide we would presumably have to rely on our best judgements regarding other human needs and values as well as more contextual factors.

Fourth, the Kantian legislative perspective also needs to be distinguished from rule-utilitarianism.[27] Both propose ways of thinking about what moral rules there should be and how they should be specified. But from the rule-utilitarian perspective the aim of deliberators is exclusively to find the set of rules that, if generally adopted by the appropriate community, would maximize utility. Utility can be defined, of course, in different ways—for example, as happiness, satisfaction of actual preferences, or fulfilment of a purified set of informed and considered preferences. But the point is always to find the rules that produce the most utility, without prior constraints regarding its distribution or the means of achieving it. Kantian legislators, by contrast, are trying to find rules they can reasonably endorse and justify to one another under the severe constraint of their overriding commitment to the dignity of each person.

By hypothesis, Kantian legislators respect each other as persons with ends of their own and are not indifferent to what enhances the ability of individuals to realize their ends. But the legislators should not be conceived as having the unlimited project and authority to determine, over all matters, which ends are to be promoted and how. Although their jurisdiction is wide-ranging and their sovereignty is complete within its scope, their legislative agenda is limited. The commitments presupposed in taking up the Kantian legislative perspective, as suggested earlier, are to ideas such as the priority of conscientious judgement, acceptance of constraints on self-interest, some form of reciprocity, respect for human dignity, autonomy as an ideal of deliberation, recognition of the autonomy of others, and abstracting from morally irrelevant concerns when deliberating about rules. These commitments are substantial, but they do not, even in theory, propose for legislators an overarching goal of maximizing some given value. Importantly, they do not imply that the law-makers have unlimited authority, or any rational basis, to make whatever rules they prefer or think best as they try, God-like, to empathize completely with the wishes of everyone. In taking up the

---

[27] There are many versions, but one classic is Richard Brandt's 'Toward a Credible Form of Utilitarianism', in Hector-Neri Castañeda and George Nakhnikian (eds.), *Morality and the Language of Conduct* (Detroit: Wayne State University Press, 1965). See also Richard Brandt, *A Theory of the Good and the Right* (Oxford: Clarendon Press, 1979), and R. M. Hare, *Moral Thinking* (Oxford: Clarendon Press, 1981).

Kantian legislative position one does not magically become this empathetic, nor does one commit oneself to obeying the rules of those who do. One does not, as it were, agree to join others in placing all one's preferences into an anonymous pool so that impartial rule-makers, more empathetic and less morally constrained than we, can decide what rules will satisfy the most preferences in the pool. Though they must be prepared to accept the constraints of the rules that, as Kantian legislators, they make, they are not committed to legislate from a point of view that places all their life-plans on the agenda for decision by legislators concerned only to maximize global happiness, preference satisfaction, or even realization of ends.

PROBLEMS OF BRINGING THE KINGDOM DOWN TO EARTH

Comparisons of the kingdom of ends principle with rule-utilitarianism and Rawls on justice lead naturally to conjectures about how the Kantian perspective might look if developed more fully as a theoretical model that philosophers might use in trying to derive and justify a set of moral rules. But, as I said initially, my concern here has been with a more modest enquiry, namely, to see how the Kantian principle might serve as a heuristic guide for reasonable, conscientious agents who are trying to resolve some practical questions, especially concerning how to conceive, specify, and interpret moral rules. Kant presented his idea of a kingdom of ends, not as a guide to moral judgement, but as a part of a highly abstract discussion of the most basic issues in moral theory. The problem, then, is to see whether the abstract ideal can have a practical use. To deal adequately with this problem would be a large project, and here, in my final remarks, I will only mention some of the obstacles it faces and hint at strategies for meeting them.

First, since the kingdom, as construed here, is a perspective for deliberating about rules, its use requires us to make judgements about what sorts of issues are appropriately placed under moral rules. When we think there is, or ought to be, a moral rule regarding some conduct, we are presumably considering standards that are meant to be publicly acknowledged, represented in moral education, and appealed to in moral criticism, as well as used as action guides by individual agents. As rule-utilitarians have noted, there are costs as well as advantages in having conduct governed by moral rules. And advocating rules tends to make less sense the less likely one is to find agreement, within the relevant group, on how to handle the issue in question. With regard to many moral decisions, reasonable people can get along well enough without public agreement on rules, by relying instead on the individual judgements of people who internalize some basic moral attitudes. But on other matters, for example, recurrent questions of life and death, it seems essential to work towards a widely accepted common framework for decisions. Also we must keep in mind that there are rules of many kinds, defined and enforced in different ways. All this may seem obvious, but the practical point is that Kantian legislators, like rule-utilitarians, must face prior questions about what issues call for treatment by rules and then about what types of rules are appropriate. Kant makes suggestions about these matters in his *Metaphysics of Morals*, but that is only a beginning.

Second, the kingdom of ends ideal, like any rule-generating procedure, must face the possibility that, in practice, it will produce moral dilemmas, gaps, and disagreements. Given the central role of dignity, one naturally suspects that reflection from the Kantian perspective will result in commitment to rules absolutely forbidding each of two types of conduct, even though we may face situations where to avoid one is to do the other. Given how limited and imprecisely specified the commitments of Kantian legislators are, it seems obvious that some questions about moral rules will not be determinately resolvable. And finally, given the above together with inevitable human ignorance, fallibility of judgement, and impurity of heart, even the most sincere and conscientious deliberators are likely to disagree about some significant issues.

How, for practical purposes, should those sympathetic to the Kantian perspective take these problems? First, as Alan Donagan has noted, strict moral dilemmas are conceptually impossible in a Kantian moral theory, as presumably they are in any rationalist ethics.[28] That is, treating duties as absolute practical commands, the theory cannot concede that persons have all-things-considered duties that they strictly cannot meet. Thus, if it seems a duty forbids A and forbids B but we cannot avoid doing one or the other, then we must go back and rethink the issue, including if necessary the reasoning that led us initially to think that refraining from A and refraining from B were strict duties in all circumstances.

---

[28] Alan Donagan, 'Moral Dilemmas, Genuine and Spurious: A Comparative Anatomy', *Ethics*, 104 (1993), 7–21. See nn. 22 and 27 of the previous chapter. Donagan makes an exception for cases in which the dilemma-like situation was brought about through the agent's own prior wrongdoing.

For practical Kantians, then, *apparent* dilemmas pose tasks for further moral thinking rather than a reason to abandon the framework or simply to marvel at the tragic absurdity of life. A similar attitude seems advisable about both moral gaps and disagreements. The heuristic ideal, perhaps, is definitive resolution of and rational agreement on every significant issue, but the practical imperative is only to seek it and to be honest in admitting that we rarely have it. Rule-utilitarianism, we might note, usually contains stipulations that make it less likely *in theory* to generate dilemmas, gaps, and disagreements, but theoretical neatness, of course, is no guarantee of actual agreement on determinate solutions in practice.

Third, the kingdom of ends principle, unless qualified, is in danger of encouraging *utopian* thinking. That is, unless we are wary, it may lead us to draw unreasonable inferences about how we should act in our very imperfect world from our thought experiments about ideal agents in a more perfect world. If, for example, we imagine that in the kingdom of ends all citizens conscientiously obey the laws, then we will ignore the problems stemming from the fact that there is no such strict compliance in our world. Questions regarding punishment and incentives will not even arise. There is a further problem even if Kantian legislators can agree which rules are best for situations where partial compliance is all that they can expect. Our actual moral community may be deeply committed to a quite different set of rules that are not ideal but yet not bad; and in this situation, though recommending reform may be admirable, simply to follow blindly the more perfect rules, ignoring the actual forms of social life, may be morally inappropriate, and even disastrous. A rule-utilitarian theory that advocated following the 'ideal code' for a community would, of course, face a similar problem.

A practical Kantian strategy for thinking about such problems would have to concede at once that there is no unqualified imperative to follow those rules that we would legislate under the unrealistic assumptions that these rules will in fact constitute the moral code of our community and that everyone will automatically follow the rules. Perhaps thinking about what such rules would be is useful, but it must be followed by reflecting on the differences between that world and ours. We could try to decide on rules with the basic attitudes of Kantian legislators but under the more realistic assumption of partial compliance, that is, by assuming that most, but not all, can be convinced to obey the rules. This might suggest constructive criticisms and reforms of actual practices. But, as long as even these more realistic reform rules diverge from the actual moral code of one's community, it is a matter for further moral judgement whether, in any given case, one should follow the reform rules we would endorse or instead adjust to the demands of the actual situation. Kantian deliberative attitudes may help here, but it is unlikely that for such decisions further rules will be of any use.

Fourth, a final problem that should be mentioned is the currently influential objection that any two-level theory that calls for impartial thinking, like rule-utilitarianism and my Kantian perspective, alienates the living agent from what allegedly gives authority to moral rules.[29] On these theories, it is charged, 'we' are expected to live by prescriptions that 'they' would make, when 'they' and 'we' have importantly different moral outlooks. This is an important line of objection, though hard to make clear. It asks each of us to consider seriously whether the higher-order perspective recommended for determining moral rules is really one that, on honest and deep reflection, we can acknowledge as authoritative for us. Perhaps the answer is not the same for all, and, if so, it is hard to imagine a proof that it should be. I suspect, however, that the Kantian perspective on rules is in important respects more likely to meet this concern than is rule-utilitarianism.

In other words, my conjecture is that when duly qualified and adapted for practical use, the Kantian principle in significant ways comes closer than rule-utilitarianism to reflecting a deep and widely shared moral sense of *how* we should try to conceive, specify, and apply moral rules. Many of the standards of the Kantian perspective seem to be already implicit in the questions we raise in a practical context. Other constraints built into the Kantian perspective reflect a common moral conviction that certain values, such as basic human dignity and autonomy, are morally prior to any moral imperative to satisfy more preferences.

Also, despite its current reputation to the contrary, the Kantian perspective, I suspect, more nearly expresses what readers of this volume normally take for granted and would be reluctant to abandon, namely, that we are not required to place every aspect of our personal lives and relationships with others on an agenda to be authoritatively reviewed, and endorsed or squelched, by impartial legislators whose primary attitude is to maximize utility. If my conjecture is right about what most of 'us' think, then even if it happens that rule-utilitarian legislators would make exactly the rules that we would, their attitude towards rules

---

[29] See Michael Stocker, 'The Schizophrenia of Modern Moral Theories', *Journal of Philosophy*, 73 (1976), 453–66, and Bernard Williams, 'Persons, Character, and Morality', in Amelie Oksenberg Rorty (ed.), *The Identity of Persons* (Berkeley: University of California Press, 1976), 197–216.

might be so foreign to ours that the fact that they would legislate a rule carries no evident moral authority with us. Seeing rules as prescribed from an alien perspective would not help us to see why *we* count them important, that is, why it makes sense for us as conscientious agents to accept that we must constrain *ourselves* by them.

PART II

Respect for Humanity

3

Basic Respect and Cultural Diversity

PROLOGUE

History echoes with passionate pleas for *justice* and *charity*, but in our times, increasingly, what we hear are demands for *respect*. In a world where interests are diverse and often conflicting, justice is needed to assure each person a reasonable prospect of security, liberty, and other basic conditions of a tolerable life. Charity can fill gaps, rendering aid that cannot be demanded as a right and ameliorating the harmful consequences when justice fails. Respect, as a moral ideal, answers to a deep and pervasive human need beyond the more concrete needs that characteristically lead to demands for justice and charity.[1] Even though they have long benefited from charity and have now won concessions to their just demands, people stigmatized as inferior may still feel, quite rightly, that they 'get no respect'. The respect that they want is something more than material benefits, more even than such benefits offered in a charitable spirit or from recognition that they are owed. What they want, I believe, is something to which we should presume every human being has a claim, namely, full recognition as a person, with the same basic moral worth as any other, co-membership in the community whose

What I present in this chapter and the next is a slightly revised version of the Tanner Lectures, entitled 'Respect for Humanity', given at Stanford University in April 1994. I am grateful to those who were responsible for making that opportunity possible, especially Obert Clark Tanner and Grace Adams Tanner, the trustees of the Tanner Lectures, its director, Grethe Peterson, and officials at Stanford University, notably President Gerhard Casper, Susan Okin, and Michael Bratman. Barbara Herman and Jeffrie Murphy, as expected, provided encouragement and constructive suggestions as well as acute and insightful criticisms, which were highlights of the occasion. I also want to thank the audience at the lectures and participants in the accompanying seminars for their challenging, but respectful, comments.

[1] Justice, charity, and respect are different concepts, none of which reduces to the other, but this is not to deny that they can overlap in various ways. All of these may recommend the same course of action on a given occasion, for example, and one important way to demonstrate respect is to grant another person (willingly and for the right reasons) what he or she is owed in justice.

members share the authority to determine how things ought to be and the power to influence how they will be.[2]

The long and ugly history of struggles against racial bigotry, gender oppression, and cultural imperialism seems to reveal an unfortunate pattern. Deep injustices, once partially hidden by the conspicuous but inadequate charity of the privileged, become more glaring, and so the less privileged increasingly demand their *rights* rather than hope for generosity. But, unfortunately, as major battles for justice are won, mutual respect is slow to follow. For example, slavery was replaced by official segregation, and this in turn has given way to greater legal equality for African Americans; but the struggle has left a nasty residue of racial contempt. Legal disregard for women has been partially overcome, and other unjust social barriers to women may be yielding to protest; but here, again, victories for justice are often followed by a backlash of mutual contempt rather than an increase of respect. Unabashed colonial exploitation commonly passes over into a phase of hypocritical paternalism, which, under pressure, then retreats to a more distant indifference to the troubles of former colonies left behind. In each sphere, as chances for reconciliation are lost in empty rhetorical exchanges, naive hope and premature trust can easily turn to bitter resentment, cynicism, and ultimately mutual contempt.

Although less angry and violent than the reaction to open enmity, this final *contempt* poses problems that may be even harder to resolve. One can at least confront and respectfully negotiate with a single-minded, unpretending enemy; but contempt is a deep dismissal, a denial of the prospect of reconciliation, a signal that conversation is over. Furious argument and accusation, and even sharp-tongued deflation of hypocrisy and self-deception, leave some space to resume communication; but cold, silent contempt does not. The one demands to be heard, while the other walks away in disgust. Moral argument, however impassioned, is addressed to a person, acknowledged as 'one of us': perhaps delinquent, misbehaving, outrageously deviant from our common standards, but still 'one who can be reached', or so we presume. Increasingly, and sadly, it seems to me, we are in a place and time when, having at last achieved some success in combating the most overt forms of

---

[2] Note that I use here the cautious terms 'we should presume' and 'a claim', leaving open for now whether the initial presumption can be overridden and under what conditions one's 'claim' must be fully and immediately honoured. Obviously not everyone should now be trusted, without qualification, with the same full rights and responsibilities as persons who are mature, competent, and conscientious adults. Qualifications are needed regarding infants, the mentally incompetent, mass murderers, sociopaths, etc. These special cases will be discussed to some extent in the next chapter.

bigotry, oppression, and imperialism, we are in danger of sliding into a stage of mutual contempt and dismissal, affecting all sides of racial, gender, and cultural divides.

But if there is a trend toward separation, dismissal, and contempt, there are also healthy reactions as increasingly minorities make the demand for 'respect' their common theme, women refuse to put up with sexual harassment, and university students prod reluctant traditionalists toward greater respect for cultural diversity. This loud and many-sided call for respect loses much of its potential force, however, and even begins to sound thin and trite, when made indiscriminately, without ground or context. 'Respect me!' everyone shouts; but if the demand comes from intolerant racist and sexist bigots, one cannot help but doubt its force. Similarly, when the demand comes from a gang member with a knife at your throat, an ideological terrorist, or a student who refuses to read any literature written by Eurocentric white males, then one begins to wonder. Why should I respect everyone? What does respect entail? Is it compatible with deep disagreement and disapproval? Does respect need to be earned? Can it be forfeited? Is respect due to persons *as members of groups* or only *as individuals*? Does proper respect mean refusing to make comparative judgements of merit? On the contrary, are not some writings trash, some cultural practices immoral, and some people utterly contemptible?

I am not a sociologist or historian, and so it is not my place to identify and analyse social trends; but my impression that we face the broad trends that I have sketched is partly what prompts my current reflections on the ethics of respect for persons. They pose immediate practical problems to which, I believe, some old philosophical ideas are still quite pertinent.

THE PROJECT, THEORETICAL AND PRACTICAL

My plan in this chapter and the next is to return to a certain stage in Western intellectual history in order to draw out some ideas that are pertinent to current problems. To do so is to risk both distorting history and offering anachronistic solutions to new problems; but occasionally we can find in old texts bits of wisdom that are worth reshaping for current debates, especially if the problems we face are in fact perennial issues of human conflict in a new guise.

Specifically, the plan is to describe and extend the core of Immanuel

Kant's idea of human dignity, with its fundamental requirement of respect for persons. Although Kant himself is often criticized for lapses into dogmatic rigourism, his principle of respect for persons is the product of his deep dissatisfaction with dogmatic, uncritical, and pseudo-scientific moral theories that would impose their parochial norms on a world of richly diverse people who are capable of critical reflection and making their own choices.[3] Respect for persons, Kant realized, presupposes a practical conception of persons that must be normatively grounded, systematically developed, and responsive to a realistic (but not cynical) view of the human predicament. It must not merely reflect the substantive norms of particular communities or traditions, for it is needed as a framework for guiding moral reform within cultures and mediating conflicts among them.

As might be expected from any time-bound philosophy, Kant's ideas come with excess baggage that clear-thinking people cannot easily carry across centuries and continents. So among my tasks will be to propose developments, or modifications, of the initial Kantian ideas to make them more tenable to those who can draw on two hundred more years of experience and philosophical reflection. It is not immodest to suppose that we can propose improvements on venerable ideas from the past; what would be presumptuous is only to suppose that future reflection can never improve on our own proposals. In the present case, the proposals needed are of two kinds: first, that we strip from the core of Kant's ethics certain unnecessary doctrines, no matter how dear to the old man's heart these may have been; and, second, that we render some of Kant's abstractions more concrete, in particular by augmenting his abstract conception of *free and principle-governed rational agents* with a conception of *culturally embedded social persons* who do not so much 'create' values as 'find' what is valuable to them in their historical contexts. This augmentation of Kant's theory is especially important because it seriously addresses the most persistent source of dissatisfaction with Kantian ethics voiced in recent times.

[3] Although, as I shall argue, Kant's fundamental moral theory is potentially liberating and duly respectful of all persons, in his specific comments on women, unfortunately, he remained a man of his time, taking for granted stereotypes that denied the equal competence and potential intellectual, social, and political independence of women. See, for example, MM, 91–2 [316–17] various remarks in his *Observations on the Feeling of the Beautiful and the Sublime*, tr. John T. Goldwait (Berkeley: University of California Press, 1960), and *Anthropology from a Pragmatic Point of View*. Kant was also more keenly aware of conflicts between individuals and nations than of deep cultural conflicts and misunderstandings, but again his theory, I believe, is pertinent to the latter as well.

After sketching, filtering, and augmenting the Kantian idea of basic respect for humanity, I propose to draw out some of its implications regarding the attitudes we should take toward cultural diversity. Here, as we apply the augmented Kantian idea to an urgent contemporary problem, its moral significance should become clearer. In effect, it offers a reasonable ground on which mutually respecting persons can stand, despite deep cultural differences, an intermediate ground between a dogmatic moralism that would impose all of our values upon everyone and an uncritical relativism that would accept anything, no matter how cruel, in the name of diversity.

In concluding this chapter, I shall venture a few comments on how basic Kantian respect might be relevant to a more immediate issue: How far should the traditional university curriculum be modified in response to the challenge of multiculturalism? In the next chapter I sketch more fully the Kantian grounds for respect for persons and address the particular question, Why shouldn't we say that criminals and bigots, and others we perceive as immoral, have *forfeited* all respect as human beings?

The practical problems raised here are major, complex problems in the real world, and so, one may wonder, what has *philosophy* to do with them? Obviously, mere thinking will not make the problems disappear. Nor should one presume, when offering philosophical reflections, that everyone will be convinced. The major questions that moral philosophy addresses are, in the end, normative ones that each of us must answer for ourselves. They ask where a reasonable person should stand on various issues, and why. One obvious reason that moral philosophy cannot eliminate concrete problems, such as bigotry and intolerance, is that it can never make itself heard beyond a limited audience; but even when serious people listen, it has no magical power to coerce assent. At best, by doing moral philosophy one can offer *others* only the product of one's efforts to think through normative problems honestly and clearly, together with a commitment to live by the results. For *oneself*, engaging in moral philosophy can help to structure a life of integrity, by identifying what one can conscientiously live for, the normative ground where one finds one must finally stand after scrutinizing one's initial beliefs for hypocrisy, self-deception, parochialism, and prejudice. By philosophizing with others, one can hope for greater agreement, within limits; but, beyond that, when agreement proves impossible, one can only hope for *respectful* disagreement.

EARLIER MORAL THEORIES
AND HUMAN DIGNITY

In his *Groundwork of the Metaphysics of Morals*, Kant famously argued that it is a fundamental moral principle, a categorical imperative, that we should treat humanity, in every person, as an end in itself, never as a means only. The idea had many implications, for example, regarding justice and the limits of expediency in politics; but one especially important implication concerned the basic attitude that human beings should take toward each other. In the second part of his later work, *The Metaphysics of Morals*, Kant spelled out this implication in discussions of 'duties to oneself' and 'duties to others'.[4] Self-respect, he argued, requires that we avoid servility and other forms of self-degradation. The key idea was that, as a human being, everyone has an equal worth, independent of social standing and individual merits. To grovel and humiliate oneself before others, in shame or even guilt, is to deny one's equal status as a human being. If guilty, one should reform, making one's conduct more appropriate to the dignity of one's status; but that status itself is unconditional, not something one earns or can forfeit.

Equally, Kant maintained, it is a duty to respect others as human beings. Contrary to aristocratic doctrine, he argued for a basic respect for persons as human beings that is not grounded in (and so should not vary with) heredity and social rank. Contrary to meritarian individualism, he claimed that this respect is also not based on (and so should not be extended or withheld according to) individual talents, accomplishments, earned social position, or even—surprisingly—moral goodness. The requirement of respect, instead, is rooted in the dignity of humanity, an unconditional and non-quantitative value attributed to everyone with the potential capacities to be a moral agent.[5] This value, Kant maintained, is 'above all price' and 'without equivalent'. It sets firm limits to what one human being may do to another, even in a good cause. And, significantly, it is fundamentally a requirement of attitude and policy, not a specific act-principle.

Kant's idea of human dignity was bound up with his particular conception of persons and embedded in a many-sided, systematic ethical

---

[4] See MM, 173–93 [417–44] and 254–64 [462–73].
[5] G, 102 [434–5]. References and more interpretative comments on this basic idea of human dignity can be found in my *Dignity and Practical Reason in Kant's Moral Theory* (Ithaca, NY: Cornell University Press, 1992), esp. chs. 2 and 10. See also Alan Donagan, *The Theory of Morality* (Chicago: University of Chicago Press, 1977).

theory that I shall not describe in detail. What I propose to do instead is to survey some background in the history of ethics that may help to explain the appeal of Kant's basic idea.

Oversimplifying, we might characterize some major steps in previous moral philosophy as follows. Through many centuries, beginning with Plato, moral philosophers asked their audiences to pose *for themselves* the questions, What is a good life? and What sort of life would a wise and reasonable person choose, given the human condition, the assets and limits of human capacities? The answers were partly given in terms of the kinds of ends these philosophers thought worth pursuing, but the ancient philosophers also acknowledged, in various ways, that the fact we live among other people imposes limits on what we can wisely and reasonably conceive to be the good life for ourselves. Justice, the bonds of friendship, and the needs of the *polis* were seen not merely as pragmatic, prudential constraints but also as limits inherent in the structure of a good life. These philosophers differed, of course, about what the good life is, and so certain higher-order philosophical questions became prominent: *Why* is one way of living better than another? What *reason* is there to prefer the life of an Athenian over the life of a Spartan, or vice versa? How can one know or justify one's opinion that a life of so-called virtuous moderation is better than a life of pleasure? In other words, how are values grounded? What, if anything, makes them more than mere preferences?

Responding to early Sophists who regarded values as conventional and relative, Plato offered one of the main answers that has influenced the Western tradition: true values are grounded in an unchanging reality beyond this world we see and feel. Like numbers and other abstractions, they exist independently of all human thought and history. They can be known through reason, but only through the trained and dialectically disciplined reason of experts, who, as it happens, are none other than philosophers. Although dialectical argument must precede the discovery of what is good, in the end the good must be 'seen' or intuited by the most highly educated. Common folk are only dimly aware of true values and so must be instructed by the experts. Ordinary feelings and thoughts about what is valuable are essentially worthless. The Platonic idea, however obscure, has persisted in modern and less elitist guises. Later versions concede that most human beings, with a bit of effort, can 'see', intuit, or have revealed to them the realm of independent values, which somehow exist 'out there' as models, but are not made or changed by human needs, thought, or social development.

Later Greeks, including Aristotle, realized the implausibility of the

Platonic vision, even if they were not as repelled as we are by the elitism that accompanied it. For them, starting with Aristotle, the biologist, the good life could be determined by the study of human nature. They saw nature as having a purpose or *telos* for our species, and this is supposed to be discernible in common human tendencies. The purpose of human life, and the virtues that enabled the wise and fortunate to achieve it, turned out to be remarkably reflective of the ideals and needs of the particular cultures in which these philosophies developed and competed: a balanced and moderate life of activity, guided by reflection, according to Aristotle; a life free from pain, according to Epicurus; a life of disciplined self-mastery, according to the Stoics. These theories rested upon what now seem dubious assumptions about human nature: a *teleological* structure and *common* capacities, aims, and requirements for happiness.

Medieval thinkers introduced a theological perspective and eventually grafted this on to the ancient teleology. Ultimate values are grounded in the mind or will of God, they argued; voluntarists saying that God created values by his arbitrary will, and traditionalists saying (with Thomas Aquinas) that eternal values were not created by God but merely promulgated to us, finite beings, as divine commands.

All three views sought to ground values in something deeper, more lasting, and more impressive than fluctuating human desires and preferences. But modern thinkers, notably at first Thomas Hobbes, challenged their basic presuppositions. Abstractions do not exist as things to be perceived, he argued; and, famously, David Hume later added that even if they did, mere 'perception' of them (by 'reason') would not move anyone to action. Human motivation, for good or ill, is rooted in desire and feeling, and so, Hume and his friends said, any plausible conception of objective value must be grounded in universal, or almost universal, human sentiments. According to the British empiricists, the good life is not grounded in anything outside of the lives of ordinary human beings, but rather in certain mundane commonalities in what we like and dislike. Platonic forms, ancient teleology, and even theology were increasingly rejected as ultimate grounds for value judgements; and, especially after Hume, it seemed more and more plausible to see values as little more than matters of taste and useful conventions. Privileged access to values by the elite became a less popular idea, for, though philosophers were supposed to have a more 'scientific' understanding of values, the feelings that make up 'the moral sense' (as well as other matters of taste) were thought to exist in everyone—everyone, at least, who grew up with the benefits of Western civilization.

The British empiricists helped to bring the idea of values down to earth, but their positive views raised problems. Would the empirical study of human nature really confirm the uniformity of human feelings on which their account of morality rested? Could the fact that human beings happen to be disposed to similar feelings of approval and disapproval adequately account for the common belief in the authority, binding force, and universality of basic moral principles? Wouldn't conventional theories of justice, like Hume's, leave dominant societies without any good reason for respecting weaker societies?[6]

Natural law theory and social contract theory, in many varieties, also developed in the same, modern period. Though almost always tied to theological premises, the former offered the hope that *reasonable* people, of all cultures, could survive and thrive together if they would just govern their interactions by a minimum common framework that respects the rights and value of all human beings.[7] But the idea that natural laws are simply 'discerned by reason' was too reminiscent of Plato. It invited philosophers to declare dogmatically which precepts were 'laws of nature', thereby enabling them to dress up their favourite maxims in a cloak of authority. Increasingly one could wonder how one can know what laws of conduct nature or God prescribes. How was the thought of such external laws supposed to *motivate* free and critical thinking persons, who have desires and plans of their own? When, as was common, natural law theory reverted to divine sanctions to provide motivation for obedience to its laws, it took on again many of the old problems of traditional theological ethics. For example, its appeal to divine sanctions left unexplained the common moral idea that one should do what is right without regard for reward or punishment.

Social contract theories came in many varieties, and they offered some promise of grounding moral and political values more squarely in the problems and possibilities of the human condition. But various difficulties undermined the promise. Some theories, such as John Locke's, presupposed a historical fiction; others, such as Hobbes's,

---

[6] Hume said, for example, that justice could not bind us with respect to animals, even highly intelligent animals, if they lacked the power to *make* us respect them, and tragically Europeans continued to treat members of less powerful cultures as if they were animals.

[7] In theory natural rights and equal (basic) moral standing were typically extended to all human beings, 'men' or 'mankind', but in recent years many have raised reasonable doubts about the extent to which various natural law and social contract theorists actually intended to include women and 'savages' when they wrote grandly of the rights of 'man'.

underestimated the human resources for peace and so proposed draconian means to end war. Jean-Jacques Rousseau deeply influenced Kant with his vision of what it would be for a community of free persons to live in mutual respect, listening to each other, working together, despite their differences, and governing themselves, in their public life, by the general will of all citizens. Though human-centred, egalitarian, and inspiring, Rousseau's political ideal none the less invited abuse of power by the self-appointed interpreters of the general will; it required invasive measures and a secular religion to promote patriotic spirit; and it gave little reason for decent treatment of 'aliens', i.e. those outside the ideal community.

This, briefly (and oversimply), was the context of moral philosophy as Kant might have seen it in 1785. Previous moral theories had failed. They preached specific values without adequate grounding, or else they undermined the authoritative mediating role of morality by reducing it to something contingent, relative, and in effect variable with culture. Crucially, Kant thought, they did not seek the source of all human values in humanity itself, that is, in the distinctively human capacities for thoughtful evaluation. Kant proposed a new perspective, which acknowledged contingent values that vary from person to person, and from society to society, and yet also endorsed a common formal framework for moral thinking. He tried to draw *both* of these, the variability of particular values and the common framework, from the idea that human beings themselves are the ultimate source of all our (human) values, moral, aesthetic, and personal. Endorsement under conditions of reasonable reflection, not mere sentiment, is what grounds values; and, significantly, the idea of *reasonable* reflection presupposes a willingness to listen to the voice, and heed the interests, of others. Reasonable reflection also requires a kind of deliberative freedom, which, in practice, implies that one must try to see one's situation realistically, counteracting one's natural tendencies to self-deceit, self-serving bias, and local prejudice. A central point was that, although the values of individuals and societies may vary widely, their expression must be constrained by whatever basic framework for human interactions would be accepted by reasonable, autonomous, and mutually respectful persons.

Kant's theory is complex, and, whatever its virtues, they are entangled in metaphysical and moral views that are at least controversial, at worst obscure and unduly rigouristic. I propose simply to set aside these features for now, in order to concentrate on the central idea of human dignity and respect for persons.

1. For example, let us disregard Kant's conviction that reason prescribes quite specific absolute duties, such as that one ought never to tell a lie, and also set aside his empirically unfounded and obviously culture-bound ideas about the particular nature of women, sex, and animals.[8]

2. Also, when Kant tried to *interpret* everyday moral concepts in a larger philosophical context, he introduced certain metaphysical Ideas that he thought presupposed in the moral perspective. These Ideas, including 'the intelligible world' and a 'free will' independent of space and time, have understandably led to scepticism about Kant's whole philosophical system. I believe, however, that these metaphysical extensions of Kant's normative concepts are to a considerable extent separable from the central points in his moral philosophy, at least separable from the main points that I shall stress in this chapter and the next.

3. Again, although Kant himself was optimistic that all reasonable and autonomous persons would agree to *the same* moral principles, that optimism is very difficult to share in our contemporary world. But, as I explain later, sharing that optimism is not necessary for our purposes; for we can treat Kant's proposals as a standard of *conscientiousness*, rather than absolute moral truth, and for this purpose assurance of universal agreement is not needed.[9]

4. Similarly, though Kant may have assumed it, we need not insist that every sane adult member of *Homo sapiens* has a conscience and that all human children have the capacity and predisposition for it. Instead, one can say more modestly that, for practical purposes, our morality of respect presumes, until proved otherwise, that virtually all human beings, except perhaps the severely brain-damaged, have enough potential for developing the capacities for reciprocity and self-restraint to qualify for human dignity. Again, unless proved otherwise, we presume that aware, functioning adults, who have a language and engage in social interactions, are not beyond the reach of reasonable moral discussion.

All of these modifications, I would argue, are compatible with the core idea of human dignity: that is, human beings are to be regarded as worthy of respect as human beings, regardless of how their values differ and whether or not we disapprove of what they do.

[8] See, for example, MM, 182–4 [429–32], 178–80 [424–6], 193 [443–4], and also 'On a Supposed Right to Lie because of Philanthropic Concerns', in the 3rd edn. of *Grounding of the Metaphysics of Morals*, tr. James W. Ellington (Indianapolis: Hackett Publishing Co., 1993), 63–7.

[9] I discuss this modification, or extension, of Kant's moral theory, and the need for it, along with some other needed developments, in ch. 2 of this volume.

To avoid misunderstanding, I should anticipate now a point to be discussed more fully in the next chapter. That is, it is crucial to notice that in our ordinary ways of thinking we often use an idea of *respect* quite different from Kant's idea of respect for persons *as human beings*. This is the idea of respecting individuals for *their achievements or special merits*. Respect for merit must be earned and can be forfeited. Kant's more controversial idea, by contrast, is that, simply by virtue of their humanity, all people qualify for a status of dignity, which should be recognized respectfully by everyone.[10]

PERSONS CONCEIVED AS THE SOURCE OF VALUES

The idea of respecting persons remains rather empty until the underlying (normative) idea of persons is specified. *How* we respect persons as sources of value, as well as *why*, depends on how we suppose they come to value what they do.[11] This is not to say that we need, or could use, a full-blown metaphysical theory or complete human psychology here. To base an ethics on either would introduce complexity and controversy of the very sort that simple respect principles are meant to bypass. What should suffice, for present purposes, is a review of some general points about how human beings come to form values—points that, on reflec-

[10] The basic distinction here and its refinements have been frequently discussed. See, for example, Stephen L. Darwall, 'Two Concepts of Respect', *Ethics*, 88 (1977), 36–49, and my *Autonomy and Self-respect* (Cambridge: Cambridge University Press, 1991), chs. 1, 2, and 11.

[11] My main concern in this chapter is, not with the grounds, but with the *content*, or practical implications, of the Kantian idea that human beings should be respected as valuers, i.e. as rational persons whose valuing various sorts of things, under appropriate conditions, is the source of all values (at least as we can know them). The *grounds* of this basic Kantian notion that what is valuable is somehow constituted by the reflective endorsement, under certain conditions, of rational agents (conceived in a certain way) are, of course, open to controversy. Although in the next chapter I reconstruct some aspects of Kant's defence of this idea, there is much more that needs eventually to be said. In particular, I want to make clear that I do not endorse a simple argument pattern which says *without further argument and explanation* that: persons should be respected as such; they are sources of value (i.e. their valuing things, in appropriate conditions, makes those things valuable); human persons, we discover empirically, value such-and-such things in these-and-those ways; therefore, persons should be respected, as valuers, by helping them continue to value things in these-and-those ways (as in fact they tend to do) and by providing them as far as possible with such-and-such things (the things they in fact value). There is something to this line of thought, but, as it stands, there are too many gaps. My subsequent list of 'ways human beings value' (in this section), then, is meant only to point the way toward certain principles (spelled out in the next section) about how we should respect human beings, but it is not meant, by itself, to establish or justify these principles.

tion, may be obvious but help to specify what it might mean to respect human beings as sources of value. I shall distinguish six points. The first few are Kant's; but the rest are necessary supplements.[12]

1. Most obviously, individuals value the realization of various personal goals and projects and, derivatively, many other things as means to this. Traditionally, human beings, as opposed to inanimate things, plants, and animals, are conceived as having characteristic capacities of understanding, memory, foresight, language use, rational reflection, and awareness of others.[13] They have, at least potentially, an ability to constrain themselves by principles and norms seen as providing reasons for acting. They have some capacity to reflect on their immediate desires, impulses, and preferences and from this to form more settled goals, plans, and policies, while being aware of elementary facts of life, such as that desires conflict and one 'cannot have it all'. They adopt ends, recognize means, and are disposed to take the necessary means to their ends, when available. These points correspond in Kant's theory to the ability to 'set oneself ends', to use hypothetical imperatives, and to make plans free from immediate control by animal instinct and impulse.[14] Having these general capacities implies little or nothing about the specific values that human beings have. It does not imply, for example, that they are selfish; nor does it imply that they are altruistic.

2. The capacities of 'humanity' that qualify persons as 'ends in themselves' include some minimum capacity for reciprocity and recognition of the moral standing of others.[15] This is not to say that everyone is

---

[12] Here I sketch these points about values only briefly. Each needs further explanation, and the relations among them should be clarified. All but the first two points, in effect, propose incorporating into Kantian moral theory ideas that are usually thought to be reserved for theories hostile to Kantianism. These ideas are admittedly important and yet either omitted or not stressed in Kant's writings and in Kantian ethics as usually interpreted. To develop these ideas and to show their compatibility, even fruitful companionship, with what I consider the most important, basic features of Kant's moral theory is a large project, to which I hope to contribute in future work.

[13] I say 'characteristic' here to avoid controversies about how to classify infants, severely brain-damaged (human) accident victims, etc.; issues to be considered, at least briefly, in ch. 4.

[14] G, 80–8. Later Kant calls these capacities 'the predisposition to humanity,' as opposed to the (moral) 'predisposition to personality.' See R, 21–3.

[15] This feature of what, in his *Groundwork*, Kant calls 'humanity' corresponds to what, in *Religion*, he calls the 'disposition to personality' R, 22–3 [27–8]. Kant regarded *humanity* (and later *personality*) as more than a latent capacity, like the ability to learn French or set theory. This included a predisposition toward developing and exercising the capacity, a predisposition that sometimes fails to develop fully, but, absent conflicting tendencies (e.g. sensuous desires), does. Kant regarded these dispositions to be innate, not learned, aspects of human nature, but contemporary Kantian theory, I think, might concede that it is sufficient that the capacity to *acquire* (or 'learn') the predisposition is

morally good or even has a developed conscience. The point is just that basic respect is attributed on the presumption (even if it is merely faith) that the persons respected have at least the capacity to be touched and moved by considerations of reciprocity and recognition of (all) other persons as having moral standing.[16]

On the Kantian view, we conceive of persons as (at least potential) *valuers*, whom we respect as the *source of all (human) values*. But persons are valuers in different ways or senses. Under point 1 above, we consider them as *valuing* goals, policies, and derivatively means, where *valuing* involves some degree of reflective endorsement, which is more than merely *desiring*. Under point 2 above, we consider persons as at least potentially recognizing the (equal) status of all persons and then as valuing being in reciprocal relations with others on mutually agreeable terms.[17] But there are still other ways in which persons may be considered sources of value.

3. People do not merely have ends and means according to their likes and dislikes, they also tend to have some values that are essential or virtually indispensable to them. I have in mind two quite different sorts of things. First, there are some general aims, characteristic of human beings, apparently so common, so deeply rooted, and so vital to decent human life everywhere that they are understandably taken, for practical purposes, as *essential* to human nature. Happiness, broadly construed, is perhaps the most common term for these aims, when appropriately combined, but more specific elements often cited include self-preservation, freedom from pain, the development and exercise of our physical and mental powers, companionship, social standing, self-respect, and so on. Less controversial are associated needs that (virtually) everyone seems to recognize as vital to human life, whatever its

---

a natural or almost invariable feature of human beings. Such a concession would not be without consequences, but I shall not pursue the issue further here.

[16] I am inclined to add 'equal moral standing', but Kantians should want the threshold for respect kept low enough to include, for practical purposes, virtually every functioning adult human being. Perhaps capacity to recognize equality is not so essential here as the capacity to recognize everyone as having *at least a quite substantial moral standing* ('substantial' here implying much more than a minimum recognition of someone's 'moral standing', say, as 'lowest-caste human'). For now I leave open just what is involved in 'recognizing moral standing' and 'reciprocity'. Eventually, of course, these need to be spelled out, but for now the main point is just that human beings are presumed to be, in some appropriate sense, able and disposed to acknowledge and respect rights and interests of others and to join others in accepting (and following) various mutually advantageous principles and conforming to them.

[17] This corresponds, roughly, to 'a capacity for a sense of justice' and to the capacity for being 'reasonable', in John Rawls's *Political Liberalism* (New York: Columbia University Press, 1993), 81 ff.

particular forms: for example, food, water, shelter, community support, and freedom and opportunities of various kinds. Second, there are the various particular projects, associations, and cherished ideals with which individuals come to identify themselves. Among these are the 'ground projects' that Bernard Williams talks about, commitments so deep that the person who has them might not care to live without them and such that we might say that the person would not be 'the same person' if he or she lost them.[18] Kant himself acknowledged indispensable values of the first kind but not, at least explicitly, those of the second kind.[19] Nevertheless, that people often have such individual ground projects and ideals is an important fact about them as persons, a fact that needs to be recognized in any full account of what it is to respect persons as persons.[20]

4. Human beings do not form values as abstract, ahistorical rational beings completely free from cultural context, but neither are they fully programmed robots lacking in the critical ability to contribute to the shape of their lives. As many have recently emphasized, people come to value what they do in a particular setting, influenced by dominant cultural patterns as well as cross-currents of contrary social influences.[21] We are embedded in intertwining networks of cultures and subcultures; and however independent and thoughtful we may become, these no doubt constantly influence and impose outer limits on what we come to like and to dislike, to cherish and to hate. However, for practical purposes, the Kantian warns that we should not overestimate the irresistibility of these cultural bonds by assuming that reflective persons can never see good reason to set aside a part of their heritage. As existentialists saw (but exaggerated), we are not like *personae* in a play of life for which the script has already been completely written. We stand neither totally outside, nor totally within, the roles in which we find ourselves. Up to a point, at least when the cross-currents of the context permit, people can take responsibility, and hold others responsible, for

[18] Bernard Williams, 'Persons, Character, and Morality', in Amelie Oksenberg Rorty (ed.), *The Identities of Persons* (Berkeley: University of California Press, 1976), 197–216.

[19] See MM, 149–52 [385–9], and C3, 317–21 [429–34]. The significance for Kantian ethics becomes clear in Jeffrie G. Murphy, *Kant: The Philosophy of Right* (London and New York: Macmillan, 1970), 94–108, and Barbara Herman, *The Practice of Moral Judgment* (Cambridge, Mass.: Harvard University Press, 1993), ch. 3.

[20] I thank Cynthia Stark and Robin Dillon for helping me to appreciate this point.

[21] Alasdair MacIntyre is perhaps the philosopher who has, in recent times, most vividly and influentially emphasized the importance of this point. See, for example, his *After Virtue*, 2nd edn. (Notre Dame, Ind.: University of Notre Dame Press, 1984).

trying to resist and remould features of a culture deeply at odds with respect for humanity.

5. Human beings are disposed to seek what is valuable to them, and sometimes they find it—often where they were not looking.[22] Too often Kantians, like existentialists, talk as if 'free' individuals 'choose' their non-moral values, picking them from thin air, as it were, for no reason. They suggest, misleadingly, that (acausally) free agents simply 'dub' certain goals as valuable to them, by sheer radical choice, thereby *making* them rationally important to themselves and morally significant to others.[23] In fact, I think, for the most part we simply *find* certain things in our experience to be valuable to ourselves and others like us, and other things we find indifferent, ugly, deplorable, despicable, or disgusting. Like what is 'funny', 'interesting', and 'entertaining', what is seen as intersubjectively 'valuable' in this way is judged to be, as we say, 'worthy' of attention among some relevant group, but this carries no implication that 'value' is a real intrinsic property of things in the world or even the dispositional property of causing pleasure to everyone who experiences the thing. To say that we *find* things valuable even when we were not especially looking for value (e.g. suddenly coming upon a gorgeous sunset) is not to make a metaphysical point but only a phenomenological one.[24] It is *as if* we *just see* that some things are good to us

---

[22] Here, as in 1 and 3, and to some extent in 4, I am thinking of 'values' as the various things people cherish other than morality itself (e.g. other than the minimum framework of respect I have referred to): for example, art, customs, rituals, religious traditions, family relations, work, games, foods, literature, myths, patterns of humour, etc., of various kinds, the sort of things, aside from morality, that characteristically differentiate one culture from another.

[23] Some of my earlier papers (e.g. 'Pains and Projects', in *Autonomy and Self-respect*, ch. 12, and 'Kant's Theory of Practical Reason', in *Dignity and Practical Reason in Kant's Moral Theory*, ch. 7) may veer close to these implausible claims. Christine Korsgaard too at times seems to suggest something of the sort, but I suspect she intends something more subtle.

[24] I mean here to make clear that, despite my talk of 'finding' values, this point does not imply commitment to G. E. Moore's theory of intrinsic value or to any 'naturalistic' reduction of 'value' to 'fact'. I also want to leave open the plausible *psychological* explanation of judgements of value as rooted in natural responses of persons of a certain kind, developed in a certain way, to facts they encounter or at least perceptions they have. Thus, the causal account of value judgements may refer to a relation between persons, as responders, and facts or perceptions about the valued objects. But this is not to say that to *experience something as good* is to *think of it as* causing favourable responses in me and persons like me. I assume here too, as earlier, that to value something, to find it valuable, and to judge it of (intersubjective) value are more than merely desiring, liking, or experiencing some inclination toward the thing. In the first case one finds, or judges, or sees something as *worthy* of desiring and endorsing for choice, at least in appropriate contexts. More needs to be said on these distinctions, of course. Finally, I conjecture that these common-sense points about how we find various things valuable, and dis-

and, we assume, to others like us, and other things bad; these 'discoveries' come and go, whether we are looking or not, often not all at once, but gradually.

I should emphasize that none of this implies that exactly the same things will be, or even can be, found valuable in every culture; to the contrary, I assume that we cannot even understand, much less appreciate, some experiences without the cultural background of those to whom they are valuable.

6. Finally, human beings value much, if not most, of what they do *as social beings*. Kant, too much influenced by Hobbes, tended to think of the moral life as a constant struggle between reasonable moral constraints and *self-serving* individual desires. But it is part of our problem, as well as its solution, that as social beings we care deeply for joint projects, interlocking social networks, and common histories. It is a misleading but all too familiar Enlightenment picture that independent individuals are always beset by discrete self-referring desires and then from these choose for themselves a series of personal 'ends' that are definable without mention of others, except perhaps as competitors. But this picture of what and how people value what they do is seriously distorted in several ways.

Consider, for example, the fact that many of our projects are *joint projects*. That is, like members of an orchestra we aim to produce something, over time, that cannot be done alone. More significantly, the goal itself is conceived as doing something well *with others*, where each does his or her part not in isolation but with the aim and wish to do it with the others.[25]

Moreover, *historical particulars* are typically important in what we value. We do not, for example, want just that some good music be played by someone, but that we, the orchestra members (Ursula, Kareem, Hsu, Dmitri, Joe, *et al.*), play Beethoven's Seventh Symphony well together now. Feuding families want not just to confirm the abstract

valuable, are denied by philosophical extremists regarding value—both voluntarists and realists—because they overreact to the inadequacies of the opposite extreme view. Once we concede that values are neither 'created' as such by free, unmotivated 'dubbing' nor discovered as intrinsic features of the world we experience, then there should be little resistance to the commonplace observation that we typically 'find' some things valuable and others not.

[25] This general point is recognized by many people, but I am indebted especially to the following: Robert M. Adams, 'Common Projects and Moral Virtue', *Midwest Studies in Philosophy*, 13 (1988), 297–307; Nancy Sherman, 'The Virtues of Common Pursuits', *Philosophy and Phenomenological Research*, 53 (1993), 277–99; and various works of Michael Bratman.

proposition 'Unprovoked aggressors will be made to suffer'; they want to make sure that they themselves avenge the aggression of their particular enemies immediately.

Some of our deepest values may also be *reciprocal and layered*.[26] For example, I value the fact that you respect and trust me, and you value the fact that I respect and trust you; moreover, I value the fact that you value the fact that I respect and trust you, and you value the fact that I value the fact that I respect and trust you, and so on. The values here are obviously deeply entwined and not individually satisfiable.

Again, philosophers often oversimplify life by treating all values as present-time desires for goals which are seen as discrete states of affairs or events, but many of our values, I think, are *cross-time wholes*, involving our joint histories with other people.[27] Producing a piece of music, with a temporal beginning, middle stages, and conclusion, is an example. As Aristotle suggests, we can assess a human life as exemplifying the final good for human beings, and as a 'happy' life, only by considering the whole life as it has been (or is anticipated to be) completed.[28] Moreover, what counts, as we reflect, is not just whether the discrete moments were (or will be) pleasant (or intrinsically desirable) but also the pattern and the conclusion, how the parts of the life fit together, how each stage complements or completes the earlier stages, for good or ill. A meaningful life is not measured, on the model of accounting, in terms of pluses and minuses for independently good or bad moments; but rather, as Alasdair MacIntyre has stressed, its value is often assessed more in the *narrative terms* of stories (e.g. histories, biographies, novels, legends, and folktales). Here the connections between the parts of a life matter, like the connections among the chapters of a book. The terms of assessment, not reducible to any fixed rules, include initiation, unfolding, tensions, disruptions, growth, character, climax, resolution, and fitting (or unfitting) endings.

We can observe, too, that the whole of a life, a personal history with loved ones, and significant episodes within these often have for us an *organic value*, that is, a value in the whole that cannot be equated to any sum of values of 'parts'.[29] Like the beauty of a painting or the per-

---

[26] This idea is vividly presented by Thomas Nagel in his essay 'Sexual Perversion', *Journal of Philosophy*, 66 (1969), 5–17.

[27] This is a major theme of MacIntyre's *After Virtue*. I note its potential relevance to a practical problem in 'The Message of Affirmative Action', in *Autonomy and Self-respect*, ch. 13, esp. 201–11.

[28] Aristotle, *Nicomachean Ethics*, in Richard McKeon (ed.), *The Basic Works of Aristotle* (New York: Random House, 1941), i. 10–11 [1100a–1102a], 946–9.

[29] G. E. Moore emphasized the idea that intrinsic values have an organic unity, the intrinsic value of the whole not always being equal to the sum of the intrinsic value of

sonal 'meaning' of complex social experience, such things cannot be evaluated by dividing them, assessing the parts, and somehow 'adding up' the results. The great moral philosophers, including Kant, must have had some practical awareness of these rather obvious facts; but, as contemporary critics are fond of repeating, their value theories are often expressed in special, semi-technical terminologies that over-simplify the familiar experiences of evaluation that they were meant to clarify.

A final caution. These various complex ways in which social beings have values should not be confused with the simple idea that people (at times) care for the welfare of others. That, I think, is obviously true, but such simple benevolent desires are far from the whole story of our being social. We also hate, resent, and despise others; we find our lives deeply attached and entwined with others we do not even like; many joint projects of one group are aimed at the destruction of another group; and many prefer narratives and histories that end with their group gleefully gloating over the suffering of some group of outsiders. Human sociability, and the sense of connectedness with others, is part of the context of human life, for good or ill; it is not, by itself, the solution to its conflicts.

WHAT WOULD IT BE TO RESPECT PERSONS AS VALUERS?

To review, on the Kantian perspective the ultimate source of human values is not Platonic forms, natural teleology, God's will, or universal human sentiment. Ultimately all that is valuable for us stems some-how from the reflective endorsements of human beings. *Particular* ends, means, ground projects, discovered delights, joint endeavours, social networks, and histories are valued differently by different indi-viduals and cultures. But the common framework Kant proposes as worthy of reflective endorsement by all is a basic requirement, across cultures and individual differences, to respect every human being as a source of value.

---

its parts. However, Moore worked with a metaphysical idea of intrinsic goodness as an intuited, simple, non-natural property, which is opposed to the Kantian conception, and Moore was also more willing than one should be, I believe, to talk as if intrinsic values could be compared in terms of the *quantity* of value in each, thereby taking too literally the metaphor of 'sums' of value. See G. E. Moore, *Principia Ethica* (Cambridge: Cambridge University Press, 1903), 27–36.

How can we make this more specific? The key is that persons are to be respected as the sources of (human) value and that we value things in the six ways reviewed in the last section. More specifically, then, how should we respect every person?

1. In so far as we value and respect persons as capable of reflecting on their desires, setting their own ends, and rationally pursuing means to them, we have some (presumptive) reason to allow them the space and opportunity to do so and even to aid them in the pursuit to some extent, provided their means and ends are compatible with due respect for all others. Since there are millions of people on earth, each with many diverse ends and entitled to some life of his or her own, the general duty to *aid* their pursuits, as Kant said, can only be an 'imperfect' one: a relevant consideration but indefinite as to whom, when, where, and exactly how to help. The presumption against interference with others' innocent projects, however, stands as a constant constraint on our pursuit of our own interest as well as a permanent bar against excessive paternalism—the attempt to make people happy only according to *our* vision of the good rather than theirs.

2. In so far as we value and respect persons as moral agents, with the capacity to reciprocate and acknowledge the moral standing of others, we must not 'write them off' as creatures who can only understand and respond to power, bribery, and manipulation. Morality itself is constituted, on the Kantian view, by what fully reflective, autonomous, and reasonable persons would agree to as a fair and mutually agreeable framework for human interactions. Hence no one has privileged access to what morality prescribes, and no one's voice on moral matters should be arbitrarily discounted. What mutual respect requires more specifically must itself be worked out, in many-sided conversations, in which the biases of each of us are amply exposed to the contrary perspectives of others. The (modified) Kantian conception of morality does not entail that to be respectful one must indiscriminately celebrate, accept, or even tolerate all the different practices endorsed by some cultural group. Given cultural diversity, the lesson to draw, rather, is that we cannot have proper respect and work out what this requires in particular contexts unless we try to think from an inclusive human perspective, with moral humility, willingness to listen, to rethink, at times to suspend judgement, and often to compromise.

3. In so far as we value and respect persons as having the two kinds of indispensable values—(a) the necessary means of life and (b) self-identifying ground projects—we have presumptive reasons both for non-interference and for aid, provided the projects and the means them-

selves are compatible with due respect for others. Importantly, we have here grounds for setting limits to our tolerance and approval of what others do; for when the powerful are denying the weak the basic necessities of life, standing up for the weak is often more respectful to all than standing idly by.

Respect for persons as deeply identified with certain (permissible) ground projects requires respect for them as the particular individuals they are, not merely as fellow members of common humanity. That is, what is called for is not merely respect for the general capacities and rights they share with others but also appropriate attention and response to what they, as individuals, count as most significant about 'who they are'.[30] Respecting humanity, then, requires more than a proper attitude toward people in the abstract; it requires respect for people as particular individuals, whose 'identity' (as we say) is bound up with particular projects, personal attachments, and traditions.[31]

4. In so far as we respect persons as embedded in a cultural and historical context, though capable to some extent of reflectively criticizing and rejecting it, we must avoid two extremes. On the one hand, we must not discount the significance of culture in determining what treatment is properly respectful; but, on the other hand, we must not simply assume that to treat them *as their dominant culture dictates* is always respectful to *them*, the individuals. Understanding the individuals' own conception of their relation to their culture is important, but not always decisive. For example, to condemn them for what we regard as immoral conduct, in total disregard of what that conduct meant and whether it was prescribed or condoned in their own culture, would fail to respect them as human beings, like us, who are partially shaped, unconsciously limited, and deeply influenced by cultural environment. But to refuse to make any judgement at all about those in 'other cultures' is disrespectful to them, for it treats them as the fixed product of societal influences with no moral power to understand and be moved by moral criticism of it.

5. In so far as we respect persons as generally 'seekers' and sometimes 'finders' of value, we should be ready to make some effort to

[30] *Appropriate* respect here does not mean indiscriminate aid or toleration of all personal projects; it must take into account the fact that some personal projects, even 'ground projects' crucial to an individual's 'identity', may be deeply immoral and contemptuous of others.

[31] The notion of 'identity' here is normative and slippery, though important. It is not the same as the thinner concept of 'personal identity' generally discussed in the metaphysical debates of philosophers concerning split brains, brain transplants, memory discontinuity, etc.

appreciate the different values others have found. At the same time we should not assume that they are perfectly set and satisfied with what they have found, and thus uninterested in communicating and sharing new experiences. Ideally, value systems of individuals and groups would evolve, as people have the power and freedom to explore, and to widen the range of their experience, as well as to retreat and protect themselves from constant massive exposure to unwelcome forms of life. Diversity should not be valued just for the sake of diversity, but for the way it allows some to live out the best values they have found and enables others to seek out something better.

6. Finally, in so far as we take seriously the idea that persons have social values (joint projects, reciprocal and layered values, etc.), we can no longer imagine that we can respect persons just by dealing with them, one by one, as if they were isolated sources of individual interests. We respect someone only by acknowledging and taking fully into account the importance to that person, and others, of the networks of relationships in which that person finds life meaningful. Group ties, traditions, family connections, and deeply layered hopes may mean more to persons than anything they value just for themselves. Respect for individuals, properly understood, should not compete with community values, for the only way to respect the social values of individuals is to honour, so far as one legitimately can, the groups within which the individual finds his or her life valuable. The limits to how far we can honour group ties, of course, lie in the general requirement to respect all persons. In so far as group loyalty feeds on hatred and contempt of others and expresses itself through war and humiliation, those who would respect all humanity must disengage their basic *respect for the individual members* from the *respect for their group* that would otherwise be its corollary.

BASIC RESPECT AND MULTICULTURALISM IN THE UNIVERSITY

So far my remarks have been quite abstract, wide-ranging, perhaps too concerned with theory for the general reader. Thus, in conclusion, let me try to compensate in a small way by talking more specifically about how the idea of basic respect for persons might apply to the controversial question, How should universities respond to the facts of cultural diversity?

The issue is complicated because of the diverse nature of universities themselves. They are many-sided institutions that have evolved for various purposes, serve different constituencies, and are answerable to many contributing and engaged parties. What these elements should be, and how they should be ranked, will no doubt always be a matter of controversy. To simplify, then, I shall comment only on the educational or teaching commitment of universities, particularly in undergraduate general studies courses.

The question, then, is this: What is a reasonable and respectful attitude to take, when confronting decisions about university general education, given heightened sensitivity to (what I shall call) the facts of cultural diversity? First, let us review some of these facts. I take it that the following four points are fairly uncontroversial.[32]

1. People in different cultures, both across time and now, differ deeply in their ways of life, their social norms, their conceptions of law and interpersonal relationships, their highest aspirations, and also in their mundane everyday tastes and preferences. There may be also overlapping similarities, perhaps even some universal convergence points; but because of difficulties of cross-cultural understanding, we do not know how deep and pervasive these similarities, or differences, are.

2. Although cultures evolve and intermingle, and individuals sometimes rebel and advocate radical changes, most people tend to seek and find what is valuable and meaningful to them within their own cultural settings. Individuals are embedded in cultures and often identify themselves and their ground projects in terms intelligible only in their cultural contexts.

3. Although, when conditions are right, social criticism and independence of mind are possible and important, we all inevitably tend to misinterpret others and to be biased by our own heritage whenever we try to think through issues that cross cultural borders. This includes, of course, philosophers who lecture on respect and cultural diversity.

4. The various cultures, and subcultures, are not equal in power, and throughout history powerful groups have tended to persecute, exploit, and try to dominate weaker groups, sometimes with open group enmity but often in the name of universal ideals. The means have been many,

---

[32] The 'facts' that I select to emphasize here are, admittedly, far from all the relevant facts that need, ultimately, to be taken into account. I deliberately stress what I take to be facts about deep differences, difficulties in cross-cultural communication, and oppression of the weak by the strong because these are, I believe, major sources of the most urgent obstacles to mutual respect in multicultural contexts.

including not only war, slavery, and genocide but also subtler symbols of moralistic disapproval or contemptuous dismissal. These are reflected in folklore, histories, literature, and philosophy, as well as in everyday jokes and conversations. The almost universal tendency to bias and the frequent moral imperialism of dominant groups understandably lead to scepticism about the objectivity of cross-cultural judgements, especially the judgements of the relatively privileged.

Some apparently think that these facts warrant an attitude of extreme relativism about values, which draws no limits. Since there are such deep differences in beliefs, they say, there is no good reason not to accept 'respectfully' whatever values prevail within a culture. Or, if they confess disgust for foot-binding, clitoridectomies, wife burning, child prostitution, or other practices condoned in different cultures, they must be careful, they think, to explain that this is a mere 'personal preference'. Since whatever passes within a culture is to be respected for that place and time, extreme relativists have no moral ground, besides changing local fashion, for trying to reform even their own society. 'Whatever is, is right'; or, to put the point in more postmodern terms, the ideas of 'right' and 'wrong', and 'better' and 'worse', need to be deconstructed and then discarded with other myths of the past.

As elementary philosophy texts have explained time and time again, admitting the facts of cultural diversity in no way supports this wholescale resistance to making cross-cultural value judgements, with its indiscriminate acceptance of whatever has the endorsement of some culture. Moreover, the rejection of all cross-cultural standards opens the door to the very sort of power-driven cultural imperialism that culturally sensitive, gentle relativists want to resist. Controlling and subordinating those who are weaker may be an essential value in some dominant cultures, as, for example, in the American subculture of macho men with respect to 'their' women. When this happens, indiscriminate toleration amounts to politely condoning abuse, exploitation, and humiliation. Even the *hypocrisy* of oppressors who dominate others in the name of high moral ideals cannot be condemned by the extreme relativist, except perhaps with the mild rebuke, 'My friends and I dislike what you are doing.'

We should not be smug, though, just because we can see the self-defeating character of the extreme relativist position. The facts of cultural diversity do not support *that*, but we should not be so arrogant as to think that they have no implications for us at all. In particular, for those who, like me, endorse at least basic respect for persons, there are strong implications. Among these, I believe, are the following.

First, we cannot fully respect people of diverse cultural backgrounds, within our own country or elsewhere, without making a serious effort to understand and *appreciate*, so far as we can, features of their cultures that they cherish and see as crucial to their particular identity. Given the inevitable predisposition to cultural bias, we can progress toward such understanding and appreciation only by engaging with the voices of the people within those cultures, through their literature, their histories, and their folklore, and ideally with the help of teachers who themselves represent the cultural heritage.

Of course, limited time, opportunity, and other circumstances severely limit the extent and depth to which any one person can study and engage with other cultures. As teachers and students, perhaps, we have more contact with other ethnic groups than the average person does; but the more diverse our local environment, the more obvious it becomes that we can begin to understand only a small fraction of the many traditions represented by the people we meet. To study a wide range of cultures superficially, like sampling many dishes at a smorgasbord, may be personally rewarding, but is unlikely to contribute significantly to overcoming the problems of cross-cultural misunderstanding and disrespect.

A more realistic ideal would be deeper engagement with one or a few different cultures. Becoming fully 'bicultural' in one's experience, analogous to being truly bilingual in speech, is probably beyond the reach of most of us, nor is it clear that this is generally desirable. What is important, however, is to challenge one's customary ways of thinking, feeling, and perceiving so that one becomes more open to the possibility of values that one could never imagine when bound within a single cultural experience. This increased sensitivity to alternatives may lead to new sources of personal enrichment, in music, art, literature, and personal friendship; but, more important, it is needed for *meaningful* tolerance and respect. Without the openness stimulated by appreciation of some other cultures, we might proclaim commitment to these ideals but fail to see *when and how they give us reasons* for acting (and for restraint) in contexts of cultural conflict. Respect is blind if uninformed about relevant values and the reasons they provide; and it inevitably remains uninformed if nothing shakes us from our habits of seeing everything exclusively from our primary culture's perspective.[33]

---

[33] Barbara Herman has been particularly helpful in stressing that what is needed (and possible) is not so much full knowledge of every culture but rather *openness* and sensitivity to possible facets of the cultures we confront that may affect what reasons we have to act one way or another.

Second, in trying to understand and appreciate different literary values, traditions, rituals, music, languages, patterns of personal relation, and so forth, respect calls for us *to confront our biases*, to try to recognize and counteract our initial inclination always to judge by comparison with what is most familiar. With regard to diverse *moral* practices, basic respect calls all the more for modesty and caution to curb our arrogant bias in judging others whom we hardly understand. This requires not merely self-discipline but also, so far as possible, respectful confrontation and communication with representatives of cultures whose practices we are initially inclined to condemn; for, on the modified Kantian view proposed here, moral insight is not the special endowment of any group but is something that can only emerge gradually as diverse but mutually respectful human beings engage seriously in communication about how best to live together despite their differences. Thus, openness in confronting other cultures is needed, not only to respect individuals who are different from us, but also, more generally, to curb our moral arrogance and to further moral understanding. This is not to say that morality is simply a hodgepodge of standards picked indiscriminately from a variety of cultures and thrown into a multicultural pot. The point is rather that no single group, within the bounds of one heritage, can by itself achieve that diminution of bias, awareness of options, and appreciation of human limits and possibilities necessary to warrant confidence that it possesses the best, or most humane and just, moral system.

Third, it is not respectful to people of other cultures, or to ourselves, to condone and tolerate all cultural practices, no matter how harmful and restrictive they may be. On the modified Kantian conception that I am proposing, human beings are seen as culturally embedded but none the less as (to some degree) capable of critical judgement, independent thinking, recognition of the moral status of other persons, and constraining themselves by principles based on the ideal of mutual respect among all persons. To respect this moral capacity, as the key to a morality of respect, we must, however modestly and cautiously, condemn practices that, even after closest study, seem deeply dismissive of certain classes of human beings. To condemn cultural practices, elsewhere or at home, one must take a stand, and in taking a stand one takes a *risk* that bias has corrupted one's judgement. But respect for all, unlike more parochial principles, can be conscientiously defended to all, and those who endorse it show no respect to themselves or others when, through excess caution, they refuse to condemn what they see as deeply contemptuous practices. An important implication for issues regarding curriculum is that the respect that calls for widening cultural understanding does not require, or allow, us to suspend our most basic standards of judgement—for example, to read the diaries of Anne Frank and Joseph Goebbels, or the autobiography of Frederick Douglass and the speeches of John C. Calhoun, with the same morally detached interest that might be appropriate in the study of set theory, abstract art, and geology.

Fourth, to say that moral judgement should not be suspended when reading, discussing, or selecting curricular materials does not imply that moralistic criteria should dictate what is to be read. To purge the reading lists of everything considered immoral, replacing these with works more uplifting or 'politically correct', would be to undermine any hope of the sort of cross-cultural understanding to which universal respect aspires. Listening appreciatively to history's victims is no doubt long overdue, but we should also hear the false rhetoric of oppressors and the banal excuses of the overly tolerant, if we hope to gain more than a skewed and superficial grasp of the complex dynamics of cultures. Curriculum development requires judicious selection, but understanding and respect require listening to many voices we dislike and deplore—not listening merely passively, but with minds and hearts fully engaged.

Fifth, how far should a curriculum go in replacing the old, Western, white male authors, such as Shakespeare, Hobbes, Gibbon, and Darwin, with writers representing other perspectives (e.g. contemporary, non-Western, non-European, and feminist)? I do not pretend to have a definite answer; and, even if I did, it would be most appropriately presented, with due respect, as a proposal to a diverse deliberative committee with the authority and commitment to work out the details together. One implication of what I have been saying today, however, seems clear and relevant. As human beings, we tend not only to hold on to what we now value but also to seek out more of what we may find valuable, and we find it in many places we could not initially anticipate. But finding something valuable is not the same as having an initial untutored desire for it or even liking it upon first exposure. Many, if not most, of the long-revered works in the now much disparaged 'canon' for college students were there because people who devoted time to them experienced in them something that enriched their lives. These works have, then, a strong, though not exclusive, claim on our attention. The claim stems not so much from our respect for the authors themselves, much less from their origin in a European, white male tradition, but from respect for those who might be the readers. One does not have to argue that these works are 'better' than each competing non-standard selection, by some standard neutral among all cultures, but only that they have been persistently found to be among the best or most valuable to the reflective readers within the tradition they represent. Nor, for reasons just given, need they be 'morally pure'. What does matter is that they have been challenging, stimulating, illuminating, and life-enriching to a sufficient number of intelligent and diligent readers to warrant a prediction that they will continue to be found so by others.

My remarks here are not meant to favour 'the canon' more than innovation and diversify in the curriculum, for the case for each seems strong. Here, as elsewhere, dogmatism is out of place. There are no precise lines to be drawn in choosing among a wealth of riches. So what proper respect calls for, surely, is open discussion and listening, broadly inclusive procedures for decision-making, and eventually compromise. If a curriculum did not give substantial place for *long-recognized excellence* within the dominant Western tradition, it would not respect those who are deeply influenced by that tradition and so have special reason to try to understand it and find what has been thought most valuable in it. If, however, a traditional curriculum did not diversify in a serious and substantial way, it would continue to reinforce cultural bias or at least fail to help students to develop their resources to fight it. Moreover, this extreme conservatism would fail to respect students as persons who, despite being embedded in a culture, can enrich their lives by learning to appreciate values of another kind—or at least to respect those who do.

4

Must Respect be Earned?

In my last chapter I sketched (and modified) an old idea drawn from Immanuel Kant, the idea that the ultimate source of human values is humanity itself, rather than Platonic forms, natural teleology, God's commands, universal human sentiments, or particular social conventions. Humanity is attributed only to those presumed to have certain basic normative capacities and dispositions. These include the ability to reflect on one's desires and circumstances, to set ends for oneself, to form coherent plans, and to be willing to reciprocate with others in endorsing principles that respect each person as a potential source of legitimate values. In Kant's philosophy these ideas were accompanied by a moral rigourism and a radical 'two-perspective' metaphysics that few philosophers today can accept; but I treat these as associated ideas that are inessential to Kant's central moral insights. In his vigorous defence of individual responsibility, Kant seems to have exaggerated the power of autonomous individuals to set themselves ends and to adopt principles independently of others, but his view can be coherently supplemented, I suggested, with a more realistic account of how, rather than dubbing individual goals to be valuable by acts of free choice, we tend to *find* our values, as social beings, within our familiar cultural contexts. Applying this suggestion, I argued that *if* we respect persons as sources of value, understood in this more realistic way, *then* we are committed to certain attitudes about cultural diversity. In particular, this respect has implications for *how* different cultures should be represented in a university curriculum. For example, proper respect calls for caution and modesty in moral judgement but not for unlimited tolerance or passive acceptance. It requires effort to appreciate other cultures but not moralistic dismissal of our Western heritage. Mutual respect, in a pluralistic world, urges us to acknowledge that we are all embedded in cultural contexts that unavoidably *limit* our understanding and skew our judgement, but do *not preclude* our responsibility to confront and diminish our prejudices in wider cross-cultural communication.

Supplementing Kant's own account of how we form our values, I called attention to six points about how a commitment to basic respect for human beings as sources of value might work out in practice. Each of these prescriptions should be considered, for now, as *prima facie* or *defeasible*, for in particular cases what is recommended by one consideration may be in tension with what is recommended by another. For example, the presumption that one should not tolerate or condone cultural practices that are deeply contemptuous of women can be in tension with the prima facie consideration that we should respectfully acknowledge that individuals tend to identify themselves by their traditional roles within a culture. How in practice these tensions should be resolved will require further reflection, perhaps case by case. Inventing further rules for these problems may not be helpful. In any case, my argument left the details of these matters open, in order to stress more general points. That is, *if* we accept basic Kantian respect, *then* (1) there are limits to what cultural practices we can condone, but (2) we have at least prima facie reason not to interfere coercively or manipulatively with the cultural values that others find, and reflectively endorse, as central to 'who they are', and (3) we must try, so far as possible, to encourage changes in disrespectful cultural practices, at home or elsewhere, but only by means that respectfully address, as moral agents, those with whom we disagree.

Although these conclusions may seem obvious to many, they are not uncontroversial. Even if our values stem ultimately from the reflective endorsements of human beings, we may wonder, *why* should we respect and value every person as a source of values? It does not follow from the fact that everyone *has values*, or finds things valuable, that these things *are valuable*, or ought to be regarded by all as valuable. It is natural to wonder *why* we should respect those who refuse to respect others, who blatantly disregard even the minimum demands of a morality of respect for persons. To be blunt, are not some people, as a former colleague would say, 'moral garbage', mere 'scum' that pollutes rather than enriches life for the rest of humanity? How can we respect such people in any meaningful sense? Why suppose that we are committed to respecting those who have done nothing to *earn* it? Even if we grant that everyone is initially owed some respect as a human being, is there any reason to deny that some extremely bad characters, by their immoral deeds, *forfeit* all respect, justifying our viewing them with utter contempt?

These are the issues to which I now turn. Whereas before we focused on *how* to respect humanity (in multi-cultural contexts), we now ask *why* and *within what limits?* These are large questions that I cannot pretend to answer adequately here. What I can offer is only a sketch of some ways a Kantian might interpret and respond to them. The sketch is meant partly to reflect Kant's own basic strategy of argument, fine points aside, and partly to suggest lines of response, broadly consistent with Kant's ethics, that might be developed more fully in time.

RESPECT FOR HUMANITY VS. RESPECT FOR MERIT: REFORMULATION OF THE ISSUES

One might suppose, mistakenly, that doubts about the propriety of respecting *all* human beings could be dismissed by making a simple distinction. To those who think that we should respect only those who have *earned* respect, for example, we can imagine an analytic-minded philosopher responding as follows. We need a distinction, he or she says, between two kinds of respect: *respecting persons for their merits* and *respecting persons for their social positions*.[1] Consider the first. When we mean to acknowledge individuals' distinctive merit or excellence, we can say such things as 'One must respect Perlman as a violinist,' 'She won the respect of the team for her efforts,' 'I respect him as a politician, but not as a saxophonist,' 'I respect her as an artist, but not as a person.' Respect here amounts to confidence in a person's ability or esteem for her excellence in a context of comparative or scalar evaluation.

Again, we often respect persons for *performing well in a social position*, but then we are not respecting them merely because they occupy the position but rather because they are good at the tasks associated with the position. When we have in mind respect for merit, for example, to say 'I respect her as a lawyer' means 'I respect her because she is a *good* lawyer,' not 'I respect her because she *is* a lawyer.' For similar reasons, respecting someone as a safe-cracker does not mean respecting the person simply *because* he or she *is* a safe-cracker but rather respecting the person for his or her safe-cracking skills.

Now consider the second kind of respect: respect for a person's social position. Suppose someone says, 'She has not been a particularly good mother, but she is my mother, after all, and I must respect her as such.'

---

[1] See Stephen Darwall, 'Two Concepts of Respect', *Ethics*, 88 (1977), 36–40. His terms are 'appraisal respect' and 'recognition respect'. A similar distinction is an important part of my discussions in *Autonomy and Self-respect* (Cambridge: Cambridge University Press, 1991), esp. chs. 1 and 11.

Here the point is not to make a comparative evaluation, but rather to acknowledge that merely holding a certain position, or standing in a certain relation to another, is sometimes enough to warrant a (presumptive) claim of respect. This should not be surprising, because social roles, positions, and relationships are often defined in normative terms, by the rights, responsibilities, and privileges that are constitutive of them. To take another example, suppose I say, 'I cannot abide his views, and I do not trust him, but he is, after all, the president, and we must respect him as such.' Here I would imply that office-holders are to be respected on account of the position they hold, not because they are doing well at fulfilling that position.

How is this distinction relevant to our concerns? Consider our previous question, whether we must respect those who refuse to respect others. Armed now with the distinction between two kinds of respect, our hypothetical defender of the Kantian position might try to dismiss this worry as a mere verbal confusion. Of course, he or she might say, immoral, vicious people do not deserve *respect* in the first sense, for they are not especially good or meritorious as persons; but, none the less, we must *respect* them *as human beings*, in the second sense, for *humanity* (or being human) is itself a moral status or position that calls for respectful recognition. In support, he or she might cite the point, noted by Locke and others, that 'person' often functions as a 'forensic notion', defined, as it were, as 'one who possesses such and such rights and duties'. Similarly, he or she might argue, the terms 'humanity' and 'human being' are often used as labels for those presumed to have a certain moral status worthy of respect. If so, it seems we can coherently respect even viciously immoral people *as human beings*, even though, as individuals, they fall far short of how human beings should conduct themselves.

This reply calls attention to an important distinction, but it fails to meet the underlying concern of those who wonder why they should respect all human beings. To be sure, if we share the same moral attitudes, we may come to conceive of 'being human' as a moral status with given rights and duties, just as aristocrats once conceived of 'being a duke' as a quasi-moral status with rights and duties. In this context of agreement, to say 'She is a human being, so treat her accordingly,' would be a way of expressing a familiar moral judgement. This would be like saying, in an earlier time, 'He is a duke, so treat him accordingly.' But playing with these conceptual implications will not get us very far toward a deep justification. Even if it is, for some speakers, a tautology that human beings should be treated with respect, we may still wonder why we should elevate even the most vicious members of our biological species to the normative status of 'human being'. Similarly, even if, for some, 'Dukes are entitled to special honour' is true by definition, we may still doubt whether certain corrupt characters who were called 'dukes' are entitled to that richly normative label. Building entitlements into the definition of the terms 'human being' and 'duke' makes it all too easy to defend the propositions 'Human beings should be respected' and 'Dukes are owed special honour,' for it simply turns them into tautologies. Once we do this, however, the moral controversy merely shifts to another question, namely, what entitles anyone to the labels 'human being' and 'duke'? We may still wonder why we should respect *this or that particular* lying freeloader or sociopathic murderer.

The moral of these linguistic reflections is simple: although the demand to *respect people as human beings* treats 'being human' (or 'having humanity') as a moral status, it leaves open to question what rights and responsibilities should belong to that position. 'Respect her as a human being' does not mean 'Esteem her as a comparatively superior human being' but rather 'Accord her all the respect (presumptively) due to anyone who has the status of being human.' But specifically *what* respect is (presumptively) due to all human beings, and whether it can be forfeited, so far remains an open issue. Given this, our initial question about why we should respect all human beings can be re-expressed, in a more refined way, as follows: *(1) Why grant to all members of our species, or even to all with certain basic normative capacities, a moral status (of 'humanity') that includes the presumption that anyone who has the status should be respected by all?*

If we can answer these concerns about the *presumption* that respect is owed to every human being, then a further question still arises: *(2) Granted that all human beings have a defeasible right to respect as human beings, is there any reason to suppose that they cannot forfeit this right?* This question is pressing because analogies suggest that all role rights can be forfeited by gross misconduct. For example, even though 'doctor' and 'president' refer to roles that are usually accorded a presumption of due respect, some doctors and presidents are so corrupt that, by general agreement, they forfeit their initial claims to respect on account of their positions.

Suppose that we can see *some good reasons* for *trying* to respect even the worst persons as human beings *if this is possible and compatible with our other responsibilities.* Our agreement with Kant that no one can altogether forfeit respect as a human being would still be *conditional* on satisfying ourselves regarding a remaining question: *(3) How, in practice, can we defend ourselves, punish criminals, and express our outrage at bigotry and corruption if we must treat all unjust, corrupt bigots with respect?* This question seems pressing especially if we come to doubt the answer so often given in theory, but rarely in practice, namely, 'Condemn and despise the sin, but not the sinner.' With experience, we may well wonder: Is this psychologically possible? Even so, would it really be respectful? Can we respect either ourselves or the perpetrators of heinous crimes if we refuse to hold them *responsible* for their choices?[2]

In what follows, I address all of these concerns briefly. To preview: First, I sketch a Kantian line of reasoning for the presumption that respect is owed to all human beings. There are two main steps, outlined in the next two sections: (1) a description of a Kantian moral framework and efforts to show that this articulates and develops moral concepts to which we are already committed and (2) a claim that some formal requirements of respect are implicit in the Kantian framework and more substantive requirements can be defended by reasoning from it. Second, I consider how a Kantian perspective might lead us, for moral and practical reasons, to try to adopt the attitude that no one can completely forfeit all respect as a human being, provided this is possible and compatible with our other responsibilities. Third, to satisfy the last proviso, I suggest reasons for thinking that basic respect for all humanity, as understood here, is possible and fully compatible with our responsibilities to protect ourselves, to support just punishment, and to censure the perpetrators of evil (not merely their 'deeds').

Together, these points have important practical implications regarding how we can legitimately respond to immorality and crime. We should respect even vicious and unremorseful people *as human beings*, but we can do so without tolerating their behaviour, trusting them to reform, or forgiving them. Far from being empty, however, the requirement of respect limits the kinds of moral censure and punishment that we can fairly use. The Kantian ideal of respect should also temper our responses on campus to those whom we believe to be racists and sexists, replacing contemptuous dismissal with firm but respectful confrontation.

---

[2] The general policy of separating the 'sin' from the 'sinner', condemning the former while never attributing blameworthiness to the perpetrators, seems disrespectful to oneself as it denies one the expression of legitimate resentment and indignation, and it seems disrespectful of the offender because it places him or her in a category outside normal interactive moral relationships.

INTERPRETING THE ISSUE: WHY SHOULD WE RESPECT ALL HUMAN BEINGS?

At first glance, this seems a simple question, for we are used to many ways of answering questions of the form 'Why should we . . . ?' On reflection, however, it is not so obvious how we should understand the question. What sort of answer might one be looking for? Often we answer 'Why should we . . . ?' questions by pointing out desirable consequences, but the basic Kantian claim is not amenable to this sort of defence. Even if we could show empirical evidence that adopting a policy of universal respect proves to be generally advantageous to everyone, this would not justify holding it, as Kantians do, as a deep, necessary feature of the basic moral framework for deliberating about all specific issues. Granting everyone due respect is a basic moral requirement not derivative from the desirability of promoting other good consequences. Although it is a welcome fact that according people due respect tends to promote other goods, Kantians take the principle of respect for humanity as standing independently of this fact and serving as a limit to what we may legitimately do in our efforts to promote the general welfare.

Again, given Kantian denials of intuitionism, naturalism, and sentimentalism as theories of value, it is not open to 'justify' respect for humanity by pretending to find 'in' humanity some intuitable, natural, or sentiment-evoking property of 'worthiness of respect'.

Kant himself wrote eloquently of the reverence and awe that seem forced from us as we contemplate 'the moral law within', and this may suggest that Kant's only ground for making universal respect so central in his ethics is his belief that everyone will, necessarily but inexplicably, 'find' that this moral predisposition commands their respect wherever it is found, even in those who in fact flagrantly fail to follow it. One famous passage in Kant's *Groundwork*, in fact, might seem to offer just this sort of argument. That is, one might take Kant to be arguing as follows: All of us first recognize 'humanity' in ourselves; we cannot help but regard this humanity in us as 'Awesome!' ('an end in itself', loosely interpreted); seeing that the 'awesome' thing is also in every other moral agent, we should acknowledge that the same attitude is appropriate to humanity in everyone;[3] hence we should respect everyone's humanity.

---

[3] See G, 96 [428–9]. The argument would be fallacious in moving to the requirement to respect humanity in others if what one recognized in oneself was just that one's own humanity was of great value to oneself (as, perhaps, one sees one's own pleasures). The

Now even if Kant at times suggests this sort of argument, it does not provide the kind of deep grounding that one might hope to find for his central principle of respect for humanity. Many will no doubt refuse to concede that they find either 'humanity' or 'the moral law within' as awesome as Kant does, and by Kant's own principles he should not be appealing either to intuition or to contingent sentiments (as, it seems, the argument above does) to support his account of the basic features of the moral point of view. One might try to argue that the initial recognition of humanity as 'awesome' is neither an intuition nor an emotional response, but rather a *necessary* aspect of a *rational* agent's inevitable consciousness of being subject to moral constraints (i.e. part of 'the fact of reason' that Kant discusses in his second Critique).[4] But, for this proposal to amount to more than an appeal to 'intuition' or common sentiment, it needs to be more fully explained *why* seeing one's own 'humanity' as an 'end in itself' is necessarily something we do *because we are rational.*[5]

What, then, is the Kantian ground for the idea that we should respect all human beings as such? With apparent simplicity we can say, as commentators often do, that the ground is 'humanity' itself, or 'rational nature', or 'autonomy'. This, however, only indicates *what* qualifies moral agents as objects of basic respect as human beings; it does not spell out *why*. The reference (to 'humanity', etc.) points to what *Kant believed* a creature needs in order to be owed such respect; but it does not, by itself, provide an argument that addresses the concerns of those who have yet to accept the Kantian moral framework. Is there more we can do?

We can 'justify' some features of a system of thought by showing their connections with other beliefs we share, for example by showing how they are entailed or presupposed by deep and pervasive commitments that we would find difficult, if not impossible, to discard. Proofs and 'justifying' arguments come to an end at some point, but we can often satisfy the actual 'Why should we . . . ?' concerns that prompt the search for justifications. Sometimes we do this by revealing that the 'We should

argument presupposes that one sees humanity, in one's own case, as *in itself worthy of respect*, not just something valuable to one because it is one's own.

[4] C2, 30–2 [30–1].

[5] Even if it gives a plausible reading of Kant's argument, the fuller explanation needed would make the argument in question far more complex than the simple, facile ('intuitive') line of thought that the interpretations I am examining in this section take it to be. That fuller account would need, I think, to make use of at least some of the background ideas that I develop in the next two sections. Thus, although I believe there is something to the proposed interpretation, I shall not try to develop it here.

. . .' in question turns out to be, in effect, the expression of an attitude to which we are already committed by other beliefs and attitudes that we see no adequate reason to abandon. The conceptual connections may be far from self-evident, revealing themselves only by deep analysis of the normative concepts we employ. The mode of argument, then, would not be a quick appeal to intuition, linguistic or otherwise, but a process of gradually unfolding and articulating more clearly the implications of modes of thought that we actually rely upon and could not give up, at least not without radical reorientation of our lives.

This is the sort of 'justification', I believe, that Kant offers in response to the concerns underlying the question 'Why should we respect all human beings?' Briefly, we should because such respect is an essential aspect of the moral framework for deliberation to which we are in fact committed by our concept of ourselves as moral agents, subject to duties, once this is properly understood. In the next section, I describe some general features of the Kantian moral framework (as I reconstruct it) and sketch strategies Kant suggests for showing that in fact we pre-suppose it. Then, in the following section, I consider how this basic moral framework leads to the presumption that all human beings should be respected in certain (formal and substantive) ways. As always for Kant, 'we should' refers to what 'we would' do if, though able and sometimes tempted to do otherwise, we acted in a fully rational way. 'Why should we . . . ?' questions, then, in effect translate into questions about what is rational, or reasonable, for us to do.[6]

THE KANTIAN MORAL FRAMEWORK AND KANT'S STRATEGIES FOR SHOWING IT IS PRESUPPOSED IN COMMON MORAL CONCEPTS

Kantian ethics acknowledges a need for a common moral framework for thinking about specific moral issues. That is, its ambition is to attempt to resolve more particular controversies by appeal to widely shared standards for moral deliberation and argument, standards pro-viding criteria regarding what is morally relevant and procedures for working toward reasonable resolutions of conflict. Many familiar

---

[6] As will be evident, I often use 'reasonable' to express in common-sense terms what Kant seems often to mean by 'rational'. The latter term in recent times is usually used to describe conclusions based entirely on instrumental reasoning and individual prefer-ences rather than prescriptions based on thinking from the common point of view of all moral agents (i.e. what I call 'reasonable').

perspectives on morality (for example, those inherent in various religious sects) quite frankly call for an antecedent conversion to a quite specific value system. Thus, they do not well serve, and were not meant to serve, the desired mediating role of a general framework for discussion, mutually acceptable to a wide range of people with diverse moral convictions. Utilitarianism, in its several forms, has been attractive partly because it seems to serve that mediating role, in effect asking people who are quarrelling over particular day-to-day moral issues to frame their disputes in terms of a common overarching commitment to whatever seems, on best evidence, to promote the greatest satisfaction of human preferences, impartially considered. Utilitarian theories, however, raise many (now familiar) problems, most notably that, even though committed to 'counting' each person's preferences, they leave open the possibility that, in the end, the good of some may be totally sacrificed to satisfy the preferences of others.

What I propose, then, is to sketch an alternative moral framework, drawn from Kant, which is meant, like utilitarianism, to be a mode of thinking that can help to mediate moral disputes. But, unlike utilitarianism, this Kantian alternative refuses to reduce moral deliberation to unconstrained quantitative thinking that treats all individual aspirations as just so many preferences in a common pool, which are to be denied or approved according to a global maximizing strategy. The framework I shall sketch is Kantian in a broad sense because it draws from several of Kant's formulations of the Categorical Imperative, but I do not have time here either to trace its heritage or to fill in all the necessary details.

The basic idea is that, for purposes of thinking about what particular moral principles we should endorse, how they are to be interpreted, and what exceptions should hold, we can appropriately think of moral principles as principles that all *reasonable* human beings would accept, as justifiable to themselves and others, under certain ideal conditions. The idea of the 'reasonable' here, as in John Rawls's work, is broader than the idea of 'the rational', as contemporary decision theorists understand this; for reasonableness includes a willingness to reciprocate with others on mutually agreeable terms.[7]

The conditions for ideal reasonable legislation include sober and realistic awareness of the contexts in which the principles are to be applied,

---

[7] Common-sense and Kantian ideas of the reasonable, as I understand them in contrast with other models of the rational, are discussed more fully in my paper 'Reasonable Self-interest', in *Social Philosophy and Policy*, 14 (1997), 52–85. Unfortunately, the same term serves for both the rational and the reasonable in Kant's texts.

sensitivity to the diverse values that people have, willingness to set aside personal differences that are morally irrelevant to the task, and effort to review principles on their merits, without undue reliance on one's own familiar traditions, antecedent cultural or religious loyalties, and personal attachments.[8] A key stipulation is that each person, in reviewing possible moral requirements, must acknowledge that, ideally, every person subject to the requirements shares equally the authority to make and interpret them. Everyone is, as it were, an equal co-legislator in what Kant calls 'a kingdom of ends', in which the legislators together must 'make' the 'laws', settling on moral standards that, they agree, should take precedence over their individual policies. That is, they are seen as, ideally, the joint authors of principles that trump the policies that *otherwise* they might adopt to satisfy their personal desires.

This ideal 'moral legislation' is not arbitrary but is supposed to be guided by legislators' mutual commitment to essential features of a moral perspective that, like constitutional constraints, are not themselves 'legislated'. The latter, basic ideas implicit in the various forms of the Categorical Imperative are meant to be constitutive aspects of the ideal of living in community with other free, equal, and reasonable moral agents who constrain their personal pursuits by mutually agreed standards. We are to think of substantive moral principles, beyond the constitutive standards, as binding a person only if they are justifiable to that person in so far as that person too considers the issue from the ideal perspective of a co-legislator. Thus, human beings are viewed as if they were jointly authors of binding principles and individually subject to them, once the principles are finally decided.

In this ideal model, all moral agents are assumed to have *autonomy*, which means, in part, that no one is morally bound by demands imposed from any other source, unless such demands are backed by more basic principles that all rational agents with autonomy would accept. Autonomy implies, further, that in moral legislation one does not accept principles simply because they are traditional, currently accepted, sanctioned by religious authorities, or especially favourable to the interests of one particular group rather than another. The *humanity* of each person is treated by the others as an 'end in itself', at least in the 'thin' sense that the 'reasonable will' of each person, along with every other, is what counts as the final authority. Hence all accept the constraints that they jointly will as legislators, giving them priority over the various

---

[8] My idea of Kantian moral 'legislation' as a framework for deliberating about more specific issues and various problems it raises are discussed more fully in 'A Kantian Perspective on Moral Rules', ch. 2 in this volume.

(contingent) ends and means that otherwise they might like to adopt. That is, if they believe that the appropriate joint deliberation of all who have humanity, or reasonable wills, would converge on certain general principles, then they acknowledge those principles as the final, unconditional authority regarding what ends they should seek and what means they may, and may not, use.

The general idea here has affinities, not only with Kant, but with Rousseau's political ideal, John Rawls's theory of justice, Thomas Scanlon's idea of moral justification, and no doubt other views as well. Many details need to be filled in, and problems must be faced, before any heuristic model of this kind can be fairly assessed or confidently used. But, long before that, it is natural to wonder: What could lead one to think of ideal moral reflection in this way? Kant tried to show that the Kantian legislative perspective is implicit in the attitudes of ordinary conscientious people. His reasoning took two lines, which converged on the main point.

One line of thought starts this way. What fundamental priorities express the attitude of conscientious persons, independently of the specific views they may have about what is right and what is wrong? Well, at least this: they have the attitude that if they judge, upon full and reasonable deliberation, that they are morally required to do something, then they must do that, even if other goods have to be sacrificed. In other words, they treat what Kant calls their 'good will' as good 'above all else', 'without qualification'.[9] This is not to say that they hold that morality generally requires the radical sacrifice of other goods, such as health, wealth, knowledge, and happiness; it means only that, if the only way they can gain one of these other goods is by doing what they are convinced is wrong, then they are committed to forgoing that other good. This is an old and, to many, trivial point: one should not sell one's soul (or moral integrity) for anything, no matter how attractive it may appear. So far, of course, this tells us nothing substantive about what sorts of acts are immoral; but it reveals a conscientious attitude as one that accepts that there are reasonable constraints on the pursuit of personal goods, including happiness. Upon further analysis, this attitude is revealed as a matter of *respect* for moral principle, something distinct from wanting to achieve a desired goal.[10] The attitude turns out, on reflection, to be respect for 'objective principles': that is, principles to which anyone, *if fully reasonable*, would conform his or her personal policies ('maxims').[11]

[9] G, 61–2 [393–4].   [10] G, 68–9 [400–1].
[11] G, 69–70, esp. 69 n. [401–2, esp. 401 n.].

Another line of thought runs in the same direction, but a bit further.[12] Different people have different ideas about what particular duties they have, but what is it *in common* that they are thinking when they think they are morally required to do or to refrain from various acts? For one thing, they think they *ought* to do it; and this thought may be interpreted as the idea that what they ought to do is what, upon full and reasonable deliberation, they would do if completely rational and reasonable, though they are quite aware that they might not do it.

There are many things, however, that they believe they ought to do that they do not regard as *moral* requirements, and so more must be said. The something more is apparently this: when conscientious persons accept something as a moral requirement, they see it as non-optional, that is, as what they ought to do, whether or not they feel like doing it, and not just because it serves their personal interests. Unlike what is 'necessary' to fulfil an optional plan, they feel, one cannot simply change one's plans and thereby escape the 'ought' judgement. What accounts for their sense that they 'must' or 'ought to' do what they believe is morally required, then, is not their belief that doing it will get them something they want, such as wealth, friendship, or happiness. Since thinking one *ought* to do something, in general, implies thinking that it is reasonable to do, they must presuppose that there is some other kind of reason why they ought to fulfil particular moral requirements. They must, then, be presupposing, among their deep commitments, some general principle, or point of view, that would explain why they regard it as reasonable to judge that they ought, on particular occasions, to do the morally required things, whether they want to or not.[13] In other words, they are committed to there being some standards of reasonable

[12] The following paragraphs, to the end of this section, are meant to be a very loose reconstruction of lines of thought in *Groundwork*, ch. 2, esp. 80–104 [412–37].

[13] The point is independent of whether there is general agreement on the particular duty. Some may think that it is a duty to lie on a certain occasion, and others think that it is a duty not to lie; but what they have in common is the supposition that reason requires them to do the various things that they believe to be morally required, whether this serves their particular wants and plans or not. And this, presumably, needs explanation and support from a more general account of what it is to be reasonable. As I noted earlier, I am systematically substituting 'reasonable' for 'rational' in the discussion of moral deliberation because I think this is less misleading to modern audiences. Also note that the argument presupposes an internalist view of reasons and 'ought'; that is, if I judge that I have reasons to do something, or ought to do it, I am thereby to some degree disposed to do it and I acknowledge that there is something I favour or am committed to that is positively connected with it. 'Committed' here, though, does not mean whole-heartedly or all-things-considered finally resolved to do it, but leaves open that I could merely acknowledge its 'authority', believe it is what I would do if doing my best, etc.

conduct, which they count as authoritative for them, that indicate that certain things ought, and others ought not, to be done, and not just because this serves the specific aims and interests that the agent happens to have.

To put the thought in Kant's terms, the idea of duty presupposes that there is a Categorical Imperative, that is, a general principle reasonable for all, that can guide moral judgement and support particular moral beliefs. This cannot be merely the Hypothetical Imperative, 'It is rational to take the necessary means to your ends,' for this supports no requirement independent of one's aims and wants.[14]

At this point we must look around for candidates. Most alleged moral principles are too specific and substantive to be plausibly advanced as principles reasonable for everyone to adopt, no matter how diverse their aims, values, and traditional ties. For example, 'Follow the will of god X,' 'Follow the example of those judged wisest and best in your community,' 'Live by the code of your ancestors,' 'Obey the law,' 'Follow the promptings of your natural sympathy'; all these, and many more, are too limited in application, or too controversial in their priorities, or both, to gain wide acceptance as the comprehensive, universally reasonable standard that people who believe in moral requirements presuppose as the source of these requirements. Many people may be persuaded to accept them, but why should one expect all reasonable people, regardless of their particular differences, to find such specific, substantive principles authoritative for them? If they fear the consequences of violating tradition, law, or religious precepts, this would make conformity to those principles quite sensible, but it could not justify thinking of them as *moral requirements*, that is, as how one ought to act regardless of one's personal wants, hopes, and fears.[15]

The inadequacy of the other candidates to explain the idea of duty makes the Kantian proposal look more promising. The core idea is that the Categorical Imperative, that most comprehensive principle behind the belief in particular duties, is 'conform to universal law', which, liberally reconstructed, means to restrict one's personal acts and policies to those compatible with whatever general principles everyone would accept if 'legislating' from the moral perspective that I sketched earlier.

---

[14] My understanding of this non-moral general principle of reason is more fully spelled out in my collection of essays on Kant's ethics, *Dignity and Practical Reason in Kant's Moral Theory* (Ithaca, NY: Cornell University Press, 1992), chs. 1 and 7.

[15] See G, 108–12 [441–4], and contrast 88 [420–1]. Here I try merely to articulate the spirit of Kant's opposition to substantive accounts of the fundamental moral principle, deliberately omitting Kant's more direct lines of argument for his 'universal law' formulation of the Categorical Imperative and its relation to later formulations.

Morally binding 'laws' are not to be found in a vision of Plato's world of Forms, in God's mind, or in secular conceptions of nature. Rather, we must try to work out together what a moral point of view requires in various situations by trying to think realistically, to transcend particular biases and special interests, and to find a common core of ideals and standards that we can justify to each other, despite our differences. What makes this formal prescription a candidate for being a 'principle of reason' is that what it enjoins is simply an interpretation, for the human condition, of the abstract rule 'Govern yourself, constrain your desires and plans, according to what is reasonable.' The interpretation, which begins to add some teeth to the precept, holds that what is reasonable is (ideally) to be worked out jointly in ongoing, mutually respectful deliberations in which everyone must try to justify proposed policies and principles to everyone else who is willing to reciprocate.[16]

FORMAL RESPECT FOR ALL IS IMPLICIT IN THE KANTIAN MORAL FRAMEWORK AND SUBSTANTIVE RESPECT DEFENSIBLE FROM IT

The Kantian moral perspective implicitly contains within it an important, though relatively formal, requirement of respect. In accepting moral constraints as what, ideally, all human beings would agree upon in reasonable joint deliberations, we are, in a sense, respecting each person as a potential co-legislator of the basic principles we must all live by. The aim is to see that our conduct can be justified to others who are able and willing to take up the moral point of view. This does not mean that we may do only what others like, but only that we must avoid conduct that we believe would be prohibited by principles that all reasonable people (taking the moral perspective) would agree on.[17]

---

[16] Here I interpret and extend ideas Kant presents in G, 88–104 [420–37] along lines discussed more fully in *Dignity and Practical Reason in Kant's Moral Theory*, and some later essays, including 'Donagan's Kant', ch. 5 of this volume.

[17] Perhaps it is worth calling readers' attention here to an important qualification I introduce later when trying to accommodate the ideal Kantian model to the reality that reasonable people will not always agree: that is, one can view the model as a standard of individual *conscientious decision*, rather than *moral truth*. Moral truth, one might say, would be the ideal point on which all reasonable persons' moral deliberations would converge. But since we do not often know that, we can say that a conscientious choice is one based on what, after due deliberation, consultation, and consideration of the opinions of others, the moral agent sincerely judges to be the best candidate for reasonable acceptance by all, even though he or she is aware that reasonable people may disagree.

If some people are not now willing and able to deliberate morally, though they have the potential capacity to do so, their interests and voice can to some extent be represented by proxy: that is, by others trying to give weight to what those not now able to deliberate would agree to if they could and would take up the requisite point of view.[18] In this way we may think of children as represented in the moral deliberation process, even though not now ready actually to take part.[19]

A different sort of proxy argument from the Kantian framework might call for decent treatment, kindness, and even a kind of 'respect'

[18] In this way, I am supposing, infants (at least all but the severely brain-damaged) might have their interests represented and protected. Those who can now deliberate morally must do so in such a way that they could reasonably hope to justify their principles, eventually, to all with 'humanity', the basic capacities and dispositions that enable a person to be a moral agent in human conditions. These capacities can be ready and developed, as Kant seemed to be supposing in most of his ethical writings; or they could be latent, as in young children. Much discussion would be required to decide, as interpretation of Kant or as independently defensible theory, where to draw these lines; but for now I assume that those with the latent capacities of humanity (e.g. young children) are among those to whom moral deliberators must try to imagine themselves justifying their policies. This involves trying to estimate, difficult as this might be, what particular children would say when they are mature and aware of their basic human needs, but have not lost sight of their childhood interests. Alternatively, perhaps the hypothetical justification should be addressed to proxies who both understand and are fully devoted to the children's interests. These issues, I realize, are too complex and difficult to resolve here, and the same can be said of foetuses, the comatose, the permanently retarded, etc. They are issues that should not be swept aside; for unless they can be satisfactorily addressed within a Kantian framework, that framework remains subject to significant doubt.

[19] The same might be said for any adults whom we *knew* to be so blindly devoted to *authorities* for answers to moral questions that they actually cannot yet engage in reasonable deliberation about moral issues on any other ground. Jeffrie Murphy feared that my presentation implied that many Roman Catholics must be denied basic respect because of their loyalty to their church and scriptures; but I cannot see how this follows from my reconstructed Kantian view. First, it would be arrogantly presumptuous to suppose we *know* that the believers in question have no grasp of the moral considerations themselves, only blind acceptance of 'orders' understood only as that. Typically, to the contrary, Catholics that I know have a good sense of morality *together with* a faith that, properly understood, authoritative church prescriptions are based on good moral reasons. Second, even if a given believer is not currently able to engage in moral dialogue and deliberation with anything more than appeals to authority, the Kantian perspective, as I understand it, does not deny that person respect as a human being; for we have no good reason to suppose such a person permanently and unalterably unresponsive to moral considerations presented as reasons for action rather than as commands.

The practical point of insisting on active capacities of independent reflection, autonomy, etc. in the *ideal* of moral deliberation is not to deny respect to imperfect deliberators, but just to indicate that in our *hypothetical* reasoning from that ideal construct we need not imagine that good moral arguments are constrained by a need to convince people when they are relying exclusively on authority.

for non-human animals and members of our species born without any potential for moral deliberation; but such an argument, obviously, could not support a presumption of *respect for them as* (even potentially) *fellow 'legislators' of moral principles.*

Although I shall not try to construct the argument for decent treatment of animals and brain-damaged human beings here, one point at least is worth noting now. Critics often assume that basic Kantian ethics can offer no better case for decent treatment of animals than the contingent, empirical argument Kant himself offered for an 'indirect' duty not to be cruel to animals: that is, cruelty to animals is likely to foster habits of cruelty that are likely to be turned against human beings.[20] A common cause of this mistaken assumption, I suspect, is a confusion between the essential point in basic Kantian theory that 'humanity' is *the source of moral duties* and the independent and, I believe, inessential point (unfortunately also accepted by Kant) that 'humanity' fully specifies and restricts the range of creatures toward whom we have direct moral duties. The latter implies, for example, not only that we have no duties 'to' animals, but also that decent treatment of animals is morally required only in so far as indecent treatment of them would damage vital human interests. But this repugnant doctrine does not follow from the fundamental Kantian point that moral duties get their authority and direction from the ideal deliberations of reasonable human beings. If, as most of us believe, there are good reasons to deplore and prevent the needless suffering of animals, one should not assume, without further argument, that our reasonable Kantian moral 'legislators' are precluded from taking these considerations into account and setting their moral standards accordingly. Some ways of expressing such reasons, admittedly, are incompatible with Kantian value theory, but we are not restricted to these.[21] The crucial point to remember in debates on this issue is that the fact that only human beings have moral duties (and the capacity to determine specifically what their duties are) does not entail that they can reasonably ignore the miseries of the beings who lack the capacity for morality but who nevertheless suffer in many of the ways that we do.

The idea of all human beings as potential co-legislators is admittedly

---

[20] See MM, 192 [443].

[21] Here I have in mind, for example, the old utilitarian idea that pains, whether human or animal, are 'bad in themselves', where intrinsic badness is interpreted as a real metaphysical property that exists and is discernible as such independently of considerations about what it is reasonable to choose to pursue or to avoid. The contrast with a Kantian value theory, as I see it, is characterized in my *Autonomy and Self-respect*, ch. 12.

a metaphor that abstracts in many ways from the imperfect conditions of real moral deliberation and discussion. Nevertheless, it is an ideal that makes vivid and brings together important aspects of what moral deliberation may be thought, at its best, to be. If we take the ideal seriously, we can see that it implicitly presupposes certain standards of respect that are, comparatively speaking, formal or procedural. For example, legislators sincerely trying to find reasonable agreements must *listen* to one another, take seriously the arguments of those who reject one's initial position. They must be *sincere* in their proposals and *non-manipulative* in their arguments, for their aim is not to gain power through debate but to *convince* others that their position is justifiable. Efforts to *broaden one's knowledge*, to *see issues from others' point of view*, and to *invite criticism* of one's reasoning are all needed in honest attempts to locate and remove the sources of disagreement. Granting that no one has privileged access to moral truth requires us to *acknowledge the fallibility* of our moral judgements when we realize that others sincerely disagree. Even when we acknowledge persons only as *potential co-legislators*, as we do with young children, this suggests we should promote the development of their capacities to become mature moral deliberators. There is reason, then, to make education undogmatic, to encourage critical thinking, empathy, and communicative skills. Manipulative, seductive, deceitful, and overpowering rhetoric should be out of bounds both in moral education and in public discussion of moral issues. All these requirements are implicit in the idea that all are potential authors of the moral law, and, importantly for our purposes, they are all forms of respect. Thus, to accept the Kantian moral framework itself is already to acknowledge at least a presumption that all human beings should be accorded these forms of respect in moral discussion and education, in the ways appropriate to their level of development.[22]

Importantly, a ground for presuming more substantive requirements of respect for all human beings may be found when we actually try to take up the Kantian moral perspective,[23] rather than merely thinking

---

[22] Note that the first reason for the presumption of respect for all, which I try to draw from the moral perspective itself, corresponds to what in the next chapter I call the 'thin' notion of humanity as an end in itself. It is a minimum kind of respect built into the relatively formal idea that morality requires treating what 'humanity', or rational willing, in each person legislates as supremely authoritative over one's other concerns.

[23] By 'substantive requirements of respect' I have in mind the more specific prescriptions, beyond those I have just labeled 'formal', that I discussed in the previous chapter. Ideally, in a fuller argument, these would be reviewed and explained in detail, but for now I am concerned mainly to sketch the *pattern* of the argument from the Kantian legislative perspective to justify requiring more substantive forms of respect.

about the formal constraints implicit in it.[24] Each rational person, Kant says, necessarily regards his or her own humanity as an end in itself, on the same ground as do others; and so, Kant argues, we must regard humanity in every person as an end in itself. There are various ways to read this argument; some render it fallacious, others (including one I discussed earlier) merely make it implausible.[25] A more promising idea suggested by the passage is this. Suppose we ask what people, despite their diverse backgrounds and values, typically regard as especially important, of highest priority, about themselves and how they are to be treated by others. Deep reflection, we can conjecture, will typically downgrade many of the momentary, superficial concerns we have, and focus our attention on matters such as having a life, freedom, security, opportunities, self-respect, and the substantive forms of respect from others. We tend to regard concern for these things, which Kant associates with our 'humanity', as more than mere personal preferences, in fact as (objectively) higher-order values on which we have a legitimate claim. Placing a high priority on being respected for one's humanity, or rational nature, may even be thought to be implicit in the common (rather thick) concept of a rational person, one who lives a life governed by reason.[26] In any case, the key assumption for present purposes is just that, in the absence of strong contrary evidence, we can reasonably presume that, when thinking clearly and deeply, people tend to place a high priority on being respected as human beings, in important substantive ways, independently of whatever respect they might earn for special merit.[27]

[24] This corresponds to my conjecture, in 'Donagan's Kant', that one might argue from the moral perspective defined with a 'thin' idea of humanity as an end to a 'thicker' or richer normative conception of humanity as an end. The key would be arguing that any reasonable person who acknowledges all persons as 'ends in themselves' in the thin sense would, because of some plausible but contingent premises about what people deeply care about, try to protect as nearly absolute (and as not subject to trade) certain other values that earlier (in *Dignity and Practical Reason*, ch. 2) I described as implicit in Kant's idea of 'humanity as an end in itself'. For example, the value of (honourable) life, not being deprived of one's rational capacities, claims to a fair share of external liberty, symbolic expressions of respect from others, etc.

[25] See the second section of this chapter ('Interpreting the Issue'), third paragraph.

[26] This suggestion is in line with the interpretation I mentioned but did not pursue in the fourth paragraph of the second section. I intend to return to this on another occasion.

[27] Note I did not say 'absolute priority'. The point is compatible with people thinking that they would sacrifice, subordinate, or only conditionally value this respect under some imaginary circumstances (e.g. if the price of insisting on universal respect was tolerance of evil). But if they realize that, as I suggest later, we could give an unconditional respect to every human being, as such, without losing our right to self-protection, moral criticism, and punishment, then they may see no need to qualify the value they place on

Supposing this is generally true of human beings, then we all have reason to *propose* moral constraints to protect these essential or high-priority values, including substantial forms of respect, and on the same grounds we have reason to *hope that others will endorse* these constraints as well. In the moral legislative model, the condition of insisting on protection for oneself is willingness to concede that one must grant a similar protection for others. So, assuming, as I suggested, that having the respect in question is among the higher-priority shared values, then we can suppose that everyone deliberating from the Kantian legislative perspective would endorse at least the presumption that every human being is to be respected so far as possible in the substantive ways that we so highly value. Since not all human beings have special skills or unusual merit compared to others, the respect we presume required cannot be *respect for a person's merit* but rather *respect for a person's position*, which in this case must be just the position of 'being human'.

Having now sketched the patterns of argument for presuming that respect for all human beings is morally required, we must face a recurring objection. Kant's arguments assume that all 'human beings', or persons with 'humanity', have, at least potentially, the capacity and predisposition to deliberate from a moral perspective and to act accordingly, and Kant apparently had faith that virtually all the (adult) people we are likely to meet, perhaps outside institutions for the insane, in fact have the essential attributes of 'humanity'. Today, however, we may question this assumption. Are there reasonable doubts sufficient to undermine even the modest claim that we should, *for practical purposes*, presume that all the cognitively competent, functioning people we encounter in daily life qualify for our respect as human beings?

Kant, like most others in his era, seemed to accept without much question the predisposition to morality as a basic feature of human nature.[28] He granted that human beings have, in addition, an innate tendency to evil, but even that, as Kant interpreted it, was just a tendency, under temptation, to refuse to follow a moral law that in our hearts we acknowledge as authoritative for us.[29] No human being, he supposed, loves evil for evil's sake; and no one mature enough to understand morality could be indifferent to it. Even the worst murderers when

---

such respect. We can conceive a world where everyone unconditionally respected every person as a human being (though not for merit), where this respect is never forfeited, without supposing that in that more respectful world we would have to tolerate, avoid censuring, or even try to like people who behave outrageously.

[28] R, 21–3 [25–8].   [29] R, 23–40 [28–44].

facing the gallows, he thought, could not help but feel remorse and sense the justice of their punishment. There are two aspects to the human will: one, our practical reason (*Wille*), acknowledges the reasonableness of moral considerations and makes us respect their authority; the other, our power of choice (*Willkür*), enables us to choose in practice to follow that authority or else to violate it. A moral choice, Kant thought, preserves integrity and self-esteem, but an immoral choice inevitably results in internal conflict of will and discontent with oneself; conscience, an internal judge, is inescapable.[30]

Are there, despite Kant's faith, functioning adult members of our biological species who do not have, even potentially, the capacity for morality? There are several different categories to consider. First, literature is full of grand tales about *defiant immoralists*, who, like Milton's Satan, take as their motto, 'Evil, be thou my good!' There are also stories about completely *innocent amoralists*, who somehow manage to grow up and interact with others, like gentle but intelligent animals, but remain conscience-free and impervious to moral concepts. Turning from fiction to more troublesome real cases, *sociopaths*, we are told, can have an intellectual grasp of moral concepts but remain inwardly unmoved by them. They can manipulate others by moral arguments, but, having never internalized any moral standards, they have no conscience to violate.

Obviously, the severely brain-damaged can lack moral capacities, but our question is a more difficult one: Can human beings with a full range of cognitive and linguistic capacities none the less be *utterly unable* to acknowledge and be moved by moral considerations? If so, our previous Kantian arguments would apparently give us no reason for respecting them as human beings, for those arguments presupposed that they were potentially among those whose acknowledgement of the basic moral framework made them respectworthy co-legislators of moral principles. Even if morality is like a fair, mutually beneficial game for all who can accept and play by its rules, we could not be sure that everyone has the *ability* to do so. Given this, for all we know, some who otherwise appear mature and responsible adults deserve neither the benefits nor the burdens of being respected as human beings with moral capacities. It is often thought, for example, that empirical evidence shows that this is how 'sociopaths' should be viewed.

The issue whether in fact those labelled 'sociopaths' really lack all capacity and disposition to morality can be settled only by empirical

---

[30] MM, 188–91 [437–40].

investigation, not philosophical speculation. It should be noted, however, that the issue is not as easy to resolve as it might at first seem. Sociopaths no doubt display ample evidence that they *do not* constrain themselves by familiar moral principles, but much more is needed to demonstrate that they *cannot*. They have developed their amoral habits and policies in response to particular circumstances, and we lack adequate evidence whether they would remain equally unresponsive in all circumstances. Perhaps they have seen all too well how cynically some self-professed moralists use moral discourse to their own advantage. Perhaps they have never experienced anything they trusted as genuine, rather than self-serving, judgemental, and manipulative, moral discourse and interaction with others. Like everyone else, they display evidence of their predispositions by their responses in a certain corner of our very imperfect world, which is not a world ideally designed always to bring out a latent moral predisposition if there is one. Therapists working within a mental health model are not trained or expected to engage their clients in genuine moral dialogue, as equals, providing the recalcitrant with the good and sincere moral arguments needed to elicit a moral response if that is possible. So a sociopath's resistance to therapy is not necessarily the same as irremediable insensitivity to moral concerns.

Given our uncertainty about the empirical issue, there is a practical moral consideration that should suffice to make us quite reluctant to identify classes of aware and functioning people as none the less utterly lacking in the potential for morality. History is stained with a bloody record of what happens when people too lightly dismiss as 'inhuman' other people they dislike and fail to understand. Greeks thought the barbarians incapable of reason and virtue; Europeans and early Americans viewed black Africans and their descendents that way; and there is a long record of men thinking that women are human enough to follow but not to lead, to be gentle and compassionate but not to be just and courageous. We are obviously tempted to take the failure of others to conform to *our own* moral ideas as sufficient evidence that they *cannot* think morally and do not deserve the respect of moral dialogue. Since this temptation has been for centuries an unfair source of misery to people misjudged to be 'less than human', it seems wise to counteract the temptation with a strong contrary presumption that, until *proved* otherwise, virtually all the cognitively able and functioning people we meet have at least the *potential* capacity and disposition to engage with others in mutually respectful, reciprocal moral relations.

Since we must act under uncertainty about whether sociopaths, and other apparent amoralists, are *incapable* of morality, we risk error however we treat them. The practical question, then, is: Which error would be worse? From a moral point of view, I suggest, it is generally worse to risk denying respect where it is due than to risk granting respect where it is not due. In the first case, we risk wrongfully casting a potentially responsible human being out of the moral community, whereas in the second case we only risk wasting our moral scruples where they are not needed. So, again, for practical purposes, we should presume that respect is due to all.

CONDITIONAL GROUNDS FOR REFUSING TO ALLOW THAT BASIC RESPECT CAN BE FORFEITED

Assuming for now that there is a strong presumption that every human being should be respected as such, can they, by persistent and unrepentant immorality, *forfeit* all the respect that was presumptively due to them as human beings? In other words, can a person's conduct be so contemptuous of others that it defeats and cancels our (presumed) obligation to respect him or her as a human being? Many seem to think so; Kant did not, but, in any case, it is a practically important, but complex, issue.

To avoid misunderstanding, note that *forfeiting* occurs when *moral agents*, who are responsible for their actions, violate important rules so flagrantly that their *culpable* misconduct removes from others the moral obligation to treat those persons (in certain respects) as their standing would have otherwise required. Thus, for example, an ordinary felon forfeits the right to vote, and club members delinquent in their dues may forfeit their club privileges. If a creature that we formerly took to be a responsible moral agent did things so wild, destructive, and unresponsive to reason that we concluded that we owed 'it' no moral consideration whatsoever, this would not necessarily be a matter of judging that a person *forfeited* all his or her rights. Forfeit presupposes responsible moral agency, and our changed attitude might simply reflect our opinion that earlier we misjudged the *causally responsible* agent to be morally responsible as well. Rather than grounds for forfeit, the person's deplorable conduct may be viewed as evidence that we should reclassify the agent, supposing 'it' more like an animal or an unsocialized, wild child than a responsible human adult.

Two quick caveats are needed here. First, there are strong practical and moral reasons, as I noted earlier, for being very reluctant to

reclassify any functioning adult as 'merely an animal', and my hypothetical example above is not meant to deny this. The point of introducing it is simply to stress that saying that a moral agent *forfeits* all
rights and standing as a human being is quite different from saying that
someone does not qualify as a moral agent, responsible for his or her
conduct. Second, because of the extraordinary difficulty of fully understanding the psychology of Hitler, Attila the Hun, Jeffrey Dahmer, and
the like, these extreme cases are not good test cases for a *general policy*
about what rights criminals and other moral offenders forfeit. So, for
now, let us concentrate on more easily intelligible cases, admitting that
more may need to be said about cases in which the evil—or madness—
is apparently so extreme as to defy understanding.

From the Kantian perspective, there are several possible ways of
arguing that no one should be seen as having totally forfeited all respect
as a human being. Our considerable ignorance of the deep motives and
character of offenders is significant. Also, since lawful conduct is no
guarantee of moral attitudes, we are to a considerable extent ignorant
of the *comparative* moral worth of overt offenders and law-abiding citizens. Again, since we cannot help risking that we will misjudge people,
we need to consider whether it is better to err one way rather than the
other. Is it not better to err by giving offenders more respect than they
are due than to err by denying offenders respect that is due? Can any
of us with genuine moral humility, rooted in honest scrutiny of our own
characters and motives, confidently deny all force to the thought 'There,
but for circumstance (the grace of God, luck, or whatever), go I?' Are
we willing to live in a world where everyone judges us, up to the point
of utter contempt, by standards of evidence often too loose to reach a
reasonable verdict on another's ultimate moral deserts? Further, would
not treating criminals and other offenders with utter contempt cast a
shadow of dishonour on all human beings, as Kant suggests?[31] After all,
by hypothesis, if culpable, those we condemn are 'responsible' moral
agents, and so they retain at least some minimum responsiveness to
moral concerns. Moreover, their failings, broadly speaking, are similar
to ours in kind even if not in degree.

The Kantian framework, as presented here, suggests another line of
argument. This relies more heavily on empirical assumptions than Kant
would have liked, but none the less it seems relevant. If we address
the issue of forfeit from within the Kantian framework, it boils down
to whether appropriately situated 'legislators' of (derivative) moral

---

[31] MM, 212 [466], 209–10 [462–4].

standards would cancel the presumed obligation to respect all human beings for the special case of heinous crimes and moral offences. Since this is a question about real, quite imperfect human circumstances, it requires a shift from ideal to non-ideal theory and hence some appropriate adjustments in how we conceive the Kantian moral deliberators addressing the issue.

Let me pause briefly to explain. In ideal theory we ask, What principles would moral legislators make under the assumptions that the legislators will agree and that each will accept and follow their joint decisions? But the principles that would be reasonable if we could assume universal conscientious compliance may be quite unreasonable, even disastrous, if applied to the real world, where non-compliance is frequent and compliance must often be forced by threat of punishment. This does not mean that ideal theory is useless. It is often helpful to think *first*, What would be the ideal principles, that is, the principles most reasonable to adopt *if* all would conscientiously follow them? This is helpful, however, only so long as we are willing to think again, more realistically, about the differences between that ideal world and ours. Then the issue becomes, How must those ideal rules be modified to accommodate the facts of the actual world—for example, the facts that even the most conscientious people commonly disagree about moral principles and that the less conscientious often violate even their own principles? If we accept the legislative model, the strategy for addressing such issues is to consider what modifications ideal legislators would make in their principles if they knew they were legislating for people who are quite imperfect in specified ways.

Consider, for example, the problem raised by *moral disagreement*. In the most abstractly conceived Kantian moral legislature, 'the kingdom of ends', individual differences among members are discounted and so no disagreements are anticipated. But how are we to apply the ideal to our circumstances, where, even with the best efforts to eliminate bias, disagreements persist? The best move toward a solution, I suggest, would be to adjust the Kantian framework as follows. As more ideal moral legislators presumably would recommend *for moral deliberation in our imperfect world*, where moral disagreements are pervasive, our best possible human deliberators should (1) acknowledge their liability to disagreement while continuing to seek as broadly based and well-grounded agreement as possible. To this end, they would also (2) prescribe a variety of strategies to reduce deep disagreements, such as encouraging cross-cultural understanding, broadening the scope of moral dialogues, looking for common values beneath superficial differences, accepting mediating procedures when substantive disagreement proves unresolvable, and so on. Then, aware that these strategies are not always successful, they would (3) recommend both *moral humility* and *conscientiousness*, as the best attitudes in a world where moral certainty and universal agreement are impossible. By this I mean that when moral disagreements persist, despite our best efforts to reduce them, then the best we can do is to admit our fallibility,[32] and then, each of us, act on the principles that we honestly judge to be *the most plausible candidates* for being justifiable to all. With this amendment, reflections from ideal theory can help to guide *conscientious* personal choice even though they offer no assurance of moral '*truth*'.[33]

Now to return to the issue of forfeit, we need to consider how such moral deliberators would modify ideal principles if deciding standards for a world (like ours) that is imperfect in another important respect besides its liability to moral disagreement—namely, even when there is agreement on what is morally required, *non-compliance is frequent and coercion is necessary*. In particular, would they withdraw the presumption that everyone should be respected as a human being?

Recall that our hypothetical moral deliberators are now concerned to settle on rules for an imperfect world, like ours, in which even conscientious people have lapses and no one is completely immune from corruption. Although character and conduct are not entirely matters of luck, they know that, in our imperfect world, luck provides very unequal opportunities, temptations, and social pressures. Even if, as relatively comfortable and educated folk, they are fairly confident that they, and their loved ones, will never commit the most serious crimes, they know that less fortunate or more impulsive people will do so despite the fact that they are not beyond redemption or utterly lacking in concern for others. They know too that children and partners loved by many respectable people will turn to crime, for reasons we cannot fully understand. Their confidence that they themselves, and their own children and loved ones, will never turn out like this may not be as justified as they think. In any case this special feature of their own case is more relevant to their private wishes than to what they should approve as general moral policy.

---

[32] Strictly, one should admit not only fallibility (i.e. that one may be in error about what is the best candidate for justifiability to all), but also that there may be no fact of the matter about which of several candidates is better.

[33] By moral 'truth' within the framework considered here we must mean what all human beings, as ideal co-legislators, would agree on from the moral point of view. Conscientiousness requires merely trying one's best to think issues through from that point of view, in consultation with others, and acting on the outcome.

Another important fact that they must keep in mind is that all systems for imposing punishment and moral sanctions are subject to error, both unintended mistakes and deliberate abuses. Adding this to the previous considerations, the result is that the moral deliberators should be aware that a policy allowing that serious offenders forfeit all respect would, over time, authorize utterly contemptuous treatment for some innocent people, many of mixed character, some who now fully intend to be law-abiding, and many loved by them.

Before a policy is settled, moral deliberation should also include vivid representation of what utterly contemptuous treatment can amount to. First, there are many practices actually employed in prisons today: for example, de-emphasizing individuality by giving prisoners generic hair-cuts, uniforms, cells, and identification tags; moving them by physical force whether needed or not; using basic comfort and opportunities for physical exercise, mental stimulation, and companionship as special 'treats' to manipulate behaviour; ignoring prison rapes and beatings; and unrestrained verbal abuse from guards. Next, we must recall the many contemptuous forms of punishment employed in various places throughout history: physical beatings and burnings, sleep deprivation, prolonged solitary confinement, 'silent treatment', exiling, ostracizing, public humiliation by branding, tarring and feathering, coerced false confessions, 'brainwashing', drawing and quartering, public display of heads on pikes, refusal of burial, expunging names from records, and blacklisting heirs. More informal expressions of contempt should also not be forgotten: cursing, spitting, mocking, gratuitous denial of inno-cent wishes, and other efforts to express disdain (treating someone 'like dirt', 'like a worm', or 'like garbage'). Especially when based on the thought that the guilty person has *forfeited* all moral standing, these punishments and symbolic humiliations are ones that we are naturally very reluctant to risk incurring or imposing on anyone about whom we care. This is not only because we hate pain but because we could hardly bear the utter contempt these practices express, which is far more, and far worse, than mere retribution, vengeance, indignation, and angry rebuke. It represents the will of others, collectively, to deny any remain-ing worth to our existence, and it would be a rare person who could maintain his or her self-respect, or even self-love, when forced to con-front that message.

Recall, too, that those who accept the Kantian framework are not self-centred or 'mutually disinterested', like Rawls's members of the 'original position'. They are committed to regarding humanity in each person as an end in itself, and at least formal requirements of respect for persons as co-legislators of moral standards are implicit in the basic framework for deliberation. Also, with some minimal empirical assumptions, we can argue *from* the Kantian framework *to* reasonable presumptions of further (substantive) respect, as we did above. Similar argument would support prima facie requirements of mutual aid and promoting the happiness of others, since no appropriately impartial legislator would deny that meeting vital needs and promoting happiness are good to do at least *when there is no relevant reason not to*.

Given all this, it seems incredible to suppose that all Kantian deliberators would agree that criminals and other moral offenders can altogether forfeit respect and that, therefore, we may treat them with utter contempt. There is good reason to suppose that to be subjected to such contempt is too awful to risk, not only from an individual's point of view but from that of any representative person reflecting on general policies in advance of involvement in particular cases. They would not want to risk being treated with utter contempt; nor would they want to risk this for anyone else because, by hypothesis, they care (to some degree) about everyone.

This conclusion needs to be qualified, however. All have *good reasons* not to accept a policy that risks utterly contemptuous treatment for them or anyone they care for; but, for argument's sake, we must concede that there could be *overriding reasons* warranting the risk. Our conclusion that respect cannot be forfeited seems clear, then, provided one further condition can be met. This remaining condition is that the attitude of not permitting respect to be forfeited is possible for us and is compatible with our other responsibilities, in particular to protect ourselves, to maintain just punishment, and to speak out forcefully against moral atrocities. Do we need to treat serious offenders with utter contempt in order to protect ourselves, to give them their just deserts, or to express our reasonable outrage? In the next, and final, section, I suggest that, to the contrary, we can continue to respect offenders as human beings without sacrificing any of these concerns.

THE POSSIBILITY OF RESPECTFUL SELF-PROTECTION, PUNISHMENT, AND MORAL CENSURE

My claim in this final section is the following. The proviso we left open in the argument above is satisfied because we can treat everyone with basic human respect and still meet our other responsibilities. Thus, our presumption that all moral agents should be respected as human beings should stand even for perpetrators of serious crimes and moral offences. Even they should not be seen as forfeiting all respect.

First, is self-protection compatible with respect? Many of us would agree with Kant that, properly constrained, self-protection is a right and a responsibility. We may resist unlawful threats with force, and we should not let anyone 'walk all over us'. Measured, proportional responses to unwarranted threats, however, are not contemptuous of the attacker. Even lethal force in self-defence is permitted by traditional moral standards, widely agreed to be justifiable to virtually all reasonable persons. Nor do we need to return mockery and degrading insults to those who hurl them at us, for there are more effective ways to combat verbal abuse. A policy of trusting the demonstrably untrustworthy is not a requirement of respect, but merely foolishness. Tolerating others' abuse and contempt is not a way of respecting them, or oneself; it only smooths the way for continuing maltreatment. Respectful self-protection leaves the door open for negotiation and reconciliation, when possible, but it does not require dropping one's guard prematurely.

Even when self-protection warrants lethal force against an aggressor, readiness to kill *when absolutely necessary* need not express the *contemptuous attitude* that the aggressor has forfeited all considerations as a human being. The respectful self-defender would *prefer*, if possible, that aggressors retreat peacefully, that they not suffer permanent pain and humiliation, and that ultimately they rejoin the law-abiding community and thrive in their legitimate concerns. Utter contempt is shown in the use of unnecessary force, disregard for peaceful options, and, generally, regarding unjust aggressors as nothing but obstacles to be eliminated.

Second, is basic respect compatible with reasonably effective and just punishment? What is needed are public systems that protect legitimate interests, discourage further violations of reasonable laws, and yet also respect everyone, including criminals, as human beings. Granted, our own coercive social systems fall short, but that does not mean that effective systems of protection, deterrence, and punishment must necessarily deny basic respect to offenders. Surely neither the draconian methods of punishment nor the attitudes of utter contempt reviewed in the last section are necessary; and history does not record that they have been remarkably effective.

In any decent social order with a proper respect for its members, there will need to be fair, public rules designed to ensure its members a secure life with opportunities to pursue what they find valuable, provided the pursuits are compatible with others' right to similar pursuits. Universal respect does not require *tolerance* of wilful violations of the rights of others. In principle, and approximately in practice, a society can respect all its members by maintaining laws and other social norms, guaranteeing, to all who will cooperate, security and opportunities that would be impossible without rule-governed mutual constraints. By limiting surveillance and the constant presence of armed guards, members trust each other, conditionally, to comply with the laws from a conscientious regard for what they can see as a fair basis for cooperation. Even this (cautious) trust is a form of respect. Once this trust has been breached, we can show basic respect by providing fair trials, access to legal defence, consideration of mitigating circumstances, avenues of appeal, respectful demeanour and speech in legal processes, abolition of degrading forms of punishment, resources to encourage reform, appropriate criteria for parole, and prison conditions that do not add gratuitous degradation to just punishment. To ensure *respectful just punishment* we need reforms in both our practices and our attitudes, but neither experience nor philosophical argument has shown that this is an unattainable goal.

Third, similar considerations apply when we turn to moral censure outside the legal system. Just as some systems of punishment are disrespectful and others are not, moral blame and disapproval can be respectful or not. There are many ways these can be disrespectful. For example, an unwarranted, disrespectful superiority is displayed when we self-righteously blame others for overt offences no worse than our private ones. Again, we show disrespect when we make oral accusations based on flimsy evidence, class stereotyping, and no genuine effort to understand. Also, manipulative blame, meant merely to condition subjects to associate unwanted behaviours with bad feelings, ignores the reason and judgement of those who are blamed, in effect denying their moral agency. It is how we train pigeons and rats, which we regard as incapable of responsible choice. Finally, hurling epithets at someone in contempt, merely to vent one's hostility, to cause pain, or to please a sympathetic crowd, fails to address the offender as a person because there is no willingness to hear a response.

We are not forced to choose between disrespectful blame and cold, contemptuous dismissal, because *respectful moral accusation, argument, and censure* are possible. Moral blame, properly conceived, is a judgement addressed to someone presumed capable of hearing it as such and responding appropriately. Blame is not merely a pain inflicted to deter future misconduct by inducing an expectation that similar pains will recur when misconduct recurs. The most painful and disturbing moral censure, in fact, presupposes that the person blamed is "one of us", guilty of betrayal of shared commitments and capable of feeling the bite of the censure just because he or she has internalized moral ideas of mutual respect under which he or she stands accused. To express moral disapproval is all the more appropriate when the accuser is not a moralistic busybody, quick to judge, but is the very person the offender has most disrespected by his or her conduct. Judicious moral blame is a judgement that itself respects the accused as a moral agent, capable of hearing and heeding the relevant moral point. Although notoriously those of us in glass houses should be reluctant to use it, moral blame can be loud, vehement, and pointed while at the same time respectfully addressing the conscience of the accused.

I hasten to add that my remarks here are not meant to encourage a moralistic, judgemental attitude, for this too is a serious vice that mutually respectful people have many reasons to avoid and discourage.[34] My point is just that since *respectful blame* is an option in response to extreme immorality, one cannot argue that all respect is forfeited by serious moral offenders because to think otherwise would be to condone their offences. Since just and respectful punishment and moral censure are available to express appropriate moral attitudes and protect legitimate interests, there is no good reason to set aside our initial presumption that all human beings have dignity, a respectworthy status that need not be earned and cannot be forfeited.

This conclusion is pertinent to our initial concerns, in the previous chapter, with moral debates on university campuses. For example, all sides in disputes about sexism and racism are usually convinced that their stand is conscientious and correct. No one admits to being either a bigot or an unfair accuser of bigotry; and so the problem has more to do with 'erring conscience' and moral insensitivity than with wilful immorality. Here, more than ever, there is a need and an opportunity for mutually respectful moral discussion because, unlike in criminal cases, typically all sides are already publicly committed to being conscientious in their judgements. Moreover, these confrontations

[34] In fact in my previous writings I have so emphasized the merits of not being judgemental, rather than the possibility of respectful moral judgement and censure, that I fear this may have encouraged the suspicion that Kantian respect is incompatible with vigorous moral blame. My last remarks are meant, in part, to correct that impression.

take place within universities, which are institutions, more than any other, opposed to dogmatism, empty rhetoric, and manipulation of opinion and committed, instead, to listening to evidence, accepting criticism, and understanding alternative points of view. That is the theory, anyway; and mutually respectful moral debate should be part of the practice.

5

Donagan's Kant

FEATURES OF DONAGAN'S CONTRIBUTION

Alan Donagan combined, to a rare degree, an acute and insightful mind, an extraordinary breadth of scholarship, and a deep sense of the need to treat philosophical issues systematically. He helped contemporary audiences to understand and appreciate classic texts often seen as inaccessible. He took a stand against several current trends in philosophy, defending his convictions with such an evident integrity, clarity of mind, and civility that even those who remained unconvinced could not fail to respect him. He treated the works of Aquinas, Kant, Spinoza, Collingwood, and his own contemporaries respectfully but also with a critical eye. Despite his unusual knowledge and appreciation of their works, to him these were not voices of authority but, rather, sources of insights that must be tested by reason in public discussion. With characteristic modesty he gave credit to traditional philosophers for many of his ideas, but he transformed and supplemented these ideas with his own insightful commentary.

Donagan is rightfully acknowledged as one of the most important Kantian moralists of our time. This is remarkable when one considers that he wrote relatively little that is direct commentary on Kant's works. Rather, his main contribution to the understanding of Kant's ethics was interpretation in a broad sense. That is, Donagan tried to capture the sense and spirit of Kant's central ideas about morality, reading sympathetically but not slavishly, and presenting the core, as he saw it, as a whole system of thought that unifies common moral opinion, a metaphysics of action, and traditional moral philosophy. In fact, his major work related to Kant's ethics, *The Theory of Morality*, was not a commentary on Kant's work but, rather, an articulation of the moral theory

Earlier drafts of this chapter were presented at the University of Chicago, University of California, Riverside, and University of California, San Diego, and I am grateful for the comments made in discussion there. I also want to thank David Cummiskey, Russell Hardin, Barbara Herman, Robert Johnson, Geoffrey Sayre-McCord, Andrews Reath, and Bart Schultz for helpful comments.

embedded in Jewish and Christian thought and for the most part well articulated by Kant.[1] Donagan honoured Kant by making his own attempt to work through Kant's project and to defend its major theses in a way suitable for our times. It is not surprising, then, that his Kantian ethics is partly constructive and creative, revealing without pretence the author's process of purposefully focusing, selecting, and rephrasing Kant's ideas, using the resources of contemporary philosophy and his own critical judgement to modify Kant's ethical system.

An important part of Donagan's contribution to the development of Kantian ethics lies in his extensive work on action theory. Although he traced his conception of human action to Aristotle and Aquinas and suggested that Kant obscured this conception by associating it with transcendental idealism,[2] Donagan vigorously opposed contemporary trends in action theory that are alien to Kant's perspective and that tend, if taken for granted, to undermine any effort to understand Kant's position and arguments. Moreover, in *The Theory of Morality* Donagan explicated aspects of Kant's action theory that are independent of any reference to the noumenal and gave a central place to this conception of human action in the exposition and defence of Kantian ethics.

In addition to his work in action theory, though not independent of it, Donagan made a major and more direct contribution to the development of Kantian ethics by offering a substantive interpretation, systematic application, and subtle defence of Kant's formula that humanity is always to be treated as an end in itself. The significance and difficulty of Donagan's undertaking can be seen most clearly against the background of objections that have been persistently raised against Kant's ethics. Many critics object that Kant's formulations of the Categorical Imperative are too formal to be of any use in moral deliberation and discussion. Others grant that the principles are action-guiding but object that they lead to moral dilemmas and intuitively unacceptable choices in hard cases. A few concede that Kant's theory can escape these problems but insist that it can do so only when recast as a kind of consequentialism. Donagan's special contribution was to develop systematically a Kantian theory that addresses all of these concerns. While granting that Kant's universal law formula is a formal principle, Donagan presented Kant's humanity formula as a substantive require-

---

[1] Alan Donagan, *The Theory of Morality* (Chicago: University of Chicago Press, 1977), 29–31, 63–6. References will hereafter be given in the text, identified as TM.

[2] Alan Donagan, *Choice: The Essential Element in Human Action* (London: Routledge and Kegan Paul, 1987), 139–40.

ment of respect from which, with some further specificatory premises, one can derive a set of quite rigorous moral constraints on what one may do. Moreover, Donagan argued forcefully that the humanity formula is a non-consequentialist standard that leads to consistent and morally acceptable judgements, at least when applied judiciously to actual human problems rather than to fanciful stories dreamed up by philosophers.

In applying the Categorical Imperative, those sympathetic with Kant's ethics usually try to use Kant's formulas as direct guides to moral judgement in particular cases. Donagan, however, followed more closely Kant's own major attempt to work out the practical implications of his general moral theory. In his *Groundwork of the Metaphysics of Morals*, Kant articulated and defended several abstract formulations of his basic moral principle but discussed only a few examples of how they might guide moral deliberation. Later, in *The Metaphysics of Morals*, he turned seriously to the task of applying his basic principles, and did so by trying to work out a well-defined and ranked set of derivative principles rather than by using the Categorical Imperative directly to decide each particular case as it might arise. Donagan respected Kant's intentions here more than most commentators. In *The Theory of Morality*, in fact, Donagan used his basic principle of respect to derive a system of more specific moral precepts that resembles, but also judiciously modifies, the system that Kant presented in *The Metaphysics of Morals*. In a subsequent paper commenting explicitly on the structure of *The Metaphysics of Morals*, Donagan seemed to reaffirm his confidence that moral judgement regarding particular cases can be guided by a set of rigorous moral precepts, derivable from the basic moral principle and valid for all human beings.[3]

Like Kant, Aquinas, Whewell, and others whom he admired, Donagan believed that moral principles are requirements of practical reason. In a rationalist ethics, as he conceived this, moral principles are 'comparatively few' and express 'side-constraints' (in Nozick's sense) on what we can do in real-world conditions.[4] Specific moral requirements can be derived from these only with some additional premises that interpret the terms of the principles and specify constraints already

---

[3] Alan Donagan, 'The Structure of Kant's *Metaphysics of Morals*', *Topoi*, 4 (1985), 61–72. It should be noted that, though both the systems of Donagan and Kant include quite 'rigorous' standards ('perfect duties'), each allows some indeterminacy and room for choice in other principles ('imperfect duties'), such as beneficence.

[4] Alan Donagan, 'Moral Dilemmas, Genuine and Spurious: A Comparative Anatomy', *Ethics*, 104 (1993), 11; repr. in *The Philosophical Papers of Alan Donagan*, ii, ed. J. E. Melpas (Chicago and London: University of Chicago Press, 1994), 158.

established. Rationalist moral theories may be presented as deductive
systems because 'this is the form most convenient for applying and
testing them', but the deductive form 'neither exhibits the steps by which
they were arrived at nor is meant to'.[5] Both the general moral principles and the additional premisses needed in the system, on Donagan's
view, are 'adopted on the basis of informal dialectical reasoning'.[6] As
he responded to one critic, 'in morality as in mathematics middle truths
are grasped before their foundations are'.[7] It is a 'disabling mistake', he
argued, to assume that rationalist moral theories must be 'would-be
axiomatic systems' or 'deductive theories that purport to begin with
principles that are self-evident'.[8]

In *The Theory of Morality* Donagan aimed to exhibit the structure of
Jewish and Christian traditional morality as a deductive moral system,
while readily acknowledging that neither presenting it in deductive form
nor showing that it has been long accepted establishes that it is a rational system. He also, however, took on this further task of defending the
rationality of the traditional system as he presented it.[9] In *The Theory
of Morality* he reconstructed a Kantian argument for his basic principle
of respect (TM, ch. 7) and defended his derivative precepts against the
charges that they are inconsistent, impose impossible demands, and are
unacceptably inflexible in hard cases (TM, chs. 5 and 6). In responding
to these objections, Donagan was often ingenious and wise, even if not
always convincing. The distinctions, commentary, and subtle casuistry
that he employed raised the level of discussion and need to be taken
into account by anyone seriously trying to understand and evaluate
Kant's ethics.

For example, against the charge that his system generates moral
dilemmas, Donagan pointed out, quite rightly, that a system of
principles cannot be rational in a Kantian sense if, properly applied, it
both prescribes and prohibits the same act to one who is not already at

---

[5] Alan Donagan, 'Moral Dilemmas, Genuine and Spurious: A Comparative Anatomy',
Ethics. 12.

[6] Ibid. See also Donagan, 'The Relation of Moral Theory to Moral Judgments: A
Kantian Review', in Baruch Brody (ed.), *Moral Theory and Moral Judgments in Medical
Ethics* (Dordrecht: Kluwer Academic Publishers, 1988), 171–92; repr. in *Philosophical
Papers of Alan Donagan*, ii. 194–216.

[7] An unpublished comment to John Danley.

[8] Donagan, 'Moral Dilemmas', 12.

[9] TM, 29–31, 143–243. Donagan held not only that general acceptance is not sufficient to establish rationality but also that it is not necessary. See his 'The Relation of
Moral Theory to Moral Judgments', 171. However, he apparently thought that general
acceptance of a morality over a long time was at least some evidence that it is rational.
See TM, 28–9.

fault.[10] It must be possible for one to fulfil all the precepts of the system, at least if one has not already violated a precept. Many apparent moral dilemmas, he argued, are cases where the agent is already at fault, and it is no objection to the theory that it implies that one can immorally put oneself in a situation from which one cannot then extricate oneself without 'doing a lesser evil', that is, violating a precept that everyone, in an initial position of innocence, should resolve never to do. Other apparent dilemmas, as well as hard cases, depend on fanciful hypothetical cases, and against these Donagan insisted, reasonably, that moral principles need to be justified only for real-world conditions. Let justice be done, even though tragedy befalls; and there is no way, in the real world, that doing justice will cause the heavens to fall.

Often Donagan's defence made use of metaphysical distinctions between 'doing' and 'letting' and between the *consequences* of one's acts and the *effects of another's responses* to one's acts, but he acknowledged that moral responsibility does not track these distinctions in any direct and simple way (TM, 50–1 and 112–42). If all these defensive devices fail to remove an apparent moral dilemma generated by the system, Donagan admitted that it was necessary to rethink the system, no doubt attempting to save its central doctrines by admitting further exceptions.[11]

TOPICS AND AIMS OF THIS ARTICLE

The process of reconstructing the work of traditional writers is always in danger of blurring the lines between the initial author and the creative commentator, and, as Donagan was fully aware, creative reconstruction should build upon meticulous historical scholarship. None the less, I share Donagan's belief that the reconstructive approach to classic texts, at its best, pays traditional authors the respect of taking their views seriously. By focusing on texts from new angles, it can help to illuminate aspects of a theory obscured by equally selective standard readings. And, by addressing objections stemming from inessential features of a theory, the reconstructive approach can encourage those who have turned away from a theory for those reasons to reconsider its merits.

[10] Moral dilemmas are discussed in Donagan, TM, 143–9, 'Consistency in Rationalist Moral Systems', *Journal of Philosophy*, 81 (1984), 291–309, and 'Moral Dilemmas'.
[11] See Donagan, 'Moral Dilemmas', 12–13.

It is hard at times to draw a precise line between Donagan's account of Kant's ethics and Donagan's own development of the ethical theory that he believed largely Kantian in type as well as embedded in a larger tradition. For many purposes this uncertainty is not particularly worrisome, but it poses a difficulty for those of us who want to contrast the moral theory Donagan defended with other readings of Kant's texts and other ways of developing a Kantian ethics. One can argue that a different account better fits Kant's texts at some points, but this is no criticism if at those points Donagan was not aiming to do textual exegesis; and one can argue that a different development of Kant's central insights is more promising as an ethical theory, but, again, that is no objection to Donagan's work so far as that work was meant to be expository. My point in mentioning this difficulty is not to criticize Donagan's reconstructive project but just to explain the approach I will take in my discussion. That is, rather than attempting to assess Donagan's success by making assumptions at each point about whether his aim was to express or extend Kant's ideas, I will simply contrast features of Donagan's theory with alternatives that, in my opinion, should be considered. Some of these alternatives, I think, have merit both as expressions of Kant's ideas and as ideas worthy of development in ethical theory of a broadly Kantian type; but at times, I admit, my suggestions amount to rejections of aspects of Kant's own beliefs that Donagan found acceptable.

My discussion will focus on Donagan's method for *identifying* the basic (or 'supreme') moral principle behind common moral *belief* and his *interpretation* of that principle, *not* on his arguments that the traditional system is *rational*.[12] More specifically, my plan is as follows.

First, I review some important similarities between the views of Donagan and Kant regarding the need for moral philosophy and its major tasks.

Second, I sketch Kant's radical method for identifying the basic principle of common moral opinion, which is to analyse the *form* of ordinary moral consciousness rather than its content. I contrast this with

[12] I shall use the terms 'basic principle', 'fundamental principle', and 'supreme principle' interchangeably, meaning a general moral principle supposed to be implicit in common moral *belief* or *opinion* and *presented* in a moral system *as* a comprehensive first premiss or guiding standard for choice, without suggesting that it is 'self-evident' or even dialectically certifiable as rational. For Kant the content is supposed to be expressed in the several forms of the Categorical Imperative, and for Donagan it is expressed in just one of these forms of the Categorical Imperative, i.e. the formula of humanity.

Donagan's approach and note how the differences between Kant and Donagan on this methodological point could, quite understandably, lead them to different ideas of what the basic principle says.

Third, I discuss how the basic principle in Donagan's system should be interpreted. After surveying a number of different ways one could read its crucial term, 'respect every human being as a rational creature', I suggest that to see how Donagan himself understood the term we need to look at the specific moral precepts that he thought were derivable from his basic principle. What this reveals, not surprisingly, is that Donagan understood his basic principle as a substantial, rigorous, non-consequentialist constraint that accords with Kant's firm stand on most specific issues but remains controversial.

Fourth, I review some familiar, but persistent, doubts about substantive Kantian principles, such as Donagan's. These doubts, which I share, provide reason for considering more formal readings of Kant's humanity formula, which I do in the next section.

Finally, I contrast Donagan's substantive interpretation of the humanity formula with a more formal reading suggested by the pattern of argument in Kant's *Groundwork*. My conjecture is that Kant worked with a quite substantive (or thick) version of the humanity formula (primarily in *The Metaphysics of Morals*) but also with a more formal (or thin) version (mainly in the *Groundwork*). The thick and thin versions may be compatible, but argument is needed to move from one to the other.

BACKGROUND BELIEFS AND THE
TASKS OF MORAL PHILOSOPHY

The background beliefs behind Donagan's investigation in *The Theory of Morality* are similar in many respects to those Kant had in undertaking his *Groundwork*. Like Kant, Donagan believed that the basic moral principle in his ethical theory was not new, that it was implicitly accepted in traditional morality as a rational requirement, and that in fact it is so. Moreover, both Kant and Donagan held that from this basic moral principle, with good judgement and some general facts about the human condition, one can derive a consistent and coherent system of moral principles that are more specific than the basic principle but still general enough to hold for all rational human beings. The system of derivative principles, they believed, would correspond (more or less) to what other traditional moral philosophers and most ordinary conscientious persons accept.[13] They anticipated that it would be a system of *duties*, positive and negative, that primarily categorizes *actions* as permissible or impermissible.[14]

Some principles, they agreed, would imply that it is impermissible not to promote certain ends (e.g. others' happiness) to some degree over time and, more specifically, impermissible to fail to promote them on certain particular occasions (e.g. when another is in dire need, you can help easily, and only you can help) (TM, 86; G, 90 [423]; MM, 201–6 [452–8]). But neither the supreme principle nor the specific principles, Kant and Donagan thought, would identify an overriding basic end to be produced, by reference to which actions in general are to be judged right or wrong. Moral principles, on their view, are not merely means to an end. That is, they are not simply norms useful for promoting an independently desirable end, not even such an important end as human happiness.[15]

In saying that these were shared background beliefs, I do not mean to imply that they were assumed without reason or held dogmatically as beyond question. My point is just that, as initial opinions and antici-pated conclusions, they naturally helped to shape how Kant and

---

[13] Obviously they knew that not all previous Western philosophers agreed on the same moral principles, and so the term 'traditional' here must be construed as referring selec-tively, but indefinitely, to a large and influential group of philosophers in whose work certain common threads were discerned. Also it seems Donagan was more confident than Kant that his views were shared by philosophers, moralists, and theologians, whereas Kant may have been more confident of the concurrence of ordinary people. Note Donagan's emphasis of the point that 'the moral conscience may be vitiated by a corrupt consciousness' (TM, 141–2).

[14] I add the qualification 'primarily' because Kant seemed to include as a part of the system both (1) duties to adopt certain maxims, e.g. to promote the ends of others, and (2) the general prescription to make duty one's motive, or, in other words, to count the fact that an act is a first-order duty as a sufficient reason, in one's own ordering of maxims, for acting accordingly. There is for Kant no official category of supererogatory action, though it is controversial whether in effect he acknowledged an analogous concept. See my *Dignity and Practical Reason in Kant's Moral Theory* (Ithaca, NY: Cornell University Press, 1992), 147–75, and Marcia Baron's 'Kantian Ethics and Supererogation', *Journal of Philosophy*, 84 (1987), 237–62. Donagan denies that there are supererogatory acts in the sense 'morally good to do but not obligatory'. Supposed supererogatory acts, he suggests, are either 'nonmorally good to do but morally nonoblig-atory' or else 'an action which promotes an end which it is morally obligatory to promote but in a way which is not obligatory because it demands too much of the agent' (TM. 56).

[15] The belief that moral principles are not merely means to an end (i.e. 'end' in the sense of 'something desirable to be produced, promoted, or sought after') contrasts with typical consequentialist views about all principles *except*, of course, the basic conse-quentialist principle itself. Consequentialists, I suppose, do not view *that* principle as a means to an end but as the basic assertion that the end ought to be promoted.

Donagan conceived their tasks as moral philosophers. Given their shared view, they would hardly suppose that a moral theorist's task is to invent new principles, to convert the masses to true morality, to persuade amoralists that conforming to moral principles promotes their self-interest, to make people care about morality by some other means, or to explain empirically why in fact they do care. Moreover, Kant and Donagan would have little reason to conceive their special responsibility as moral theorists as the project of investigating empirically which particular social institutions are most useful and which personal life-styles most rewarding.[16] It is not surprising, then, that Kant and Donagan viewed their tasks as moral theorists rather differently, and in some respects more modestly, than many contemporary moral theorists.

On their shared conception, the primary tasks included at least these: first, to identify the basic principle of common moral opinion;[17] second, to articulate and interpret this principle in a perspicuous way; third, to derive from the basic principle a structured set of more specific moral requirements valid for all human beings; and fourth, to 'establish' the fundamental moral principle, confirming, if possible, by philosophical

[16] Donagan not only denied that the moralist's task is to design institutions *to promote happiness* but also held that, according to the weight of Hebrew-Christian morality, the moralist's task is not to design institutions at all. Though some institutions, such as slavery, are wrong, he wrote, 'most institutions, and a fortiori most of their forms, are neither ordained nor forbidden by common morality' (TM. 30). See also his distinction between legislative draftsmen, on the one hand, and moralists and judges, on the other (TM. 73–4), and 'Moral Rationalism and Variable Social Institutions', *Midwest Studies in Philosophy*, 7 (1982), 3–10. Kant, of course, allowed a role for 'moral anthropology' and commented scathingly on sexual practices he disapproved of, but he distinguished moral anthropology from pure moral philosophy, and his notorious remarks on adultery, masturbation, sodomy, etc. were at least supposed to illustrate the application of general principles of perfect duty rather than empirical judgements about what practices are, and are not, rewarding to participants.

[17] 'The basic principle of common moral opinion', as intended here, need not be a principle that ordinary people explicitly affirm and use. Nor is it implied that everyone's 'intuitions', prior to critical reflection, would instantly agree with its practical implications. Donagan thought, however, that, despite obvious moral disagreements (especially among those influenced by contemporary philosophers), reflective moral opinion in a Jewish and Christian tradition tended to converge on a set of moral precepts that can be reasonably seen as having a certain basic principle as their foundation. Kant was confident that ordinary folk, when not corrupted by philosophy or distracted by self-serving inclinations, know quite well what their specific duties are, and he thought that these moral opinions correspond to judgements one would reasonably make if guided by a certain basic principle and that this same principle is also presupposed in their very concept of duty. Donagan and Kant, I think, held that these points are true even if it should turn out that their belief that the basic principle is rational turns out to be unprovable or even illusory. Thus 'basic principle' in this context does not imply 'self-evident' or even 'rational to believe'.

argument the common conviction that the source of its *authority* is reason, not tradition, common sentiment, or religious faith.[18] My subsequent discussion will focus only on the first two tasks, beginning in the next section with the first.[19]

CONTRASTING METHODS FOR IDENTIFYING THE FIRST PRINCIPLE

In Kant's terms, the task is 'to seek out' the supreme principle of morality. This does not mean 'to establish' it as rational, but it means more than merely to articulate it. That is, the aim is to give reasonable considerations for believing that what one calls the supreme moral principle really is what common moral opinion presupposes as its most basic, comprehensive requirement, from which particular duties derive their moral force. What method is appropriate to the task? Here Donagan and Kant seem to diverge, and the difference foreshadows differences in their interpretations of the principle.

Donagan's method is to look for the fundamental moral principle in

[18] In a response to Dan Brock, Donagan expressed the view that, contrary to his earlier view in TM, he believed that Kant was right to suppose that Kantian duty-based theories 'belong in a religious setting'. But, like Kant, even then he denied that the theories presuppose the truth of any religious beliefs. The point, he added, is that 'if Kantian duty-based theories are true, the *either* something like Judaism or Christianity must be true, *or* human life is ultimately tragic' ('Comments on Dan Brock and Terrence Reynolds', *Ethics*, 95 (1985), 874–86; italics mine). Also note that, although in TM Donagan reconstructed one of Kant's abstract arguments for the humanity formula with approval, his rationalist method did not require an abstract proof of the first principle and, no doubt for this reason, he seemed not particularly worried about the possibility that no abstract proof, by itself, can convince moral sceptics.

[19] It is extremely important, to avoid misunderstanding, to keep in mind that these first two 'tasks' mentioned here, which are my main concern in this chapter, are distinct from the project of justifying the basic principle as rational or 'true'. In chs. 1 and 2 of the *Groundwork* Kant sought to 'discover' the supreme moral principle without assuming that there really are duties, allowing for the moment that morality might be an illusion. Donagan too tried to identify and articulate the basic principle of Jewish and Christian moral tradition while still admitting the possibility that this tradition is fundamentally in error. In doing so, he appealed to tradition, assuming that those acknowledged as the greatest spokespersons for the traditional morality had best expressed its supreme principle. When addressing what I take to be the separate issue of justifying the supreme principle as rational, Donagan *also* appealed to tradition (as well as abstract argument) by granting some rational credibility to firm convictions of many people regarding middle-level moral truths that survive dialectical reasoning over long periods of time. (This, incidentally, he distinguished from an intuitionistic approach that gives weight to, and seeks to harmonize, virtually all unreflective moral feelings one may have.) My discussion, and comparison with Kant, concerns the former, rather than the latter, purpose of the appeal to tradition.

the works of 'traditional' moralists and moral philosophers. These, apparently, are writers who shared with Kant and Donagan many of the background beliefs mentioned earlier and whose attempts to express a basic moral principle seem to converge. Since the aim is to develop 'that part of common morality according to the Hebrew-Christian tradition which does not depend on any theistic belief', it seemed appropriate to look for its fundamental principle in the consensus of writers within that tradition who tried to articulate it (TM, 29). Donagan thought that in Aquinas and Kant he found the best formulations of the basic principle that others in the tradition were trying to express, and he judged Kant's version to be preferable to Aquinas's because it is simpler, makes applications more straightforward, and seems more amenable to defence by philosophical argument (TM, 65). Apparently (and, if so, reasonably) Donagan also thought that it would confirm a formulation of the supreme principle *as the presupposition of the common moral tradition* if one could successfully derive from it a system of more specific moral principles that is substantially congruent with the particular judgements of most traditional moralists.

Donagan's appeal to 'tradition' for these purposes may be unusual among contemporary moral philosophers, but, given some assumptions, it makes good sense. The question, it must be remembered, is not whether, contrary to sceptics, the supreme moral principle is rational to believe and obey. Rather, it is, How can we identify the basic guiding principle behind the moral *beliefs* of many generations of people presumed to share a common moral outlook and a broad consensus on its implications for practice? Donagan did not assume that people in this tradition had a common faculty of intuition, so that we could take their convergence of opinion as evidence of intuited moral facts. Nor did he argue that the consensus was achieved by the use of a God-given power to discover God's will, seen as the ultimate source of moral duty. He did not rely on a coherence theory of moral truth or a constructivist idea of 'reflective equilibrium' as justification for the supreme principle.[20] The point, rather, was simpler and more modest: assuming convergence and consensus within the tradition to be studied, one can find its fundamental principle by looking to the general pronouncements of the reflective and articulate thinkers who spoke for the tradition and checking to see how well these fit the consensus on specific kinds of cases.

---

[20] One must keep in mind here the distinction between justifying a principle, i.e. showing it to be true or reasonable to accept, and convincingly identifying a principle as the basic principle of some group.

Though reasonable given its assumptions, this method of investigation raises the worry that, apart from verbal assent to familiar (but variously interpreted) biblical texts, there may be far less moral consensus in Western culture, even in its Jewish and Christian branches, than is assumed by the method. A method that proceeds by trying to trace the constant threads in the *content* of traditional moral opinion cannot yield significant results unless the supposed consensus is really there, and it is at least an open question how extensive the agreement is among all Jewish and Christian moralists.

Even if there were deep disagreements among moralists who counted themselves Jewish or Christian, the idea of a common *tradition* can be, and perhaps has been, constructed by selectively dubbing some Jewish and Christian writers to be mainstream and others to be outsiders. By prior selection, then, one could ensure a measure of agreement and so make easier the task of finding a common basic principle in the writings of one 'traditional' author, such as Aquinas or Kant. If the 'discovery' of a common principle is to have more than parochial interest, however, one would need to show that there were good independent reasons for counting some writers as 'traditional' and others not, reasons other than one's desire to affirm a common thread. Perhaps this is possible to some extent in the case of Jewish and Christian moralists, but where to draw the lines, and why, will no doubt remain difficult and controversial questions.

Donagan's seeking the supreme moral principle in the content of a moral tradition makes it no surprise that the principle he finds is quite substantive rather than formal or procedural. The method seeks a basic principle from which, with descriptive specificatory premises, one can derive a rich system of substantive action-guiding norms, and the supplementary premises that interpret the terms of the basic principle are to be found largely within the same moral tradition. Naturally, one can expect that any first principle identified by this method will have quite substantial action-guiding content. Whether this is an objectionable feature of a theory is controversial, but later I suggest that on a plausible reading of the *Groundwork* even Kant's 'humanity as an end in itself' principle, prior to supplementation, should be understood as more formal and procedural than Donagan's supreme principle.

The method by which Kant tried to identify the supreme moral principle presupposed in ordinary moral opinion contrasts with Donagan's appeal to traditional writers.[21] In fact, though Kant repeatedly affirmed

---

[21] One might suppose that Kant would not have complained about Donagan's identifying the supreme principle of common opinion by judiciously selecting among the ideas of the great moral philosophers within the tradition, for, after all, Donagan selected

his faith in ordinary moral consciousness, he was rather distrustful of previous moral philosophers. After all, he insisted that all moral philosophy before him was based on a fundamental error (trying to draw moral laws from the idea of a will without autonomy). Thus, while he thought that the basic ideas expressed in his formulations of the Categorical Imperative would be familiar to everyone, he could not be expected to support his view that these express the fundamental principle of common moral belief by citing the concurrence of earlier philosophers, whom he regarded as deeply misguided. Moreover, given his vehement warnings against using examples and empirical methods in basic moral theory, he wanted to establish that he had identified the basic principle without having to undertake the sort of empirical investigation needed to show that the specific implications of his principle actually match ordinary moral judgements (or those that survive critical reflection).[22]

Kant's method of seeking out the supreme moral principle, in contrast to Donagan's, focuses on the form rather than the content of common moral consciousness. In other words, instead of looking for agreement about *what* duty prescribes, he concentrated on the *way* we conceive duty and *how* it binds us. He tried to identify certain general features constitutive of how rational moral agents conceive themselves and the relation between their inclinations and their duties, whatever these may be. Even if such agents were to disagree about what their specific duties are and how the basic moral principle should be expressed, they share (Kant thought) a common sense of what it is to be an agent who has inclinations and duties. By identifying this and analysing its presuppositions, Kant hoped to show that all rational moral agents are committed, by the attitude that constitutes them as such, to no more and no less than the quite formal prescriptions expressed in the several formulations of the Categorical Imperative. Kant's practical use of these formulations suggests that he took it for granted that, for purposes of

Kant's own formulation of the basic principle and, one might conjecture, Donagan may have selected Kant's formulation with full awareness and approval that Kant had already successfully employed the alternative method which I am about to sketch. But some doubt is cast on this conjecture by the fact that Kant's method points to a formal reading of the humanity formula whereas Donagan interprets the formula quite substantively.

[22] Although I think that Donagan would have considered this matching as confirmation that he had correctly identified the fundamental principle of the moral tradition, he did not in fact claim to have carried out the empirical investigation in any thorough way. Kant, it should be noted, does say in the preface to the *Groundwork* not only that working out the applications of the supreme principle 'to the whole system' would help to illuminate the principle but also that its 'adequacy' in application would 'afford strong confirmation'. He quickly notes, however, that 'its seeming adequacy' provides 'no safe proof of its correctness' (G, 60 [392]).

application, these basic prescriptions could also be interpreted more substantively, that is, as the same principles fleshed out with more content provided by some supplementary ideas about what rational agents, or at least rational human agents, in fact will.[23]

This method for identifying the basic moral principle has long been suspect, for it has seemed doubtful that Kant could draw his large rabbit (the basic principle saying what, if anything, duty requires) out of his small hat (the commitments inherent in being a rational agent who has inclinations but acknowledges duties). But the method makes more sense the smaller the rabbit and the larger the hat. That is, the more formally we interpret the supreme moral principle and the more fully we fill in the initial Kantian idea of moral agency and duty, the more plausible will be Kant's claim that the supreme principle merely reflects those initial ideas.

A proper reconstruction of Kant's attempts would be long and complex, but a bare sketch may suffice to convey the strategy. There are two converging lines of argument. In the first chapter of the *Groundwork* Kant begins by attributing to common moral consciousness the attitude that a good will is unique in being unqualifiedly good. Moral agents acknowledge, then, that one should never abandon one's good will and that other goods are worth pursuing and approving only when one can do so while maintaining one's good will. To abandon one's good will, for human beings, is just to will contrary to what one recognizes as one's duty. So the relevant point for purposes of identifying the supreme principle is just that moral agents, as such, are committed to the priority of doing their duty over anything they could gain by violating it.

The second chapter starts with the assumption that moral agents believe that they have duties, and then analysis shows that duties are understood as rational constraints that can conflict with one's inclinations and self-interest but should always be respected none the less.

---

[23] This seems evident from Kant's attempts to justify some particular moral conclusions rather directly from the 'universal law of nature' formula and the 'end in itself' formula. What I am supposing is that when one traces the arguments leading to the formulas, one is led to a thinner (or less substantive) interpretation of the formulas, but when one traces Kant's applications of the principles one seems to find that a more substantive version is presupposed. Thus there is something to be said for both sides of the long-standing dispute about whether the principles are substantive action guides or thin 'formal' principles useless without supplementary moral assumptions. The idea that there are both thinner and thicker readings need not be a deep problem *if* one can see how to reconstruct a reasonable argument from one to the other and *if* one can make sense of Kant's texts by trying to keep straight which version is at work in various contexts.

Transposing and supplementing in a complex series of steps, in both chapters Kant arrives at essentially the same point. That is, the most general and basic prescription to which every moral agent, as such, is committed is 'conform to universal law' (G, 70 [402], 88 [421]).

This is the principle that a good will, when acting as such, must be acting on, and it is also the principle to which anyone believing in duties, by virtue of that fact, must be committed. What the principle says is quite 'formal', and it is not implausible when understood simply as the prescription which moral agents would have to acknowledge by virtue of their presumed attitude toward maintaining a good will and being subject to duties (as Kant analyses these). Since the idea of a 'universal law' is that of a rationally necessary requirement applicable to all moral agents, the basic import of the prescription 'conform to universal law' seems to be just this: one must always act consistently with whatever principles are required by reason for everyone. And 'reason' here, as the argument makes clear, cannot refer to the instrumental reason that prescribes means to agent-relative ends. Rather, it refers to a further capacity, presumed to be shared by all moral agents, to recognize some constraints as interpersonally objective, personally binding, and of higher priority (in cases of conflict) than satisfying one's inclinations and pursuing happiness.

The next steps are attempts to argue that this central idea can be expressed appropriately in the various formulations of the Categorical Imperative, which Kant claimed to be versions of the same basic principle. Although there are many twists in the road before Kant reaches the formulation of the supreme moral principle that is analogous to Donagan's, Kant's starting points and method of investigation strongly suggest that even that formulation should, at least first and most strictly, be interpreted as expressing essentially the same message as the formal prescription 'Conform to universal law.' If so, the basic message, in effect, should be, 'Always choose (or "will...") as reason demands, respecting the priority of its claims (on everyone) over any other concern that may conflict with it.'[24] Given the Kantian understanding of 'reason',

---

[24] One might suppose that this means that the supreme moral principle condemns even minor imprudence and inefficiency, which are typically regarded as non-moral faults. But it should be remembered that for Kant 'counsels of prudence' and 'rules of skill', though 'imperatives', are not 'universal laws'. Strictly, on Kant's view reason does not unconditionally demand specific acts in the name of prudence or efficiency, for hypothetical imperatives always leave us options. See *Dignity and Practical Reason*, chs. 1 and 7. Rutiger Bittner, in *What Reason Demands* (Cambridge: Cambridge University Press, 1989), expresses this contrast forcefully and then argues that there is nothing reason *demands* in Kant's strong sense.

this is just the basic constraint to which all moral agents are presumed to be committed in conceiving themselves as bound by duties and acknowledging the special value of a good will.

To summarize, the main relevant points so far are these. First, although Kant (like Donagan) knew that his supreme principle was not a new discovery and granted that ordinary people know their duties, Kant (unlike Donagan) did not look to previous writers or the *content* of traditional moral belief to show that what he called its supreme moral principle was in fact so. Second, Kant used a method of investigation which presupposed that conscientious moral agents have a common understanding of *what it is to be bound by duty* but not that they agree substantively about *what their duties are*. Third, the fact that Kant thought that he could identify the supreme moral principle by his special method strongly favours construing the primary message of that principle, in its several (supposedly equivalent) forms, as the quite formal moral requirement to conform one's will to the demands of reason.[25]

One final remark about methodology and the relevance of previous philosophers. Donagan found the closest approximation to Kant's supreme moral principle in Aquinas (TM, 8–9), but Donagan hardly mentions Rousseau. Perhaps because so many others have commented on Rousseau's influence on Kant, Donagan thought it better to stress other matters. I suspect, however, that if one takes more seriously the parallels between Rousseau and Kant, one can see in Kant's ethics a somewhat different, and less rigid, framework for moral deliberation than Donagan accepted and attributed to Kant.

To illustrate, even Kant's method of identifying the supreme principle is analogous to how Rousseau proceeds in the early parts of *The Social Contract*. Despite his disagreements with other Enlightenment figures, Rousseau shared their aversion to approaching philosophical questions by respectfully retracing the writings of traditional authorities. In the *Discourse on the Origin of Inequality* Rousseau showed, and eloquently defended, his extreme suspicion of official doctrines about *who* has *what* rights and duties, and *why*. Then in *The Social Contract*, taking for

---

[25] The formal/substantive distinction here marks a relative difference which may vary with context. Thus 'formal' does not mean imposing absolutely no effective constraints on what practical conclusions one can reach, and 'substantive' does not mean definitively action-guiding even in the absence of further normative and empirical assumptions. Also, in saying that a principle is 'formal' I do not mean that it is about the 'form' of willing as opposed to its 'matter' (or 'end'), for the formula of humanity, for which I suggest a 'formal' reading, is considered by Kant to be about the 'matter' or end that reason prescribes.

granted a common understanding of the distinction between mere force and moral authority, he poses a quite Kantian ('regressive') question: Given that everywhere people live under the coercive power of others, what could make that legitimate? That is, assuming the widely shared common concept of *rightfully* exercised power, what would we have to supposed about the parties, their wills, and their laws in order to judge that if exercised under those conditions and laws coercive power would be justified? Kant proceeds in an analogous way: Start with a shared idea of a rational moral agent legitimately but internally constrained by a sense of duty, and then ask what we must presuppose about such agents, their wills, and their principles in order to judge that if operating under those conditions and principles the internal constraints of a sense of duty would be justified.

Along the way to a fuller answer, both Rousseau and Kant identify basic prescriptions that reflect the constitutive attitude of those committed to respecting rightful political authority (Rousseau) and moral duty (Kant). In both cases, too, the basic prescription can be seen as identifying legitimate constraints by the procedures from which they are derived rather than by their content. For Rousseau the idea is 'Conform to the laws backed by the general will of the people,' and for Kant, in its barest essentials, it is 'Conform to the principles required by reason.'[26] But, again, for both, this is at best only part of the story.

DONAGAN'S SUPREME MORAL PRINCIPLE

The principle that Donagan endorses as the basic principle of traditional morality is Kant's formula: 'Act so that you treat humanity, whether in your own person or in that of another, always as an end, and never as a means only.' This, Donagan says, 'takes the ends of actions to be human beings themselves', in that they are the existing beings *for whose sake* dutiful action is done (TM, 63). It is a way of expressing the biblical command 'Love your neighbour as yourself.'[27] In its canonical

---

[26] For Kant, on my reading, 'conforming to reason' is eventually unpacked as conforming to the rational willing of moral 'laws' by all from the perspective of members of a legislative 'kingdom/realm of ends'. (See my *Dignity and Practical Reason*, 58–66 and 226–50, and 'A Kantian Perspective on Moral Rules', ch. 2 in this volume. Thus the analogy with Rousseau's basic prescription is even closer than my initial summary makes it appear.

[27] Lev. 19: 18; Luke 10: 25–8. Compare Kant's remarks on the commandment in c2, 86–7 [83].

form, according to Donagan, it says: ' It is impermissible not to respect every human being, oneself or any other, as a rational creature.' This principle, Donagan thought, is not equivalent to Kant's universal law formula, which Donagan treated as a non-substantive requirement of impartiality: that is, for a moral system justifiably to treat what is permissible as different for different persons there must be a 'reasonable ground' in the nature or circumstances of the individuals (TM, 58–9).

The crucial question, then, for understanding Donagan's interpretation of the fundamental moral principle is how we are to understand 'respect . . . as a rational creature'.[28] Since this phrase often plays a role in discussions of Kant's ethics, it is worth noting that it can express (or conflate) several different ideas. When we speak of respecting, or otherwise treating, persons 'as a . . .', this phrase can indicate scope, argument, mode of treatment, or some combination of these. The point, for example, could be to indicate the range of those who should receive this treatment. Here the idea might be better expressed, 'As rational creatures, human beings should be respected.' Often, however, the phrase alludes, perhaps at the same time, to a crucial 'grounding' premiss in an unspecified argument or rationale for treating human beings with respect. This thought might be better expressed by saying, '*Because* they are rational, human beings should be respected.' (It is well to keep in mind, however, that there is generally much more to a rationale for respect than can be adequately conveyed in a short summary phrase.) Finally, the phrase can indicate the prescribed manner of treatment. If so, the relevant question is *how* we should respect the persons in question. To answer 'as a musician', 'as a boxer', 'as a sorority sister', 'as a judge', or 'as a rational creature' at least gestures toward the sort of treatment, attitudes, and judgements that are recommended.

For Donagan the phrase 'as rational creatures' apparently served all of these functions. Respect is prescribed for the whole class of rational creatures, and their being rational is the key premiss in the argument that they should be respected. But for purposes of interpreting the supreme principle, the important point is that the phrase 'respect human beings as rational creatures' is supposed to specify the required mode of treatment. According to Donagan, it is a descriptive phrase that is used and understood in non-moral contexts: 'anthropology and psychology' and 'everyday descriptive discourse' (TM, 66). Thus, he

---

[28] The fact that Donagan uses 'rational creature' instead of 'rational being', as Kant does, may reflect something about the prominence of theism in their thinking, but this, I take it, is not relevant here.

argued, further moral premisses do not need to be supplied (or assumed) in order to derive from the basic moral principle substantive principles regarding veracity, promise-keeping, force, culture, beneficence, and so forth.

But what mode of treatment is indicated by the general phrase 'respect human beings as rational creatures'? Perhaps wisely but unfortunately for those who want to summarize his view briefly, Donagan held that the concept was 'not usefully definable' for his purposes. He thought that defining it in Kantian terms, as 'treating a human being, by virtue of his rationality, as an end in itself', might be 'clarifying' but 'does not furnish us with a useful substituend' (TM, 67). Although it helps to eliminate some obvious misunderstandings, Donagan's belief that his idea of respecting human beings as rational creatures expresses what Kant meant by treating human beings as ends in themselves still leaves open important interpretative questions, for few ideas in history have been so diversely interpreted as Kant's idea of an end in itself. Donagan's treatment of specific moral issues, I think, best conveys a sense of what he had in mind, but even so, as he warned, his idea cannot be usefully encapsulated in a brief definition.

Given this situation, it may be helpful to adopt an indirect approach. That is, rather than trying to define Donagan's sense of 'respect . . . as rational', we can try to contrast it with several other ways this expression might be interpreted. This would at least locate Donagan's view relative to some others that might be confused with it. Along the way, we can note some distinctions that are needed in discussions of respect for persons, independently of our interest in Donagan's work. Consider, then, several ways of construing 'respect . . . as rational' that seem not to fit Donagan's project even though they may express how some others understand the crucial phrase.

First, some might read the phrase very broadly, as including place-holders for further moral premisses not yet supplied. For example, respecting human beings as rational could be construed as 'granting to human beings all the *rights, privileges, and honour* that are *due* to rational creatures'. Even if comprehensive enough to stand as a 'first principle' in a scheme of duties, this is obviously not the sort of substantive supreme principle that Donagan needs to derive specific duties *without further moral premisses*.

Second, others might read the central phrase quite narrowly. For example, in some contexts to respect a person as rational might be to rely on that person to use good sense, to give the person credit for effective intelligence, and perhaps to be disposed to defer to that person in contexts calling for rational judgement in mutual projects. Alternatively, but still narrowly, respecting persons as rational might be understood as treating the person with the conventional symbols of honourable status (as 'higher-order' beings) and refraining from displaying toward the person any signs of contempt (as 'lower-order' beings). Neither of these narrow readings captures Donagan's meaning, however. Donagan included as 'rational creatures' all moral agents and so, presumably, all (or virtually all) human beings, including the not-so-bright, the foolish, and the immoral as well as the paradigms of intellectual power and self-control;[29] and he did not advocate relying on the unreliable, giving false credit, or deferring to the judgements of fools, idiots, and scoundrels. Not displaying contempt to anyone is a specific moral requirement, according to both Donagan and Kant, but this obviously cannot be the *comprehensive* moral standard from which all specific principles of duty are derived (TM, 88; MM, 254–9). That standard must be broad enough to guide conduct in all sorts of contingencies.

Third, since merely showing conventional signs of respect is not enough and we cannot respect the undeserving for actual merit, one might suppose that what the basic principle requires is adopting a *genuine* attitude of reverential recognition of the rational *capacities* of human beings and so seeing human beings as quite splendid by virtue of that capacity (or its 'sublime' expression, a good will). More specifically, since Kant suggests that respect for persons is essentially respect for the moral law in them, one might consider the respect required by the supreme principle to be a special feeling of awe upon recognition that human beings, as rational, are in a sense authors and subjects of the moral law. This will not do for Donagan, however, at least if he follows Kant, for it is fundamental for Kant that the recognition of the moral law and the reverential feeling that accompanies it are not things that moral agents can fail to have.[30] They are not voluntarily acquired

---

[29] He added that, in applying the supreme principle under which respect is due all human beings, the irrational and immoral behaviour of others could justify setting aside the usual moral precepts, e.g. not to lie or to use force against another's will (TM, 85 and 89). Regarding the scope of the requirement of respect see TM, 238–42 and 82 ff.

[30] C2, 75 ff. [71 ff.]. Donagan, like Kant, presented moral imperatives as requiring that we *act* in a manner that respects persons, not that we feel respect or merely cultivate a respectful attitude. Donagan seemed to agree with Kant that so far as we use reason we inevitably do ('must') acknowledge rational nature as an end, but he thought (unlike Kant, I suspect) that it is possible (though contrary to reason) for human beings not to conceive their humanity as an end, seeing it instead as 'utterly pointless'. In fact he adds that Kant's moral theory 'becomes utterly unintelligible' if Kant meant to deny this when he asserted that human beings necessarily conceive their existence as an end in itself (TM, 237 and 230).

but, rather, something constitutive of us as moral agents (or, meta-phorically, 'forced' from us by the moral law). It cannot be an impera-tive or requirement of duty, then, to adopt an attitude or to have a feeling of 'respect' in this special sense. By acting from duty, Kant thought, a person would express this respect, but the supreme duty cannot be to acquire it.

Granting this, someone might suggest that the supreme moral princi-ple says something like, 'Get in touch with this special feeling of respect, dispel distractions, let it fill your consciousness, and then just act however the feeling prompts you.' (This might be regarded as a Kantian analogue to the principle of 'situation ethics', 'Love, and do what you will.') But, whatever its merits (which I suspect are slight), this is not the supreme moral principle that Donagan wants, or needs, for it lacks the substantial action-guiding content that Donagan needs in his supreme principle in order to derive specific principles without further moral premisses.[31] Nor is such a principle likely to yield the quite strict duties, invariable from person to person, that Donagan seeks to justify.

Fourth, an interpretation more appealing to those who are drawn to both Kantianism and consequentialism is the following. We start, again, with the idea that the rational capacities found in human beings are 'splendid things', understood now as valuable at an order above market value, sentimental value, and the like ('mere price'). But now the command of the supreme principle is not (as before) to acquire or to act spontaneously from the special attitude and feeling of reverence for moral law in persons. Rather, to respect human beings as rational creatures would be *to follow principles* that reflect the higher value, or greater moral importance, of rational living over the various other things that people want. Such principles, for example, would reflect a lower priority on promoting pleasure and personal projects than on pre-serving (human) lives; preventing debilitating (human) pain, disease, and drug use; combating superstition and prejudice; advancing education; and increasing opportunities for people to determine effectively the course of their lives in a rational way.

So far the interpretation just affirms some controversial priorities that Kant, and perhaps also Donagan, accepted. Suppose, however, that these priorities were considered the *only* Kantian constraints inherent in 'respecting human beings as rational'. Then the system of moral prin-ciples could be worked out in the manner of rule-utilitarianism, except

---

[31] Also note Donagan's vehement rejection of situation ethics in TM, 62–5.

that the values of 'rational living' would have a higher ranking than other intrinsic values. The point would be to find the rules that, when generally accepted by most people, tend to promote the most valuable results, considering everyone impartially and taking into account the priority of rationality-respecting values over other kinds.[32]

This 'Kantian consequentialism' is clearly not Donagan's view, any more than it is Kant's, for it allows one to *trade off* the value of one person's thriving as a rational being for *more* value of the same kind in several persons. For Kant, an 'end in itself' is not only 'above price' but also 'without equivalent' even among other things that have 'dignity'. Donagan's vehement denunciations of consequentialism and his defence of strict precepts regarding deception, promise-breaking, murder, and so forth make it clear that he accepts Kant's view as implying that human dignity is an incommensurable and absolute value, not subject to trade-offs even among other things with that higher-order value.[33]

By contrasting Donagan's interpretation with these other ways of construing 'respect for human beings as rational', I have given an indirect, negative, and still indefinite characterization of his view. For a positive and more specific understanding of his own concept of 'respecting human beings as rational', one needs to look directly to the list of moral precepts that Donagan thought to exemplify proper respect.

The first-order precepts, stated in preliminary form, include the following:

1. 'It is impermissible for any human being to take his own life at will', 'to mutilate himself at will', or 'to do at will anything that will impair his health' (TM, 76 and 79).

2. It is impermissible not 'to adopt some coherent plan of life accord-

---

[32] See David Cummiskey, 'Kantian Consequentialism', *Ethics*, 100 (1990), 586–615, esp. 598–9. This theme is developed in Cummiskey's later book, *Kantian Consequentialism* (New York: Oxford University Press, 1996).

[33] On this point, Donagan's reading of Kant is the same as mine. See *Dignity and Practical Reason*, 38–57 and 196–225. There are points of difference, however. For example, in 'Making Exceptions without Abandoning the Principle: How a Kantian might Think about Terrorism', in *Dignity and Practical Reason* 196–225, I suggest a way in which the humanity formula might be applied in two-level (but non-consequentialist) moral thinking, and this is a proposal which I suspect Donagan would not approve. Also, the formal or 'thin' account of the humanity formula briefly suggested in the last section of my present discussion is different from Donagan's account and, I should note, from the 'thick' account that I earlier presented (when drawing heavily from Kant's *Metaphysics of Morals*) in *Dignity and Practical Reason*, ch. 2. I do not claim that the ideas in these accounts are incompatible, but only that they are not the same and that, given Kant's thinner account, argument is needed if, like Kant, one also accepts a thicker principle of humanity.

ing to which, by morally permissible means, his mental and physical powers may be developed' (TM, 80).

3. 'It is impermissible for anybody at will to use force upon another', and so 'at will kill another', or 'at will inflict bodily injury or hurt on another', or 'hold another in slavery' (TM, 83).

4. 'It is impermissible not to promote the well-being of others by actions in themselves permissible, inasmuch as one can do so without proportionate inconvenience' (TM, 85).

5. 'Even for a good end, it is impermissible for anybody, in conditions of free communication between responsible persons, to express an opinion he does not hold' (TM, 89).

6. 'It is . . . impermissible for anybody to break a freely made promise to do something in itself morally permissible' (TM, 92–3).

Donagan states other principles concerned with property, law, family, and military service, but the above list gives a sense of how 'respecting as rational' is to be understood. Without trying to define it, we can at least say that it is the sort of attitude one shows by refusing to kill, impair, hurt, force, deceive, and break promises with another human being, assuming one is doing so for the sake of the other and in circumstances where certain respect-based exceptions do not apply.[34] One also shows respect for oneself by developing one's own mental and physical powers (for one's own sake) and respect for others by promoting their well-being (for their sakes), assuming appropriate circumstances.

What is absolutely impermissible, on this view, is acting in any way that fails to respect a human being. A number of specific precepts, however, are stated initially with the important qualification 'at will' in order to leave room for specified exceptions to be built into the final versions. Donagan did in fact argue for many exceptions, more than Kant allowed, but the exceptions, like the rules, were to be justified by the basic moral principle. That is, no exception could be allowed unless permitting it was compatible with proper respect for *every* human being, including the very persons whom we imagine we may deceive, harm, and so forth, owing to special circumstances. Respect was not quantified. Exceptions were not to be justified by arguing that by a *little* disrespect to one person we can respect *more* people to a *greater* extent.

Donagan apparently thought that, in deriving the specific precepts and assessing possible exceptions, we could judge whether an act is disrespectful simply by focusing on how one treats another (or oneself)

---

[34] I add that the respect-showing activities are 'for the sake' of the person to whom respect is shown because, on Donagan's view, treating persons as ends, and giving them proper respect, is acting for their sake (TM, 64).

directly, for example, when one lies to another (or impairs one's own health). We are not invited to estimate overall, long-range consequences of the general acceptance of the various principles. For example, telling lies (except under duress or to irresponsible persons) is always wrong; and so it seems that one could not justify a particular lie by arguing indirectly that, given its overall effects on everyone and the values that would be expressed by lying in this case, reflective, impartial, and mutually respecting moral agents would approve of lies in such cases.

It is not surprising, then, that the list of exceptions that Donagan allows is quite short and narrowly circumscribed. He does allow some significant exceptions, disallowed by Kant, that most people today would probably consider humane and sensible (e.g. lying to a murderer to save a friend). None the less Donagan rejected the idea of 'prima facie duties' as too indeterminately permissive (TM, 22–3, 93), and, like Kant, he defended a system of specific moral principles that is significantly more stringent regarding a number of issues (including lying and promises) than many conscientious and reasonable persons seem to find acceptable.

PERSISTENT DOUBTS ABOUT SUBSTANTIVE KANTIAN PRINCIPLES

Donagan offers a systematic development of certain prominent strands in Kant's moral thinking. In particular his moral system reflects much of the spirit and rigour of the particular moral views that Kant expressed, for example, in *The Metaphysics of Morals*. As is well known, however, doubts about Kant's rigorous system of moral principles have been persistent. Some of these concerns stem from more general doubts about the idea that the most comprehensive and basic moral principle is a quite substantive action-guiding principle, capable of generating specific duties for all without further moral premises. Donagan was aware of these concerns, and he and others have had much to say about them. I cannot engage in the debates on these issues here, but I want at least to mention some of the main doubts, for two reasons. The first is that these are doubts that I share and so should mention in an otherwise laudatory commentary on Donagan's Kant. The second, and more important, reason is to set the stage for a contrast between substantive readings of Kant's basic principle, such as Donagan's, and a more formal reading, suggested in the previous section of this chapter.

First, the objection has often been made that Kant's strict system of moral principles will generate unresolvable conflicts of duty and morally unacceptable judgements in hard cases. Despite Donagan's good sense and ingenuity in defending his own system of principles against many particular counterexamples, one may still reasonably worry that these problems persist for him. For example, unexpected events can result in a person's inability to keep both of two innocently made promises. Generally, as Donagan noted, we can consider one of the promises annulled by virtue of some 'tacit condition' understood by both parties; but it seems to me unrealistic to suppose that this escape is always available (TM, 93). Apparent dilemmas of this sort, as well as more dramatic hard cases, readily come to mind and seem all too familiar. Donagan rightly insisted that putative counterexamples must be described in realistic detail and examined case by case, but it is not easy to share Donagan's conviction that their apparent force will always dissolve upon close, judicious scrutiny.

Second, substantive readings of Kant's absolute requirement to treat persons as ends often tempt us to focus attention too narrowly on simple interpersonal exchanges. For example, Donagan's main method of deriving the principles of veracity, promise keeping, and so forth from his supreme principle is apparently to focus exclusively on the parties in a particular interaction and to judge whether in that interaction each was 'respected as rational' in a familiar sense. But, understanding 'respect' more broadly and taking seriously that *every* human being is to be respected and valued as an end, it seems we must take into account a larger context. What appears on the surface disrespectful to an innocent person (e.g., a lie) may at times be the only option to causing (or failing to prevent) humiliation and grave harm to others outside the particular interaction. If so, principles permitting the surface disrespect might in some cases be justifiable (e.g., later) even to the person who suffers from it, assuming that the person has a basic commitment to a moral point of view that deeply respects everyone. If the surface disrespect was consistent with principles that can be justified even to the person who suffers it, it would not seem to be the sort of deep disrespect that Kantians must always condemn. In any case, one's method for working from the supreme principle to specific moral principles should not rule out this way of thinking.[35]

Third, a moral theory with one basic moral principle, one might

---

[35] In *Dignity and Practical Reason*, ch. 10, I try to illustrate this reflection from a broader perspective about how to act in hard situations consistently with valuing everyone as an end.

think, needs that principle as more than a source for deriving a 'meta-physics of morals.' That is, even if a first principle can generate a system of specific principles categorizing some acts as impermissible for all human beings, and some other acts as not, we also need that first principle to frame moral deliberation and guide judgement for purposes beyond this.[36] This is partly because a moral reflection is concerned with attitudes, ideals, and institutions, as well as what is permissible to *do*.[37] But there is a further point.

That is, given the vast diversity among cultures and individuals and our deep ignorance of conditions different from our own, we are quite limited in what we can say with confidence about what 'all rational human beings' should and should not do. Given some broad features of a Kantian moral perspective, we can reasonably infer some pre-sumptive moral considerations of the sort Donagan initially states (e.g. not to use force on another *at will*). But we are not in a position to leg-islate, as appropriate to all conditions, quite specific rules with all their exceptions explicitly defined. A 'supreme principle' so substantive that it enabled us to do this would risk losing its credibility as a rational and widely shared moral commitment.

A first principle need not become useless or lose its credibility, however, just because, due to our limitations, we cannot derive from it Kant's or Donagan's specific, rigorous, and universal principles of conduct. Modestly but still usefully, without reverting to consequen-tialism or merely 'prima facie duties', a Kantian basic principle could guide moral judgement to policies and decisions for the conditions that we know and understand. For familiar reasons, we must admit that if,

---

[36] Note that Donagan seems to suppose not only that it is possible to derive a system of universal precepts declaring certain sorts of acts impermissible for everyone but also that particular moral judgement is always a matter of applying these universal precepts. If so, then unless a specific rule in the system of *universal* precepts forbids an act, it *is morally permitted*. This is a more extreme position than merely saying that there is a system of universal precepts that forbids some acts and does not forbid others, for the latter leaves it open that the *basic* moral principle may give guidance in cases where there are no (derivative) *universal* precepts that apply.

[37] Kant acknowledged this in several ways. P. 1 of *The Metaphysics of Morals* gives standards for institutions; to have a good will one needs more than conformity to duty, and sympathetic feelings should be cultivated. Donagan acknowledges the need for 'dispositions of affection' (TM, 11) and avoiding a 'corrupt consciousness' (TM, 138–42), which are more than merely acting in accord with moral precepts. Importantly, he adds, 'Nobody can act well unless he acts morally; but, for the most part, to act well it is not enough to act morally. A life the sole object of which was to obey the moral law would be aimless and empty' (TM, 11). However, both Kant and Donagan seem to treat the primary function of the basic principle as determining whether acts are right or wrong.

in our conditions, an act is wrong, then it must be wrong in any conditions *relevantly similar*; but we can make reasonable judgements about our conditions even though, because we know too little of other conditions, we cannot specify the exact scope of the prohibition. If so, the suggested conclusion is that we need a supreme moral principle, or framework for moral deliberation, that can guide moral judgements in familiar local conditions even if we are not in a position to derive Kant's or Donagan's ideal 'metaphysics of morals' with specific and rigorous precepts binding on all human beings.[38]

Fourth, moral disagreements among human beings are apparently deep and persistent. This suggests that we should rethink the reasons for wanting to articulate a basic moral principle and the practical role such a principle is supposed to play. The systems of moral precepts advocated by Donagan and Kant, for better or worse, are far from being the common understanding of everyone, even in Western culture, and those who doubt them cannot all be dismissed as unreasonable. Given that substantive basic principles lead quite directly to these precepts, doubts about the precepts also reflect doubts about the substantive basic principles. Disagreement and doubts do not prove error, of course, but ideally one of the functions of a moral theory is to offer a framework for moral reflection, quite widely acknowledged as reasonable, that can help to resolve or mediate particular moral disagreements or, if this is impossible, to guide us to tolerable ways of accommodating moral diversity.

The more controversial the framework is, the less helpful it will be for this purpose, and the more the framework has already incorporated within it the values of one side of particular moral disputes, the less authoritative its resolutions will seem.[39] Respect for persons as rational creatures requires that we take their moral opinions seriously, even when they disagree with us, and ideally the basic principle of a moral theory can serve as a reasonable common starting point for working toward more agreement, or at least mutual understanding.

[38] I do not mean, however, that we should simply follow the common textbook practice of trying to crank out answers to particular moral problems by a quick intuitive application of the universal law formula or the idea of persons as ends in themselves.

[39] There are obviously two important considerations here which can be in tension. The least controversial, or most 'formal', frameworks will be of little use for resolving particular moral disagreements, and so a helpful moral theory must take a moral stand on central points. But the price of 'loading the theory' with controversial values is to turn it into a platform for a narrow moral party.

TOWARD AN ALTERNATIVE ACCOUNT

The arguments leading up to Kant's identifying the supreme moral principle in both chapters 1 and 2 of the *Groundwork*, I suggested earlier, favour interpreting the supreme principle in a relatively thin, non-substantive way. From these lead-in arguments we expect the humanity formula to rephrase the often repeated core message that fully rational moral agents do, and so we all should, conform to principles of reason, even when in conflict with our inclinations and self-interest. The thin description of what the universal law formula says, that is, 'Conform to universal law as such' (G, 70 [402] and 88 [421]), satisfies this expectation, though Kant claimed that this could also be interpreted as the (apparently) more substantive formula, 'Act as if the maxim of your action were to become through your will a universal *law of nature*' (G, 88 [421]).[40] Since the formula of humanity as an end in itself was supposed to be essentially a version of the same principle, there is some reason to expect that formula to have more or less the same relative formality or substance. In fact we should not be surprised to find that, though he did not say so explicitly (as he did for the universal law formula),[41] Kant worked with thinner and thicker versions of the formula of humanity. Presumably, if Kant had acknowledged this shift, he would have argued that any extra substance in the thicker version also had certifiable credentials; that is, the thicker version follows from the thinner together with some other reasonable assumptions.

Donagan offers us what I call a 'thicker' (or more substantive) version of the humanity principle, and others, including myself, have suggested interpretations that are similarly rich with prescriptive content.[42] So I confine my concluding remarks to conjectures about the possibility of a thinner conception of the humanity principle. Reasons for doubting that there is a thinner version of the humanity formula, I suppose, would be mainly three, but none is decisive.

First, because of what other philosophers have typically meant in calling something an 'end in itself', one might understandably suppose at first that, like these, Kant's formula was meant to prescribe some sub-

[40] Between the two formulas just quoted, of course, Kant offers the unqualified universal law formula, the interpretation of which has always been controversial.

[41] C2, 70–1 [67–8].

[42] *Dignity and Practical Reason*, 84–90. Christine Korsgaard gives an illuminating discussion, different, rich, but apparently less loaded with implicit direct prescriptions than Donagan's or mine. See her 'Kant's Formula of Humanity', in *Creating the Kingdom of Ends* (Cambridge: Cambridge University Press, 1996), 106–32.

stantive goal to pursue. But further reading quickly dispels that impression.[43]

Second, Kant remarked that the formula of humanity, unlike the universal law formula, was concerned with the 'end' or 'matter' of maxims, as opposed to their 'form' (G, 436). This requires that the formula be understood as *about* the ends or matter of maxims, but it does not necessarily mean that the principle is not formal or relatively thin in the sense I have been supposing. That is, we need not assume that the formula, in its unsupplemented form, restricts the permissible ends of maxims by prescribing a higher 'end' (or value) conceived so definitely that one could derive from it, together with merely descriptive premises, a useful system of action-guiding principles.

Third, when one examines Kant's use of the humanity formula in arguments (especially in *The Metaphysics of Morals*), one seems to find a quite substantive principle at work. Donagan found his apparently quite powerful principle of respect for human beings as rational creatures, and in an earlier paper I concluded that Kant's working principle prescribed placing an extreme priority on preserving, developing, exercising, and honouring rational capacities in each person.[44] This consideration seems stronger than the previous ones but still not decisive, for Kant may have slid from a thinner to a thicker conception without fully realizing it. This conjecture would seem plausible especially if one could reconstruct how Kant could think that both the thick and the thin versions are morally valid and that the second follows from the first (given ideas Kant thought obvious).

What would a thinner version of the humanity formula look like? To begin negatively, if it were characterized as saying 'respect every human being as a rational being,' the expression 'as a rational being' would not be construed as by itself specifying the particular modes of treatment prescribed (as in 'as a boxer', 'as a computer programmer'). The prescription, strictly, is to treat 'humanity', that is, rational nature, 'in' human beings as an 'end in itself', that is, as something of 'absolute value', 'unconditional and incomparable worth', and 'an end against which we should never act' (G, 95 [428], 102–3 [434–6], 105 [438]). By doing this, we treat the individual persons as 'ends in themselves'. But the question remains, What is it to acknowledge rational nature, or reason, in each person as of unconditional and incomparable worth?

---

[43] Humanity (rational nature) as an end in itself is contrasted with 'objects that can be produced', and it 'exists as an end in itself' (G, 95 [428]); it is 'not an end to be produced, but a self-existent end' (G, 105 [437]).

[44] *Dignity and Practical Reason*, ch. 2.

My earlier paper, and perhaps Donagan's book, at times come close to presenting Kant's claim in a way that might invite the following caricature: 'Human beings have reason; that is a splendid thing ('awesome!'); so treat *that rational aspect* of human beings as you would a treasured, even sacred, object—preserve it, protect it, polish it, display it, and honour it.' But, though this may express an attitude Kant thought that we should have, it does not seem to be the point that the arguments in the *Groundwork*, before and after the humanity formula is introduced, are leading to or proceeding from.

The course of the argument before the humanity formula, to summarize grossly, analyses the idea of the wills of fully rational moral agents as wills committed overridingly to following the dictates of their reason over their inclinations. The conception of reason, of course, presupposes that reason prescribes the same, objectively and overridingly, for everyone in the relevantly similar situation. The universal law formula focuses our attention on our maxim as we imagine it (also) *in others* (in relevantly similar situations), and it asks if *then* we can suppose, as initially we may have expected, that our use of reason coheres with our adopting the maxim. Then the humanity formula, by Kant's report, asks us to consider the end or 'matter' of our maxim (or the purposes, values, and priorities that we would take for granted in acting on it). But now the exercise is not so much to try to imagine our *maxim* as permissibly shared by everyone. Instead it can be seen as asking us to take seriously our presupposition that the authoritative *reason*, or rational will, that must assess all maxims is in everyone, not just ourselves. This focuses attention not, as before, on what others may *do* (e.g. if adopting our maxim) but on what their rational wills *prescribe* (e.g. about how we propose to treat them).[45] This, when the story is all told, will turn out to be just what everyone else wills, in so far as they take the appropriate point of view, but the shift in focus helps to remind us that the 'reason' with which fully rational moral agents check maxims is not the 'instrumental reason' that serves each as a means to coherent pursuit of personal ends.

The point of focusing on reason, or rational will, in others, one might say, is not initially and primarily to recognize it as an awesome thing to be preserved, protected, and so forth but to prepare us to acknowledge that, as conscientious moral agents, we are committed to counting their

[45] The relevant question, of course, is not what their use of instrumental reason prescribes as a means to their desired ends but what their use of the supposedly common faculty of reason prescribes when legislating objectively and independently of personal inclination.

rational willing, together with ours, as the ultimate source of moral authority. It is significant that, after the humanity formula, the next stage in Kant's argument to reveal more fully the content of the supreme principle is the introduction of the formula of autonomy.[46] That is, now that the humanity formula has told us to count rational nature in each person as unconditionally valuable, the autonomy formula reveals more about how we are to do this. We honor the unconditional value of rational nature in another primarily by counting that person's rational willing, together with everyone else's, as the authoritative source of moral laws.

For moral theory the point to which this is leading is that moral laws are not to be conceived as having authority because they are willed by God, found in tradition, discovered in a Platonic heaven, or responsive to universal human sentiments. Rather, by analogy with Rousseau, they derive their authority, somehow, from the 'general will' of everyone, in so far as people are willing in the appropriate public-spirited way.[47] For purposes of practical application, the important implication would be that the process of trying to determine what the specific moral principles are, and what exceptions they permit, must be one that tries to respect the interests and voice of every conscientious person.

Ideally, on this view, a completely authoritative moral demand of reason would be a principle upon which there is, or would be, a convergence of the rational willing of everyone when taking the appropriate legislative point of view.[48] Perhaps in fact, despite Kant, there are few, if any, actual convergence points in the moral judgements of all human beings. And even if we have faith that moral opinions would tend to converge (at least on some defeasible principles) as people more nearly approximate the ideal conditions for moral legislating, we may

[46] This is 'the idea of the will of every rational being as a will which makes universal law', or the idea that the will of each is not only 'subject' but also 'author' of the moral law, i.e. when willing rationally without personal 'interest' as a motive (G, 98–9 [431–2]).

[47] Rousseau and Kant diverge in many ways, but both thought that the 'general will' was an aspect of the will of everyone in the appropriate group (good citizens for Rousseau, moral agents for Kant) and an aspect which at their best they acknowledge as having for them an overriding authority over their 'private wills'. How one determines just what the appropriately conceived 'general will' prescribes is, alas, a deep problem for both Rousseau and Kant.

[48] Any plausible reconstruction of the Kantian moral legislative perspective, I think, must be more 'formal' and procedural than Donagan's fundamental principle, but it cannot be empty or devoid of morally significant constraints. In earlier discussions I suggested a quite thick reading of the formula of humanity as a constraint on thinking from the legislative perspective, but my reflections on Donagan suggest that perhaps that constraint is too controversial for a basic moral framework and that at least it needs more argument.

still disagree about what those convergence points would be. If so, then, facing deep conflicts of principle, the best one could do is to try to work out, with due respect to the divergent opinions of others, moral principles that one could honestly recommend (and would defend) to anyone as *one's best candidates* for rational acceptance from the moral legislative perspective. Despite disagreements, by following such principles we could be morally conscientious even if not assured of the 'moral truth' of our judgements.

The core message of the humanity formula, on the thin reading, is that we must treat not merely our own reason, but also reason in each, as authoritative over inclinations, our own and theirs as well. To treat reason (or rational willing) in each as of unconditional and incomparable worth is not merely or primarily to protect and treasure it like a valued object but to respect the principles or 'laws' that (in our best judgement) it prescribes.

Persistent doubts about this or any 'formal' reading of Kant's formulas arise when we try to use the suggested framework for resolving specific moral issues. To get any further action-guiding substance from the thin humanity principle, I think, we need at least two things. First, the conception needs to be fleshed out theoretically by the formula of autonomy and the idea of legislation in a kingdom/realm of ends, which more explicitly present the rational wills (or reason) of each as jointly determining specific moral principles by reflection under certain minimal moral constraints.[49] Second, for application purposes, we need to exercise our own reason, from the prescribed point of view, in conjunction with others and in the light of ample empirical information and (inevitably) moral assumptions not captured in the bare bones of the theory.

This, one might suppose, is in effect what Kant did in shifting from a thinner to a thicker conception of the humanity formula. Kant apparently thought it obvious, if not analytic, that fully rational agents care, above particular inclinations, about preserving themselves as such, exercising rational control over their lives, being respected as higher-order beings, and many of the other values and priorities that Donagan (and I earlier) found in *The Metaphysics of Morals*. If so, Kant might suppose it an easy step from the thin version of the humanity principle to the

---

[49] My still inadequate efforts in this direction are in *Dignity and Practical Reason*, chs. 3, 5, 10, and 11, and 'A Kantian Perspective on Moral Rules'; but there are important and different suggestions in the work of Barbara Herman, Christine Korsgaard, Onora O'Neill, Andrews Reath, Roger Sullivan, and others. The general line of thought here obviously has affinities, too, with ideas of John Rawls and Thomas Scanlon.

thicker versions that Donagan, and Kant himself, seemed to endorse. But if I am right, argument is needed between the steps, and I suspect it is harder than Kant or Donagan thought to show that the rational wills of all would converge on as inflexible a set of moral precepts as they accepted. Moreover, given persistent deep moral disagreements on these matters, the fundamental Kantian principle would direct our attention not just to our own independent judgement of what should be done but, crucially in our non-ideal world, to fair procedures of mutual dialogue and accommodation.

These brief remarks point toward a way of developing Kantian ethics that is different from Donagan's but similar in spirit. In sum, the alternative I favour would treat the basic moral principle as more formal (or less directly substantive) than Donagan's reading, give a more central role to certain ideas of Rousseau, and see the foundations of ethics as more practical than metaphysical. The account would lead to, or at least permit, the following extensions of Kant's basic theory in the *Groundwork*: first, that a reasonable 'metaphysics of morals', or system of duty-specifying principles, can admit even more exceptions than Donagan allows; second, that the moral attitude expressed in the basic principle implies more than any list of universal *action-guiding rules* that can be derived from it; and, third, that a significant part of the implications of the basic principle has to do with procedures of moral judgement and accommodation. The latter become especially important as we face the fact that moral disagreements and uncertainty are more common and deeper than Kant, and perhaps Donagan, supposed.

PART III

Justice and Responses to Wrongdoing

6

Kant on Responsibility for Consequences

In *The Metaphysics of Morals* and also in *Lectures on Ethics* Kant makes brief, thought-provoking, but puzzling remarks about which results of an action can be imputed to the agent. The most crucial for my subsequent discussion are the following:

If someone does more in the way of duty than he can be constrained by law to do, what he does is *meritorious (meritum)*; if what he does is just exactly what the law *requires*, he does *what is owed (debitum)*; finally, if what he does is less than the law requires, it is morally *culpable (demeritum).*[1]

The good or bad results of an action that is owed, like the results of omitting a meritorious action, cannot be imputed to the subject. The good results of a meritorious action, like the bad results of a wrongful action, can be imputed to the subject.[2]

My aim in this paper is to raise some questions about these (and related) remarks. My purpose in doing so is both to seek a better understanding of Kant's moral theory and to focus thoughts regarding the independent question: How, Kant aside, can moral responsibility for consequences be reasonably determined? The context of the quotations above suggests that Kant was thinking primarily of *legal* responsibility, at least as far as *bad* consequences are concerned. My main interest, however, is in questions about *moral* responsibility. Judgements of moral responsibility, of course, often underlie the attribution of legal responsibility, but they also extend to cases in which legal enforcement is inappropriate. My discussion of Kant's remarks about the imputation of bad results, then, will admittedly move beyond the context with which Kant was mainly concerned in order to consider whether what

---

[1] MM, 19 [227].
[2] MM, 19 [228]. These passages are well discussed by Jan C. Joerden, 'Zwei Formeln in Kants Zurechnungslehre', *Archiv für Rechts- und Sozialphilosophie*, (77) (1991), and by Andrews Reath, 'Kant's Principles for the Imputation of Consequences', *Jahrbuch für Recht und Ethik*, 2 (1994), 159–76. Another helpful source is the richly informative, analytical, and scholarly discussion of types of imputation in law, with critical comments on Kant's view, in Joachim Hruschka's 'Imputation', *Brigham Young University Law Review* (1986), 669–710.

Kant has to say about legal imputation has a reasonable extension beyond the law.

In so far as Kant considered imputation outside the context of the law, he concentrated on imputing *credit* for bringing about *good* consequences and on an alleged parallel between the principles for imputing good consequences and the principle for imputing bad consequences. But, for present purposes, I set aside questions about credit and this alleged parallel as well as Kant's thoughts on *degrees* of responsibility. Instead, my ultimate concern here is with the question: How are we reasonably to determine *when* (not 'how much') a person is *morally* responsible for the *bad* consequences of his acts? As a step towards addressing this larger issue, I ask the more immediate question, namely: What answer to the above question can we draw from Kant's remarks regarding imputation, and is that answer reasonable, as it stands?

My area of concern may seem puzzling to Kantians, for it seems not to fall squarely into either of Kant's paradigms of law (*Rechtslehre*) or 'ethics' beyond law (*Tugendlehre*). The cases of moral responsibility for bad consequences on which I want mainly to focus are those in which we judge the following: a person did something morally wrong; this resulted in something bad for someone else; this bad result is the agent's fault; so the agent owes something in response, for example, he ought (morally) to acknowledge legitimate criticism, apologize, and make some compensation to the person whose loss he caused, even though the duty violated and the compensation owed may not be of a kind that a legal system should enforce. Suppose, for example, that, to avoid embarrassment, A tells a lie to B that has the effect of lowering B's opinion of C's cooking skills, appeal as a lover, etc. Even if legal enforcement is out of the question, A's wrongdoing had a bad consequence for C, and so A should 'make it up', for example, at least by apologizing and trying to correct B's opinion of C. Or again, if I fail to keep an informal (not legally binding) promise to a friend to keep her informed of a forthcoming event and my failure results in my friend's missing a special evening's enjoyment, then her disappointment is my fault and I ought to try to compensate her somehow. To mention an even more common case, the needless pain and worry suffered by one's spouse or colleague because of an undeserved insult, which one made in a moment of anger, is a bad result that is morally one's fault. Here, though the spouse or colleague may lack grounds for a lawsuit, it would normally be one's moral responsibility to apologize and make some constructive efforts to restore the relationship.

These are cases that seem to fall outside the judicially enforceable duties of the *Rechtslehre*, and in any case I think that they *should not* be the business of the law. They are not, however, merely cases of being inattentive to imperfect duties, such as beneficence and gratitude. Kant treats lying as contrary to a perfect ethical duty to oneself.[3] Since he counts a lying promise as contrary to a perfect ethical duty to others, presumably he would place my case of promise-breaking (which is not illegal) in the same category.[4] Insults reflect a failure to comply fully with an ethical duty of respect to others, which again is more serious than an omission of a meritorious act under a wide imperfect duty.[5] In his brief remarks about imputation quoted above Kant may have been thinking of only two paradigm categories: legally enforceable perfect duties ('what exactly the law requires') and imperfect ethical duties ('more in the way of duty than one can be constrained to do'). Since my examples are cases of morally impermissible acts that are not illegal, they do not fall into either of these two categories. They suffice, however, to illustrate my present concern, which is to enquire how Kant's principles of legal imputation would work out *if* treated as a standard for *moral* responsibility for consequences.

INTERPRETATIVE QUESTIONS

Regarding bad results, Kant's claims are these: (1) the bad effects of an act that was owed (exactly required) cannot be imputed to the agent, (2) the bad effects of not doing what is meritorious cannot be imputed,[6] (3) the bad effects of a wrong act can be imputed. Already a number of questions arise.

What is imputation? In the moral sense, Kant says, it is 'the

---

[3] MM, 182–3 [429]. For an interpretation of these categories, see my *Dignity and Practical Reason in Kant's Moral Theory* (Ithaca, NY: Cornell University Press, 1992), ch. 8. I think that there are serious gaps in Kant's system of moral categories. For example, there should be room for perfect non-juridical duties to others, covering cases where there may be enforcement by informal social sanctions, as well as by conscience, but not enforcement by the state. This is a large issue, however, that need not be settled for present purposes.

[4] G, 89–90 [422].   [5] MM, 209–10 [462–3].

[6] Presumably, since Kant considers the bad results of not doing what is meritorious not imputable, he would also regard the bad results of all 'merely permissible' acts as not imputable. An example of the former would be someone's business losses that result from one's refusal to volunteer a morally optional loan (when the person was not in dire need). By 'merely permissible' I mean acts not morally required, not morally forbidden, and not even falling under an imperfect duty, i.e. not 'more in the way of duty than duty requires'. Examples would include, under normal circumstances, buying an ice-cream cone, playing games with friends, reading a novel, telling jokes, etc.

judgement by which someone is regarded as the author (*causa libera*) of an action, which is then called a deed (*factum*) and stands under laws.'[7] It can imply 'rightful consequences of the deed', e.g. that it warrants punishment or reward; or it can be a mere 'appraisal', which apparently is a moral assessment not implying warranted punishment or reward. Judgements that a person did something *culpable* or *meritorious* illustrate the former, whereas judgements that a person did something *owed* or *merely permissible* would seem to be examples of the second. Basically, then, to impute an act to a person implies that the person *did* that deed, while satisfying both the general conditions for being a responsible free agent and the specific criteria for having acted freely on the particular occasion. It implies, further, that the act stands in some relevant relation to a moral law or a (morally significant) law of the state. The relation can be 'more than the law requires' (meritorious), 'less than the law requires' (culpable), or 'exactly what the law requires' (owed).

This official explanation concerns imputing an *action* to an agent, but Kant goes on to speak of imputing the 'results' or 'effects' of acts. What does this amount to? Some act descriptions themselves contain reference to 'effects'. For example, we might say that 'what the butler did' was 'to kill the cook' and the effect was 'the cook was then dead'.[8] Here the act and the so-called 'effect' are conceptually inseparable, and so to impute the act is to impute the effect. But, in his discussion of imputing consequences, Kant apparently had in mind cases where the effects (results, consequences) are only contingently related to the acts, as with 'the butler killed the cook' and 'the dinners were then less tasty'—or, more seriously, 'the butler stabbed the cook' and 'the cook died'. In such cases imputing the act is conceptually distinct from imputing the effects.

But what is it to impute the effects? This implies, no doubt, that the effects were a *causal consequence* of an act (deed) of a responsible agent; i.e. it is, in a descriptive sense, an effect or result of an act of which he

---

[7] MM, 19 [227]. In Kant's *Lectures on Ethics* the account is similar: 'To impute responsibility is to judge, in accordance with certain practical laws, how far an action is due to the free agency of a person. Responsibility presupposes free agency and a law' (LE, 57).

[8] In such cases many would argue, following Hume, that no genuine causal relation exists between the events *as described* because in genuine causal relations the cause and the effect are logically independent. This seems to be Kant's view as well since he regarded particular causal laws as contingent and empirical. I mention the case of conceptually related 'cause' and 'effect' only to distinguish it from the cases that are pertinent for discussion.

or she was the 'author' (*causa libera*). But it must imply more than this, for the effects of morally required (owed) acts are said to be not imputable even though they are causal consequences of what a responsible agent does. It is central to Kant's ethical theory that dutiful acts are not identified as those that produce, or even aim to produce, beneficial consequences. Similarly, wrong acts are not to be identified as those that promote, or aim to promote, harmful consequences. Thus dutiful acts can, and often do, in fact have natural effects that are very harmful and 'bad'. In many cases these bad results will be unforeseen and unintended, as when, due to unknown physiological peculiarities of a particular patient, a doctor's reasonable efforts to save a patient's life result in that patient's death. In other cases the bad results of a dutiful act might have been completely foreseen in advance, for example, when one knows that revealing a certain truth is professionally obligatory and necessary to assure fairness but also that doing so will surely cause great pain to someone. Dutiful acts, then, often have bad consequences even though Kant says that bad consequences are not imputable to the agent who acts dutifully. It follows, then, that to *impute* a bad consequence to an agent's act must be distinct from simply determining that a state of affairs is in fact a bad consequence of the act.

Further, to impute the consequence of a deed cannot be to imply that the agent is *more or less morally deserving or worthy because of the consequence*. This is because moral desert and worth for Kant cannot depend upon contingencies and 'luck', whereas whether a particular consequence follows upon a given act does depend on contingencies. Suppose two equally malicious and undeserving agents each drop a boulder from a freeway bridge, intending to kill motorists, but only one boulder happens to land on a passing automobile, killing the driver. The death is imputed to the one whose boulder struck the motorist, but he is morally no worse than the other for what he did. We say that the one person, and not the other, 'is to blame for the death' and is guilty of a kind of offence (murder) reasonably punishable more severely than the offence of the other (attempted murder). But, for Kant, the 'inner worth' of the two offenders, so far as it is revealed in what they did, is the same.

The last case involves a violation of a legally enforceable duty, but that is not essential to the point. Suppose two agents independently acted with an equally bad will to embarrass and humiliate an innocent person with malicious (but not illegal) insults and, by luck, only one succeeded in his aim. (The intended insults of the other, we might suppose, fell on deaf ears or were perceived as ridiculous by all who heard them.) In this case, although we can impute bad results only to the agent who succeeded in humiliating his victim, the inner moral quality revealed by that successful agent is no worse than that of the agent who, by luck, failed to humiliate his intended victim. Doing something morally blameworthy, or at least doing something freely (a 'deed') which is 'less than the law requires', is for Kant a necessary condition of responsibility for bad consequences, but what the consequences of a blameworthy act are, and even whether there are any bad consequences, depend upon empirical contingencies that are independent of what makes the agent blameworthy.

It is tempting to suppose that Kant's idea of imputable consequences is identical with the common-sense idea of *consequences for which a person is to blame*, but this, I think, is not evident in the text and would make Kant's thesis less plausible. Normally, of course, the bad results for which we *hold someone responsible* are also bad results for which we *hold him to blame*, but the ideas here are not quite the same. Holding someone to blame *for an act* implies that the agent was at fault, did something morally unworthy, reprehensible, without (full) excuse or justification. Given this, what would it mean to hold a person *to blame for* the bad *results* of an act? This is not, I take it, *simply* to judge both (1) he did a blameworthy act and (2) this act had bad results; it also suggests blameworthiness, fault, reprehensibility *for* having intentionally caused the bad results or *for* having let those results come about by not having anticipated and taken special steps to avoid them, as one should have.[9] Typically one is to blame for damages when one meant to cause them or knowingly and culpably took a risk that one would cause them. But to say that an agent is responsible, or liable, for certain bad outcomes does not imply being to blame for them in this sense. The basic judgement that the agent is responsible for the bad consequences of his deed, I take it, is just that by his deed he has incurred an obligation to try to compensate for damages, rectify the situation, or accept other appropriate costs in response. It is at least conceptually possible, though morally controversial, that a person can be 'strictly liable' for utterly unforeseeable consequences, that is, responsible for making compensation or bearing other costs even though one has not violated any duty of due care, taken unreasonable risks, etc. Kant's view seems to be that

---

[9] The 'special steps' here need not be extraordinarily difficult or unusual; it might be, for example, simply refraining from speeding when driving on city streets. The point is just that a person regarded as *to blame for* bad consequences did not merely neglect the general duty 'to do what is right' but in particular failed to anticipate and avoid bad results that he should have anticipated.

one is not responsible for the bad consequences of one's deeds unless one has done something wrong, and typically this means that one is *to blame for one's misdeed* as well as *responsible for its bad consequences*; but this does not mean that one is necessarily *to blame for those bad consequences*, in the ordinary sense. In any case, for purposes of further discussion I shall understand 'imputable bad consequences' as 'bad consequences for which one is responsible', not as 'bad consequences for which one is to blame'.

To summarize, so far it seems that imputable bad consequences are (1) among the causal consequences of a deed, (2) not a measure of the agent's moral worth or desert, (3) consequences for which the agent is responsible (e.g. to compensate or rectify), and (4) usually, but not necessarily, consequences for which the agent is to blame. What more is required for consequences to be imputable? Clearly this is an appropriate relation between the act and its consequences and relevant laws, legal or moral. In the case of bad effects, we might understand this as follows. Bad effects are rightly imputed to an agent within a moral or legal system when the second-order precepts of the system determine that, given his situation, the agent's having brought about those effects imposes liability to penalties and/or obligations to make compensation, liabilities that the agent would otherwise not have (e.g. from the deed itself, considered apart from its effects). In a legal system the liability could be to pay restitution or even to serve (more) jail time; in a social morality the liability could include being subject to informal demands for compensation and, in some cases, an obligation to acknowledge the legitimacy of others' resentment and blame *for having caused* the untoward effects.

On this interpretation, then, assuming that a responsible free agent is 'author' of a wrong act that has bad consequences, what determines whether in the particular case those consequences can be rightly imputed to the agent (as liabilities to penalties, etc.) must be relevant rules, or second-order precepts, of law or morality.[10] Although, as noted above,

[10] Here I use Alan Donagan's idea of 'second-order precepts' as a set of responsibility-determining rules that operate in a background of first-order precepts that say what is and is not permissible. See Alan Donagan, *The Theory of Morality* (Chicago: University of Chicago Press, 1977), chs. 3 and 4.

It should perhaps be noted how, on the present interpretation, one can understand Kant's idea that the bad effects of any wrong 'deed' *can* be imputed. This suggests the possibility that in some such cases the bad effects are not in fact imputed, perhaps even rightfully not imputed. The most plausible interpretation, in my opinion, would be that the possibility that 'can' holds open is just that sometimes there may not be 'judges' in a position to make the judgement (imputation) that law or morality authorizes. A criminal may in fact not be apprehended, for example, or a moral offence with harmful 'luck' and uncontrollable causal contingencies cannot affect one's *inner moral worth*, this is not to say that such factors cannot play a role in the way such rules determine liability. Legislators constructing legal and social codes, and critics assessing them, may have good and just policy grounds for letting such factors influence their decisions as to what penalties and obligations should be attached to various cases of wrongdoing.[11] It is arguable, for example, that a fair and reasonable legal system, as well as informal moral attitudes, can (regarding some matters) exact a higher penalty for successful attempts to harm others than for failed attempts, even when the only difference between the cases may be the fortuitous deflection of a bullet by a falling object.

The next question, naturally, is: What are the criteria for considering the results of an act to be 'bad'? This may seem an obvious matter, and perhaps for most practical purposes it is. But since serious liabilities depend upon the answer, it requires some attention. Surely it is not enough that someone merely *does not like* the effect of another's wrong act, for then liability would turn too much on the variable whims and tastes of spectators. Damage to *permissible interests that everyone has as a rational agent* surely should count as 'a bad result', but bad results cannot be restricted to these. If, for example, someone's vandalism destroys my (monetarily worthless) personal mementos, causing me only the loss of private enjoyment, even this, surely, should count as a 'bad result' of the sort that law and social morality can reasonably take into account.[12] Although these few negative points seem obvious, what should count as a bad result will no doubt vary with the context. This is among the things that need to be determined, by appropriate moral and legal reflection, in the process of constructing and assessing the

consequences may go unnoticed. Actual imputation requires an actual functioning judge (legal or moral), whereas whether an imputation *can* rightfully be made is determined by the relevant legal or moral rules together with the facts (an agent was 'author' of a deed with bad consequences, falling under the rules).

Further, note that a distinction can be made between (1) the claim that a bad result is imputable under a *given* legal or social system and (2) the claim that the bad result is imputable under such a system *which is itself justified* with respect to the issue at hand. Kant's precepts about imputability, I take it, are meant to characterize the latter.

[11] Note that in 'On a Supposed Right to Lie because of Philanthropic Concerns' Kant acknowledges that 'accident' may affect whether one is punishable: Immanuel Kant, 'On a Supposed Right to Lie because of Benevolent Motives', in *Grounding of the Metaphysic of Morals*, tr. James Ellington, 3rd edn. (Indianapolis: Hackett Publishing Co., 1993), 63–7.

[12] One might argue that the mementos, as 'property,' are in a category of things in which every rational person has a permissible interest, but the property value of the mementos might be negligible and the main morally relevant harm might be the personal non-monetary loss, which is peculiar to the individual.

second-order laws and moral norms that attach liability to the 'bad results' in question.

Finally, there are important questions about what counts as a 'result' in the morally and legally relevant sense. In effect Kant offers just one, seemingly simple, second-order precept for imputing bad results: we can impute bad results when but only when they are caused by an agent's wrongdoing.[13] But are unintended and unforeseen events that are caused, in a descriptive sense, by one's wrong acts always 'results' of them, in a relevant normative sense?[14] Is an event an imputable consequence even if the event fell outside what any reasonable person could anticipate as a 'risk' of the sort of (wrong) activity in question? Does it matter whether other agents are involved in the 'causal chain' from the act to the bad result? For example, suppose a trespasser flips a light switch while wrongfully but unmaliciously looking around someone else's apartment, thereby triggering a bizarre and unusual chain of natural events leading to the burning of the house. Is the burning of the house to be imputed to the trespasser? Suppose the burning of the house wakes the neighbour's dog, whose barking arouses his owner, who as a result discovers his daughter in bed with the gardener, who from fright leaps out a window to his death. How much of this is to be imputed to the trespasser?

These, of course, are familiar sorts of problems, well discussed by Hart and Honoré, Alan Donagan, and no doubt many others.[15] But unfortunately Kant simply mentions 'bad results' without adding any qualifications. Strictly, given what Kant says, it seems that moral considerations enter, not into determining what counts as a 'result' for moral purposes, but only into determining what acts 'the law' forbids

---

[13] Here I am assuming that, though Kant does not explicitly say so, he does not think that bad results that unfortunately follow from meritorious acts are imputable. This is suggested by the fact that Kant only mentions the good results of meritorious acts (above duty), and he explicitly denies that bad results can be imputed to omissions of meritorious acts. Could choosing to help others beyond what is required always incur liabilities that one could avoid simply by refusing to help in such cases? Also, Kant maintains a parallel between imputing good results for meritorious acts and bad results for wrong acts. Without my assumption (i.e. bad results of meritorious acts are not imputable), the parallel would require imputing the good results of wrong acts, which seems bizarre. For example, if you make a fortune because I deceive you into investing in what I take to be a losing business, do I then get the credit?

[14] The terms 'effect', 'result', and 'consequence' may be distinguishable linguistically in subtle ways, and for some purposes one might stipulate a distinction (e.g. reserving 'consequence' for imputable results). But here I use the terms interchangeably. Each, I suspect, can be used in either a descriptive or a normatively loaded sense.

[15] H. L. A. Hart and A. M. Honoré, *Causation in the Law* (Oxford: Clarendon Press, 1959); Donagan, *The Theory of Morality*, 32–52, 112–42.

and whether the agent, at the time of the wrongdoing, satisfied the conditions for being a responsible agent or 'author' of deeds.[16] This interpretation seems confirmed by Kant's argument in the infamous paper, 'On a Supposed Right to Lie because of Philanthropic Concerns'. There Kant claims that if you told a lie to divert an assassin from killing a friend but then, unexpectedly, the lie led the murderer to the friend, who was then killed, the friend's death can be imputed to you (as well as to the murderer, no doubt). Here neither the fact that the effect was unintended, unforeseen, and highly improbable nor the fact that another agent wrongfully intervened in the causal chain was viewed by Kant as blocking the imputation of the friend's death to the liar.[17] Since he was willing to accept this implication, it seems we must conclude that Kant intended his unqualified second-order precept regarding imputation of bad effects to be taken quite literally. That is, assuming they are bad, *all* results or effects, in the descriptive sense, of an imputable wrong act can be imputed to the agent, regardless of whether or not the bad results were foreseeable, expectable risks, independent of other agents, etc.

QUESTIONS REGARDING THE ADEQUACY OF KANT'S VIEW

If, as may be, I have misunderstood Kant's position, I welcome corrections, especially in so far as they reveal that position to be more subtle that I have supposed. But rather than pursue matters of interpretation further, I want now to turn to questions about the *acceptability* of the views I have attributed to Kant. The most general critical questions are these: (1) Are the bad results of *wrong* acts *always imputable*? (2) Are the bad results of acts that are *not wrong ever imputable*?

To begin with a few remarks regarding (2), one would need to consider the possibility of imputable bad results from (*a*) *doing exactly* what duty requires and (*b*) *omitting to do* 'more than duty requires'. These are the cases Kant explicitly addresses. But a thorough discussion would need to consider also the possibility of imputable bad results from (*c*) *doing* 'more than duty requires' and (*d*) doing what is *merely permis-*

---

[16] In saying that, for Kant, moral considerations 'enter' into the determination of what law forbids, I do not mean to imply that Kant held that immorality is always a sufficient reason for making conduct illegal. Moral considerations, in the broad sense, are relevant, but in a complex way.   [17] 'On a Supposed Right to Lie', 65.

sible.[18] Is there anything to be said for imputing bad results in any of these cases?

Regarding (c), Julia Driver has called attention to doubts that might be raised by reflecting on the recent film *Howard's End*.[19] Here going 'beyond duty' in a well-meant effort to help a man, two well-connected women lead the man to make a (seemingly good) job change that unfortunately proves to be disastrous for him. When later one of the women becomes wealthy by marrying the very person reliance upon whom led to the disaster, we are easily moved to think that she owes something to the poor man whom she tried to help because, though she went beyond duty to do him a favour, her meddling in his life resulted in his poverty. This seems to be a case in which, contrary to Kant, the bad results of a woman's act are imputable to her even though her efforts were meritorious and 'beyond duty'.

The obvious Kantian response, however, seems plausible: If she really did *nothing* wrong, then his poverty is not her *fault*; and her passing on credible information and advising a job change was not wrong *in itself*. What prompts the intuitive feeling that the woman owes something to the man whom she tried to help is probably the suspicion that she is guilty of a more subtle wrong. For example, one might argue that she was wrong to induce a vulnerable and ignorant 'social inferior' to place such an unqualified trust in her, asking him, in effect, to rely on her to make major life-determining choices for him that he should have been warned to face autonomously. Alternatively, if she was not wrong in doing this, one might argue that, by taking on the role of patron or trustee for a dependent, she incurred a quasi-contractual obligation to help the man when her advice turned out badly.[20] In either case, the source of the subsequent obligation to help, if any, need not be seen as imputation of the bad result of a perfectly innocent act.

Are bad results ever imputable if one is 'minding one's business' or even 'just doing one's duty'? Given that such acts are *merely permissible* or *owed*, they are not *wrong* and so one cannot be 'faulted' *simply for doing them*. But one can do what is permissible or owed in an obnoxious *manner* and for despicable *motives*. Perhaps then, one might

---

[18] I assume that (a) represents fulfilment of a perfect duty, (b) represents (permissible) omission of a relevant imperfect duty, (c) represents fulfilment of an imperfect duty, and (d) represents acts that are none of the above and yet also not wrong or 'less than duty'.

[19] In an unpublished paper, 'Failed Favors'.

[20] Her role as 'trustee' was also complicated by the fact that she gained her wealth by marrying the man about whom her misjudgement causally contributed to the disastrous outcome for the man she advised. All in all, the *Howard's End* example may be too complex to be a good test case for a philosophical thesis.

think, the bad results of doing what is permissible or owed could be morally imputed. Suppose, for example, I have a right by law and custom to burn dry leaves in my yard at any time, but I meanly choose to do so only when my neighbours have hung their white linen on their clothesline. When, predictably, the smoke from my fires spoils the fresh scent of their linen, am I not morally responsible for the bad result? Or consider the professor who dutifully criticizes a struggling student who is failing to meet course standards, but who delights in doing so in a cruel and insulting manner. Should he feel no moral responsibility for the student's subsequent misery and depression? In both cases, I think, the agents can be faulted for bringing about bad results, and they should do something, if they can, to make up for the harm they caused. Are these, then, counterexamples to Kant's precept regarding imputability?

The Kantian response, again, seems clear, and plausible. What were merely 'an obnoxious *manner*' and 'despicable *motive*' relative to the descriptions under which the acts in question were 'permitted' or 'owed' turn out, under other descriptions, to be *morally wrong acts*. For example, considered as 'maliciously producing smoke to foul the neighbours' linen', my burning leaves was not morally permissible; and considered as 'taking cruel pleasure in insulting and demeaning a student', the professor's criticism was not 'owed' or 'exactly what duty required'. So, given the morally relevant descriptions, the bad results are imputable because the agents did wrong or 'less than duty'.

Although the examples do not constitute convincing counterexamples to Kant's precept, they do provide a lesson. That is, whether Kant's precept regarding imputability is morally acceptable as a working standard depends crucially on how one describes the 'acts' in question. At least regarding some moral judgements beyond the law, the precept gives reasonable results when the act description already includes morally relevant features of *motive* and *manner*, or *why* and *how* one did something (described more thinly). Failure to see this would give false comfort to the callously self-righteous who would too readily wash their hands of responsibility for harms they cause simply by citing the excuse 'I am only doing my duty' or 'I was just minding my business.' In principle, at least, Kant acknowledged that considerations of motive and manner are relevant to moral assessments, for they can be reflected in the agent's *maxim*, which is what must be tested to see if the agent acts rightly or wrongly. Unfortunately, however, the problem of determining exactly what features belong in the characterization of an agent's maxim notoriously remains as a problem for Kantian moral theory.

Another putative counterexample to the thesis that the bad results of dutiful and permissible acts are not imputable concerns what is called 'doing the lesser evil'. Suppose that one faces what Alan Donagan, following Aquinas, labels a perplexity *secundum quid*. That is, because one has already done something wrong, one finds oneself now in a situation in which all of one's options are condemned by the primary moral precepts that every *innocent* person can and should follow without exception.[21] Donagan regards this as a 'moral dilemma' in which whatever one does will be wrong, an 'evil' even if 'the lesser one'. Kant, as I understand him, would not concede the possibility of such a situation. Instead, he would insist, for all alleged cases of this sort, that the conflict is only in the 'grounds of obligation' and that one's actual duty, all things considered, given the options, is to act as the stronger ground of obligation requires.[22] Since to do so is a duty, it is also permitted; since the act is permitted, it is not 'evil' even though its consequences may be very bad. The peculiarity of such cases is that it seems that the bad consequences should be imputable even though the act itself is dutiful.

To illustrate: Suppose a burglar has immorally and illegally broken into a house and knocked over a lamp, which then starts a fire. Wanting to prevent the owner from losing his whole house, he (dutifully) puts out the fire by the only available means, which involve irreparable damage to valued property (e.g. water stains on carpets, books, etc.). Once the fire started, he acted rightly and conscientiously; but some of the results of what he did then were bad and, surely, they are imputable to him.[23] To consider another example, suppose that, having made a solemn promise to drive a friend to a meeting, I knowingly and wrongly make a second promise to do a service for someone else that is incompatible with my keeping the first promise. Seeing that I cannot do both, and sincerely regretful that I got myself into the 'dilemma', I conscientiously choose to do what seems less offensive and damaging in the situation, say, breaking the second promise. This is the right thing to do, and so 'my duty' in the situation, but surely I am morally liable to compensate for the inconvenience I caused to the second promisee.

---

[21] By 'innocent' here I mean, of course, not in violation of any moral precepts *relevant* to the situation, e.g. not having committed any offences that necessitate further prima facie wrongs to avoid even greater prima facie wrongs. In short, an 'innocent' person here is simply one who has not wrongfully put himself or herself into a situation where important grounds of obligation pull against one another. See 'Alan Donagan, *The Theory of Morality*, 152-3, 155-6, and 'Consistency in Rationalistic Moral Systems', *Journal of Philosophy*, 81 (1984), 291-309.   [22] MM, 16 [224].

[23] The *overall* or net results for the house owner, we may suppose, were better because the burglar doused the fire than they would have been had he not. But the fact remains that something bad happened as a result of the burglar's dousing the flames and it seems the burglar should be liable to compensate the owner for that damage. Whether or not this is generally the law, it seems a reasonable moral position.

Like the previous putative counterexamples, I think that these cases can be interpreted in a way that is consistent with Kant's thesis. Although the damage to the books and carpet in the first case was a result of the burglar's dutifully putting out the fire, it can also be seen as a consequence of his unlawful entry and knocking down the lamp. So we can impute the bad results to the burglar for his earlier unlawful acts. Since these immoral acts 'set up' the situation in which he had no moral alternative but to cause the damage, the damage can be seen as a consequence made 'necessary' (in a morally relevant sense) by the initial wrongdoing. Similarly, in the second case, causing inconvenience to the second promisee was made morally necessary by my earlier wrong act of making a morally impermissible promise. Thus, even though it resulted from my dutiful act of keeping the first rather than the second promise, it is imputable as a bad consequence of my (earlier) wrongdoing.

The thesis that the bad effects of dutiful and permissible acts are not imputable is subject to another, perhaps more difficult challenge. Why could there not be a moral analogue to strict liability in the law? That is, might there not be cases where a justified moral code, for good reasons, holds a person morally responsible for bad effects even without fault?[24] The judgement could not be pronounced in condemnatory terms, of course, only in terms of liability to pay a price. Whether bad effects can be imputed, as we have seen, does not depend upon whether the agent was *morally worse*, or *less deserving*, than otherwise for having caused the bad effects; for luck might have prevented the bad effects without affecting the agent's moral worth. So the fact that luck can play a role in determining liability has already been conceded. Also, we have seen that even in standard cases (imputing bad effects for *wrong* acts) what is imputable must be determined by reference to a (justified) legal or moral code, and thus many crucial factors (such as what counts as a 'result', as 'bad', etc.) need to be determined in the process of constructing and assessing the codes. These considerations lead one to conjecture, then, that even *whether fault* (or wrongdoing) *is necessary for moral liability* should be open to decision as one tries, from a moral point of view, to construct or assess specific moral codes.[25]

The cases that prompt the conjecture are necessity cases of a kind

---

[24] This speculation then concerns cases which lack one feature in my earlier general characterization of the main subject, in the fourth paragraph of this chapter.

[25] Fairness and justice will constrain the construction of any system, on the Kantian view, and thus will no doubt limit the role of liability without fault, but my conjecture is that this is not absolutely ruled out.

familiar to lawyers. For example, an innocent man pursued by killers takes another's horse as a necessary means of escape; he escapes, but only by running the horse so hard that it dies. A seaman pulls his boat up to another's dock in a life-threatening storm; the dock is thereby damaged, though the seaman was justified in doing what he did. Or, again, a motorist swerves to avoid hitting his own child who has just run into the road, thereby striking a parked vehicle; he damaged the vehicle, even though he only did what he had to do. From a moral point of view, I assume, the agents did what was (at least) permissible. In the last case, and perhaps even in the others, the agent did exactly what duty required.[26] Clearly, assuming they were innocent in falling into their crisis situations, what they did was not wrong, they were not at fault, and they are not *morally to blame* for the damage they caused. But nonetheless what they did caused the owners of the horse, the dock, and the parked vehicle to suffer losses, which were not their fault either; and, given the dangers, each of the agents gained from what they did. The question is, under a reasonable system of *moral* principles, should the owners bear the whole loss by themselves or should the agents bear some liability to compensate them?

Kantians should reject any suggestion that for pragmatic reasons agents should be blamed and treated as if guilty when in fact they are not. But if innocent liability to compensate for damages can be effectively stripped of the common condemnatory message associated with standard imputation, then there may be no reason in principle why liability cannot be imputed for justified, and even dutiful, acts of the sort described above. And there may be practical reasons for doing so. For example, having everyone know in advance that they are morally obliged to help make up the losses in such cases should have a useful deterrent effect, discouraging facile judgements that necessity justifies (or duty requires) damage to others' interests and instead causing us in crisis situations to look harder for better solutions. By asking the agents to assume or share the costs of the damage they caused, a moral code would be telling them to convey a healing message to those whose interests they have set back. Having done what *in normal circumstances* would be an insulting disregard for another's standing as a person with rights, the agents need to convey a counter-message, in effect, saying, 'Though I intentionally benefitted at your expense, I do not discount

---

[26] The first two cases will also be cases of doing exactly what duty requires if we add to the stories certain stipulations, for example, that the agents had other-regarding, if not self-regarding, duties not to give up their lives at this time and that there were no other available means to avoid death.

you as a moral agent and here is some tangible evidence of my sincerity.' When not legally compelled, offering compensation might convey this sort of message and thus help to counteract distrust and to restore normal moral relations.[27]

Finally, there are many cases that challenge Kant's positive thesis that the bad results of wrong acts are always imputable.[28] The example offered earlier of a trespasser whose minor offence starts a chain of disastrous events is just such a case. By flipping a light switch, which he admittedly had no right to touch, the trespasser caused the house to burn down; and what he did led eventually to a gardener's leaping out of a window to his death. But, whatever the law may say, I suspect that many will agree that it is quite counter-intuitive to suppose that the burning of the house and the death of the gardener are the agent's fault and that he is liable to compensate for them.[29] When an effect is completely unintended and unforeseeable, utterly beyond what any reasonable person could anticipate, and when in addition it depends on the voluntary choices of other responsible agents, it may be too incidental and remote for moral sensibility to count it as the agent's fault or responsibility.

To take Kant's own example, let us suppose (implausibly) that it would be morally wrong to tell a lie to a would-be killer for the altruistic purpose of saving one's friend's life. (The claim becomes more plausible to me if I imagine that there was another, morally unproblematic means available, equally or more likely to divert the killer.) If it was overwhelmingly improbable in the situation that the lie would lead the killer to the friend, so that no reasonable person would have considered that as one of the risks of lying in the situation, and given that the mur-

---

[27] This point was suggested by Gerald Postema in conversation.

[28] Here I return to question 1 in the first paragraph of the second section of this chapter ('Questions regarding the Adequacy of Kant's View').

[29] Some might argue that the trespasser is liable but only to a small degree. Then they might appeal to Kant's cryptic remarks about degrees of responsibility to try to justify the claim that the liability is small. Since the 'moral obstacle of duty' (i.e. the stringency of the moral requirement not to trespass) was relatively small (compared, say, to murder, malicious injury, and even theft), the degree of imputation (Kant implies) tends, other things equal, to be relatively small. Kant says, 'the less the natural obstacles and the greater the obstacle from grounds of duty, so much the more is the transgression to be imputed (as culpable)' MM, 20 [228]. Strictly speaking, this claim refers to degree of imputation of the deed, not of the bad consequences, but one can perhaps extrapolate to the view that one should be less liable for the bad consequences of less culpable deeds. This sort of argument would make Kant's claim less strikingly counter-intuitive, but still I suspect that it goes beyond what most would acknowledge. Some completely unforeseeable consequences of minor offences, with chains of events including the acts of other agents, seem to me not morally imputable at all.

derer killed the friend by his own choice contrary to the liar's full intent and desire, then it seems to me quite bizarre to impute the friend's death to the liar. By hypothesis, he did something culpable, but his friend's death is not his responsibility.

Even foreseeable consequences in some cases may be not imputable. To take a soap-opera-style example, suppose that Mary has promised her mother that she will not marry until she is twenty-one but she plans to marry Tom at once, though she is only twenty. She feels (rightly, let us suppose) that she will be wrong to break her promise, even though she plans to do it. Quite independently, Harry, the jealous poet, confronts her with a jilted lover's manipulative threat, saying, 'If you persist in your determination to marry Tom tomorrow, I will burn all the love poems I have ever written.' She marries Tom as planned, let us say, and in response Harry burns his quite valuable poems. Here, by hypothesis, Mary did something wrong, and it had a foreseeable bad consequence.[30] But most of us, I imagine, would hesitate to say that Mary is responsible for the loss of Harry's poetry. Perhaps redescription can remove the problem, but it is not evident how.

Admittedly, there is a way of construing 'imputable' that would circumvent these last objections, namely, treating imputability to mean merely 'satisfying certain *necessary* conditions for correct imputation'. Given this, one might reply to the counter-examples above by saying, 'Kant only held that bad consequences of wrong acts *can* be imputed, that is, they are candidates for correct imputation by virtue of two salient features, the wrongness of the act and the badness of the results; but this does not imply the counter-intuitive result that the loss of Harry's poems should actually be imputed to Mary or that the gardener's death should actually be imputed to the trespasser.' The problem with this response is not only that it makes Kant's thesis about the imputability of bad consequences quite weak and indeterminate; the problem is also that it seems at odds with Kant's treatment of the altruistic lie to save a friend from murder. There Kant seems clearly to think that the friend's death, if a causal result of the lie, should be imputed to the liar as something for which he is responsible. In the context Kant's thought experiment would lose its rhetorical force if he were merely to say that the death is imputable to the liar in the weak sense that it meets *some*, but not all, necessary conditions for its being the liar's responsibility. Kant's point, I take it, is this: if you lie and if, even

---

[30] At least this is so if we can assume, as Kant apparently did, that the intervention of an immoral choice of another agent does not break the causal chain, preventing us from calling the bad event even a 'consequence' of the initial act.

unforeseeably, it turns out badly, then you are (not 'might be') to blame for the disaster, and so it is clear that even the altruistic lie should be avoided. A Kantian revisionist, however, noting that Kant's position about altruistic lies is unsatisfactory in any case, might settle for the weaker sense of 'imputability'.

POSTSCRIPT

The only problems and challenges to Kant's position that I raise above are intuitive ones; that is, the charge is merely that its implications conflict with how I, and perhaps 'we', would judge moral responsibility for consequences in various cases. Noting such objections is important for moral philosophy, I think, but the problems it flags are merely provisional and tentative ones. The next stage of discussion of these matters should be enquiry as to whether our intuitive judgements can withstand critical scrutiny, can be systematized in a principled way, and can be justified from a clearly articulated fundamental moral point of view. The criteria for imputation are, in effect, second-order precepts, about how to respond when first-order principles of duty are violated (or transcended). As such they should be assessed within the overall context of a system of moral thought that includes, importantly, the basic framework for moral deliberation about what the specific moral precepts should be. What the principles of imputation should be may well depend on what exactly the first-order principles are as well as how the moral notions of 'consequence' and 'free cause' are interpreted. As said before, what counts as a *bad* result and the role that contingencies and luck may play in fairly assessing responsibility need, ultimately, to be determined at this more comprehensive level of reflection. Intuitive objections provide a starting point for discussion but cannot be decisive. Whether Kant's simple formulas about imputation can stand as part of such a moral system, reasonably constructed, remains an open question.

7

Kant on Punishment: A Coherent Mix of Deterrence and Retribution?

For many years Kant was widely regarded to be the arch-retributivist regarding punishment, and many, even now, would accept that characterization without hesitation. Recently, however, scholarly studies have cast doubt on this widely accepted picture. Retributivism, we can now see, is not the name of one simple doctrine; rather, what has been called by this name comes in many different forms and degrees. By reinterpreting or seeing past Kant's most off-putting rhetorical remarks on punishment in *The Metaphysics of Morals*, several writers have explored more deeply the structure of Kant's justification of punishment, noting the tension between Kant's recognition of the need for punishment as a deterrent and his stern and (apparently) retributive remarks about how and why punishment must be carried out.[1] A careful reading reveals both elements as quite prominent, and leaves the desired reconciliation, if any, obscure.

After years of trying to find an acceptable interpretation, Jeffrie Murphy has finally concluded that Kant did not really have anything that deserves to be called 'a *theory* of punishment'.[2] Recently Sharon Byrd, Don Scheid, and Sarah Holtman, and earlier Jeffrie Murphy and I (more sketchily), proposed mixed interpretations that try to make sense of the tension by postulating different roles for the deterrence and retributive elements in Kant's writings.[3] I remain convinced that this

---

[1] Kant's most sustained discussion of punishment is in *The Metaphysics of Morals*, esp. MM, 104–10 [331–7], 130 [362–3], 23–34 [229–42], 89–98 [311–23].

[2] Jeffrie G. Murphy, 'Does Kant have a Theory of Punishment?', *Columbia Law Review*, 87 (1987) 509–12; italics his.

[3] B. Sharon Byrd, 'Kant's Theory of Punishment: Deterrence in its Threat, Retribution in its Execution', *Law and Philosophy*, 8 (1980), 151–200; Donald Scheid, 'Kant's Retributivism', *Ethics*, 93 (1983), 262–82; Jeffrie G. Murphy, *Kant: The Philosophy of Right* (London and New York: Macmillan, 1970), 109–49, and 'Kant's Theory of Criminal Punishment', in *Retribution, Justice, and Therapy: Essays in the Philosophy of Law* (Dordrecht and Boston: D. Reidel Publishing Co. 1979), 82–92; Thomas E. Hill, Jr., *Dignity and Practical Reason in Kant's Moral Theory* (Ithaca, NY: Cornell University Press, 1992), chs. 9 and 10; and Sarah Holtman, 'Toward Social Reform: Kant's Penal Theory Reinterpreted', *Utilitas*, 9 (1997), 3–21.

recent emphasis is a significant advance in understanding Kant's moral and political thought, but I retain the lingering worry that even the best of this work, in the effort to highlight Kant's appeal to deterrence, has not yet fully done justice to the retributive current in his thought. It seems as if the pendulum has swung too far in reaction to earlier caricatures of Kant's retributivism, and we are still missing, or only partially articulating, the whole story about why Kant's account of punishment seems so distinctively different not only from familiar deterrence theories but also from any of the ways of mixing deterrence and retribution that readily come to mind.

Kant's expressed views on punishment are like intriguing pieces of a large jigsaw puzzle. It is obvious enough how some pieces fit together, but not quite how others complement and unite the rest. Moreover, there seem to be gaps, and so some pieces may be missing. As Murphy says, Kant's writings on punishment are too brief and incomplete to enable us to call them, as expressly presented and without supplement, a full-fledged '*theory* of punishment'. We might have to conclude, as Murphy now does, that Kant really has no coherent theory of punishment, only a jumble of half-connected thoughts. But, not ready to despair yet. I suspect that if we will just diligently *look for* or *construct* the missing pieces, many of the apparent gaps can be filled and the puzzle may yet yield a whole picture that makes sense, whether or not in the end we see it as one we can endorse. To lay out the whole picture remains the ideal, but here I can only offer some suggestions.

My plan for discussion is the following. In the first section, I comment on Kant's position on *who should be punished, how, and how much*. These are pieces of the grand picture puzzle that we have more or less ready to hand. That is, the main points are familiar in outline, even though interpretations vary on matters of detail.[4] My concern in this section is to emphasize that Kant thought that, even under bad governments, breaking the law is a moral offence, except in one special case. Thus, for Kant, normally we can presume that the legally guilty are

---

[4] The *level and status* of Kant's ideas about who, how, and how much we should punish may also be controversial. Many seem to assume that Kant held his answers (such as *ius talionis* or 'an eye for an eye') as self-standing, fundamental moral truths, but the structure of his moral theory as a whole seems clearly to imply that such relatively specific principles, if justifiable at all, must ultimately rest on the more basic moral ideas contained in the various forms of the Categorical Imperative. If so, Kantian moral philosophers need to question whether Kant's specific principles of punishment, without modification, can really be derived from Kant's basic theory. It is quite possible, even likely, that due respect for Kant's main insights into the foundations of morality and its supreme principle will prove to require reflective present-day Kantians to abandon these and other particular moral opinions that Kant endorsed, even vehemently defended.

morally guilty as well. By itself, of course, this presumption does not warrant retributive punishment, but it is a significant part of the background of Kant's idea that principles of punishment are warranted by justice rather than purely pragmatic or consequentialist considerations.

In the second section, I distinguish some paradigms of retributive theory and deterrence theory, as well as various ways of trying to mix elements of these. Once the paradigm cases and simple mixed cases are spelled out, it should be plain that Kant's expressed views on punishment do *not* add up to any theory of *these types*. If his theory is best understood (or reconstructed) as a mixed theory, the retributive and deterrence elements must be mixed in a more subtle way. More subtle mixed accounts have in fact been proposed recently, but none, I believe, fully captures all of the retributive elements in Kant's understanding of punishment.

In the third section, I call attention to some familiar features of the concept and practice of punishment that I believe Kant took for granted. Assuming that Kant took these background features very seriously, his 'retributive' remarks on punishment begin to make more sense. More to the point, adding these assumptions to the subtle mix of deterrence and retributive elements already identified by recent commentators contributes to an understanding of Kant's theory (or partial theory) of punishment as quite distinctive and more deeply 'retributive' than even recent 'mixed' interpretations suggest.[5] Here, I admit, one must 'read between the lines' or 'construct' some of the ideas that help to fill out Kant's picture because the ideas that are needed are not so much explicit in the text as they are assumptions that it would be natural for Kant to make, given his other views and the fact that they are commonplace ideas, perhaps even implicit in our *concept* of punishment.

My main proposal can be summarized as follows. The deterrence elements in Kant's account of punishment serve an important but restricted role, well designed to avoid any slippery slope to consequentialism. Some (though not all) retributive elements are also central to the theory. They are not mere 'side-constraints' on a deterrent 'price system' of social control. They reflect the view that, given human conditions, the institution of *punishment* is required by *justice*, that fairness requires its impartial, regular, principled imposition, that just punishment is inflicted *for* violations of public law that one is *both legally and morally bound* to obey, and, finally, that, since punishment serves to express

---

[5] By 'mixed' interpretations I mean those that attribute to Kant's account of punishment both a deterrence and a retributive aspect.

public moral disapproval, it should be honest, well grounded, and proportionate to the gravity of the offence.

THE SCOPE, DEGREE, AND KIND
OF PUNISHMENT

A fully developed theory of punishment would provide systematic, clearly related answers to many different questions. Jeffrie Murphy, for example, lists the following as the central questions: (*a*) What is the nature of crime and punishment? (*b*) What is the moral justification of punishment? (*c*) What is the political justification of punishment? (*d*) What are the proper principles of criminal liability? (*e*) What are the appropriate punishments? Each of these questions, of course, serves as a heading for more specific questions, and there are, no doubt, many other ways of organizing the issues that need to be addressed.

My own main interests are the standard questions of *moral* philosophy: What ought one to do (in various situations), and why? Thus my organizing perspective on a theory of punishment is to ask: First, what does the theory say about who should be punished, to what degree, within what limits, and how? Then, second, how does the theory purport to justify its answers to these questions? That is, how do these answers follow from its conception of morality and basic moral principles together with whatever further conceptual and empirical assumptions it relies upon in the course of its argument? In Murphy's terms, my first question overlaps his questions (*d*) and (*c*), and my second question is primarily his question (*b*), but to answer it a theory would need to address his (*a*) and (*c*), and more. In this section I review three parts to Kant's answer to my first question.

1. *Who should be punished?* The context is restricted to official punishment through criminal law, and so we set aside parental punishments, vigilante 'punishments', divine punishment, etc. In the relevant context, then, Kant's answer, in general, seems clear: *all and only those who commit crimes* ought to be punished. Crimes are offences against antecedently specified, public laws that prohibit certain 'external' conduct and prescribe a sanction to be applied for non-compliance. The laws that define such offences need not themselves be morally warranted in order for punishment to be appropriate; they need only be laws laid down and enforced by a sovereign that has *de facto power* and so also *authority* to declare (in the name of 'the united will of the people') what

is law. The sovereign may have been unwise or even wicked in making a given criminal law, but state officials (prosecutors, judges, juries, jailers, etc.) generally have the legal and moral responsibility to see that violators are punished as prescribed by the law, with one possible exception.

The possible exception is a situation where carrying out a legally ordered punishment would be so heinous as to be 'wrong in itself', either because the type of punishment is strictly immoral to impose, or because the *legally* guilty defendant is manifestly *morally* innocent, or both.[6] In discussing revolution and again in *Religion*, Kant concedes that, morally, one may refuse to follow a tyrant's legal orders to do what is in itself wrong, even though one may not participate in revolutionary activities.[7] Thus, Kant might allow exceptions to the general precept 'All the (legally) guilty ought to be punished,' or to the right of legal officials to enforce it,[8] if law enforcement officials had to decide whether

[6] I should warn the reader at this point that here, and more often than not in this chapter, I am using the terms 'legal' and 'moral' in familiar English senses which do not correspond exactly to Kant's use of the distinction between the juridical and ethical in *The Metaphysics of Morals*. Juridical duties in Kant's sense belong to morality or 'ethics', broadly construed, but not to virtue and the ethical as Kant distinguishes these from the realm of *Recht*. See MM, 9–14 [214–21], 145–9 [379–84].

[7] At MM, 98 [322] Kant allows that a people 'in parliament' may refuse 'negatively' to accede to every demand the government declares necessary for administering the state. At MM, 136–7 [371] Kant qualifies the categorical imperative 'Obey the authority who has power over you' by adding parenthetically 'in whatever does not conflict with inner morality'. See also R, 142n. [154n.], and Hans Reiss's 'Postscript' in Hans Reiss (ed.), *Kant: Political Writings* (Cambridge: Cambridge University Press, 1991), 267–8. Reiss notes that, in *Religion*, 142n. [154n.], Kant expressly cites a qualification to the duty of obedience to state authorities that he expressed without explicit qualification in *The Metaphysics of Morals*, 137–8 [372]. Kant writes, 'When it is said (Acts, V, 29) 'We ought to obey God rather than men,' this means only that when statutory commands, regarding which men can be legislators and judges, come into conflict with duties which reason prescribes unconditionally, concerning whose observance or transgression God alone can be the judge, the former must yield precedence to the latter.' See also Sven Arntzen, 'Kant's Denial of Absolute Sovereignty', *Pacific Philosophical Quarterly*, 76 (1995), 1–16. Arntzen apparently sees Kant's position in *Religion* as inconsistent with his position in *The Metaphysics of Morals*, but, in my opinion, they can be reconciled. The former maintains the moral duty to resist certain grossly immoral state orders whereas the latter insists that there can be no legal right, enforceable against the sovereign, to such disobedience and also that 'ethics' in the broad sense requires us in general (possibly excepting the extreme case of orders to do what is in itself immoral) to obey the law, arguing for reform of unjust laws but in the meantime conforming to them. (Here I use the terms 'law', 'moral', and 'legal' in a standard English sense, acknowledging that there is no simple, unqualified way to translate these into Kant's German without confusing the point.)

[8] There are a number of cases where Kant seems to be admitting that, although in some sense a defendant ought to be punished (even with the death penalty), special circumstances undermine even the legal right and duty to punish (or to apply the death penalty), e.g. shipwreck 'necessity' cases and, in defence of 'honour', a soldier killing in

to prosecute someone guilty of violating a tyrant's heinously unjust law that would have required him, the defendant, say, to slander, torture, rape, kill, and desecrate the bodies of innocent persons. Assuming that the defendant's compliance with the law in this case would have been morally wrong in itself, though 'legally' mandatory, the defendant's legal guilt would not carry with it, as in the typical case, the moral guilt of having failed to live up to his or her moral responsibility to obey the law. If so, making an exception to 'All the (legally) guilty ought to be punished' might be morally justified, even though contrary to law. Conceivably, Kant *might* have wanted to insist, to the contrary, that officials have an absolute moral duty to carry out the legal punishment even though the accused had an absolute moral duty to refuse to obey the law; but, having admitted moral grounds for citizens' conscientious refusal to obey laws in extreme cases, he would be hard pressed to justify such an absolute stand against conscientious refusal of officials to punish in those cases.

My understanding of Kant on the exceptional cases, in sum, is the following. According to Kant, unlike Aquinas, even grossly immoral 'laws' laid down and enforced by a tyrant are still really laws, are genuine parts of the *legal* system, even though contrary to the norms of practical reason, the principles of natural law, as expressed in *Rechtslehre* and elsewhere.[9] The sovereign in Kant's theory, in contrast to Hobbes's, is morally bound by these norms and morally ought, therefore, to make and reform laws to conform with *Recht*. This does not mean, however, that when the sovereign fails in this responsibility and enforces unjust statutes, the statutes automatically lose the force of law. Most unjust statutes, Kant thought, are not only part of the legal system but also laws we are *morally* bound to obey.[10] There is, however, one

a duel and a mother killing her illegitimate newborn infant. Apparently, these are not bizarre cases of a legal duty of officials to punish despite a moral prohibition against doing so, but rather cases of moral grounds for limiting the legal right to punish in special circumstances. See MM, 27–8 [235–6], 108–10 [336–7].

[9] Here I am using 'legal' in a familiar contemporary sense in which 'legal' does not imply 'morally required', but, to avoid confusion, I should note that there is a different idea of 'legal' within Kant's moral theory, implicit in his distinction between legality and morality. Roughly, for Kant, the latter is a distinction between the conduct required merely to 'conform to duty' and this together with the motivation to render the act 'from duty'.

[10] For example, oppressive taxes, unnecessary curfews, prohibitions on publishing works on religion, etc. To obey these unjust laws seems clearly not 'wrong in itself' in the sense Kant intended, and so obedience would be morally obligatory. To suppose that we are morally permitted to violate any law that we, personally, judge to be unjust is clearly contrary to Kant's arguments for sovereign authority in MM. In fact those argu-

exception that Kant acknowledges, namely, that unjust legislation requiring a person to do what is *morally impermissible in itself* (i.e. in *all* conditions) may and must (morally) be disobeyed.[11] This leaves open the possibility, and makes it plausible, that a law requiring officials to punish *all* law-breakers, no matter what, might itself be morally impermissible to obey in some extreme circumstances.

There is, admittedly, an alternative way to reconstruct Kant's theory, but this is less plausible as an interpretation, I believe, than the account sketched above. The assumption there was that the exceptional cases are to be understood as instances of *legal* requirements that are *not morally binding* (but in fact morally obligatory to disobey). An alternative interpretation might say, instead, that those exceptionally unjust statutes lose the status of *law* altogether, so that, for these special cases, Kant's view is like Aquinas's: an unjust 'law' is no law at all. There is perhaps some reason to expect that Kant would take this position. Given his absolute stand against revolution, and on other matters, it seems natural to suspect that he would think that obedience to law is an unconditional moral duty. The fact that he rarely even mentions possible exceptions no doubt contributes to this impression. Given this assumption, it might be thought an advantage of the alternative (Thomistic) interpretation that, despite Kant's *presumed* view that we always ought (morally) to obey genuine laws, this alternative interpretation would allow Kant none the less to maintain, without inconsistency, the humane view that conscientious refusal to obey extremely unjust state orders (*alleged* laws) is sometimes morally right.

On balance, however, the evidence seems opposed to the alternative

ments, like parallel arguments in Hobbes, seem to imply, as Hobbes acknowledges, that to authorize a sovereign at all we must always subordinate our personal judgement about what justice requires when it conflicts with the sovereign's judgement, acting then as if 'The sovereign must be right, after all, and so his laws are not unjust, and so I am morally bound to obey.' Obviously Kant could not conscientiously endorse this as an unqualified conclusion, especially since his sovereign's judgement, unlike Hobbes's, does not constitute justice but only (at best) aims to conform to it as an independent rational norm. So, despite his arguments, Kant slips in the needed exception without much explanation: one may trust one's own conscientious judgement against the sovereign's if the latter's commands seem clearly to order one to do what is wrong in itself (as opposed to, say, suffering an injustice to oneself or doing merely what would be wrong if not legally commanded).

[11] Kant writes as though such disobedience, in contrast to active participation in revolution, must be 'passive'. But that seems unwarranted by his own standards. Suppose an unjust statute commanded one not to interfere actively when racially despised people were brutally beaten, raped, etc., even though one could easily stop this. Would not the same sort of arguments that Kant acknowledges for passive disobedience warrant active disobedience in this case? See the next chapter.

interpretation. Though only rarely, Kant *does* mention exceptional cases, as we have seen; and then what he says is not that the bad 'law' ceases to be law but just that non-compliance with it is morally permissible. The alternative account also introduces a significant deviation from Kant's expressed views about what constitutes public law. That is, though rational moral principles *should* guide actual lawmaking, the actual legislation and judgement of the sovereign in power, no matter how tyrannical, in fact determine what the laws of the state are.[12]

Some may be surprised, even doubtful, that Kant might admit an exception to a policy ('Punish all the guilty') that he seems to defend so adamantly and often without mentioning exceptions. They should, however, consider the passages (mentioned above) about conscientious refusal to obey the law.[13] Also, they should note that in the passages where Kant seems most clearly to accept as unqualified '*All* the (legally) guilty ought to be punished,' his attention is focused, not on the sort of (quite appealing) exception discussed above but rather on the dubious practice of making exceptions (1) on consequentialist grounds,[14] (2) on the general excuse that the law is unjust,[15] or (3) for whatever special personal interests a sovereign might have in 'pardoning' someone.[16]

Let us now set aside the exceptional cases of legal orders to do what is intrinsically immoral. The interpretation of these cases may be controversial and they obviously were not the standard cases that Kant had in mind in his brief discussion of the principles of punishment. For all other cases, Kant holds that those who commit crimes are also morally guilty. Even if what they did was in itself morally innocent, i.e. not morally wrong unless made illegal, it becomes morally impermissible when a law, even a bad law, forbids it. All juridical duties are indirectly ethical duties, for all duties, even those that also require 'external legislation', have their ultimate source in categorical requirements of practical reason and so 'belong to ethics'.[17] In other words, setting aside the special cases where to obey the law would be to do something in itself

---

[12] Confusion on this point is probably encouraged by the fact that 'Recht' can serve for both the English words 'justice' and 'law' and also by the fact that, according to Kant, justice does typically require citizens to obey the commands of the de facto ruler even when those commands are unjust.

[13] That is, cases where to carry out a punishment as required by one's legal office would be something of a kind wrong in itself or where the person legally liable to punishment is so only because of his or her passive refusal to obey a legal order to do something in itself wrong.   [14] MM, 104–6 [331–2].

[15] MM, 136–7 [371–2].   [16] MM, 109–10 [337].   [17] MM, 20–1 [219–20].

immoral, whenever law forbids (or requires) an act, one has an indirect ethical duty to refrain from (or to do) that act and even to refrain (or to act) from the right moral motive.

To summarize Kant's position, as I understand it, morally objectionable acts are of different types. (*a*) Some, such as private drunkenness, gluttony, neglect of one's talents, ingratitude, breaches of friendship, and mockery of others, cannot or at least should not be prohibited by law and yet they are morally wrong or manifestations of vice. (*b*) Other acts are permitted by some actual legal systems but *should* be forbidden by law and are morally wrong to do (as contrary to natural right) even when permitted by law, e.g. private 'punishment' of servants by maiming them or beating them to death. (*c*) Many common acts, like malicious murder, rape, and theft, are doubly wrong, morally speaking, i.e. wrong because inherently contrary to natural right but also wrong because forbidden by lawful authorities. (*d*) In any imperfect legal system, there may be some acts that are morally wrong (if at all) only because they are illegal, for example, violating arbitrary state restrictions on travel, trade, and publications. (*e*) Finally, there are the special exceptional cases mentioned above: that is, acts that are morally objectionable in themselves even though in fact they are *required* by (corrupt) law.

Without ignoring these distinctions we can still say that, setting aside the special cases (*e*), Kant holds that *all and only those both morally and legally guilty should be punished*. That is, those who should be punished are all those guilty of legal offences and (so also) morally guilty (at least for violating the duty to obey the law). Only the legally guilty may be punished because punishment is inherently an official act within a practice whose officials are authorized only to punish those guilty of specified offences. Again setting aside the exceptional cases (*e*), only the morally guilty may be punished because only the legally guilty may be punished and all who are legally guilty, aside from (*e*), are also morally guilty.

Since in general (special cases aside) moral guilt is necessary for legal guilt, those justly liable to punishment must have been 'free', in various relevant ways, to have conformed to the law: e.g. mentally competent, physically able, morally permitted, not innocently ignorant of relevant facts, not tried under secret or *ex post facto* 'laws', etc. If some legal systems grossly ignore these conditions, their contrary rules and commands are unjust. Thus, I assume, in saying that, the special cases aside, all and only the guilty should be punished, Kant presupposes freedom conditions for guilt. It is not enough for justified punishment that offenders have behaved observably in ways to which the government regularly and intentionally responds by inflicting pain and deprivation; conformity to the law must have been within their power in the ways required for moral responsibility.

Kant, I think, took for granted a background context for his discussion of punishment, except for special type (*e*) cases, that included these standard conditions: the legally guilty knew what they were doing; they were aware that they were breaking the law; they recognized (with some inner conflict) that doing so was morally wrong; they chose from non-moral incentives to violate the law anyway (though able to do otherwise); they were liable to pangs of conscience afterwards; and they were, on some level, disposed to acknowledge that they had no just complaint about being punished up the limit of *ius talionis*. These assumptions, which often do not match what we find in our courts and jails, are important to keep in mind when we try, critically, to draw practical lessons from Kant's theory for our world. For now, however, my point in mentioning the apparent background of Kant's discussion is just to note that in that context it is more plausible to speak (as Kant does) of punishing the legally guilty as just, as a categorical imperative, as returning what their deeds 'deserve', as morally (as opposed to pragmatically) based, even as a response to 'sin [*peccatum*]'.[18]

2. *How much ought the guilty to be punished?* Kant, like many others, holds some version of the idea that the severity of the punishment ought to be proportionate to the severity of the crime. But how is severity to be measured? Examples suggest that the relevant standard of severity of punishment is something like the ranking that people, if rational, would normally give about how undesirable it would be, from a self-interested point of view, for them to receive the different punishments. Thus, capital punishment gets a very high ranking, castration lower but presumably still quite high, small monetary fines quite low, etc. 'Normal' rankings, certain examples suggest, may be adjusted when it is known that certain types of people will care less, and others more, for certain punishments, e.g. the rich find small fines less burdensome than the poor do.[19]

What is the criterion of severity of offence? It cannot be the degree of the offenders' inner unworthiness stemming from their bad or weak will; for that is not generally available to public view, and the legal system should restrict its assessments to whether 'external acts' were legally and morally wrong and yet 'freely' done. Inner motives, on which

---

[18] MM, 106–7 [333], 104–5 [331], 130 [363].
[19] See MM, 105–6 [332].

fine-grained moral assessments depend, are not the business of the public law to judge. That the offender was morally guilty is important to warrant punishment, on Kant's view, but how gravely guilty by all the relevant moral criteria (of motive, character, moral effort, etc.) is not at issue. The severity of offence intended, then, must be something like the degree of harm or 'hindrance to liberty' that the offender has illegally inflicted. Kant's remarks on proportionality suggest that severity of offence should be measured in roughly the same way as severity of punishment. If so, since severity of punishment varies with normal aversion from a rational self-interested perspective, then severity of offence should vary according to how the victims of crime would normally rate the harm or loss from their rational self-interested perspective. This seems in line with Kant's idea that punishment should be such that if you (illegally) strike another, you strike yourself, and if you kill another, you kill yourself, etc.

A passage that seems at first in conflict with my claim here is Kant's remark that the fittingness of the death penalty for murder (and other capital crimes against the state), judicially imposed by the law of retribution, is 'shown by the fact that only by this is a sentence of death pronounced on every criminal in proportion to his inner wickedness [*inneren Bösartigkeit*]'. We should note, however, that even here, in the special case of capital crimes, Kant continues to affirm that the operative judicial principle is the *ius talionis* or 'law of retribution', which for Kant is not a principle urging judges to match up the inner wickedness of criminals with appropriate degrees of punishment. Rather, *ius talionis* calls for giving back to criminals something undesirable equivalent in worth to what they have taken or destroyed.[20] Both what was taken and what is to be repaid must be identifiable and (roughly) measurable by a public court, which (unlike conscience) is focused on 'external' actions rather than 'inner' motives.

The context of Kant's reference to 'inner wickedness' is a discussion of the execution of Scottish rebels (1745–6). Some had rebelled believing it their political duty; others rebelled for private gain. Kant offers a brief (and weak) argument to show that by being executed they each suffered proportionately to their degree of inner wickedness: that is, honourable rebels will not find the death penalty as undesirable as the dishonourable ones will, so the death penalty is less severe for the former than for the latter. The point here, it seems clear, is simply to assuage the discomfort that some may feel about executing even well-intentioned

---

[20] The German term ('Wiedervergeltungsrecht') indicates this more clearly, I think, than the English ('retribution').

revolutionaries, as Kant thought the law of retribution required. Kant tries to console those worried about such executions by saying, in effect, that, since death is not as great a loss to honourable rebels as to self-serving rebels, the actual result of applying the law of retribution, as it happens, is that the more honourable rebels suffer less than the dishonourable ones. Thus, at least in this case, criminals turn out to suffer in proportion to the degree of their 'inner wickedness'. The point, I take it, is that even though the court must apply the strict law of retribution, which disregards the difference in the motives of the rebels, critics need have no moral concern about using that strict judicial standard for the rebels because the actual outcome satisfies even the standard commonly associated with divine justice (suffering according to degree of inner wickedness). The passage in question, on this reading, seems quite compatible with Kant's position as presented above. It fits what Kant implies elsewhere, namely, that 'suffering proportionate to inner wickedness' should be neither the rule nor the aim of a system of criminal laws.

We should also note that the law of retribution, absent special psychological assumptions, does not guarantee that normal and rational persons' incentives to avoid a particular punishment would sufficiently counteract their drives to commit the corresponding crimes, even under conditions of perfect enforcement. The formula is designed to ensure that normal potential *criminals*, if self-interestedly rational, rank their aversion to various punishments on the same relative scale that normal potential *victims*, if self-interestedly rational, rank their aversion to being subjected to the corresponding kind of treatment illegally. But the intensity of (self-interestedly rational) potential criminals' *drive to commit a crime*, say, of jealousy, revenge, or glory-seeking, may not, all things considered, correlate well with their aversion to being treated (by punishment) as they propose to treat their victims. My aversion to being illegally whipped may equal my aversion to being officially whipped, but my desire to whip someone else illegally may outweigh my aversion to being whipped as punishment. Perhaps this is why some suggest that the appropriate policy is, so far as (physically and morally) possible, to make the threat of punishment for a crime just sufficient to counteract normal (rational self-interested) drives to commit that crime.[21] It seems doubtful, however, that this proposal would yield the regularity that Kant wanted; and, furthermore, it seems far removed from the tradi-

[21] See Byrd, 'Kant's Theory of Punishment', 192.

tional 'eye for an eye' formula that Kant explicitly endorses (with some qualifications).[22]

To maintain its generality, presumably the law needs to 'round off' and work primarily with typical cases, for example, assuming for the most part that everyone would give roughly the same ranking to the seriousness, from their perspective, of being illegally murdered, maimed, beaten, slandered, robbed, etc. Even though Kant apparently favoured quite simple, unqualified definitions of crimes, a complex legal system could give a finer-grained classification of offences without violating Kant's idea that the legal system should not try to judge and rank the ultimate moral worth of law-breakers. The system could, for example, take into account differences in the (empirically discernible) circumstances, opportunities, obstacles, etc. in specifying what counts as 'same offence' and 'equal severity'.[23]

3. *In what manner ought the criminal to be punished?* Kant acknowledges that public justice 'makes its measure and principle' the *ius talionis*, the traditional idea that justice demands 'an eye for an eye', etc.[24] This expresses more or less the idea of proportionality discussed above, but it adds a (qualified) suggestion about the type or manner of punishment appropriate to each offence, namely, the punishment ought to be, when morally and physically possible, the same kind of harm or loss the offender has wrongfully inflicted on his victim. The immediate reason offered is just that 'all other principles are fluctuating' and 'extraneous considerations are mixed into them'.[25] Though death is always the required punishment for murder, in other cases, Kant concedes, punishments strictly like the offence in kind may be impossible or immoral (e.g. as with rape, pederasty, and bestiality) and so permissible 'equivalents' (in severity) may be used instead.[26] Except for the suggestion that punishments *similar in kind* to the offence (e.g. the death penalty for murder) may often, though not always, be appropriate punishments, the

[22] The criminal's aversion to losing an eye in punishment may correlate well with his (and others') aversion to losing an eye in an unlawful attack and yet the threatened punishment (loss of an eye) may often be more than enough, and yet sometimes less than enough, to counteract an impulse to put out someone's eye. The same sort of point could be made regarding more common crimes. Here I use 'an eye for an eye' as a simple illustration of the law of retribution, even though Kant himself considered mutilation as degrading to humanity and so presumably not an appropriate punishment.

[23] At MM, 19–20 [228] Kant notes briefly that the degree of culpability that can be imputed to an agent varies with the different kinds of obstacles he or she faced when choosing to break the law.

[24] MM, 105–6 [332].   [25] MM, 106 [332].   [26] MM, 130 [363].

'eye for an eye' principle merely affirms the idea that the severity of punishment and offence ought to be proportionate in the sense I suggested
above. At least if everyone would rank being treated in ways they dislike
(being robbed, defrauded, maimed, killed, etc.) in more or less the same
way as others do, whether the unwanted treatment stems from crime or
punishment, the 'eye for an eye' principle would make the offences and
punishments approximately proportionate in severity.[27]

Kant explains the content of the principle of retribution by noting
that, under the principle, 'whatever undeserved evil you inflict upon
another, . . . that you inflict upon yourself.'[28] More vividly, under the
principle, the credible threat of punishment puts a would-be offender in
a situation such that 'If you insult him, you insult yourself; if you steal
from him, you steal from yourself; if you strike him, you strike yourself; if you kill him, you kill yourself.'[29] Again, the principle is merely
explained by saying it 'brings [the offender's] evil deed back to himself'
and the punishment does to the offender 'what he has perpetrated on
others, if not in terms of [the law's] letter at least in terms of its spirit'.[30]
These remarks are often taken to be quick and intuitively appealing *justifications* of the retributive principle, perhaps because many people do
accept as a primitive and comprehensive moral truth, or ideal of justice,
that, so far as possible, each should get back exactly what harm or loss

---

[27] 'An eye for an eye' provides a suitably 'external' standard applicable to many cases,
but, applied literally, it would not always capture the intuitive idea that severity of punishment should be proportionate to severity of offence, morally or measured by its value
to the victim. For example, being subject to armed robbery of $1,000 seems a quite
serious offence from the perspective of most victims whereas a (forcefully extracted) criminal fine of $1,000 does not seem a very severe penalty, as penalties go, from the per-
spective of offenders. To revert to the old (but illegitimate) practice of taking an eye for
an eye, even if we assume that keeping one's eye means more or less the same to everyone, taking an eye for an eye overlooks the fact that an eye means more to the one-eyed,
to visual artists, etc. Public insult or slander means more to some than others, as Kant
recognized, so adjustments would be needed to capture the 'spirit' of proportionality. See
MM, 130 [363]. In these cases, as always, problems of relevant act description enter the
picture. In one sense, 'what he did' in wilfully blinding a one-eyed visual artist or slandering one whose public life depends on his pristine record is different from merely
'taking an eye' or 'slandering someone', and one might argue that the experience of being
forcibly robbed is a personal violation quite dissimilar to having to pay an equivalent
fine for one's offence. The main point to note relevant to my discussion, however, is that
Kant's (limited) endorsement of the retributive policy need not be taken as commitment
to any deep, basic principle of punishing according to moral deserts, evil for evil,
vengeance, etc. Its main appeal to Kant, apparently, was that it was traditional, not utilitarian, less variable than other standards, and a criterion that allowed legislators and
courts to confine themselves to making and enforcing criminal laws regarding 'external'
(though intentional) actions (independently of the degree of moral motivation of
defendants).

[28] MM, 105 [332].   [29] Ibid.   [30] MM, 130 [363].

he wrongfully inflicted on others. Those who take that general premiss for granted might well be tempted to suppose that Kant thought that the law of retribution is justified *as a public policy of state law enforcement* because it is simply an application of that (alleged) basic, comprehensive principle to the system of criminal law.

Taking the remarks quoted above as attempts to *justify* the law of retribution, however, strikes me as a serious mistake. In the sections where they appear, Kant is engaged in systematic exposition of his particular principles of punishment, not laying down foundations.[31] Moreover, the remarks can perfectly well be understood as doing nothing more than explaining, and making vivid, what exactly the *ius talionis* prescribes. More importantly, nowhere, I believe, does Kant commit himself to the law of retribution as a comprehensive, act-guiding moral principle. It is not implicit in any form of the Categorical Imperative, and Kant's moral principles of gratitude, beneficence, and even respect for others contain no qualification urging us to withhold our gratitude, kindness, or basic human respect in an effort to help God, or whomever, distribute suffering proportionately to moral ill-desert or even overt wrongdoing.[32]

Kant, of course, argues in the second *Critique* that we must believe that virtuous individuals will ultimately be happy, despite apparent empirical evidence to the contrary.[33] Kant's argument seems to assume that the virtuous *deserve* to be happy, and from this one might suppose that he also held that the vicious deserve to be unhappy. From such weak beginnings one might mistakenly infer that making the vicious suffer is our responsibility and so the criminal law should operate with this purpose. But there are serious problems with this line of thinking. Among them, I suspect, is misconstruing the sort of ground Kant has in the second *Critique* for thinking we should presume perfect virtue and happiness can and will go together. This, I think, is not an inference from an alleged self-evident abstract premiss, 'Virtue deserves happiness,' or an intuition that it is 'intrinsically valuable' for the virtuous to be happy. The starting point is that each rational-yet-sensuous human being has two deep dispositions, to maintain a good will and to pursue happiness, and therefore we are subject to two sorts of rational commands, categorical and hypothetical, the latter being subordinate to the former but no weaker or less rational for that. We must, as rational

---

[31] Foundations, by contrast, are clearly being laid, for example, at MM, 23–6 [229–33].

[32] See my *Dignity and Practical Reason in Kant's Moral Theory*, ch. 9.

[33] C2, 116–38 [110–32].

beings, strive for *both* moral virtue and happiness together, though the latter only on condition of the former. (The *morally* required ends are primarily *our own* virtue and *others'* happiness, but the highest good, all considered, would be the union of virtue and happiness in all.) Assuming that the ideal combination is not logically or metaphysically impossible, Kant argues, we need to believe and should have faith that it is in fact possible, even reasonably to be hoped for. Kant's argument may be doubted, but for our purposes the point is that it does not entail the practical 'ideal' of making the vicious suffer.

Admittedly in the *Groundwork* Kant calls attention to our moral discomfort at the thought of unregenerate scoundrels living prosperously in continuous happiness, but he does not infer that spoiling their happiness and making them suffer is in general our moral responsibility or even right (except when necessary for further reasons).[34] In this remark and in his discussion of the union of happiness and virtue in the second *Critique* Kant was concerned with virtue as inner good willing, and he clearly holds that inner moral motivation (beyond the moral guilt that we can infer from overt criminal acts) is no business of the public law. Comparative degrees of inner moral worth, whether of criminals or ordinary citizens, are too opaque to us to allow us fairly to employ our guesses about such matters to govern our ways of treating people. Non-criminals may be morally worse than criminals. Although the practice of punishment serves to discourage and express moral disapproval of overtly offensive types of acts (and their agents for doing them), we are so ignorant of the inner moral worth of individuals that we cannot fairly guide our actions, in law or otherwise, by the principle, 'Make immoral people suffer proportionately to their inner viciousness,' even if (as some think) that would be an ideal outcome.

WHAT KANT'S THEORY IS NOT: PARADIGMS OF DETERRENCE, RETRIBUTION, AND SOME WAYS NOT TO MIX RETRIBUTIVE AND DETERRENCE ELEMENTS

To establish some reference points, let us consider how we might characterize very extreme forms of deterrence theory. The function and justification of punishment, such a theory might begin, is to deter those who might otherwise violate the law. Mixed theories often combine this

---

[34] G, 61 [393].

with various constraining principles of justice, but the most extreme deterrence theory would be one which insists that all further rules and procedures of punishment are to be derived solely from this basic dominant aim (to deter citizens from breaking the law). This simplistic theory would warrant *any degree and kind* of punishment, no matter how harsh, to deter violations of law, *no matter how oppressive and crazy* the law might be. Surely, no one wants to endorse this.

Since deterrence, by itself, is a flexible and consequence-oriented standard, it has often seemed naturally at home in a general utilitarian theory. At the extreme this would say that intrinsic values are commensurable and the standard of all right action is to simply to promote (most say 'maximize') intrinsic values. This implies that not only what citizens should do, but also the kind and degree of official punishment, depends entirely on what promotes utility in the particular circumstances. Since regular, pre-announced, public imposition of negative consequences for destructive conduct often deters repetition by others, punishments that effectively deter crime would often be recommended. Officials, however, must be ready to deviate from their usual policies, secretly if necessary, whenever making exceptions would best promote utility. Harsh punishment might be warranted for minor offences if it would frighten away most potential offenders, and grave offences might be treated lightly in special cases when the offenders were popular or had powerful allies. Clearly, Kant would reject both these exceptions and the basic act-consequentialist principle that could prescribe them.

A less orthodox consequentialism could grant that justice is an especially important value, but still not a value that *constrains* our attempts to promote the greatest good. The idea is that justice itself is a primary intrinsic value that should be maximized. In other words, while acting justly is in itself a good thing, our dominant aim should be to promote justice as much as possible, everywhere, in the long run.[35] In an imperfect world, we may need to do injustice now in order to promote just practices later. Here again is a mix of consequentialism and deontology that is obviously not Kant's position. It implies, for example, that *if*, however unlikely this might be, we could bring about a world of many fewer serious rights violations in the future by deliberately deceiving,

---

[35] David Cummiskey proposes a general 'Kantian' standard that is similar in structure to what I sketch here, though the good to be maximized in his account is not simply 'justice'. See his *Kantian Consequentialism* (New York and Oxford: Oxford University Press, 1996).

slandering, torturing, and murdering innocent people now, then it might be right to do so. Clearly, that is not Kant's mix.

Turning to the other extreme, what would a thoroughgoing *retributivist* theory of punishment be? Its standard for amounts and kinds of punishment might be *ius talionis*, as Kant presents this, but this is not the only possibility. An alternative might be: 'Punish in the way and the degree appropriate to the "inner deserts" of offenders,' a policy that requires us to take into account their characters, commitment to morality, obstacles, effort of will, etc. This alternative standard has as much claim to be 'retributive' as Kant's, if not more, even though it is incompatible with Kant's idea that public law should concern itself only with 'external' actions, eschewing attempts to assess the relative quality of the agents' motives, overall moral character, etc.

A theory does not qualify as thoroughly retributivist, however, simply by adopting either of these standards as the proper measure of degree and kind of punishment. We need to consider *why* it recommends the standard. Given a certain view of the empirical facts, even a utilitarian might recommend 'an eye for an eye' (or the 'inner desert' alternative) as the most efficient deterrent policy (given other countervailing utilities). That position would be what I call a mixed one. To be thoroughly retributivist, a theory must adopt *a deep retributive ground* for punishing and for meting out punishments by 'an eye for an eye' or any alternative 'retributive' policy. Possible grounding retributive principles might include the following, if they are treated as foundational principles: 'The virtuous should be happy, the wicked should be unhappy, each proportionately to their character,' or 'It is self-evident and basic that the unjust should suffer proportionately to the harm they cause,' or 'Independently of all further considerations, justice simply demands taking from wrongdoers an equivalent to what they have gained by their misdeeds,' or 'Everyone should be treated by whatever principles they employ in dealing with others.' Kant claimed none of these as a comprehensive basic principle, I believe, and there are other ways, consistent with Kant's basic principles, that his particular retributive policy regarding the amount and kind of punishment could be defended.[36]

For merely speculative purposes, it may be worth mention that such basic retributive principles might, after all, support particular punishment policies more flexible than Kant allowed, hence a 'mixed' theory

---

[36] This is not meant as an endorsement of Kant's policies regarding punishment, but merely as recognition that there are other possible strategies its defenders might employ.

with retributive first principles and different, more consequence-oriented working policies. For example, suppose a theory held as its basic principle that *inner evil should always suffer proportionately* and, by placing no further moral constraints on its application, the theory in effect endorsed any means whatsoever to promote that 'ideal' proportionality. The implications are horrifying to contemplate. For example, the theory might warrant (1) extra-legal vigilante efforts to make the wicked suffer, (2) intrusive court procedures to enquire into criminal's minds, motives, and character, (3) punishments proportional, not to overt harm wrongfully inflicted, but to (unreliably) court-estimated 'inner worth', (4) wide discretion for judges or juries to vary severity of punishment case by case for externally 'the same' crime, in order to adjust for the estimated degree of bad or weak will of the offenders, and (5) exceptions made to normal judicial rules and procedures in order to 'punish' the immoral friends and allies of the accused (by making these suffer vicariously). Kant was clearly opposed to these practices, and so his 'mix' of retributive and deterrence elements must have been of another kind.

In an article years ago, mainly concerned to note how little Kant's action-guiding principles ask us to assess the 'inner worth' of other people, I suggested that even Kant's theory of punishment was mixed, with deterrence and retributive elements, neither of which requires assessment of moral 'inner worth'.[37] The basic idea was that Kant endorsed deterrence of crime as the primary purpose of having a practice of punishment, but the practice itself, Kant thought, reasonably included policies and constraints commonly associated with retributivism.[38] But this sketch of a two-level theory left open troublesome questions. What *justifies* having a practice with such a purpose and such policies of implementation? Are the supposedly derivative 'retributive' policies plausibly justified as the most efficient way to carry out the aim of deterrence? What distinguishes *punishment*, so construed, from a mere behaviour control mechanism that employs regular, rule-governed, proportionate application of 'disincentives' to ensure a desired outcome? My account noted the important role of deterrence in Kant's justification of punishment in general and suggested that Kant's more specific 'retributive' policies might be ultimately justified by their deterrence value, but this last suggestion now seems to me implausible and,

---

[37] *Dignity and Practical Reason*, ch. 9.

[38] In sum, these policies and constraints were that all and only the guilty should be punished, offence and punishment are to be proportionate, *ius talionis* determines kind as well as degree of punishment, but all degrading punishments are forbidden.

in any case, it does not fully explain the retributive 'tone' of Kant's discussion.

More subtle and thorough mixed theories have been developed in recent years. Donald Scheid, for example, has developed the 'two-level' interpretation, following H. L. A. Hart's distinction between the particular rules of a practice and the justification for having the practice.[39] The idea is that Kant is only a partial retributivist because, although familiar 'retributive' formulas appear among the particular rules, the justifying aim of the practice of punishment is supposed to be deterrence. That is, *why* we punish in general is to deter crimes, but *how* and *whom* we punish is determined by retributive rules. This view of punishment is similar to 'rule-utilitarian' accounts.[40] The context, however, is more restricted, and the particular rules for distributing punishment need not maximize general utility but must merely serve the general aim of deterrence.

Sharon Byrd also attributes to Kant a subtle mixed account. Making use of legal ideas familiar in Kant's time, she distinguishes between two facets of punishment, namely, threat of punishment and execution of punishment. Regarding the former, she maintains that, according to Kant, the justifying aim (purpose, function) of threatening punishment is to prevent crime by providing deterring (non-moral) incentives for obedience to law. Punishment as threat 'was a tool in the hands of civil society to counteract human drives towards violating another's rights'.[41] Importantly, she shows how Kant grounded the right and duty of the state to use this 'tool' in the basic natural right to freedom, the corollary right (in a state of nature) to 'hinder hindrances to freedom', and authorization of the head of state to represent the united will of the people.

Byrd argues, however, that the execution of punishment is not guided by the aim of deterrence but rather 'by the demands of justice stated in the principle of retribution'. Thus the specific punishments threatened in the criminal law (for the purpose of deterrence) are supposed to be carried out without deviation simply 'because the actor violated the

---

[39] H. L. A. Hart, 'Prolegomena to the Principles of Punishment', in *Punishment and Responsibility* (New York: Oxford University Press, 1968), 1–27.

[40] Classic, but different, versions of rule-utilitarianism are expressed in John Rawls, 'Two Concepts of Rules', *Philosophical Review*, 64 (1955), 3–32, and Richard Brandt, 'Towards a Credible Form of Utilitarianism', in Hector-Neri Castañeda and George Nakhnikian (eds.), *Morality and the Language of Conduct* (Detroit: Wayne State University Press, 1963), 107–43.

[41] Byrd, 'Kant's Theory of Punishment', 151.

norm'. The intrinsic value of humanity as an end in itself constrains what punishments can be carried out (and so presumably also restricts the kind and degree of punishments that can be honestly threatened). This, according to Byrd, accounts for the upper limit on just punishments specified in the *ius talionis*: to deter future crimes by punishing a particular criminal more than the equivalence suggested by 'an eye for an eye' would be to treat him or her 'merely as a means'. Here a 'retributive' policy serves as a side-constraint limiting the amount (and kind) of punishment, since an unqualified aim of deterrence would sanction draconian punishment, whatever works best.

These more subtle attempts to mix the deterrence and retributive elements in Kant's writings, in my opinion, have made significant progress in ridding us of stereotypes about Kant's views on punishment. They raise questions, however, that should be addressed in a fuller discussion, which they deserve. For example, are the two levels (Scheid) or facets (Byrd) of punishment as separable as they suggest? If the need for credibility supports the carrying out of deterrent threats to punish, is it not necessary in deliberating about 'what to threaten' to consider antecedently 'what threats we can legitimately carry out'? Similarly, can reasonable deliberation about what threats to execute (without 'using' persons as mere means) proceed without taking into account whether, and how much, deterrent threats are needed to safeguard mutually just relations among citizens? Is not Kant's 'humanity formula', as a form of the Categorical Imperative, a basic moral assumption, governing both threats and execution of punishment and both justifying the practice and the rules of the practice?

The most important question, for present purposes, is this: Is the retributive 'tone' of Kant's discussion adequately captured by merely supplementing a general justifying aim of deterrence with side-constraints, or particular rules, that restrict judicial sentences to punishments that respect humanity and 'return like for like'? My suspicion is that, despite its merits, this way of mixing deterrence and retribution does not adequately distinguish systems of *punishment* from *other behaviour control systems* that employ threats to deter with various pragmatic or moral side-constraints on the execution of threats. Since, as Byrd rightly notes, the presumed injustice, and so moral wrongness, of criminal acts plays an important role in initially establishing a state right and duty to punish, it seems plausible that it would serve a further role in explaining *how* punishment deters and why punishment, as opposed to other control systems, is especially appropriate for the task. Emphasis on the expressive function of punishment, I suspect, would help answer these questions and so might serve as a reasonable supplement and partial modification of the mixed accounts of Scheid and Byrd.[42]

THE ELUSIVE RETRIBUTIVE ELEMENT

What accounts for the retributive tone in Kant's writing on punishment, besides the features cited by Byrd and others, is not that Kant assumed *as a basic premiss* the familiar 'retributive' slogans, such as that the wicked deserve to suffer, that the purpose of law is to satisfy victims' legitimate desires for vengeance, that law aims to restore the just balance of burdens and benefits among citizens that was upset by an act of injustice,[43] or that criminals must be 'taught a lesson' by being made to experience the harm they wrongfully inflicted on others.[44] Even though Kant insisted on a qualified version of the so-called 'law of retribution' (*ius talionis*) as the rule for determining how much to punish (and, when appropriate, how to punish), doing so does not make a theorist deeply retributivist. It depends on whether the theorist treats that law or rule as a fundamental, justifying reason for the practice of punishment or rather as a policy within the practice of punishment justified by some further end, such as crime reduction or the general welfare, or a more basic principle, such as the Categorical Imperative. Although Kant is no consequentialist in his fundamental principles, he did not, I believe, regard the law of retribution as an absolutely fundamental, self-standing moral principle, in need of no further justification. Rather, he accepted the familiar law of retribution in his system as an important but derivative policy to guide both legislators and judges. Along with other principles, it was to stand as a morally necessary feature of any practice of punishment that, as a whole, could be justified as fair, workable, and mandated (for imperfect human conditions) by the most fundamental principles of morality and justice. The only way to keep public punishments definite, 'unfluctuating', and free from 'extraneous considerations', Kant argued, is to be guided, in a manner sensi-

---

[42] The idea of 'the expressive function of punishment' is central in an influential article by Joel Feinberg, but I do not mean to suggest that Kant's account of punishment is just the same as Feinberg's. See Joel Feinberg, 'The Expressive Function of Punishment', in *Doing and Deserving* (Princeton, NJ: Princeton University Press, 1971), 95–118.

[43] See Herbert Morris, 'Persons and Punishment', *Monist*, 52 (1968), 475–501.

[44] See Jean Hampton, 'The Moral Education Theory of Punishment', *Philosophy and Public Affairs*, 13 (1984), 208–38.

tive to context, by the old formula, 'an eye for an eye,' which imposes on the criminal a pain or loss equivalent, in some sense, to the harm he or she wrongfully inflicted on others.[45] But this is not because inherently immorality (or criminality) should bring unhappiness or because we have a general duty to try to redistribute happiness and unhappiness so that, more nearly, the righteous prosper and the wicked suffer.

To the contrary, I suggest, the key to the elusive retributive element in Kant's thinking is to be found in certain background beliefs that Kant took for granted, either as conceptual truths or as ideas so widely acknowledged that they could be treated as a priori relative to other, more controversial matters.[46] These can be summarized as follows: punishment presupposes pain or deprivation inflicted *for* a legally defined *offence*: liability to punishment is presupposed by criminal law; criminal law is a necessary condition of civil society, which is, in turn, necessary for the possibility of fully just relations among citizens (as well as of any attainable approximation to perfect justice); and, by the Categorical Imperative, we have the moral right and the duty to institute and maintain the practices necessary, in this way, for justice. The point is not that returning harm for harm is inherently required by morality and reason; but that, for imperfect creatures like us, the constraints of public criminal law, in addition to those of conscience, are necessary to provide even the minimum conditions for just mutual relations, and an inherent part of criminal law is the practice of punishment, a constitutive element of which is expression of public disapproval of wrongdoing by deliberate infliction of undesirable consequences in response to overt injustices. To the offenders, and those who contemplate following them, the (just) law, on behalf of citizens, says in effect, 'Our wills, not just our feelings, resolutely oppose the sort of thing you have done (or are contemplating doing), and we express this to you, in language you can understand, by forcibly hindering you, the offender, in your

---

[45] Kant shows some sensitivity to context by ruling out types of punishment he regarded immoral in themselves (e.g. raping the rapist) and adjusting the sentence for 'verbal insult' for the rich person who would not mind the usual small fine. See MM, 106 [332–3] and 130 [363]. Readers will understand, I hope, that my aim in this paper is not to endorse Kant's views on punishment but merely to offer suggestions towards developing a coherent interpretation or reconstruction that makes sense of the variety of things Kant says about punishment. For example, although Kant shows some sensitivity to context in his remarks on punishment, my own view is that this is far from enough.

[46] The elusive retributive element is what is not so obvious as Kant's use of *ius talionis* (as a limited and derivative guide to distributing punishment) but none the less helps to explain the retributive 'tone' of Kant's comments.

manifestly chosen path of disregard for others' rights and by threatening the same, equally, to those who anticipate doing the same.'[47]

The practice of *punishment*, as distinct from other 'reward' and 'disincentive' programmes of behaviour control, is deeply, conceptually bound to vocabulary and procedures expressive of the disapproval of offences and the committed, active opposition to offences by those who authorize the practice, whether or not they are the directly inflicting agents (judges, juries, jailers, etc.). This inherent *function* of punishment is not a self-standing justification of particular acts of punishment, for the practice of punishment itself stands in need of justification. (All the more, that function cannot itself justify the practice of which it is a part.) However, when we add this function to other aspects of Kant's account of punishment, including the necessity of criminal law for civil society and thus for the possibility of justice, then we are closer to a mixed theory in which punishment is seen as necessary, required for justice, expressive of moral disapproval, even (I would argue) presumptively to be meted out *proportionately* to offence as well as imposed *equally* on like offenders, all this because it is necessary for justice rather than because it is a way to maximize utility or even minimize crime.

It is important to note that my suggestion is not that the ultimate justifying aim of punishment is to give citizens a desired opportunity to express their indignation. Such expression, according to the (reconstructed) argument, is a constitutive part of the practice of punishment, but this, again, is no final justification, because we can question why we have a right and duty to maintain the practice of punishment. That justification makes crucial reference to deterrence by providing reasonable disincentives to would-be law-breakers, but it is important, I think, to see that this reference does not make the theory in which it is embedded anything like what one naturally thinks of as a 'deterrence theory' or even a 'deterrence justification'. For example, there is no guiding

[47] The claim that punishment serves to express public disapproval does not deny that it must be established independently that the public has a right to inflict punishment, i.e. to impose pain or deprivation for offences and to do so in a manner expressive of public disapproval. Just because an act is worthy of disapproval, and punishment serves to express warranted disapproval, it does not follow that we are entitled to express our disapproval in this (pain-causing, or liberty-depriving) way. The title of the state to threaten punishment and then to carry out its threats must be justified, keeping in mind not only that punishment expresses public disapproval but many other factors as well, including the rights of the offender, the necessity of law-governed coercive responses, etc. My conjecture takes up the familiar idea that punishment does in fact serve an 'expressive function', but in no way do I suppose that Kant would consider punishment justified solely, or primarily, as a device to express public disapproval.

premiss, 'Adopt whatever practices maximally deter crime' or 'Adopt whatever practices efficiently deter crime at acceptable costs (by consequentialist cost–benefit standards).' There is not even an appeal to the premiss 'Adopt whatever practices are most likely ultimately to lead to perfect justice' or the premiss 'Adopt whatever practices are expected to maximize the amount of justice in the world (or to minimize the frequency and severity of acts of injustice).' Characteristically, Kant refused to rest the justification of so important a practice on fallible and controversial predictions of future outcomes, even if the outcomes themselves are evaluated in deontological terms (justice). Deterrence has its place, but like the law of retribution, a limited, derivative place, in the justification of punishment.[48] Several versions of the Categorical Imperative, the natural right to equal (external) freedom, the fundamental principle of *Recht*, its corollary legitimating coercion as a hindrance to hindrances of freedom, the argument for the authority of the state to represent citizens' coercive rights, and further unexpressed assumptions about fairness in the treatment of equal citizens—all these play crucial background roles in any full (reconstructed) argument that punishments should be carried out in the particular ways Kant endorsed.[49]

In any system of punishment that claims to be just it is presupposed that laws define what is an 'offence' in advance and also that offenders (and would-be offenders) had, or have, a fair opportunity to conform to the law by choice; otherwise, the moral disapproval of the offender for doing the act would be inappropriate. Its inappropriateness would not lie in any failure to deter or otherwise secure desirable consequences; it would stem from the fact that the unfair 'punishment' in effect *expresses a public falsehood* (and, if deliberate, a *deceitful, manipulative message*), namely, 'We hereby publicly disapprove what we take to be your wilful refusal to constrain yourself

[48] We can say, of course, that Kant thought that we threaten punishment 'in order to deter citizens from committing crimes', but this can be misleading unless we are careful to fill out the larger picture by explaining that the point of preventing crime is to secure the conditions necessary for just relations among citizens, that justice has to do with respecting each person's equal share of external liberty, and that the right and duty of government to punish in a regular, principled, non-manipulative manner stems ultimately from the Categorical Imperative rather than an aim to maximize some independent good (e.g. happiness or even liberty).

[49] These elements are acknowledged in Sharon Byrd's thorough scholarly tracing of Kant's ideas about punishment, and so my suggestions here may not be deeply incompatible with her reading of Kant. However, I worry that, even so, her exposition misleadingly suggests that the retributive aspect in Kant's theory is a mere side-constraint, limiting the amount of just punishment, and that the deterrence element functions as the primary aim and governing guide and justification, as in some of the quasi-deterrence views which I tried to distinguish from Kant's.

by the rights of others, despite a fair opportunity to do so; and the severity of your punishment reflects our understanding of the gravity of your offensive conduct.'

This is not to say that punishment is a practice that could justifiably be used to express our disapproval of *all* immorality, and the reason for reluctance to extend its use beyond public criminal justice is not simply that this would invite dangerous abuses of government power. As Kant rightly saw, much immorality inevitably is hidden from public view in so far as it consists of bad willing not (yet) expressed in overtly wrong acts of a kind amenable to control by criminal law. Partly because of its inherently moral message, punishment can fairly be employed only when (1) the offences are clearly discernible and can usually be detected, (2) a morally defective will can be inferred from the offence, (3) the severity of the offence can be meaningfully compared to the severity of other offences so that fair equality of 'like' treatment among citizens is possible, and (4) there is sufficiently strong reason to warrant (at least a limited[50]) 'public' moral judgement of disapproval despite the facts that, for the most part, maintaining a good will and seeking 'moral perfection' are the responsibilities of individuals to themselves and individual conscience serves to constrain and 'punish' each person for violations or neglect of (directly) 'ethical' duties.[51]

My conjecture has been that punishment, as opposed to non-punitive disincentive programmes, inherently serves to express the moral disapproval of the offence by the community, which I understand not merely as a negative feeling or abstract judgement but as the community's committed opposition to that sort of act. Given Kantian assumptions about the moral law within each minimally rational person, it is tempting to add that the message of disapproval is at the same time an appeal to

---

[50] Since, according to Kant, law deals only with 'external' conduct and does not prescribe moral motives, it cannot fairly express disapproval for anything but intentional acts of injustice (violations of right) indicative only of the fact that the offender had a sufficiently bad or imperfect will to choose to act unjustly when he or she could have done otherwise. Degrees of vice and virtue in the overall character of the offender, Kant thought, cannot be fairly assessed by law, nor can the depth of wickedness or defect of will be assessed without more knowledge of inner motives and character than the law can infer from the external acts subject to its review. We can punish proportionately to the 'severity' or 'gravity' of the crime only if these are measurable by something other than the degree of bad will that moved the offender, e.g. by the degree of harm or 'hindrance to liberty' the offender has wilfully inflicted on his victim by his act (or the degree typically inflicted by acts of that type). This, it seems, is more or less the degree to which reasonable freedom-loving citizens can be presumed to want to be protected (by a system of punishment) against offences of various kinds; e.g. protection against murder and rape is generally more important to us than protection against petty theft.

[51] See MM, 160–1 [400–1], 189–91 [438–40].

the criminal to join in that disapproval. It can serve, as much as anything, to touch the conscience of the offender, making more vivid the discrepancy between what the criminal has done and what he or she cannot help but acknowledge as the authority of the moral law.

Kant's concern to employ punishments that the criminal could not complain about receiving fits with this suggestion. What is important about such punishments, it seems, is not that they serve as a criterion of what we can legitimately do back to the criminal; for, as Kant admits, we cannot permissibly 'do back' to criminals the most heinous things they have perpetrated on others. Rather, the importance of giving a punishment about which the criminal could not complain (because it gives back what he or she willed, the equivalent, or less) would seem to be that this serves best to awaken the criminal's moral sensibility. For Kant, the point would not be to use the criminal's painful self-disapproval *merely* as a means to reform and so for reduction of future crime, though this might be a welcome benefit. Nor would the justifying aim be to bring about an alleged 'intrinsically good' state of affairs in which the wicked suffer pangs of conscience. Instead, it seems more a matter of respect for criminals as 'one of us' at heart, i.e. as persons capable of seeing and disapproving their guilty acts and also as human beings whom we have a right to treat harshly against their will only on the condition that they themselves, if informed and seriously taking up the moral point of view, would acknowledge the justice (and so approve) of what we do.

8

A Kantian Perspective on Political Violence

Immanuel Kant's position on the morality of violence has long been puzzling. That Kant is a strong and principled advocate of 'law and order' is clear; and any of the forms of the Categorical Imperative, especially the humanity formula, seem to provide basic arguments against murder, mayhem, kidnapping, rape, wanton destruction of others' property, and the like. By declaring human beings 'ends in themselves', the humanity formula seems to prohibit calculated 'trade-offs' in the lives of human beings, for ends in themselves are said to have dignity, an 'unconditional and incomparable worth' that 'admits of no equivalent'. This seems sharply opposed to any revolutionary scheme designed to sacrifice a few innocents now to save or enhance the lives of many in the future. In fact, upon first reading the *Groundwork*'s eloquent passages about persons as ends in themselves, many students assume that Kant was a pacifist. But, of course, he was not. Although he deplored war, Kant endorsed killing in a 'just' war. And, whereas we might expect him to deplore capital punishment, he is adamant in insisting that there must be no pardon, clemency, or even alternative punishment for murder.[1] No matter how idealistic the killer's motive may have been and even if, in the special case, no deterrent purpose is served, 'he who kills must die'.[2] If it is morally permissible to contribute to state-endorsed violence, in the case of capital punishment and just wars, one naturally wonders how Kant can justify this from his basic moral principles. Further, one cannot help but suspect that any argument to justify such (state-endorsed) violence would appeal to premisses that would also justify

---

[1] Kant admits two possible exceptions, neither of which is likely to win much sympathy for Kant as humane regarding issues of life and death. The cases deserving of death where courts nevertheless should not impose the death penalty are when a soldier kills another in a duel to defend his honour and when a mother kills her illegitimate baby (it is unclear whether Kant thought these fully deserved to be called 'murder'). In the case of a mother killing her newborn illegitimate infant, Kant reveals more (deplorable) cultural prejudice than humanity or good sense, saying that the infant 'has, as it were, stolen into the commonwealth (like contraband merchandise), so that the commonwealth can ignore its existence . . . and also its annihilation'. He adds, 'no decrees can remove the mother's shame when it becomes known that she gave birth without being married' MM, 108–9 [335–6].   [2] MM, 106–7 [333–4].

political violence in opposition to the state, at least in very special extreme circumstances. Yet Kant, as we know, insisted that participating in revolutionary activities is always wrong.

These tensions in Kant's views about the use of violence provide the background of my discussion, but, to simplify, I shall focus upon a limited set of cases of violence, concerned with politically motivated violence *against* one's government when it is perceived as being grossly unjust. There are several reasons for discussing Kant's position and arguments about this. First, of course, the matter is of some historical interest, for how we reconcile or explain the tension in Kant's views may shed some light on how to understand Kant's basic moral principles, his political philosophy, or both. Second, anyone aiming to develop the most plausible version of 'Kantian' moral or political philosophy needs to face up to the unresolved problems, contradictions, and tensions in Kant's actual work over many years. Such problems may in fact prove to be occasions for seeing more clearly modifications that need to be introduced into any plausible moral/political theory (broadly) in the spirit and tradition of Kant and his followers. Third, and perhaps most important, the tensions identified in Kant's work are likely to be reflections of deep conflicts in common moral debates independently of Kant's special terminology. If so, clarifying the issues and looking for a reasonable framework for addressing them within Kant's ethical and political writings may be suggestive of ideas of more general interest.

My plan is as follows. In the first section, I make a few comments to delineate what I take 'political violence' to be, at least for purposes of this paper. In the second section, I review briefly a sample of Kant's actual arguments against political violence and argue that these do not provide adequate reasons for the strong position he takes. In the third section, I discuss what is needed to derive answers from Kant's famous universal law formulation of the Categorical Imperative, suggesting that a reasonable application of it seems to rule out several extreme views on political violence, including Kant's own. In the fourth section, I review several problems with Kant's universal law formula that seem to persist even on a sympathetic reconstruction, and I suggest that Kant's humanity formula is in some respects a helpful supplement but cannot by itself serve as a moral decision procedure. In the fifth section, I sketch a working conception of Kant's basic moral point of view that draws on all of his formulas. Finally, in the last section, I consider briefly how one might develop this 'legislative perspective' as a framework for thinking about the issues of political violence, and I speculate about some of the principles that might emerge. In effect, my project is to take some preliminary steps towards seeing whether, despite Kant's own inadequate arguments regarding political violence, Kant's basic moral principles, more subtly developed and applied, might support a more reasonable, flexible policy regarding this.

THE IDEA OF POLITICAL VIOLENCE AND THE BEST-CASE SCENARIO

What is political violence? Violence in general typically connotes exertion of physical force tending to injure, damage, or abuse persons or things of value.[3] Paradigms of violence against people include bludgeoning, whipping, stabbing, shooting, and forcibly dragging someone against that person's will. There is also, of course, violence to animals, to personal property, to natural environments, etc. Often violence is a 'violation' of a legal or moral norm, as in assault, murder, mayhem, kidnapping, rape, torture, etc. But this is not always required, because boxing, bullfighting, and hockey, which celebrate certain violent acts, are widely thought to be morally and legally permissible. Often unquestioned approval of the end leads us withhold the epithet 'violent' from activities that otherwise might qualify: for example, the slashing of a surgeon's knife when (with full consent) he removes a live person's healthy kidney for transplant to save his brother's life.

Political violence, I take it, has a political purpose, for example, to win an election, to force repeal of a law, to discredit a political party, to bring down a government, to gain the power to make and enforce laws among a group. These cases, the ones of which *we* most naturally think, involve the use of violent means against prevailing government or official power. But there are, of course, instances of state use of vio-

---

[3] *Webster's New Collegiate Dictionary*, first entry for 'violence', 1306. The dictionary says '*so as to* injure or abuse', which suggests the intentional use of physical force as a means to injure or abuse. This does not seem appropriate for violent storms, the violent thrashing about of someone in an epileptic fit, wanton careless play with explosives, etc. But it is sufficient for present purposes that political violence is intentional, that it employs force known *to tend* to injure or abuse, and that its purpose is some political goal. Many extend the term 'violence' to severe mental abuse in order to draw attention to moral similarities between this and physical violence; but, without objecting to that practice, I shall restrict my discussion to physical violence. Some might quibble that one might do violence by blowing up an utterly valueless garbage dump, or some other thing 'without value', but my initial characterization of 'violence' was only meant to say what is 'typically' connoted. Surely, the typical case involves injury or damage to persons or property deemed valuable.

lence, some legal and some not, as in war, suppression of riots, public executions, private torturing of witnesses, forcible detention of criminals and suspects, breaking into citizens' personal files, etc. Needless to say, there is also international political violence of many kinds: conquest, temporary invasion to bolster or undermine a ruling party, sabotage, assassination of foreign rulers, terrorist activities, embargoes, etc. For the violence to be 'political', in each of these cases, I assume that the primary aim is not *merely* profit, revenge, personal grudge, and the like, but at least in part to gain or retain control of legal and political institutions, to express an ideology, to gain or assert a perceived right, etc. It would be difficult to characterize political violence precisely enough to remove all doubts about borderline cases, but that is neither a realistic standard nor a necessary one for present purposes.

In an earlier paper I discussed terrorism, which is a form of political violence, but my focus was explicitly and entirely on the extent to which a legitimate state can permissibly exercise counter-violence in response to the (stipulated) unwarranted violence of terrorists.[4] Now, however, I want to switch my focus to violence used *against the state*, rather than (as before) violence used *by the state*. To simplify, I will also set aside violence across national borders, concentrating instead on violence used by citizens within a state for political purposes at odds with their laws, government, or other controlling powers.

Just as it is easy, after many years, to celebrate successful political revolutions from which we have profited, it is also easy to overgeneralize hostility to political violence by focusing attention on random slaughter of innocent people by crazed ideological terrorists. Some cases are obviously easier to evaluate than others. Bloody, wasteful, ineffective terrorist horrors are already before our eyes on TV daily.

Since Kant takes an *extreme* stand on political violence, it may be useful to fix our thoughts on a relatively easy case that highlights how extreme Kant's actual position was. What would the opposite extreme be, *the best-case scenario* for political violence? In outline, I suppose, it would have these features. It would be politically motivated violence against property, without resulting in death, mayhem, or loss of vital resources. It would be directed against a government (or other political institution) that was deeply, persistently, and grossly unjust and oppressive, guilty of heinous past crimes against humanity and increasing in its power and resolve to continue on the same path. All non-violent

---

[4] See 'Making Exceptions without Violating the Principle: Or How a Kantian Might Think about Terrorism', in my *Dignity and Practical Reason in Kant's Moral Theory* (Cambridge: Cambridge University Press, 1991), 196–225.

avenues of reform would have been exhausted, all reasonable appeals and compromises rejected. There would be strong, convincing evidence that the proposed violence is both necessary and likely to be successful in producing favourable change. The protestors would be well intentioned, cautious in guarding against causing more damage than necessary. The property owners, the only ones liable to suffer significantly from the damage, would be corrupt, undeserving tyrants and their cohorts. A more just, less oppressive regime would very likely result from the change, and political stability based on respect for just laws would then become possible. Finally, the proposed violence may be easier to justify if the ruling regime's initial claim to authority was dubious on historical or moral grounds, though (for simplicity) let us assume the political violence is illegal.[5] This particular combination of circumstances, I admit, is an unlikely scenario; but it is not, like some philosophical 'counter-examples', an impossible or utterly fanciful one. The hard cases, of course, are not so one-sided. Cases become morally more difficult as this paradigm 'best case' for political violence is altered along various dimensions: predictable kinds of damage, degree of oppression, alternative means, likely effectiveness, stability of expected reform, the motives of the reformers, the desert of the victims, and clear title to legality of the regime and its laws.

KANT'S ACTUAL STAND ON POLITICAL VIOLENCE

In several late works Kant discusses rebellion, revolution, and resistance to civil authorities. His rigouristic position evoked severe criticism from his contemporaries, as well as later commentators. Arthur Schopenhauer considered it evidence of Kant's senility in his later years, and most sympathetic commentators have been puzzled and embarrassed by it ever since.[6]

The content of Kant's position is clear enough. One must not obey a state command to do what is evil in itself and so some 'passive resistance' to tyranny may be justified.[7] Non-violent criticism of unjust rulers

---

[5] Here I am obviously *not* working with a Thomistic account of 'law' according to which grossly unjust 'laws' are not even laws.

[6] Christine Korsgaard, I believe, is a notable exception. See 'Taking the Law into our Own Hands: Kant on the Right to Revolution', in Andrews Reath, Barbara Herman, and Christine M. Korsgaard (eds.), *Reclaiming the History of Ethics: Essays for John Rawls* (Cambridge: Cambridge University Press, 1997), 297–328.

[7] See, for example, MM, 98 [321–2] and 136–7 [371]; also Hans Reiss, 'Postscript', in Immanuel Kant, *Kant: Political Writings*, ed. Hans Reiss (Cambridge: Cambridge Uni-

is a right and something generally to be encouraged.[8] Although the outcomes of revolutions are always uncertain in advance, some revolutions seem to promote progress. There was much in the (so-called) Glorious Revolution of 1688, the American Revolution of 1776, and the French Revolution of 1789 to admire.[9] Contrary to Thomas Hobbes, Kant held that citizens have 'inalienable rights' that all rulers are morally bound to respect. The authority for coercive state power is 'the united will of the people'. Natural rights, independent of any conventions or geographic or political boundaries, constrain what any governmental authority may justly do. Practical reason, expressed in the Categorical Imperative and the universal principle of right, take precedence, morally and rationally, over any individual or group's commands.[10] Moreover, there is reason to hope and expect that even the most cruel and unjust wars, revolutions, and counter-revolutions throughout history will eventually contribute to gradual progress to world peace and just republican government.[11] All that is the good news.

But now for the bad news (which, of course, is not really *news* to those familiar with Kant's political writings). No matter how oppressive and tyrannical one believes the state authorities to be, one has no right to rebel, to resist violently or 'actively', or to conspire to rebel against a lawful ruling power. Unlike Aquinas and others, Kant does not recognize the gross injustice of ruling powers as a condition that can deprive them of 'lawful' authority. Again, no matter how self-serving, tyrannical, and murderous a regime may have been, neither present revolutionaries nor later legitimate authorities have any right to punish the villains. Despite a posthumous note hinting the contrary,

---

versity Press, 1991), 267–8. In R, 142 n. [154 n.], Kant says, 'When it is said [*Acts*, V, 29]: 'We ought to obey God rather than men,' this means only that when statutory commands, regarding which men can be legislators and judges, come into conflict with duties which reason prescribes unconditionally, concerning whose observance or transgression God alone can be the judge, the former must yield precedence to the latter.'

[8] MM, 95 [319]; 'Theory and Practice', in Reiss (ed.), *Kant: Political Writings*, 84–5.

[9] Kant reportedly asserted (falsely) that James II 'abdicated' and that the American Declaration of Independence does not affirm a 'right' to revolution. He also thought that Louis XVI 'voluntarily' yielded sovereignty to the Estates General and then abandoned his state. See Reiss (ed.), *Kant: Political Writings*, 262 and 182 ff., respectively. None of these 'glosses', however, retract Kant's main point, which is that it is always wrong, though sometimes beneficial, to rebel against legal state authority.

[10] MM, 23–33 [229–41]. However, Kant held that the fact that the ruler's laws are unjust, contrary to the natural rights of freedom and equality of citizens, does not authorize citizens to disobey those laws; it merely imposes a moral obligation on the rulers to repeal the laws: MM, 95–8 [318–23].

[11] See 'Contest of the Faculties', in Reiss (ed.), *Kant's Political Writings*, 184–90; 'Idea for a Universal History', ibid. 50–3; 'Perpetual Peace', ibid. 108–14 and 130.

Kant's persistent public position was that it is a perfect, juridical, enforceable duty, backed by moral law, that one do nothing active to overthrow or undermine a legitimate governing power; and his standards of what constitutes 'legitimate' state power (despite 'natural law') were virtually Hobbesian.[12] 'Right', or *Recht*, for Kant refers to *legitimately enforceable 'right'* which others have a moral and legal duty to respect; but it is clear that Kant intends to say, not only that one lacks a legally enforceable right to rebel but also that one lacks the *moral freedom* to rebel, no matter how tyrannical, oppressive, and murderous the lawful regime may be.[13]

Why does Kant take such an extreme stand? First, several preliminary points may help to make his defending an absolutist position more understandable, even though they do not justify it. One is that Kant's most vigorous condemnations of participation in revolution were written in the 1790s, when Kant was elderly and not long after the bloody Reign of Terror in France. These events, and the consequent international violence that followed, tended to solidify the conservative tendencies of peace-loving people throughout Europe; and it is at least to Kant's credit that, unlike many, he hailed the republican spirit of the revolution and welcomed it as contributing to progress in history (even though unlawful).

Further, Kant had the Enlightenment's optimistic faith, which he claimed to be grounded in reason, that progress towards more just republican governments (and eventually 'perpetual peace') could and *would* be achieved by the gradual overcoming of superstition, prejudice, and public foolishness by the increasing use of reason. Free speech, rational criticism, education, and public dialogue, he believed, were available, non-violent means to the improvement of political institutions. Reform would most likely come from the top down, not by violence from the masses against their lawful rulers.

This belief was nourished, of course, by a questionable style of moral argument. That is, pure reason can determine for us what our major duties are, independently of empirical investigation. This may make some sense when the 'duties' are in the abstract form of the Categorical Imperative, and the 'empirical' data to be set aside are descriptions

---

[12] MM, 93–8 [316–23]; Reiss, 'Postscript', in Reiss (ed.), *Kant: Political Writings*, 265; and Kant, 'Theory and Practice', ibid. 79–87.

[13] The duties in the *Rechtslehre*, or first part of MM, concerned with justice and law, Kant calls 'juridical duties'; but this does not mean that they are 'merely legal' duties, for in Kant's system all juridical duties are indirectly 'ethical duties' as well. For fuller explanation and references, see *Dignity and Practical Reason*, ch. 8.

of how people in fact behave, how warmly they feel about each other, etc. The procedure is highly dubious, however, when taken to mean that we can determine more substantive duties, e.g. about political affairs, without investigating empirically what our options are and how likely each is to achieve its intended result. Kant argues abstractly that it is our duty to seek peace, justice, and happiness for all deserving people, and, from 'ought implies can', he argues that these desirable ends are possible to achieve—or at least that we ought to believe so. It is a form of argument that makes pragmatic sense in some limited contexts but is obviously dangerous if it leads one generally to ignore strong evidence against the efficacy of our (would-be) dutiful efforts. 'Ought implies can' should cut both ways; from solid evidence that we cannot accomplish certain ends by certain means we should be able to infer that it is not our duty to do so, or even to try. I mention Kant's optimistic faith here, not to endorse it, but just as a factor that helps one see his thinking as more humane than it otherwise might appear.

Kant's main line of argument, however, reverts to Hobbes's arguments against divided sovereignty, though, significantly, Kant does not accept Hobbes's view that the head of state is not morally bound by standards of justice.[14] Rulers can and do commit heinous acts of injustice, contrary to the natural rights of the citizens; but still citizens have no right, legally or morally, to rebel. Here are some representative sample passages:

since a people must be regarded as already united under a general legislative will in order to judge with rightful force about the supreme authority, it cannot and may not judge otherwise than as the present head of state wills it to. (MM, 95 [319])

The reason a people has a duty to put up with even what is held to be an unbearable abuse of supreme authority is that its resistance to the highest legislation can never be regarded as other than contrary to law, and indeed as abolishing the entire legal constitution. For a people to be authorized to resist, that is, the highest legislation would have to contain a provision that it is not the highest and that makes the people, as subject, by one and the same judgment

---

[14] Thomas Hobbes's third law of nature, 'That men performe their Covenants made,' is for Hobbes 'the Fountain and Original of Justice'. This, of course, applies *in principle* to the sovereign as well as to anyone else, but in practice, since the sovereign is not bound by the social contract, it has virtually negligible force. The one case it might bind a sovereign is if, gratuitously, a sovereign made a promise the performance of which would not be harmful to himself and the other party has already fulfilled what they promised (so that suspicion of the other's non-compliance is not an issue). See Thomas Hobbes, *Leviathan*, i. 15.

sovereign over him to whom it is subject. This is self-contradictory . . . the people wants to be the judge in its own suit. (MM, 96, [320])

And even though this constitution may be afflicted with great defects and gross faults and be in need eventually of important improvements, it is still absolutely unpermitted and punishable to resist it. For if the people should hold that it is justified in opposing force to this constitution, however faulty, and to the supreme authority, it would think that it had the right to put force in place of the supreme legislation that prescribes all rights, which would result in a supreme will that destroys itself. (MM, 137 [372])

To unravel all the aspects of these, and similar, passages would require a long and detailed exegesis, which would not serve my purpose here. Commentators generally concede that Kant's arguments fail to establish his strong conclusion, and most of us, I suspect, will find that conclusion—to participate in revolution is *always* immoral—repugnant. So I will only remark on the arguments briefly before trying to develop a more promising *Kantian* 'perspective' for rethinking the issue. For this we need to turn back to basic elements in Kant's moral theory.

The background of the case against revolution is typical social-contract theory strategy, with some new twists. A state of nature, prior to legal order, would be a condition in which deeply self-interested (though potentially moral) people lived without security, trustworthy agreements, and the opportunity to develop as rational, autonomous, mutually respecting human beings. In a state of nature they would lack rights (*Recht*) actually enforceable, but they would have proto-rights (or 'ought-to-be' *Recht*) determined by the rational ('natural law') principles of freedom, equality, and independence. The fundamental principle of justice is 'So act externally that the free use of your choice can coexist with the freedom of everyone in accordance with a universal law.'[15] This carries as a necessary corollary the idea that violations of the principle may and should be prevented; so coercion is warranted as 'hindrance to hindrances of freedom'.[16] If one were in a state of nature, one would have a moral obligation, not merely a pragmatic reason, to join with others (forcing them, if necessary) to enter a civil order. How that actually comes about is of little significance. No political conclusions are drawn, for example, from an alleged actual or tacit 'promise' to obey the ruling powers. What matters is the 'idea' of a state, once established, as resting on the 'united will of the people' authorizing the de facto ruling power to make and enforce laws on their behalf.[17] Like Hobbes,

---

[15] MM, 24 [231].   [16] MM, 25 [231].

[17] MM, 89–95 [311–19]; 'Theory and Practice', in Reiss (ed.), *Kant: Political Writings*, 73–87.

Kant believed that the only alternative to the unacceptable lawlessness of a state of nature, where individuals judge for themselves when to use force, would be a political state in which every question of ('external') liberty and coercion can be answered determinately, unambiguously, and effectively by a powerful authority presumed to be acknowledged by all citizens. Kant's belief was not based entirely on empirical grounds, for he argued that the very idea of a legal order presupposed the existence of a supreme authority, the judgements of which must be treated as definitively binding and taking precedence over the judgements of everyone else.

The influence of both Hobbes and Jean-Jacques Rousseau is evident here, an unhealthy mix. Like Rousseau, Kant held that we must act under the idea that (it is just as if) all citizens together, in a social contract, irrevocably submit their private wills to the authority of the 'general will' of the people. This, then, provides the standard of justice for laws, for the general will is supposed (perhaps by definition) to be always aimed at the 'common good'. In effect, Rousseau construed the general will as what citizens will, or would will (e.g. by voting), if fully public-spirited, concerned for the good of each and all, not making factual errors, not distracted by divisive parties, religious superstitions, and envy generated by gross inequalities of wealth.[18] But, like Hobbes, Kant also supposes that a necessary condition of lawful order is that there must be a concrete person (or group), a head of state, that is presumed always to judge and speak unambiguously for the united will of citizens.[19]

Given this set-up, it seems there can be no lawful resistance to the head of state; for 'lawfulness' requires the backing of the united will of the people, and that is presumed already vested in the head of state that revolutionaries propose to resist. But if, on the one hand, we understand the 'united will' (with Rousseau) *as an ideal moral standard*, then why should we suppose that this can be identified with the *actual legislation of any real person or group*? People are obviously fallible, and often corrupt; and it is foolish to presume, or act under the idea, that it is otherwise.[20] If, on the other hand, the 'united will' is not

---

[18] See Jean-Jacques Rousseau, *The Social Contract*, tr. Donald Cress (Indianapolis: Hackett Publishing Co., 1988).

[19] I say 'unambiguously' to contrast with Rousseau, who seems to shift between an idealistic and a concrete idea of a general will.

[20] My complaint here is of a piece with my claim in several papers that Kant has a tendency to 'utopian' thinking, in the sense of drawing illegitimate conclusions about how we, in our imperfect world, should act from accounts of how more ideal persons, in more ideal conditions, would act. See my *Dignity and Practical Reason*, esp. ch. 4, 'Kant's Utopianism'.

understood as an ideal of justice but is a mere label for the habits of obedience and acceptance citizens have accorded to their de facto rulers, then why, we wonder, should the fact that revolution would contravene the united will of the people provide any decisive moral reason against revolution?

Kant thinks it is 'self-contradictory' to suppose that one could justly, i.e. with legally enforceable right (*Recht*), will a general policy of undermining, for any reason, the political condition necessary for there to be full-fledged justice and (legally enforceable) rights. Given Kant's strong definition of *justice* and *rights* (as tied to enforceability by an absolute and undivided authority), his claim seems plausible. It does seem absurd to suppose that one could have a *legally enforceable* right to destroy the only available mechanisms for legally enforcing anything.[21] This, however, is a very limited conclusion, depending on Kant's very special definition of justice and rights. That is, it depends on Kant's construing what I called 'full-fledged' justice and rights (*Recht*) as presupposing the presence of an actual undivided ruling power to enforce the law. Neither this special definition nor the limited conclusion that follows implies that it is always *immoral*, or even *unjust* (in a non-technical sense), to try to destroy the de facto 'legal' system in one's country. Moreover, in discussing both the foundations of morality and the idea of a pre-legal society, Kant himself acknowledges the validity of moral standards, backed by reason, independent of any legal system. So, although more remains to be said, it looks from our brief sampling of Kant's arguments that it should have remained an open question for Kant whether it is ever *morally right*, and just (in a non-technical sense), to rebel violently against a tyrant.

KANT'S UNIVERSAL LAW FORMULA

If one finds Kant's basic ideas about moral deliberation plausible, or at least promising, but rejects his attempts to justify his rigid stance on

[21] To make the argument tight, some further qualifications may be needed. For example, can we imagine a legal system that allowed a 'liberty' right *to try* to destroy the legal system if but only if one was thoroughly conscientious and convinced on apparently good evidence that the system had a legally unrevisable, but in fact easily replaceable, constitution that was oppressive to many and injurious to almost all? Here I am not supposing that the system acknowledges that the conscientious revolutionaries have a 'claim right' to the system's full protection and cooperation in its revolutionary activities. That would be absurd. But is it inconceivable that the system could acknowledge their limited *liberty* right by laws providing that unsuccessful revolutionaries, once stopped and arrested, can legally avoid punishment if they can prove the 'justifying conditions' obtain (i.e. they were 'thoroughly conscientious', had 'apparently good evidence', . . .)?

obedience to law, then one must go back again to the basics of Kant's theory, suitably reconstructed, in an effort to rethink the more specific issue for ourselves. This is a large project, and here I can only sketch briefly how such an account might go.

Textbooks unfortunately treat Kant's formulations of the Categorical Imperative as if they could easily be 'applied' separately as a decision procedure to answer all questions about whether a particular act is right or wrong. In the *Groundwork*, Kant encouraged this optimism, at least with regard to the formulas for which he supplied brief examples.[22] But the examples in the *Groundwork* have a very limited, illustrative purpose, and appear almost as a digression in the main course of argument. When Kant turned to 'applications' of the basic moral law in a systematic and serious way, i.e. in *The Metaphysics of Morals* and political writings, he presents a more complex picture. The humanity formula is appealed to much more than the universal law formula, maxims are less prominent, general empirical and teleological assumptions about human nature bear much weight, the idea of hypothetical ideal agreement serves a guiding function, the moral relevance of current practices is acknowledged, types of duty are more finely divided, and an important priority is developed of (legally enforceable) considerations of justice over (non-enforceable) matters of virtue. This late work is hardly a model of clarity and rigorous argument, and, as we have seen, it contains some quite unconvincing arguments for untenably rigouristic stands. Nevertheless, it provides precedents for some flexibility in applying Kant's basic moral ideas as well as some clues about complexities that need to be taken into account. In what follows, however, I am influenced by this later work but do not attempt to give detailed textual exegesis.

Let us turn briefly to Kant's famous universal law formula.[23] Although few would deny that some important moral concern lies behind Kant's formula, the difficulties of using this as a moral decision procedure have been repeatedly pointed out by critics. Kant's defenders have shown great ingenuity by 'interpreting' or supplementing the formula to meet the objections, but none, as far as I can tell, has been fully successful. The basic problem, of course, is that the formula proposes to assess the morality of acts by submitting the 'maxim' of each act to a test,

---

[22] G, 70 [402], 89–91 [421–4], 95–8 [427–30].

[23] Here I shall speak loosely of 'the universal law formula', without pausing to distinguish what Paton calls formulas I and Ia, the latter referring explicitly to 'universal laws of nature'. The interpretations of both, and their relations, are unbelievably diverse, but I hope that my general remarks will make some sense in abstraction from these scholarly controversies.

involving a thought experiment; and, though the outcome depends upon the maxim description, we lack sufficient standards for determining, independently of moral intuition, how to describe maxims in a morally relevant way. Many familiar counter-examples to Kant's formula can be met by insisting that the 'real' or 'relevant' maxim is something other than the critic supposed. But if defenders of the formula repeatedly fend off alleged counter-examples by redescribing the maxims initially proposed, we naturally suspect that they are simply rewriting the maxim description with a view to achieving an outcome that is more intuitive or in accord with other (unmentioned) aspects of Kantian theory. Now I think there need not be anything wrong with supplementing the procedure in this way so long as the supplementary proposals are up front and defended. Until recently, however, that has rarely been the situation.

Although in the end I will suggest that we turn to a later formulation of the Categorical Imperative for purposes of application, let us consider for a moment how the universal law formula, under a sympathetic interpretation, would treat our problem of political violence. The relevant maxim is not simply 'the maxim of political violence' or even 'the maxim of using violence for political purposes'.[24] These allude vaguely to a type of activity on which one might have a policy, or maxim, but they are not stated explicitly *as a policy* that one could follow. We need to ask, what policy is meant? Is it the policy of *always* using violence to achieve political ends? That is unlikely. How about the willingness to use violence for political ends *sometimes*? That tells us something about the agent's dispositions, and Kant would no doubt require that one be ready to universalize that willingness; but it says too little to be plausibly regarded as the maxim that guides and explains a particular act. (Compare: Could 'I am willing to go to Texas sometime' be the policy I am acting on when I book a trip to San Antonio?) Maxims need to be stated definitely enough to make sense of what agents see themselves as doing, *and why*. Typically this requires some finer specification of the details of one's circumstances, features that make sense of one's engaging in described activity now but not at certain other times. For example, a maxim might be 'to use violence to achieve my political goals if the goals are of very high priority and the violent means are necessary, likely to be effective, and predicted to cost me nothing comparable to failing to achieve my goal'.

---

[24] This, I find, is a very common tendency among students, and unfortunately it is encouraged by Kant's occasional loose reference to maxims as 'the maxim of lying' etc.

This is not to say, by the way, that a policy or maxim *must* include a *detailed specification* of circumstances, for a maxim can simply refer to *all* possible circumstances at once. For example, Kant's 'maxim of self-love' (in the *Critique of Practical Reason*) is presumably the policy '*always* to do what best serves my own happiness'. My objection above to stating a maxim of political violence in this simple form was not that this would make the policy too indefinite, but rather that it is unrealistic to suppose that *anyone*, no matter how reckless, has the unqualified policy '*always* to use violence to achieve political ends, no matter what the circumstances'; for there are often easier, less costly, and more likely effective means to achieve the same ends. To be realistic, anyone seriously engaging in a conscientious effort to use Kant's guideline to determine what he or she ought to do will recognize, upon a little thought, that there are many morally relevant features of the various circumstances in which political violence might be used. As Barbara Herman points out, if there is any hope of evaluating the morality of our proposed acts by testing their maxims, then we cannot expect that the first act-description that pops into mind will be the (morally) most relevant way to express one's maxim.[25] Arriving at the best account of one's maxim may require prior deliberation, reflection on one's other moral commitments, rethinking when one's first attempts produce bizarre results, etc. (This need not render the test empty or worthless, but it requires abandoning faith in the formula as a simple moral decision procedure, independent of all other moral considerations.) On reflection, I assume, anyone seriously supposing that they can justify political violence in a particular case will have a maxim of the form 'I will use violence to achieve my political end if . . . and . . . and unless . . . and . . .'[26]

Similar remarks apply to maxims of lying. That is, (1) 'I will lie sometimes' is too indefinite to be a maxim, (2) 'I will never tell a lie' is a possible maxim but, despite Kant's example, it is not a maxim that accurately reflects a policy that most people act on (or endorse on reflection), and (3) 'I will lie if . . . and . . . unless . . . and . . .' is the form of the maxims regarding lying that most of us act on and so should be testing.[27] This is not to say, however, that the appropriate maxim to test

[25] Barbara Herman, *The Practice of Moral Judgment* (Cambridge, Mass.: Harvard University Press, 1993), esp. chs. 7 and 10.

[26] I do not mean to imply, of course, that every such maxim will have exactly two 'if' clauses and two 'unless' clauses.

[27] I realize, of course, that Kant himself referred to maxims in many vague ways and seemed not to take seriously enough the possibility of 'building into the maxims' exceptions and conditions that honestly form part of our policies.

is always the most fully specified maxim. That proposal, unless supplemented carefully, leads to all sorts of familiar problems.[28]

Various qualifications are needed to avoid other problems as well. It seems clear, for example, that maxims, as policies that one actually anticipates acting on, cannot include reference to facts of the situation, descriptions of the act, or underlying motives that are completely beyond the awareness of the agent. Suppose a person is ignorant of the fact that she is about to shoot at a bear (instead of a deer), that both bear hunting and deer hunting are illegal, and that she is driven to hunt by an unconscious need to rebel against her vegetarian father. Although these facts may be relevant to the 'objective rightness' of her acts, the person's maxim could not contain any reference to these facts.[29] As Onora [O'Neill] Nell points out, this limits the application of the maxim-testing procedure to what some call 'subjective rightness', or doing what good moral judgement prescribes on the basis of the facts as the agent perceives them.[30] Furthermore, the factors that count as making one 'unable to conceive or will' a maxim as universal law need to be circumscribed. For example, the contingent impossibility of everyone breast-feeding their infants or having genuine French champagne for their anniversaries seems irrelevant to the moral permissibility of

[28] Consider, for example, the maxim to tell a lie to a short, bald, obese, freckled-faced tourist on a full moon Tuesday at 2:37 p.m. If one is willing to lie to such a tourist in the first place, then it seems one should find it easy to will the universalization of this maxim. That everyone be willing to lie to such a person on such an occasion imposes no realistic constraint on the agent, beyond the case at hand, for the issue is unlikely to arise again. But the process of universalizing this maxim turns on factors that are irrelevant both morally and to the agent's formation of the intention. Because of these and other, less obvious but serious problems, Onora O'Neill changed her proposed reconstruction of Kant's test from a test of relatively specific, context-definite maxim-descriptions in her first book to a test of quite general, life-guiding 'ground' maxims in a more recent book. (See Onora [O'Neill] Nell, *Acting on Principle* (New York: Columbia University Press, 1975) and *Constructions of Reason* (Cambridge: Cambridge University Press, 1989).) Herman, in *The Practice of Moral Judgment*, favours applying the test to quite specific maxims (as well as, in the process of deliberation, to some quite general ones), but she requires that the details must be morally relevant and spends considerable effort trying to work out how one can determine moral relevance.

[29] What is 'objectively right' may be thought of, roughly, as what good moral judgement would prescribe on the basis of knowledge of the facts as they actually are (whether known to the agent or not). In some theories, the idea of the objective right has priority; e.g. in utilitarianism typically, the objective right is what maximizes utility whereas the subjective right is what the agent judges, from her perception of the facts, will maximize utility. For Kant, arguably, the subjective right is the prior notion. That is, the objectively right act is not defined as the achievement of a certain outcome (like maximum utility) but rather as something like the convergence of what rational moral judges would prescribe if they understood the facts correctly.

[30] Nell, *Acting on Principle*, 112–17.

these policies. Similarly, individual psychological peculiarities may be irrelevant. What matters is not so much what one *happens to like* for everyone to do but rather what one *can reasonably will* as a policy for everyone.

This qualification is crucial for purposes of averting a wide range of counter-examples, but of course it introduces (or exposes) a respect in which the universal law formula itself is indefinite and open-ended. Any plausible reconstruction needs to draw on other aspects of Kant's theory to fill out the conception of 'reasonable willing'.[31] These aspects in fact are not neatly drawn together in any one place, but are progressively revealed in later formulations of the Categorical Imperative as well as in other discussions. That *reason*, in the broad sense required for morality, requires autonomy and acknowledges humanity in each person as an end in itself is an assumption that is especially important even though it is only implicit when the universal law formula is first introduced. As John Rawls suggests, what reason, in this broad sense, 'can' and 'cannot will' may be best determined from a perspective that abstracts from various personal differences among individuals.[32] For example, the fact that a person is rich, old, self-sufficient, and obsessed with independence are special circumstances that should not be allowed to fuel his self-serving argument that he 'can reasonably will' a universal policy of refusing to give aid to the needy. The relevant conception of rational or reasonable willing is not *simply* efficiency or instrumental reason.

A further point to keep in mind is that one's aim as a rational and morally conscientious deliberator is not simply to find a maxim that appears reasonable as universal policy when considered by itself, in isolation from other maxims, against a background of institutions and norms taken for granted without question. One should be looking for a consistent and coherent set of revisable policies, at various levels of generality, with (ideally) each considered and, if need be, modified in the light of the others, with a broad view of the facts relevant to the whole set. A universal maxim that appears reasonable as a part of one set may not be when considered as a part of another set, and universal maxims that would be acceptable against one background of existing

---

[31] This in effect is what Herman attempts in her very rich and stimulating work, *The Practice of Moral Judgment*, and the same can be said for reconstructive efforts of Christine Korsgaard, Onora O'Neill, Thomas Pogge, and others.

[32] John Rawls, 'Themes in Kant's Moral Philosophy', in Eckhart Forster (ed.), *Kant's Transcendental Deductions* (Stanford: Stanford University Press, 1989), 86f. Herman, however, rejects this interpretation; see *The Practice of Moral Judgment*, 50–2.

social institutions and norms might not be so when applied to a differ-ent setting. Because of this, one's first stab at forming and universaliz-ing a maxim should not be taken as definitive, especially if its outcome is intuitively bizarre or suspicious. Finding that one cannot will a certain maxim as a universal law, one needs to ask why and consider, in a larger context, whether the blocking factor is morally significant. Or, finding that one apparently can universalize a maxim on the first try, one needs to ask whether one's ability to do so depends on one's having taken for granted some morally dubious social conditions or attitudes that should be reformed.[33] There are at least two implications of this. The first is that we need to abandon any pretence that the universal law formula, by itself, is a simple, foolproof moral decision procedure that can crank out answers, case by case, independently of all other moral considera-tions. The second implication is that, if the universal law formula is workable at all, it is to be expected that one will first apply the test to an initial maxim and then go back, perhaps again and again, to rethink and reformulate the maxim in the light of many factors, including one's other maxims, until one finally reaches a statement that both (1) reflects an honest understanding of what one proposes to do and (2) expresses a policy that one conscientiously judges to be reasonable for the cir-cumstances for anyone, despite whatever countervailing moral consid-erations there are.[34] I used to think that the practice of 'backing up' to reformulate one's initial maxim until one finds an acceptable one was subject to two objections: that it always revealed a reliance on moral 'intuition' contrary to the alleged role of the universal law formula as

[33] What I say here owes much to Herman's *The Practice of Moral Judgment*.

[34] One obstacle to using the 'back-and-forth' procedure suggested here, I suspect, is that Kant's statement of the test seems to suppose that each act has exactly one maxim, which is 'the' relevant description of what one does on an occasion. Perhaps, too, con-centrating on the assessment of *past* acts might lead one to suppose there must be a simple fact of the matter, even if we do not know it, whether 'the maxim' was *this* or *that* specified policy. But the main point of Kant's formulations of the Categorical Impera-tive, with regard to applications at least, is to guide conscientious deliberation prior to action. Here it is important to review a number of possible maxims on which one might act, rejecting or modifying them until one can find some honest account of how one sees what one is prepared to do and why, fully reflective of what one knows to be morally relevant, such that one can reasonably endorse that policy for anyone. If one cannot find such an account, or can only 'construct' an acceptable maxim by omitting reference to relevant factors one 'wishes' to overlook, then one must not do the sort of thing one ini-tially proposed. In other cases, upon finding a modified, honest, acceptable universal maxim, one may do that sort of act, or something quite similar, but only on the under-standing that it is because of some unusual distinguishing factors. Here the latter act would be permitted but the case might not be a useful precedent for further cases that are similar in many salient ways. This complex procedure in no way provides all the morally relevant materials for solving the problem of diverse maxim descriptions; it just gives the search a certain form.

a guide and that it opened the way for us to 'tinker' with our maxim description, from self-serving motives, in a bad-spirited effort to 'justify' what we suspect is morally wrong. But now it seems clear that the requirement of 'conscientious' reflection, 'reasonable' from a perspective abstracting from personal advantages, largely takes care of the second problem; and the 'back-and-forth' procedure of reformulating maxims is essential in order to have any hope of taking into account all the morally relevant factors. If an act appears to be forbidden under one morally relevant act-description, e.g. 'breaking a promise to a good friend', then it still may be permissible under another, more complex maxim that takes into account this factor as well as another, e.g. 'stopping to save an accident victim, despite breaking a promise to a good friend'. Determining which is the relevant description is no easy task, but there are reasonable ways to begin to think about this.

Now although there is much more that needs to be said on these interpretative matters, let us return to our initial problem to see what guidance, if any, we might draw from a sympathetic reading of the universal law formula. What seems fairly clear, at least, is that two extreme policies regarding political violence would prove unacceptable. Consider first the maxim, 'I shall never engage in violent resistance, rebellion, or revolution against the ruling powers in my state, no matter how tyrannical and oppressive they may be' (Kant himself in MM apparently accepted something like this).[35] Suppose we apply this to an instance of 'the best-case scenario' described earlier. Imagine: Horrible, persistent oppression and arbitrary rule persist, including incessant torture, killing, and debasing of both citizens and foreigners. All peaceful avenues of reform have been exhausted. A conspiracy of just and moderate citizens to replace the ruler without legal authorization is already under way, and this is clearly necessary and is likely to establish a more just, stable, and responsive regime. Almost certainly the only violence necessary to carry out the coup is minor property damage (e.g. breaking down doors) and forcibly removing the ruler and a few equally guilty henchmen.[36] Now, assuming that alleged a priori proofs to the contrary fail (as argued earlier), surely

---

[35] I am supposing here that Kant's concession that we must not obey state orders to do what is immoral in itself was not meant to sanction *violent* resistance, but perhaps one can imagine cases where passively refusing an order to do something in itself immoral is not an option. It depends on what turns out to be 'immoral in itself', I suppose. For example, if doing nothing violent to stop a murder that one could prevent is immoral in itself, then one would have to *violently* resist a state order not to interfere with the murder. See the last chapter.

[36] Obviously, to make the particular negative point I want to make, further conditions could be added. The point is that the absolutist policy almost certainly cannot be justified for all conceivable conditions. And, given this, we must pay attention to the many morally relevant variables.

in these conditions any reasonable person, with a basic understanding of what is morally relevant, could not will the absolutist maxim against all violent resistance, rebellion, and revolution.

Again, I should stress that the point here is not to suggest that revolutionary violence is justified *only* in this (admittedly extraordinary) situation that I call 'the best-case scenario'. Focusing briefly on this case is useful just because it only takes a little reflection on an example like this to cast doubt on Kant's attempt to cover all instances of revolution and political violence, no matter how distinct, under the same undiscriminating prohibition. The lesson is that we must be sensitive to various morally relevant dimensions of different circumstances. Once this is acknowledged and it is clear that we cannot morally assess all cases at a single stroke, then the long, arduous task of distinguishing the range of cases where the relevant factors are decisive against political violence from those where such violence is justified can begin in earnest.

The other extreme maxim I want to mention, for contrast, is this: 'I shall engage in political violence whenever it will result in more justice as well as more utility.' Although this leaves a range of cases undetermined (when justice and utility conflict), it is sufficiently determinate to count as a maxim on which an agent could act. The problem, however, is that the maxim hides the morally relevant factor that, as fallible agents, we never know with much certainty that an attempted revolution will in fact result in more justice and utility—and we know this. The truth is that, though one may feel quite confident of one's predictions, from the deliberative standpoint one always acts on fallible estimates of consequences. So, to reflect this, the relevant maxim, it seems, needs to read something like this: 'I shall engage in political violence *whenever I estimate it likely* (to degree . . .) to result in more justice and utility.' This is not an insignificant change. If one universalizes the former, unqualified maxim, then the possible worlds one imagines when trying to conceive the maxim as a universal law are necessarily worlds of greater justice and utility; but if one universalized the second, qualified maxim, the possible worlds one imagines must include many in which well-meaning revolutionaries generate nothing but disaster for themselves and others. One cannot reasonably suppose that one is an infallible judge of the consequences of political violence while others may be mistaken. The relevant consequences are what would happen if ordinary, well-meaning, but often mistaken folk followed the maxim, not what would happen if one were infallible and were allowed to declare for everyone else when revolutionary efforts will turn out for the best. When one takes seriously the constraint of endorsing the maxim for *all others who will estimate outcomes for themselves*, the upshot is a strong moral pressure to be cautious and carefully qualified in constructing one's maxim regarding political violence. History celebrates the good effects of a few famous successful revolutions, but it also records the horrors and injustices following other well-meant attempts, some failed and some 'successful'.

Let me mention briefly a possible objection, even though it is not persuasive in the end. A defender of Kant's absolutism, perhaps still partly influenced by Kant's a priori arguments against revolution, might argue as follows: 'In your universalizability argument above you assume the context of ongoing states and civil order, but we need to go back to the idea of a state of nature. About this Hobbes was mostly right, though he failed to recognize that persons in a state of nature would have moral, as well as prudential, reasons to establish a civil order with an absolute prohibition on rebellion. Given the lawless conditions of a state of nature and the untrustworthy nature of human beings in such a condition, the only way they can escape that condition and create the political conditions necessary for higher moral relations is for all to surrender completely and irrevocably the right and power to make and enforce judgements of justice to a civil authority. Since that would be the rational will of all people in such a condition, it is as if all had jointly made a social contract to obey the powers that be. In a state of nature, everyone's acceptance of policies that allowed them to resist or rebel *under conditions that they were left to judge* would not in fact generate the stability needed and so, despite the dangers of tyranny, they would rationally accept the policy of no rebellion.' Continuing the objection, Kant's defender might note that the previously sketched universalizability argument for allowing rebellion in certain extreme conditions ignored this (morally) prior (hypothetical) agreement. By treating the issue of rebellion without prior examination of how legal authority could arise from a lawless world, that argument failed to take account of the fact that the very existence of the state derives from that prior authorization.

Now this argument seems parallel to one a Hobbesian might give (on a certain reading of Hobbes), namely, an appeal to the fact that, as a subject in an ongoing state, one has already made an irrevocable commitment to yield to the sovereign's laws and judgement (except for immediate self-defence).[37] But there are serious problems in borrowing

---

[37] Notoriously the self-defence exception in Hobbes is no constraint on the sovereign, and it apparently applies only to fairly imminent lethal attack, which death-averse human beings cannot be expected not to resist.

this argument. For one thing, it presupposes the moral possibility of unconditionally binding promises; for another, it relies on Hobbes's dubious ideas that promises under duress are still morally binding and that later generations, long after the initial institution of sovereignty, implicitly authorize the sovereign to act for them. Moreover, the idea of a social contract in Kant is not a real promise but a fictional idea that serves certain heuristic purposes. Not having been party to a state of nature, actual citizens today have not actually made the alleged prior commitment. Even if it were a rational commitment to make given the special conditions of a state of nature, it is a commitment at best that is now open to reconsideration. Further, rather than reaffirm such an absolute commitment, anyone living in a more civilized world would be reasonable to consider commitment to more cautious, carefully qualified policies regarding resistance and rebellion. For it is far from clear that the only possibility of regaining civil order, upon removal of a tyrant, is for all to pledge never to resist civil authority or engage in political violence under any conditions. Kant, like Hobbes, seemed to assume, falsely, that all anarchy, however brief, is equally bad and that living in civil order for generations will make no deep difference to how people will act. That is, when they are in a transitional period between the fall of one lawful authority and the establishment of a new one, they will act the same way as they would in a pre-social state.[38]

REMAINING PROBLEMS AND THE FORMULA OF HUMANITY AS AN END IN ITSELF

So far I have considered some problems in applying Kant's universal law formula, made some suggestions about how some of these problems might be addressed, and argued merely that, on a reasonable construal, it seems that the universal law formula would warrant neither Kant's *absolute prohibition* on political violence against the state nor any *very permissive, unqualified policy* of using such violence as a means to promoting utility and justice. But there remain many problems with using the universal law formula, problems sufficiently serious to encourage Kantians to turn their attention instead to the prospect of constructing a combination of Kant's formulas. Prominent among these problems is

---

[38] I think here of Kant's idea that human nature is like a crooked piece of wood, which can never be made straight, so that the best we can hope for is that social structures (and so human *behaviour* in society) improve, not that people over time become morally better. See 'Idea for a Universal History', in Reiss (ed.), *Kant: Political Writings*, 46–7.

that, although the universal law formula implicitly asks what maxims we can *rationally* will as universal law, it does not itself specify the sense or standards of rationality that we are supposed to use. Both context and outcomes suggest that we are *not* to rely merely on means–end or instrumental rationality, with no rational constraints on permissible ends. Other aspects of Kant's stronger, moralized conception of *reason* are only gradually unfolded in the later formulations of the Categorical Imperative, and elsewhere. Consequently, beyond the fairly obvious elimination of the most extreme maxims regarding political violence, which I argued for above, there remains much indeterminacy in what one could rationally will regarding political violence.

Further, and partly as a result, Kant's claim that maxims are condemned when they cannot be conceived without contradiction as universal laws invites endless trouble. Very few maxims (including Kant's examples) seem, strictly speaking, *logically impossible* for everyone to adopt and act on; and maxims contingently impossible for everyone are often intuitively innocent. Moreover, although in special instances of 'freeloading' on social institutions the spirit of 'Don't, if everyone can't' seems an apt reminder, it is hard to see any basic moral consideration behind the completely general rule, 'If it's inconceivable for everyone to do it, it is wrong for you to do it.' Consider the maxim to let others go ahead of one in a queue, or never to buy a house but to admire others', or to adopt a child rather than having a child of one's own. One can always avoid counter-intuitive results, perhaps, by rephrasing 'the maxim'; but my point is that there seems no prima facie moral consideration against the maxims that *needs* to be overcome in this way.

Finally, until the first problem is solved, the universal law formula may give the impression that moral deliberation is a solitary activity, not essentially calling for consultation with others. Each agent, it seems, is to imagine everyone acting on the relevant maxim and then asking whether *he* or *she* can reasonably will this. Others come into account, but only in the agent's view of what sort of behaviour on their part he or she could tolerate. This fails to reflect the fact that *practical reason*, in moral deliberation, is essentially the same in all (or a construction from the reasonable reflections of all). The later formulations of the Categorical Imperative make this clearer.

Now it is tempting to suppose that shifting to Kant's humanity formula, or using that as a supplement, might suffice to resolve the problems. The humanity formula, I think, does help significantly to clarify Kant's standards of (moral) practical reason, but it raises familiar problems of its own. Treated as a rather formal constraint, as Kant's argument in the *Groundwork* suggests, the formula usefully calls attention to the fact that the faculty of *reason* which is to govern us, overriding mere inclination, is a shared faculty, in fact, *humanity* (rational nature) in each person. So when I ask whether I can treat another person as a means to my ends, the test is not just whether I can will the corresponding maxim *rationally* by some agent-relative criterion of rational choice. The test is whether anyone, including my would-be victim, can assent to the action *reasonably*, in a sense that abstracts from particular agent-relative concerns. In effect, I suggest, Kant introduces a standard of *in-principle justifiability to all*. This does not mean that a judge may not sentence a criminal because he is unwilling to go to jail, for 'justifying' to someone does not mean showing that the act in question accords with his or her personal preferences. The relevant perspective is justifiability to all in so far as they will take up the moral point of view—of practical reason, in the broad moralized sense.

Further, as I have argued elsewhere, Kant interprets treating humanity as an end in itself more substantively, as requiring a high priority on whatever preserves, promotes, develops, expresses, and honours the nature of human beings as rational, autonomous agents.[39] It implies that persons, as such, have *dignity*, an 'unconditional and incomparable worth', above all *price* and 'without equivalent'. Dignity is not a quantitative value notion by which one might justify trade-offs, say, between the dignity of one person and the 'greater' dignity of two, ten, or a hundred persons. Although weighing consequences must have an important place at some level of moral deliberation, all principles must ultimately be justified from a point of view that counts each person as having a worth that cannot be calculated.

Now although this feature of Kant's ethics has long appealed to critics of consequentialism, it raises obvious questions of application. Will there not be cases of practical moral dilemmas, where the theory makes us refuse to take any of our perceived options because each would fail to respect the dignity of someone?[40] Are there not situations where Kant's absolute insistence on dignity will require us to refuse to take emergency life-saving options which are normally wrong but intuitively

[39] See my *Dignity and Practical Reason*, ch. 2.

[40] I discuss these 'practical moral dilemmas', and the possible 'gaps' that Kantian moral theory seems to leave, in 'Moral Dilemmas, Gaps, and Residues', in H. E. Mason (ed.), *Moral Dilemmas and Moral Theory* (Oxford: Oxford University Press, 1996), 167–98.

justified in extraordinary circumstances? I have argued elsewhere that the most promising way of approaching these problems is to apply the idea of human dignity, at least in the first instance, not as a case-by-case independent moral test but as a value guideline to be taken into account, along with other aspects of morality, at a higher-order level of reflection, where general rules are decided for basic public institutions. Continuing that strategy, in the next section I sketch that legislative perspective and comment briefly on how that might help *to frame moral discussion* on political violence. This sketch of a new Kantian approach to the morality of political violence, together with some speculative remarks about its application, will have to serve as my conclusion, for the position that reasonable deliberation from the Kantian perspective would support has yet to be worked out. Indeed, to try to offer a definitive answer at this stage would be *premature*, given the complexity of the issue and the still incomplete specification of the Kantian legislative perspective. It would also be *misleading*, falsely suggesting, as too often Kantian arguments have, that these issues can be resolved in a few quick strokes without worrying about empirical realities.

A COMBINATION OF KANT'S FORMULAS: THE LEGISLATIVE PERSPECTIVE

Kant's idea of a 'kingdom of ends' (*Reich der Zwecke*) is his most explicit use of a political model for deliberation about moral principles.[41] Except for the titular head (God), all the members are both *authors* of the laws and *subject* to the laws. The Head, being a 'holy will', fails to be 'bound' by the laws only by the technicality that a holy will follows pure rational principles without any temptations and so cannot be said to be 'bound' to them. The members are *rational* and have '*autonomy*' of the will. So they are bound only by laws they legislate to themselves; they are committed to their laws as authoritative, not merely from self-interest or inclination, but from reason; they are free from threats and bribes, slavery to tradition, etc.; they make no laws without sufficient reason (so equal liberty is the starting and fallback position). They each have '*private ends*' but for purposes of

---

[41] See G, 98–107 [431–40]. In the next few paragraphs I summarize briefly the reconstruction of Kant's basic moral framework that I have been trying to develop in several papers and over a number of years. Particularly relevant are *Dignity and Practical Reason*, ch. 2, 10, and 11. 'Reasonable Self-interest', *Social Philosophy and Policy*, 14 (1997), 52–85, and Chs. 2 and 5 of this volume.

legislation they *'abstract from personal differences'*, and so work with only the abstract idea that each has a (more or less ordered) set of private ends to pursue and the knowledge that certain means are a good bet to be useful, no matter what one's ends. 'Abstracting from personal differences' need not be taken as implying an abstraction as thorough as that imposed by Rawls's 'veil of ignorance', but it implies some sort of sincere effort to set aside personal tastes and particular attachments when these are morally irrelevant to decisions about the general principles to be considered.[42] Like Rousseau's idea of the 'general will', in contrast to 'private wills', the perspective that one is to take up is that of a 'representative citizen' concerned for the good of each and all, though very much aware that individuals strongly value liberty, respect, and self-governance. The members are *'ends in themselves'*, Kant says, with *dignity*, above all *price*; and presumably they acknowledge this and constrain their legislation accordingly. Finally, the members together *'make universal laws'* by their joint rational willing. Kant seems at times to have pictured this process of 'making universal laws' as what occurs when each person, separately, 'universalizes' his or her maxims on particular occasions according to the universal law formula.[43] But it is better, I think, to conceive of the 'legislation' along the lines already suggested by the metaphor of a community of autonomous persons who together make laws for themselves, i.e. we imagine they meet, confront their problems, take into account both dignity and personal ends (abstractly considered), review possible 'bills' as candidates for laws, and then 'pass' those laws for which there is most (and sufficient) reason.

A version of the Categorical Imperative that combines the ideas of the previous versions, Kant suggests, is the rational command always to conform to the universal laws that you and others would make in a pos-

[42] Regarding the 'veil of ignorance', see John Rawls, *A Theory of Justice* (Cambridge, Mass.: Harvard University Press, 1971), chs. 1, 3, and index, and *Political Liberalism* (New York: Columbia University Press, 1993), 22–8 and index. Regarding my suggestion for an analogous, but different, Kantian legislative condition, see Ch. 2 of this volume.

[43] The 'laws' made would be intermediate principles like 'Never lie' or 'Help the needy sometimes,' between the Categorical Imperative and particular judgements, and they would be arrived at by seeing what maxims one could will for everyone to adopt and act on. For example, if each member found that all maxims that they would be acting on if they did not accept the principles above were condemned by the universal law procedure, then they are supposed to conclude that they would be wrong not to act as those maxims direct. In that case, they could conclude that 'Never lie' and 'Help the needy sometimes' are moral laws. Note that, given their 'abstraction from personal differences', if one member has sufficient reason to condemn a maxim, then so does every other person.

sible/ideal kingdom of ends.[44] Since the Categorical Imperative is a basic moral principle for personal virtue and interpersonal relations as well as matters of law and justice, the kingdom's legislators must be thought of as 'legislating' principles relevant to both areas, imperfect unenforceable duties as well as perfect juridical duties.

It is obvious, I think, how this legislative perspective incorporates the idea of humanity as an end in itself, for the legislators are stipulated to share this basic moral value. Moreover, the formal idea is expressed in their procedure: the commitment to make and obey 'laws' they can justify to each other (from their shared perspective). The complex idea of autonomy is also incorporated,[45] for the members are stipulated to have autonomy of the will, they are bound by no laws but what they agree upon together, and they are committed to abstracting from irrelevant private inclinations and particular attachments.

The universal law formula is mirrored in so far as the hypothetical legislators 'make universal laws' by their rational willing. To be sure, there is a difference between saying 'Act only by maxims that you *can* reasonably will as universal law' (FUL) and saying 'Act only as permitted by principles that you and all other rational agents *would* reasonably will as universal laws under the conditions of the kingdom of ends' (FKE). However, given that the indefinite idea of *reasonable willing* in FUL needs to be interpreted in terms of later Kantian ideas that are more explicitly spelled out in FKE, for practical purposes the kinds of moral deliberation needed to apply each formula turn out, I think, to be nearly the same.[46]

To digress from the main track to clarify this interpretive point, let us review briefly some of the differences between FUL and FKE.

1. FUL makes essential reference to the maxim on which one will act whereas FKE does not. If we adhere to Kant's idea that all intentional acts can be interpreted (practically) by reference to maxims, then FKE could easily be reformulated as follows: 'Act only on maxims permitted by principles that you and all other rational agents would reasonably

---

[44] Again, there is some textual ambiguity. At times Kant suggests that the kingdom of ends would become actual only if everyone did his or her duty and if God cooperated to see that virtue is duly rewarded. But at times it seems that we are to think of ourselves now as legislating members; in any case, use of the legislative model as a guideline does not presuppose the existence of the kingdom of ends in the first sense. At no time, it is worth noting, is the kingdom used as an 'ideal end to be produced', as if the moral imperative were 'Do whatever you can as a means to bring about a kingdom of ends.' The command is rather to conform to the laws that would be made by such ideal legislators.

[45] See *Dignity and Practical Reason*, ch. 5.   [46] But see n. 23 above.

will as universal laws under the conditions of the kingdom of ends.'
Moreover, given the persistent problems of precise maxim-description,
the fact that FKE *can* be stated (as initially, above) without reference to
maxims may well be an advantage. In any case, since the full deliberations needed to apply *either* formula require review of an indefinite
number of potentially relevant considerations, starting deliberation with
an initial statement of a maxim (as FUL demands) is no short-cut that
can replace the thorough deliberation needed for well-grounded judgements. FKE makes this clear at once, for it tells us that *'what I propose
to do'* must be cleared *under all potentially relevant act-descriptions* as
not in conflict with the principles Kantian legislators would adopt.
Moreover, what is morally relevant is either given in the principles, once
they have been worked out, or, if not, can be determined in the legislative procedure for adopting principles.

2. FUL brings in the idea of a universal law or principle in a special
way: in effect, one looks first at one's act (to find the corresponding
maxim) and then one tries to think of that act (specified by the maxim)
as a model for everyone. In effect, *one's maxim itself is transformed* into
a universal permissive law or practice, the only law to be considered
until the procedure is repeated. But FKE invites us (as Kant did in *The
Metaphysics of Morals*) first to work out a set of intermediate normative principles for everyone and only then to check our act-description
or maxim to see if, under any description, it is forbidden or required.
But this feature of FKE, again, seems all to the good, for, as we have
seen, whether any given policy or principle, in universal form, is acceptable ('can be willed') may well depend upon the context of other
universal principles into which it is to be incorporated. Adequate application of FUL needs to take that into account; FKE simply makes it
explicit.

3. FUL says *'Act only* on what you *can* reasonably will as universal
law' and FKE says, in effect, *'Do act* on what you (and others) *would*
reasonably will as universal law.' First, the addition of 'and others' in
the latter, referring to other rational legislators in the kingdom of ends,
changes the explicit model or paradigm from yourself as a solitary deliberator to an ideal legislative group; but, while this changes the 'expressive' value and intuitive appeal, the thought processes required for each
turn out not to be significantly different once one realizes that willing
'reasonably' in FUL means for Kant consulting a shared faculty of
reason that takes into account impartially the rational wills of all.
Second, the crucial factor limiting what you 'can *reasonably* will' as universal law (in FUL) is just what you and others 'would *reasonably* will'

as universal law. In other words, when one conceives a maxim as a policy for everyone and wonders, 'Can I reasonably will this?', the relevant consideration is not whether it is empirically, psychologically possible for you to choose that universal policy but rather whether *there is anything unreasonable* about choosing it. And the legislative perspective of FKE is simply a way of framing this question. One can reasonably will the universalized maxim only if everyone's acting on it violates none of the universal principles that the rational legislators would adopt. Thus, FUL seems dependent on FKE or at least the fuller specification of the standards of reasonableness that are more explicit in FKE.[47]

The Kantian legislative perspective is like that of rule-utilitarianism in some important respects. It rejects the idea that moral decisions can be made by focusing exclusively on the consequences, or other specific features, of the particular case at hand, in isolation from the merits and demerits of the general adoption of public policies that would prescribe or permit the kind of particular act in question. As with rule-utilitarianism, ideally one would first try to find a coherent and consistent set of policies, rules, and principles that one can justify from a moral perspective appropriate for the task. Particular actions are then regarded as morally obligatory if demanded by the set of constraints generated from that perspective, and are regarded as permitted if not ruled out by such constraints.

The Kantian perspective, however, is not a form of utilitarianism, and, though it must take consequences into account, it is not a form of consequentialism, as this is usually understood.[48] Crucially, when reviewing possible policies and rules from the Kantian perspective, the

---

[47] Notice that I have limited this last discussion to maxims that can be conceived as universal laws. Other maxims which fail FUL are those that cannot be conceived as universal law (without contradiction). What accounts for these being ones we 'cannot reasonably will' in universal form is not that so willing is 'unreasonable', but that it is impossible. So here reference to the standards of reasonableness in FKE seem irrelevant. FKE does not imply, as far as I can see, that a maxim is condemned simply because it is *logically impossible* for everyone to adopt and act on it, and so FKE (on my reading) does not follow FUL on this. But this seems all to the good, given the problems (mentioned earlier) about the logical impossibility aspect of the FUL test.

[48] It is distinct, for example, from the position David Cummiskey adopts in his impressive book *Kantian Consequentialism* (New York and Oxford: Oxford University Press, 1996). Most importantly, 'consequences' (though important) are not all that matters from my Kantian perspective, nor does this perspective try to find a common denominator of value (pleasure, preference satisfaction, fulfilment of rational autonomy, or whatever) the maximization (or other additive function) of which settles all moral questions. Some differences are noted in my 'Making Exceptions without Abandoning the Principle'.

legislators must constantly honour the value of human dignity—or humanity as an end in itself. The humanity formula here is not regarded as a simple, decisive action-guide to be 'applied' directly to one's proposed acts, case by case. Rather, it is a basic value, or orienting attitude, that as legislators we must adopt when deliberating about rules. It commits us to trying to find rules for a human community in which it is possible for everyone to regard each person as having, unconditionally, a basic human worth beyond his or her utility, an 'incomparable worth' rather than a quantitative value ('price') that invites calculated trade-offs. Although it is a crucial part of FKE, the humanity formula cannot be an all-inclusive *direct* guide for particular acts (independently of a system of rules) because, on that level, it leaves us with too many unresolved conflicts. That is, as a direct guide to particular action, the formula has 'gaps'; in dilemma-like cases, it pulls us very strongly towards opposite courses of action, without (by itself) giving advice as to which course to take. The hope is that many such conflicts can be resolved by taking up the higher-order legislative perspective of FKE, treating the humanity formula as specifying the *attitude* that the legislators should try to maintain when legislating and that they should try to foster 'in the real world'.[49]

What sort of constraints are implicit in this attitude? First, as legislators we are aiming to work out rules justifiable to everyone else in so far as they, like us, are willing to confine themselves conscientiously to the rules we accept, or would accept, from the Kantian moral perspective. The justification here proceeds not, as with rule-utilitarianism, by showing that a certain set of rules, if generally adopted and taught, would result in the best state of the universe, where goodness is measured by some prior standard. Rather, to justify is to show acceptability to anyone prepared to review the issue with a certain ideal moral attitude, which consists of a complex of concerns not all reducible to a desire to *produce* future goods.[50] These concerns include each person's

---

[49] It should perhaps be noted that attempts to argue that one should not treat persons in a particular way because that is merely using them as a means, not treating them as ends in themselves, often make implicit appeals to rights, as if they existed prior to and independent of the humanity formula. For example, gaining property by fraud, making a false promise, rape, sexual molestation, etc. can be understood as rights violations, and so as treating someone as a mere means as opposed to their rightful claims as human beings. That is not a bad application for practical purposes, but we need to remember that rights claims need to be justified and the humanity formula has the primary role of determining, along with other forms of the Categorical Imperative, the perspective from which we should decide what human rights there are.

[50] I am inclined to add here 'not reducible in any *very meaningful sense*' because it may be that virtually any concern *can* be formulated to look like a future-oriented concern. For example, Ross's 'backward-looking' principle of fidelity (or promise-

life as a rational autonomous agent, the liberty, means, and opportunity to live as such, his or her moral and physical capacities, and social conditions that enable and encourage rational autonomous living. Given that human dignity is 'priceless' and 'without equivalent', these values trump various special interests that individuals may develop. Some Kantians may regard these values as absolute, but in the real world occasions arise in which not all of even these most stringent values can be simultaneously honoured in practice to the extent a conscientious person would wish. The Kantian values do not merely generate future goals to be worked for; they also call for appropriate responses now, independently of what may happen later. For example, one must not only work for a future with greater mutual respect, one must also respect others as rational autonomous agents now by constraining the means one is willing to use to bring about a better future.[51] And it is not an unqualified goal to maximize human liberty over time, for all one's efforts towards this must respect each individual's right to liberty now.

Clearly, though we may continue to affirm, in abstract form, the principle that 'humanity' in each person is priceless and without equivalent, the more specific values implicit in this (somewhat vague) general idea are ones that draw us towards different policies in actual situations. There will be a need to work out adjustments, compromises, less-than-ideal temporary policies, etc. in our efforts to find the package of principles, rules, and policies that, all things considered, best respects the basic ideal of human dignity. Unlike rule-utilitarians, Kantians have no pretence to a common denominator of value in terms of which all such decisions can be made. This means that, contrary to what Kant himself thought, working out the intermediate principles for our world, a 'metaphysics of morals', will be no easy task. Rather, the principles we settle on will be complex, many-sided, full of qualifications and exceptions, constantly in need of revision, and no doubt always controversial.

But, in addition to these complexities, we must acknowledge that the basic values I have just mentioned are not all that must be considered. Each person, as an 'end in himself', has a set of personal ends that are rationally and morally optional. They are the ends we adopt, ideally

keeping) might be expressed, 'Prima facie act at each time so that the future does not include you as one who has broken his promise at this time'; see W. D. Ross, *The Right and the Good* (Oxford: Oxford University Press, 1930), ch. 2.

[51] I try to explain and illustrate this point more fully in 'The Message of Affirmative Action', in my collection of essays, *Autonomy and Self-respect* (Cambridge: Cambridge University Press, 1991), ch. 13, esp. 201–11.

upon reflection, in the light of our particular preferences, loves, hates, hopes, fears, etc. Together they constitute our conception of our 'happiness', which is not necessarily hedonistic or egoistic, but, roughly speaking, it is the life we would choose if relying solely on our desires as a particular individual. Many of these values will be shared by others, influenced by others, and have cooperative activities with others as their object; but their ground is that they are what the particular agent wants and chooses, based on experience, at least so far as permitted by morality and reason. Now part of valuing each person as a person, capable of morality but also one who (freely) adopts personal ends, is to give some weight in one's own deliberation and conduct to the *permissible* personal ends of others. What is permissible is not given in advance of moral deliberation from the legislative perspective, but is one more thing that needs to be worked out. That is, legislators must not only decide rules guided by their overriding commitment to the basic values described above (life, liberty, respect, etc.) but, that assured, they must work out principles, beyond the basics, that fairly protect and aid each person's pursuit of personal happiness. This is not simply a matter of maximizing total or average happiness after basic constraints are settled, for Kantian moral principles, I assume, must express respect for the equality and liberty of each person more directly and constantly than policies based on utilitarian impartial agglomeration of preferences will do. Besides, on the Kantian picture, there is no measure of happiness across persons.

SPECULATIVE APPLICATIONS: WHERE THE FRAMEWORK MIGHT LEAD

It is helpful to see Kant's ethics, like Rawls's theory of justice, as at least implicitly dividing its tasks into stages. Both begin with 'ideal theory', asking us to conceive a world more abstract and perfect than the actual world and then showing us what principles would be adopted as reasonable under those ideal conditions. Rawls saw clearly, and Kant at times more dimly realized, that the principles derived from such ideal conditions *for a more ideal world* (e.g. strict compliance with the rules) were not guaranteed to be appropriate for our very imperfect world. These imperfections must be taken into account. For Rawls, this is partly done by applying the theory in 'stages'—the 'original position', a constitutional convention stage, a legislative stage, and a judicial stage, where each stage introduces more information about actual conditions.

(Partly, he handles the problem by making all principles revisable in light of our considered judgements about its conclusions when we seek 'reflective equilibrium'.) Kant starts with an even more idealized notion than Rawls, the idea of a 'pure rational will'; but in his examples and systematic development of moral principles in *The Metaphysics of Morals*, he actually draws upon many (supposed) empirical facts (some of which he acknowledges, others not). Clearly any plausible Kantian-style ethics must face and adjust to the gaps between the idealized 'kingdom of ends' and real-world conditions. Here I will only mention two necessary adjustments.

Most obviously, despite what Kant thought, it is far from clear that everyone who takes up his legislative perspective will reach the same conclusions about moral issues. The more subtly the perspective is defined and the more real relevant conditions are taken into account, the more controversial particular conclusions are likely to be. The perspective helps to frame a way of thinking that might be shared and enable those who disagree to reason together towards resolutions. But resolution is never guaranteed. In hard cases there will always be some uncertainty about what is right, just as there will be for consequentialists. This may be seen as a problem of life, not of any particular theory. Some theories, however, e.g. certain ideal observer theories, yield bizarre conclusions by even admitting that ideal deliberators *might* disagree: for example, on Roderick Firth's view, it would follow that anything is permitted in any area where ideal observers disagree.[52] Kantian theory, as I see it, can avoid this problem by taking as primary the individual's conscientious judgement as to what she could sincerely recommend as a 'bill' to the hypothetical group of Kantian legislators. Practically, this means acting only by principles that one can, in earnest dialogue with others, maintain in good faith as what one judges they should all adopt when deliberating morally. Each person's obligation is to act by such conscientious judgement. The idea of something being absolutely right or wrong would be a regulative idea, or ideal, of what at best reasonable persons taking the legislative perspective would all agree upon. Our evidence, however—namely, the tendency of reflective moral opinion to converge on certain standards when reflecting well (by the Kantian perspective) in the light of their conditions—will always be imperfect. Reasonable application, then, does not depend upon universal agreement.

[52] Roderick Firth, 'Ethical Absolutism and the Ideal Observer', *Philosophy and Phenomenological Research*, 12 (1952), 317–45.

A further point that must be acknowledged is that, though it might be useful to imagine what principles would be reasonable *if* everyone followed them, we have to modify these in the light of the fact that we know that not everyone will. Real-world ignorance, weakness of will, selfishness, short-sightedness, the need for psychological props, vulnerability to social pressures, liability to chemical addictions, etc. are not features pictured in Kant's kingdom of ends or even his idealized 'idea of a social contract', but they are factors in light of which principles for a more perfect world need to be modified. To ask what legislators would think if more ideal than our congressmen is a good moral heuristic, but to stick at all costs to the principles they would adopt *for their perfect world* would be madness.

My aim here has been to describe a reasonable Kantian perspective for thinking about the problem, not to resolve it. But, in conclusion, we might speculate for a moment as to what conclusions we might expect. Here is what I conjecture.

First, beyond some quite general guiding considerations, more definite principles will not be easy to determine and are understandably controversial. There are so many factors to consider on which reasonable people may well disagree. These include not only the empirical background facts and predicted outcomes, but many moral factors to take into account. Accordingly, since the issue is vitally important, there is need for ongoing dialogue and moral humility on this issue.

Second, the most extreme positions are unlikely to survive careful reflection and dialogue from our Kantian position. To say 'Political violence is always wrong' would reflect a mode of thinking less sensitive than our Kantian perspective to the importance of securing the conditions for liberty, justice, and the legitimate pursuit of happiness; and it would ignore the fact that, in our world, we cannot affirm full respect for all unless we forcibly curtail the contemptuous acts of some. To say 'Political violence is justified whenever it serves a good end' would be to ignore the priorities of value and constraints on 'trade-offs' essential to the Kantian perspective.

Third, there are at least strong prima facie presumptions implicit in the Kantian perspective.

1. For example, despite Kant's own rigouristic position about property, it seems clear that killing and maiming human beings is worse, other things being equal, than damaging property. And doing irreparable damage to vital resources is worse than damaging replaceable property inessential to basic needs. Property conventions get their justification ultimately from their role in securing conditions in which

individuals and groups can pursue their permissible projects in a fair, orderly way with a minimum of conflict and through procedures that tend to mutual advantage. They exist to make possible good lives for human beings, which is the higher priority.

2. Another implicit presumption is that political violence targeted specifically against the grossly unjust is better than random political violence. Destroying the possessions of flagrant, violent oppressors, totally unamenable to reason, is surely better than targeting the goods of innocent people or blowing up property at random. And, if killing is warranted (as Kant thought in just war and state punishment for murder), then it is better if the victims are themselves murderous wielders of arbitrary power rather than innocent citizens or rulers who are merely inept, vain, and unpopular. This is at least in the spirit of Kant's basic principle of right/justice, which authorizes the forceful hindrance of hindrances to freedom, especially when wilful, flagrant, deeply destructive, and unpreventable by other means. Tyrants, like any common criminal, are initially entitled to a right to life and liberty equal to anyone else's under Kantian principles, and so they cannot complain that those principles treat them as 'mere means'. The only systems that can fully respect the humanity of all will have to make provision for some forfeiting their freedoms when they deliberately take away others'.

3. Perhaps, too, there is a presumption that political violence directed selectively to force specific reforms from a government that resists all peaceful appeals is preferable, other things being equal, to revolutionary violence that aims to bring down the whole governing structure, for, most often it seems, corruption and oppression are ugly aspects of lawful governments rather than rottenness at the core that robs the whole system of any legitimacy. That is, they are often more like boils to be lanced with precise surgery than rabid beasts to be put down by any means. The problem is not just the persistent fear, common among conservative philosophers, that revolution inevitably takes us back to an awful 'state of nature'. It is partly that lawful governments with pockets of corruption often still retain some of their initial claim on our allegiance, serve many of the rightful functions of government, and can be 'brought down' only by acts damaging to the interests and contrary to the strong presumptive rights of many innocent people.

4. Again, political violence used as a 'last resort' is presumably preferable from a Kantian perspective to violence as a general strategy to be employed whenever deemed likely to be effective. Kant perhaps exaggerated the prospects of reform from the 'top down' in response to calm, reasonable criticism from philosophers and other intellectuals, but his

theory, I think, rightly holds as ideal the effort to settle our differences, when possible, by rational dialogue, moral persuasion, and other peaceful means. Placing an incomparable value on 'rational nature' in each person does not mean doing *anything* that will maximize the chances that some day more people will live rationally. At least part of the message is that, up to a point, we must presume present (and treat with respect) a human potential for non-violent moral reform, even in those who have so far often acted as if deaf to reason.

5. Another consideration, more relevant for Kantians than utilitarians, is one's motive in wanting to join in political violence. Like thinkers as diverse as Gilbert Ryle and Sigmund Freud, Kant doubted that each person has infallible introspective access to one's motives. And yet why one is doing something is a morally important part of *what* one is doing. It is difficult to be sure why joining a revolution appeals to us, and not every 'high-minded', unselfish motive is acceptable from the Kantian perspective. If one adopted the extraordinary, self-diminishing 'impartiality' of act-utilitarianism as one's dominant motive, for example, this could conceivably lead one to accept murderous violence against a few for the sake of the greater good of the many, calculated in a procedure of 'trade-offs' that would be stringently opposed to Kantian modes of thinking. One needs to determine first that one has a right to be violent, which is a complex decision not turning entirely on future consequences.

6. I must emphasize that there is still an important place in thinking from the Kantian perspective, as I see it, for taking into account the numbers to be killed or injured, the odds of success, the likelihood that violence is (empirically) necessary, and the degrees of harm and misery caused and prevented. To think that these are irrelevant is either madness (as I once said, ungenerously[53]) or else to be in the grip of a philosophical theory that is assumed to take care of these matters in some other way (e.g. in an afterlife or the universal progress of history). Probably there is no barrier to the acceptance of Kantian ethics greater than the opinion that for Kantians 'the numbers don't count', the empirical probabilities of success are irrelevant, and we must blindly adhere to the rules for a more perfect world even though our own world is in fact quite imperfect, even corrupt. It is true, of course, that Kant himself held certain principles, such as 'Never lie' and 'Never actively take part in revolution,' as absolutes. It is also true that Kant insisted that con-

---

[53] *Dignity and Practical Reason*, 215.

sequences have a more limited role in ethics than many are prepared to admit. For example, the fundamental moral principle is not consequentialist; Kant's procedure for identifying and justifying the 'supreme moral principle' is, in a sense, non-empirical; and he insisted that sometimes one must refrain from doing something even though one estimates that doing it would promote more happiness. None the less, the Kantian perspective I have described, which arguably captures Kant's deepest moral insights, allows us, indeed requires us, to take into account 'the numbers' and 'the odds' at some level of moral reflection. We are looking for principles that can be justified to all who fully respect and value each person; and when it is empirically *impossible* to preserve the lives and liberties of everyone, the only way to honour the basic idea of equal dignity is to abide by principles that fairly determine whom to rescue and whom one must let go. The basic test is to follow whatever choice principles, to our best judgement in full consultation with others, we think each person, victim and survivor alike, could see as justified from the Kantian perspective. No one, then, is treated as a mere means; no thought that 'ten are *worth* ten times as much as one' is invoked. Drawing straws for the last places on the lifeboat may be more mutually respectful than all drowning together. More needs to be said about this crucial point, but it is a serious mistake, I think, to suppose that my modified Kantian perspective is not significantly different from consequentialism.

7. Finally, my personal conjecture is that the result of serious, informed debates among conscientious persons taking the Kantian perspective would be quite conservative about political violence, advocating great caution before undertaking to abandon peaceful means in order to promote peaceful and just results. We tend to celebrate successful revolutions without dwelling on the death and misery they caused to individuals, just as we celebrate wars with more focus on heroism than human tragedy. Moreover, as noted earlier, because of human fallibility, the relevant policies we must check by our basic moral standards can never be simply 'to end injustice, war, and oppression by political violence' but rather 'to resort to political violence as a means that one expects, and hopes, with some degree of probability will lessen injustice, war, and oppression'. To approve of the latter, as a public policy for fallible and self-deceiving people such as we are, would not be easy from the Kantian perspective. The risks would be enormous, and one cannot conscientiously act on such matters in ways that one knows one could not justify as a public policy for others. With too much

optimistic faith in inevitable progress and too little tolerance for exceptions in principles, Kant himself went too far in his absolutist stance against political violence, but I can imagine that his stance was at least well motivated (if not well argued) because of his deep awareness of the moral and human costs of unnecessary violence.

9

The Problem of Stability in
Political Liberalism

PROLOGUE: RAWLS'S KANTIANISM

Kantian political philosophy has been developed and extended in John Rawls's classic work, *A Theory of Justice*.[1] For many this has been a paradigm of how those inspired by Kant but critical of aspects of Kant's philosophy might construct new perspectives on old issues. Readers of Rawls's subsequent work, however, have often suspected that he has abandoned his Kantian roots and settled for a pragmatic quest for consensus.[2] Now accepting the fact that Kantian assumptions are not likely to be universally shared in a pluralistic world, he does not argue that a Kantian theory represents the truth about justice. Instead, he argues that there are reasons independent of Kantian theory for believers in other comprehensive doctrines at least to accept his *justice as fairness* as a practical framework to work with, i.e. as a 'political' doctrine. He suggests that what moved him to modify his views was the realization that the stability of a well-ordered just society would not be guaranteed even if all citizens initially accepted the basic principles of justice that Rawls had argued for. It may seem, then, that he abandons his strong Kantian

Apart from the prologue, my comments in this chapter (with minor changes) are those I presented at an 'Author Meets Critics' session of the American Philosophical Association Pacific Division meetings in April 1994. In thinking about John Rawls's recent work I have been helped by discussions with a number of people, including especially Eugene Mason, Henry West, Martin Gunderson, Carl Brandt, Andrews Reath, and a graduate student reading group at the University of North Carolina. I am also grateful to Rawls for his response at the APA session and for sending me some very helpful notes prepared for his classes.

[1] John Rawls, *A Theory of Justice* (Cambridge, Mass.: Harvard University Press, 1971). I will abbreviate this as TJ. Rawls draws significantly on Kant's ideas but readily grants that his own view differs from Kant's in some important ways. See, for example, TJ, 251–7, 586.

[2] The main subsequent work is *Political Liberalism* (New York: Columbia University Press, 1993), hereafter abbreviated as PL. This largely incorporates the ideas in his articles published after TJ, notably 'Justice as Fairness: Political, not Metaphysical', *Philosophy and Public Affairs*, 14 (1985), 223–51.

position for the sake of stability, replacing controversial Kantian arguments with pragmatic arguments that may convince people with very
different comprehensive doctrines.

My contention, however, is that Rawls has in fact a deep Kantian
reason for his more recent project. He attempts to establish the possibility of an overlapping consensus of diverse doctrines on a political
conception of justice as fairness because this is necessary to satisfy a
fundamental Kantian constraint, which Rawls calls *the liberal principle
of legitimacy*. This is the idea that the exercise of coercive political
power is not fully proper unless it is 'in accordance with a constitution
the essentials of which all citizens as free and equal may reasonably be
expected to endorse in the light of principles and ideals acceptable to
their common human reason'.[3] This principle, I think, is essentially an
elaboration of Kant's idea that a fully just constitution excludes any provision that would be impossible for all citizens to accept if they were
establishing a constitution in an original contract.[4]

WHY ABANDON OR MODIFY
A THEORY OF JUSTICE?

Despite its modest presentation and explicit limitations of scope, *A
Theory of Justice* has inspired many of us with its large vision, systematic methodology, and challenging arguments. Appearing in the midst
of a relatively stagnant period in political philosophy, the book seemed
to highlight the inseparability of moral and political philosophy and to
carry both to a deeper level. Now, paradoxically, Rawls argues that we
should see justice as fairness as a less comprehensive, less 'deep', self-
standing *political* conception that does not compete with our many
diverse (reasonable) comprehensive moral theories and religious traditions but rather appeals to these for its deep support. As before, Rawls
presents the political principles of justice as a *construction* in a certain

---

[3] PL, 137.
[4] Kant refers to a hypothetical original contract in many places. See, for example,
Kant: Political Writings, ed. Hans Reiss (Cambridge: Cambridge University Press, 1991),
77, 79, 80, 83, 99, 100, 143, 158, 162–4. An example of what Kant thinks excluded by
appeal to the possibility of an original contract is hereditary political privilege (ibid. 79,
99, 153). A fundamental principle for Kant is that citizens have innate rights to freedom
and equality, but it is not entirely clear whether this assumption plays a role in his arguments from the idea of an original contract. See, for example, ibid. 74–5. For an illuminating interpretation of the difference between Rawls's project and Kant's aim in *The
Metaphysics of Morals*, see Thomas Pogge, 'Is Kant's *Rechtslehre* Comprehensive?',
Southern Journal of Philosophy, 36, suppl. (1997), 161–87.

technical sense, but, equally important, the continuous development of his work illustrates how good political philosophy can be 'constructed' in a more ordinary sense: that is, gradually and painstakingly built up, its initial vision and insights developed over time by persistent rethinking and adjustments responsive to the thoughts of others. Having already proposed a political philosophy that has achieved acclaim unparalleled in our times, Rawls has continued his building project, patiently repairing, extending, reconstructing, and, when necessary, deconstructing his previous fine work. Reasonable persons can disagree about the truth, and even the political merits, of his proposals, but on the proposition that John Rawls has changed and enriched political philosophy as few others have there is a just and stable overlapping consensus.

To turn from the obvious to the immediate, my aim here is just to raise some questions. For this I want to focus on the relations between Rawls's two books, *A Theory of Justice* and *Political Liberalism*. The new work, *Political Liberalism*, I take it, is meant to supplement *A Theory of Justice*, not to replace it, much less to compete with it. In the essays published between the two books, Rawls offered many refinements, additions, explanations, and responses to critics, and *Political Liberalism* brings these together in a helpful and expanded form. In doing so, I think, *Political Liberalism* satisfies one of its main purposes, adding significantly to the power, subtlety, and persuasiveness of the main system of thought that underlies both works. For example, the liberty principle is somewhat altered and arguments for its priority clarified;[5] the original position is now unmistakably presented as a device of representation;[6] the relation between the 'primary goods' and the 'two moral powers' of citizens is made more explicit;[7] the revised argument for concern for future generations seems less ad hoc;[8] and now one can see more plainly what exactly, under 'constructivism', is supposed to be constructed and what is not.[9] These various revisions alone make *Political Liberalism* an important book, indeed an essential one for moral and political philosophers, quite independently of the particular issues on which my questions will be focused.

As an admirer of *A Theory of Justice*, naturally I am most interested in the *major systematic change* that *Political Liberalism* makes in the ideas of earlier work. That basic change, from which Rawls says most other changes stem, is in the way justice as fairness is now presented.

---

[5] PL, 291–371.   [6] PL, 22–8, 35, 75.   [7] PL, 75 f., 106, 178 f., 186.
[8] PL, 273–4.   [9] PL, 89–129, esp. 103–4.

Rather than treating justice as fairness as a *comprehensive* (or '*partially comprehensive*') *moral doctrine*, he now proposes it as a political conception of justice that is no longer considered as competing for the same role in our lives as other reasonable comprehensive moral doctrines (such as utilitarianism and various traditional religions). At first the change may strike us, the admirers of *A Theory of Justice*, as disappointing, because a political conception is admittedly a less grand and all-encompassing thing than a comprehensive moral theory of justice: it presupposes common ideas in the public political culture; it guides decisions only with respect to a restricted subclass of political issues; in its Rawlsian version, it foregoes any claim to truth; and it must appeal for support outside itself (to comprehensive doctrines) if it is to be deeply justified. Thus the larger questions we want to raise are: How radical are these changes? What was the problem that prompted them? Were they really necessary? Are they successful in meeting the problem? And what are the costs of making them? That is, which, if any, of the admirable features of *A Theory of Justice* have been lost by the recent move to 'downsize' the claims for justice as fairness?

Like many readers, I suspect, I was struck by Rawls's remarks in the introduction to *Political Liberalism*, suggesting that the major changes from *A Theory of Justice* stem from a problem (even an 'inconsistency') in the way that work attempted to show that a society structured by justice as fairness would be *stable*. Rawls explains the problem as follows:

to understand the nature and extent of the differences, one must see them as arising from trying to resolve a serious problem internal to justice as fairness, namely from the fact that the account of stability in Part III of [A] *Theory* [of *Justice*] is not consistent with the view as a whole. I believe all the differences are consequences of removing that inconsistency. Otherwise I take the structure and content of [A] *Theory* [of *Justice*] to remain substantially the same.[10]

To explain: the serious problem I have in mind concerns the unrealistic idea of a well-ordered society as it appears in [A] *Theory* [of *Justice*]. An essential feature of a well-ordered society associated with justice as fairness is that all its citizens endorse this conception on the basis of what I now call a comprehensive philosophical doctrine. They accept, as rooted in this doctrine, its two principles of justice. [Although not explicit in *A Theory of Justice*,] once the question is raised, it is clear, I think, that the text regards justice as fairness and utilitarianism as comprehensive, or partially comprehensive, doctrines.

Now the serious problem is this. A modern democratic society is characterized not simply by a pluralism of comprehensive religious, philosophical, and

---

[10] PL, p. xvi. A footnote follows noting some exceptions.

moral doctrines but by a pluralism of incompatible yet reasonable comprehensive doctrines. No one of these doctrines is affirmed by citizens generally. Nor should one expect that in the foreseeable future one of them, or some other reasonable doctrine, will ever be affirmed by all, or nearly all, citizens.[11]

The fact of a plurality of reasonable but incompatible comprehensive doctrines—the fact of reasonable pluralism—shows that, as used in [A] *Theory* [*of Justice*], the idea of a well-ordered society of justice as fairness is unrealistic. This is because it is inconsistent with realizing its own principles under the best foreseeable conditions. The account of stability of a well-ordered society in Part III is therefore also unrealistic and must be recast. This problem sets the stage for the later essays beginning in 1980. The ambiguity of [A] *Theory* [*of Justice*] is now removed and justice as fairness is presented at the outset as a political conception of justice.[12]

My initial attempts to understand the changes from *A Theory of Justice* to *Political Liberalism* turned crucially on this description of the project. Since the old problem was stability, I thought, the innovations of *Political Liberalism* must be seen as the proposed solution to this problem: in effect, as changes necessary to set up a new argument that, despite the fact of reasonable pluralism, a society structured by the principles of justice as fairness would tend to be stable. Many features of the text seemed to support this reading, for a major line of argument in *Political Liberalism* is that once justice as fairness is presented as merely a *political* conception, then it can win the support of an overlapping consensus of reasonable comprehensive doctrines, such as the major religious traditions and the classic moral theories. This support, despite opposition from 'unreasonable' doctrines, would naturally have a stabilizing effect. Given this reading, it seemed correct to say that changes in *A Theory of Justice* were *necessary*, but it remained far from obvious that the innovations in *Political Liberalism* would be *successful* in meeting the problem of stability. So long as the problem and its solution are seen as a simple stability problem the changes in *Political Liberalism*, I suspect, will continue to strike readers as inadequate to its aim. And, given this, many admirers of *A Theory of Justice* are likely to see the changes as too high a price to pay for the minimal increase in the likelihood of stability.

On rethinking the issue, with the help of friends and some hints from Rawls, I am convinced that I have at least partly misunderstood the *intent*, or at least the current understanding, of Rawls's remarks about how the changes in *Political Liberalism* were designed to meet the problem of stability. If so, even if I am right to suspect that there will

---

[11] PL, p. xvi.   [12] PL, p. xvii.

never *in fact* be an overlapping consensus (of reasonable comprehensive doctrines) on justice as fairness (conceived politically), or even on political liberalism, this may not be incompatible with Rawls's main point. There is another reading on which, even in the absence of actual consensus, the argument for the *possibility* of such a consensus of *reasonable* doctrines still serves an important purpose.

In my remaining remarks, I will explain my initial reading of the stability problem in *A Theory of Justice*, its apparent solution in *Political Liberalism*, and my doubts about that solution; then I will briefly sketch an alternative, hopefully better, interpretation. My point is not to draw attention to my own struggles to understand Rawls's project but rather to articulate what I take to be a quite natural, though deeply subversive, understanding of that project, so that, if it is mistaken, we can get clearer about the alternative. Towards the end of my remarks I will also briefly raise some other questions that, I suspect, are shared by a number of other readers of *Political Liberalism*.

THE PROBLEM OF STABILITY IN
A THEORY OF JUSTICE: INITIAL READING

Political philosophy, according to *A Theory of Justice*, should distinguish and address each of the following tasks: (1) it should provide a method of identifying, representing, and (in a sense) justifying fundamental principles of justice regarding the basic political and economic institutions; (2) it should interpret and illustrate the application of those principles to familiar political issues, showing the implications of the theory to be more or less in harmony with our considered moral judgements; and (3) it should offer considerations for believing that a society well ordered by those principles of justice would be stable. A scheme of cooperation was defined as *stable* when it was 'more or less regularly complied with and its basic rules willingly acted upon; and when infractions occur, stabilizing forces . . . exist that prevent further violations and tend to restore the relation'.[13] A stable system is not merely one in equilibrium, like a ball resting on a flat table, but one which under stress, up to a point, tends to return to an equilibrium state, like a ball in a cup. The first two tasks were taken up in parts I and II of *A Theory of Justice*, while the last, the stability problem, was addressed in part III.

---

[13] TJ, 6.

Whether a society well ordered by Rawls's two principles of justice would be stable was a question that, in the end, members of the original position were to consider, but Rawls did not contend that justice as fairness was the *most stable* conception of justice. For the most part arguments (in parts I and II) for the superiority of Rawls's two principles over alternative conceptions of justice *presupposed* that either Rawls's two principles, or some alternative, would be a basic public charter of a well-ordered society and so, at least initially, complied with willingly by almost everyone. Part III was designed to support this initial assumption that the two principles could win the willing compliance of citizens and to argue further that their allegiance would tend to maintain itself, despite stresses, over time. The argument was that, given conjectured psychological principles and the benefits secured to each citizen under the two principles, citizens raised in a society well ordered by Rawls's two principles would naturally develop a sense of justice and find a *just life* largely congruent with their various conceptions of a *good life*. Thus, with its three parts combined, *A Theory of Justice* argues that justice as fairness is more tenable than any other traditional conception of justice and, further, that a society well ordered by its principles would tend to stabilize itself under stress and thus tend to endure.

In *Political Liberalism*, as I said, Rawls acknowledges a serious internal problem in his previous argument for the stability of a society structured by his two principles of justice. His earlier argument, Rawls now says, presupposed that citizens accepted justice as fairness as their 'comprehensive philosophical doctrine' (or as their 'partially comprehensive doctrine'). The argument took for granted, then, not only that other competing conceptions of *justice* had been rejected but also that citizens did not believe in any general philosophies, religions, or world-views that might conflict with their allegiance to the doctrines of justice as fairness. The aim, after all, was to show that a (Rawlsian) just society would be self-perpetuating if its citizens were brought up to internalize its far-ranging conception of justice as fairness, letting this shape their thoughts, feelings, and relationships to one another.

But now, quite plausibly, Rawls grants that in any free society that we can realistically foresee, there will be a plurality of religions and other comprehensive philosophical doctrines. The very liberties of speech and conscience that justice as fairness assures to each citizen make it almost inevitable that reasonable people will continue to disagree on deep and broad issues of religion and philosophy. The problem, then, seems to be that the old argument for the stability of a just society was unrealistic in supposing that virtually all its citizens, in a climate of freedom, might come willingly to accept, and perpetually maintain, one basic comprehensive philosophical doctrine, namely, justice as fairness as presented in *A Theory of Justice*. We now see that the stability of a just society cannot be secured in that way.[14]

Even on this initial reading, I should stress, the issue of stability was never simply the general question of how to make social order durable. The issue was always how a *just* society could endure, and the aim was to show this is possible without lowering the standards of justice for the sake of securing stability. Stability was to be based on the willing consent of citizens, the idea of securing it by police-state methods being ruled out from the start. Moreover, mere durability was not the aim, but stability; that is, durability was to be achieved in large part by the fact that the citizens themselves would have developed attitudes towards justice that would prompt them to restore the system whenever its just institutions were in danger.

Now, supposing (as Rawls did) that in parts I and II of *A Theory of Justice* we already have a reasonable account of what justice demands, why be concerned about stability? As Rawls notes, moral philosophers have generally paid little attention to the question of whether their ideals will in fact become and remain widely accepted and used; so one may wonder why political philosophy should be so concerned. A natural answer, I think, is that political philosophers typically put forward a package of ideas for public acceptance, arguing the merits of the system were it to be generally accepted. (In contrast moral philosophy typically offers standards to guide the conscientious choice of individuals, whether or not others will follow their lead.) Given the difficulties of winning general agreement, and the transition costs of reforming institutions, we are understandably reluctant to bother with proposed political changes that will unravel as soon as they are instituted. Utopian writing can be enjoyable to read, but for serious political proposals we demand feasibility and a reasonable likelihood that, once accepted, they will survive long enough to make the effort to institute them worth while. Thus, in so far as justice as fairness is put forward as a political proposal that one hopes will become widely accepted, its appeal would be enhanced by a persuasive argument that a society which is just by its standard would be stable. The argument would remove a worry: the fear that such a society would only be just for a moment, its fine principles quickly giving way under predictable stresses.

---

[14] PL, p. xix.

THE SOLUTION IN *POLITICAL LIBERALISM*: INITIAL READING

Let us assume for the moment that the problem prompting the basic changes from *A Theory of Justice* to *Political Liberalism* was the stability problem as I have just interpreted it. The solution offered to this problem in *Political Liberalism*, then, seems to be not to reject or revise drastically the content of justice as fairness but to reconceive it and present it in a new light. In sum, the main steps of the solution are: (1) to treat justice as fairness as a *political conception* rather than as a *comprehensive moral doctrine*; (2) to develop a distinction, for political purposes, between reasonable and unreasonable comprehensive doctrines; and (3) to distinguish stability based on an *overlapping consensus of reasonable doctrines* from stability based on either *uniformity of doctrine* or a mere *modus vivendi* among adherents of different doctrines. Relying on these central ideas, the major step is (4) to argue that a (Rawlsian) just society can be stable in a pluralistic world because, once seen as merely political, justice as fairness can win an overlapping consensus of reasonable comprehensive doctrines. In effect, by making the claims for justice as fairness more modest and its scope more limited, thereby reducing its potential conflicts with reasonable religious and philosophical doctrines, the changes make justice as fairness more broadly acceptable. By these changes, then, and by stressing the political values secured to all under justice as fairness, Rawls seems to hope that *Political Liberalism* will persuade people of various religious and moral convictions that they can agree that it is a reasonable set of political ideas within which they can work together. Finally (5) stability based in this way on an overlapping consensus of reasonable comprehensive doctrines is supposed to be enhanced by the idea of *public reason*: that is, the idea that we are (voluntarily) to restrict our arguments, on matters affecting the basic structure of society, to political arguments drawn from within the limits of common reason and our working political conception of justice. In other words, barring emergencies, we are not to appeal to our particular comprehensive religious and philosophical doctrines in public debates about the most fundamental political institutions.[15] Such restraint should reduce divisiveness on the basic political institutions and so contribute further to stability.

[15] From correspondence I understand that Rawls may introduce further qualifications on this restriction in subsequent writings.

The key ideas here may be explained briefly as follows. First, presenting justice as fairness as merely a *political* conception means at least three things: that its main ideas are drawn from the public political culture; that it is only a theory about the basic structure of a constitutional democratic regime; and that it is viewed as a 'self-standing' idea, independent of commitments to comprehensive religious and philosophical doctrines.[16] In so far as justice as fairness is a form of 'political constructivism', this also means that its claims are not presented as 'true' but only as, in a sense, 'reasonable'.[17] Second, *reasonable* people are conceived as those who are willing to reciprocate on fair terms of cooperation when others will, and who admit certain limits on our powers of judgement. They accept only *reasonable comprehensive doctrines*, which are more or less consistent, coherent doctrines, arrived at by use of theoretical and practical reason, covering 'major religious, philosophical, and moral aspects of human life', and normally belonging to a tradition of thought.[18] Third, there is an *overlapping consensus*, as opposed to a mere *modus vivendi*, when a political conception (such as justice as fairness) wins the support of 'all the reasonable opposing religious, philosophical, and moral doctrines likely to persist over generations and to gain a sizable body of adherents in a more or less just constitutional regime'.[19]

DOUBTS ABOUT THE SOLUTION TO THE PROBLEM AS INITIALLY CONCEIVED

This initial reading of the problem and the solution at least shows why changes were necessary in the earlier account of stability. Even if part III of *A Theory of Justice* successfully established the likely stability of a society in which justice as fairness became the 'comprehensive moral doctrine' of virtually everyone, this would be irrelevant to our practical concerns because contemporary experience suggests that it is very unlikely, for the foreseeable future, that any one moral, religious, or philosophical doctrine will become accepted by virtually everyone. As Rawls says, freedom of thought and discussion fosters a plurality of doctrines; and a somewhat stifled plurality seems to persist even in those countries where freedom is suppressed. If a just society can be stable at all, it must be so despite its containing a plurality of diverse doctrines.

---

[16] PL, 11–15.   [17] PL, 93–4.   [18] PL, 48–66, esp. 59.   [19] PL, 15.

Further, we can readily grant that presenting justice as fairness as a political conception, rather than as a comprehensive doctrine, is at least a step in the right direction towards a solution. Why? The task is to show how a society that is well ordered by justice as fairness can be stable, and for now I take that to mean that a society in which the substantial majority of citizens willingly accept and use justice as fairness (regarding the basic structure) can be self-restoring and so enduring. But, given that they have many diverse comprehensive doctrines, how could (almost all) the citizens agree to accept justice as fairness? Only, it seems, if justice as fairness is rendered compatible with their comprehensive doctrines; and presenting justice as fairness as a political conception is a major step towards making it compatible. Since it does not claim to be 'true', the new justice as fairness cannot, strictly speaking, contradict comprehensive doctrines as to what is truly just, truly the nature of persons, etc. Since its scope is restricted to the basic structure of society, the new justice as fairness does not conflict with the implications of comprehensive doctrines about the more specific political issues. Since it draws its ideas from the public political culture, the new justice as fairness does not require antecedent acceptance, or even understanding, of any comprehensive religion or philosophical doctrine.

It should also be noted that the argument that there might be an overlapping consensus (of reasonable comprehensive doctrines) on justice as fairness is not merely that, when conceived politically, the view is so modest that it will not offend adherents of the diverse comprehensive doctrines. Importantly, the argument is also that justice as fairness secures to everyone, despite their doctrinal differences, certain basic liberties and an adequate floor of all-purpose means; moreover, it fosters civility and a variety of other political values.[20] Many of these advantages have already been argued for in *A Theory of Justice*, and the move to presenting justice as fairness as 'political', so far as I can see, does not undermine those arguments. So far, so good.

But, now, if the worry about stability is the practical concern that I have been assuming, it is not enough to show that it is remotely 'possible' that there could be an overlapping consensus (of reasonable comprehensive doctrines) on justice as fairness. If such a consensus is now seen as the stabilizing force of a just society, one wants some assurance that such a consensus would be likely to develop and endure. If the point of looking for arguments for stability is to see, before we attempt

[20] PL, 154–72.

reforms, whether the reforms would be lasting enough to be worth the effort, then a bare possibility is small comfort.

Is it at all likely that justice as fairness will win an overlapping consensus of reasonable comprehensive doctrines in our pluralistic world, achieving the stability of a just society in that way? On this issue, it is hard not to be sceptical. And, if we continue to see the main point of *Political Liberalism* as an attempt to assuage the practical concern about stability, then its arguments, I suspect, are bound to seem woefully inadequate.

Why be sceptical here? A main reason, I suppose, is our experience of persistent conflict of ideas in our large heterogeneous democracies. Fortunately, there has somehow developed in the United States and many other countries a considerable consensus on constitutional and associated political procedures, but when we raise questions of interpretation and philosophical justification the consensus seems to evaporate. Most people are not philosophers, and justice as fairness, even conceived politically, is a subtle and complex system of philosophical ideas. Even the distinction between a political conception and a comprehensive moral doctrine is a subtlety that may well escape the average citizen. (Think, for example, of explaining to the larger public the distinction between political constructivism, which says that the principles of justice may be *represented* as the principles agreed upon by free and equal citizens, and Kantian constructivism, which says that the principles of justice are *constituted* by the joint will of rational autonomous persons.[21]) The core tenets of political liberalism, I suppose, are more readily understood and accepted than fully specified versions (such as justice as fairness), but I suspect that the same forces that generate divergence of moral and religious comprehensive doctrines will block consensus on the less comprehensive, but still philosophical, political ideas of liberalism.

Moreover, the arguments of *Political Liberalism* seem quite inadequate, and of the wrong kind, to solve the stability problem as I have presented it. What makes for stability in society is largely an empirical question; and *Political Liberalism* does not purport to offer empirical evidence that an overlapping consensus would be likely.[22] One would

---

[21] PL, 90–107, 125–9, esp. 93, 99, and 125.

[22] Rawls offers a variety of considerations in defence of his view that such an appropriate overlapping consensus is possible, noting both the advantages of justice as fairness to all and the 'looseness' in most comprehensive doctrines that might enable their adherents to come to accept it as a working political framework (PL, 160 ff.). But he never pretends to offer empirical evidence that this is likely, and regarding even its possibility he realizes that, in the end, we must wait and see: 'Whether justice as fairness (or

expect, too, that to show there is a good chance for such a consensus, one would need to investigate the fundamental premises of the 'reasonable comprehensive doctrines' with which we are acquainted and then to argue from within such systems that they have grounds to support justice as fairness as a political framework. But Rawls deliberately sets aside this approach.

Many, if not most, people in our society, I suspect, do not have any effective commitment to a comprehensive moral, religious, or political doctrine. Perhaps a majority can name a religious affiliation, but this does not mean that they really understand and use the doctrines with which they associate themselves. Many people seem to be doctrineless ethical pluralists, with diverse opinions on particular matters but no 'theory'. If so, then even winning the allegiance of the major religions and philosophical theories (for justice as fairness) would still not ensure stability; the more or less doctrineless folk need to be convinced as well, and they are already averse to philosophical systems of ideas.

Again, if a practical concern for durability and stabilizing forces is the focus of concern, then *Political Liberalism* seems to rely too heavily on appeals to rational judgement. The factors which stabilize various societies may in fact have relatively little to do with the systems of ideas that they espouse, and more to do with habit, reinforcement, and blind emotional attachments.[23] These factors may also be highly contextual, and so not transferrable from one historical situation to another. Such non-rational factors are perhaps more prominent in tyrannical schemes that attempt to manipulate the citizens, but this does not mean that they are not a force that contributes to citizens' 'willing' acceptance in democracies.

Finally, if we understand the stability problem as the practical concern that I have assumed so far, there is a danger that Rawls's argument for an overlapping consensus will be seen as nothing more than the following caricature. Imagine representatives of all the traditional religions and other (reasonable) comprehensive doctrines meeting, together with the many reasonable doctrineless folk. They had been assigned to read *A Theory of Justice*, but, for one reason or another, they were not

some similar view) can gain the support of an overlapping consensus so defined is a speculative question. One can reach an educated conjecture only by working it out and exhibiting the way it might be supported' (PL, 15; see also PL, 167–8).

[23] Rawls, of course, recognizes that such factors play a causal role in promoting de facto stability (see, for example, PL, 161); and, as I suggest later, his focus of concern is best understood as the liberal justification of justice as fairness rather than the assurance of durability of societies that accept it.

uniformly ready to accept justice as fairness. Some, we imagine, had not understood it; others thought it denied features of their comprehensive doctrines; still others refused to endorse any public political conception, for although they believed their own doctrine best for deciding issues about the basic structure, they reasonably acknowledged that no such doctrine should be forced on an unwilling people. Now imagine that an enthusiastic (but misguided) Rawls student were to try to sell the others on *Political Liberalism*. 'We need a common, working conception of justice for basic political questions,' he says, 'and it is unreasonable for any of us to foist our *comprehensive doctrines* on anyone else, particularly since that would sanction a public denial of the truth of all the other (reasonable) doctrines. Much as we would each like to have our own doctrines control the issues about the basic structure, we cannot reasonably insist on that. So,' he continues, 'I have proposal: we Rawlsian liberals will downgrade our comprehensive doctrine to a political one, shift our claims for it from "true" to "reasonable", forgo terms not in the public culture, and restrict its use to the issues about the basic structure of society. Then the rest of you, for your part, simply agree to use this political conception as the standard that determines real issues about the basic structure. And so, when you all consent to this, we will at last have stability for a society that is just (by the standards we Rawlsians initially advocated).'

This bargain, we can suppose, would not be very persuasive, for it asks non-liberal groups to swap their share in the power to control basic decisions for mere modesty in the presentation of liberal doctrine. Careful readers will, of course, realize that this caricature of Rawls's liberal proposal is not fair. He does not, for example, offer the new political conception of justice as fairness as a bargaining chip to entice support from those who would not accept *A Theory of Justice*. The desired consensus is meant to be based on the whole range of reasons offered for justice as fairness in both his books (the reasoning from the original position, the security of basic goods, the political values, etc.), not merely on its limited scope and willingness to forgo claims to 'truth'. At best such a consensus, Rawls argued, would not be achieved in an explicit bargain but would develop gradually from a prior *modus vivendi*, as somewhat indeterminate comprehensive doctrines come to accommodate themselves so they can lend their support to what they can see to be a fair and tolerant political framework.[24] None the less, despite the distortions, the scepticism expressed in the caricature will, I

---

[24] PL, 158–68.

fear, be widely shared so long as the stability issue is understood along the lines of my initial reading.

IS THERE A BETTER READING OF THE PROJECT?

Suppose that my scepticism is correct, that is, (1) it is very unlikely that there will be ever be an overlapping consensus of reasonable comprehensive doctrines on justice as fairness (or political liberalism), and (2) the stability of (more or less) just societies, if ever achieved, will be likely to rest more on non-rational factors, relative to context and empirically discoverable, than on the prospect of philosophical arguments convincing a substantial majority of reasonable citizens. Is the main project of *Political Liberalism*, therefore, a failure, and its downsizing of justice as fairness a waste of time? Was there no point in arguing for at least the *possibility* of a just and stable society?

If we reconceive the nature of the problem that led Rawls to reconceive justice as fairness, I think we get a more attractive picture. Let us suppose that the concern with stability was not the practical concern I described earlier. (Will a just structure unravel? Will it be too short-lived to be worth instituting?) Perhaps establishing the possibility of stability 'of the right kind' is to be seen as a necessary move in a project of justifying the advocacy and use of justice as fairness as a standard. Now, however, what prompts the need for justification is not a fear that a just structure, as defined by Rawls's principles, would be short-lived but the suspicion that it would unfairly coerce reasonable people who hold other views about justice and morality generally. Asking whether it is possible for reasonable people, committed to diverse doctrines, to form an overlapping consensus on justice as fairness is a way of checking to see if there are sufficiently good reasons for making justice as fairness the determining standard regarding the basic structure, reasons which one could sincerely defend to others without denying their deepest religious and philosophical commitments. If one can make a cogent case that there are adequate reasons for diverse reasonable people to join a consensus on justice as fairness as their working political idea, then certain liberal and Kantian conditions for the legitimate exercise of power over others have been met.

If this case can be made, for example, then the maxim to use justice as fairness as a policy would be one that, in a sense, we can will as a universal law. The argument, if successful, would show that one can will the policy for everyone as reasonably acceptable from everyone's perspective, while still respecting most others publicly as no less reasonable than oneself; for the (new, political) arguments that they should adopt justice as fairness in no way presuppose that people should abandon their religion, their special conception of the good, etc., provided that they are 'reasonable' in a minimal sense. On this reading, the project is to show that advocacy and use of justice as fairness, even though inevitably warranting coercion, is reasonable and respectful of those whose use of reason leads them to disagree with us deeply. For this purpose it is unimportant whether in fact a majority of (reasonable) people will ever, in fact, come to agree on justice as fairness. Showing the possibility of stability of the right kind, on this view, would be analogous to the familiar Rawlsian strategy of justifying principles by hypothetical consent; here, though, the argument would be to allay doubts that the principles are worthy of actual consent by showing that they could, hypothetically, win (almost) universal agreement if everyone would consider them reasonably.

Several passages suggest that the point of conceiving justice as fairness as political and arguing that it can win an overlapping consensus has less to do with practical concerns about the durability of a just society than with answering the questions, 'What would be the most reasonable basis of social union?' and 'What is, for liberals, a legitimate exercise of political power?' In the fourth chapter of *Political Liberalism*, for example, this new reading seems confirmed, at least as part of Rawls's understanding of his project and the need for changes. Here he introduces the 'liberal principle of legitimacy', which says,

> our exercise of political power is fully proper only when it is exercised in accordance with a constitution the essentials of which all citizens as free and equal may reasonably be expected to endorse in the light of principles and ideals acceptable to their common human reason.[25]

This is a constraint on justification which commitment to liberalism itself imposes. Two important assumptions are that (1) so far as we are entitled to assert for political purposes, human reason does not give us grounds to rule out the major traditional religions and philosophical doctrines as 'unreasonable'[26] and (2) the political issues that arise about

---

[25] PL, 137.
[26] In his APA reply, Rawls reminded me, and stressed the importance, of the qualification in the antecedent here. It is not that, as individuals or as philosophers, we must concede that all 'reasonable comprehensive doctrines' are equally supported by good reasons. The point is that political liberalism does not permit one to assume, for purposes of deciding basic political questions, that comprehensive doctrines which meet its minimal tests for reasonableness are unreasonable or less well grounded than one's own doctrine.

the basic structure of society are such that, however these are resolved, the result will be a coercive use of political power. Given these assumptions, arguing that a political conception of justice can win an overlapping consensus of reasonable diverse doctrines is necessary to establish, from a liberal point of view, the legitimacy of using it. If there is no actual overlapping consensus, a working justice as fairness would lack the fullest justification and the deepest basis of social union,[27] but if such a consensus is not even possible, in the sense I have been discussing, then decisions based on justice as fairness would have no legitimacy at all.[28]

If my current understanding is right, then, the stability problem Rawls addresses is not, or at least need not be taken to be, whether it is likely that a society based on justice as fairness will endure. Nor is the issue even whether it is likely that such a society will in fact win willing acceptance by all the reasonable adherents of all the reasonable comprehensive doctrines. The latter, surely, is an ideal for liberals who follow Rawls, but it is not necessary. Liberals will naturally want to believe that success in achieving lasting liberal reforms is likely enough to make it reasonable to work towards such reforms; but the point of Rawls's arguments that the appropriate overlapping consensus on justice as fairness is possible is not, or is not primarily, to provide assurance on that point. The primary aim, instead, is to give a defence of justice as fairness against the charge that (even if we had power to do so) to use it as a standard for (inevitably) coercive political decisions would violate the liberal principle of legitimacy. That principle says, 'our exercise of political power is fully proper only when it is exercised in accordance with a constitution the essentials of which all citizens as free and equal may be reasonably expected to endorse in the light of principles and ideals *acceptable to their common human reason*'.[29] Given that the use of 'common human reason' will continue to leave us with diverse religions and philosophies ('the fact of reasonable pluralism'), liberals are constrained by their own principle of legitimacy not to use justice as fairness, or any other standard, in exercising political power unless they are convinced that there are sufficient reasons to defend justice as fairness to those who are reasonable but who reasonably disagree about the 'true' answers to the deepest questions of religion and morality.

To show that there are such good and sufficient reasons one needs

---

[27] This is most explicit in the unpublished class notes, but see PL, 134–72.
[28] Rawls's class notes and PL, 137 ff.   [29] PL, 137 (italics mine).

(for example) to show, without challenging the truth or reasonableness of Catholicism, utilitarianism, etc., that adherents of those doctrines have adequate grounds to accept and use justice as fairness as a practical framework if it is limited in the ways implied by calling it a mere 'political conception'.[30] To do this, it is not necessary to prove that all or most Catholics, utilitarians, etc. will, or even probably will, endorse justice as fairness some day. Nor need one show that if there were such an overlapping consensus it would in fact last.[31] What is needed is, first, a thoroughly articulated proposal of what it would be to view justice as fairness as a political conception and, second, a cogent statement of strong reasons why Catholics, utilitarians, etc., without abandoning their faith, could reasonably endorse this proposal. Rawls tries to provide both of these in *Political Liberalism*. But whether, in the end, his proposal and arguments are successful in meeting the concerns for Kantian justification, liberal legitimacy, and a reasonable basis for social union is a matter that will require further discussion.

SOME RELATED INTERPRETATIVE QUESTIONS

Rawls's rich but complex discussion raises many questions, but here I want to mention two, rather preliminary, questions of interpretation.

   1. How much of *A Theory of Justice*, I wonder, is meant to be included in 'justice as fairness' now that this is presented as a 'political conception' rather than a 'comprehensive doctrine'? Clearly portions of part III of *A Theory of Justice* are meant to be set aside.[32] No doubt the suggestions that the framework might be extended to a general theory of the right, and also of virtues, are not part of the political conception (even though they may remain fruitful suggestions for moral philoso-

---

[30] Catholicism and utilitarianism are used here as familiar examples which, I suppose, most liberals would count as among the 'reasonable comprehensive doctrines' by Rawls's criteria, but it is not important for the main point to insist that either, or any other doctrine in particular, in fact meets those criteria.
[31] Liberals will naturally hope that both are true, i.e. that a lasting overlapping consensus with reasonable Catholics and utilitarians will someday come about and will prove durable. Also strong empirical evidence against a tendency towards such consensus, even under favourable conditions, should make liberals worry that their 'good and sufficient reasons' are, after all, weaker and less free from bias than they thought. But, as Rawls might note, we are now far from having such decisive evidence for or against the emergence of a consensus; after all, the relevant ideas of a 'political conception' have only just recently been put on the table. Besides, if my reading is right, the primary concern regarding the possibility of overlapping consensus is not the likelihood of de facto agreement but the adequacy of the reasons for it.   [32] PL, p. xvi.

phy).[33] Also it is clear that certain explicit changes, e.g. in the principle of liberty and the account of primary goods, supersede the account of *A Theory of Justice*.[34] But how much of the discussion of methodology, the alternative ways an original position might be defined, and the arguments for features of the original position are still included? Does commitment to justice as fairness as political imply acceptance of the method of reflective equilibrium? It is clear that as a political conception, justice as fairness includes the idea that principles of justice 'may be *represented*' as the outcome of a procedure of construction but not as in fact 'made or *constituted*' by the agreement of free and equal persons, or their hypothetical representatives;[35] but are the details of the original position, the previous arguments for features of the original position, and the arguments that members of the original position would accept the principles part of the political conception?

The reason for asking is this. To preserve as much of the force and substance of *A Theory of Justice* as possible, it would seem that Rawls should want to include in the 'module' that is meant to be the focus of the overlapping consensus as many of these ideas and arguments from *A Theory of Justice* as is compatible with the move to a 'political conception'.[36] This seems to be Rawls's intent.[37] But then the more substantial, complex, philosophical, and controversial the political conception of justice as fairness is, the less plausibility there seems in the suggestion that it is a relatively simple, practical framework that can facilitate public discussion among people of diverse backgrounds and faiths. Also it will be more difficult even to show that all reasonable comprehensive doctrines *can* endorse justice as fairness, i.e. have adequate reasons, compatible with their doctrines, to do so.

2. The background for my second question is this. Justice as fairness, as a political conception, is just one form of *political* liberalism;[38] there are many liberalisms, presumably even many (possible) political liberalisms.[39] Political liberalisms need to identify 'fundamental questions for which the conception's political values yield reasonable answers'.[40] These are the 'constitutional essentials', which include principles regarding the structure of government and political processes and equal basic rights and liberties, but not the difference principle or 'fair equality of opportunity' (as described in *A Theory of Justice*). (Unless the difference principle appears as a guideline in a statute, for example, the idea of public reason does not allow the Supreme Court to appeal to

---

[33] TJ, 108–17, 433–9.   [34] PL, 75 f., 180–6, 290 ff.   [35] PL, 93 and 99.
[36] For the idea of the 'module' see PL, 12.   [37] PL, p. xvi.   [38] PL, p. xxix.
[39] PL, 6, 226.   [40] PL, 227.

it.[41]) The general principle of legitimacy and the idea of public reason are essential to liberalisms; and their content must include basic rights, liberties, and opportunities, an assigned priority among these, and 'measures assuring to all citizens adequate all-purpose means to make effective use of their liberties and opportunities'.[42]

There is, then, not only a distinction between the old (comprehensive) and new (political) ways of conceiving of justice as fairness but also a distinction between a fuller version of the political conception (which includes the difference principle and fair equality of opportunity) and those minimal aspects of it that are needed for it to be a form of liberalism. We might call the latter 'Rawls's basic political liberalism'. Even this, the new political justice as fairness stripped of details inessential to liberalism, is apparently distinct from other (possible) forms of political liberalism.

Now *Political Liberalism* answers the basic question, 'How is it possible that there may exist over time a stable and just society of free and equal citizens profoundly divided by reasonable though incompatible religious, philosophical, and moral doctrines?', largely by arguing that a liberal conception of justice can win an overlapping consensus of reasonable comprehensive doctrines.[43] In this extended argument are we to think of the (new) political 'theory of justice' (with the difference principle, etc.) as winning the overlapping consensus, or are we to think of (what I called) 'Rawls's basic political liberalism' as achieving that consensus?

I raise this question, like the previous one, because it seems to me that the plausibility that a political conception of justice could become widely accepted, the focus of overlapping consensus of both adherents of reasonable comprehensive doctrines and other doctrineless folk, is reduced the more detailed, philosophical, complex, and controversial that political conception is. If the whole of the (new) political 'theory of justice' is meant to be the object of the consensus, this naturally increases the difficulty of showing that there can be an overlapping consensus (of reasonable doctrines) on it. If a stripped-down conception ('Rawls's basic liberalism') is to be the object, there is more hope for showing that there are adequate reasons for a consensus but then doubts arise as to whether enough has been stabilized to call the scheme *just*. For example, a society with extraordinary affluence and gross inequalities would fall far short of justice, I think, if it merely agreed to keep

---

[41] PL, 237 n.   [42] PL, 6 and 226.
[43] The basic question is stated at PL, p. xviii.

the basic liberties fixed and provided a minimum 'safety net'.[44] Rawls himself apparently still endorses the difference principle, which would oppose such injustice, but the question now arises whether, given pluralism, the liberal principle of legitimacy allows those in power, absent actual consensus, to use it.

CONCLUDING REMARKS:
HOW MUCH HAS BEEN LOST?

Is justice as fairness now merely a political conception? Was it ever really a comprehensive moral doctrine? What have we, the admirers of *A Theory of Justice*, lost in the redescription of justice as fairness in *Political Liberalism*? There are two main points to keep in mind, I think, if one is inclined to mourn the loss of Rawls's earlier, apparently more ambitious and comprehensive, characterization of justice as fairness.

First, many aspects of what Rawls now calls 'the political conception' seem already implicit in *A Theory of Justice*, or compatible with it, and so the change may not be as radical as the introduction to *Political Liberalism* would lead one to believe. There is, to be sure, resolution of ambiguity on many points, and change on some; but *A Theory of Justice* was always limited in its focus, restrained in its metaphysical claims, and open in its use of ideas developed in modern Western political culture.[45] It was rich with suggestions about an analogous theory of 'right' and 'virtue', but that the basic structure of society was its primary subject was clear from the outset. It asked us to engage in a thought experiment about choice under a 'veil' that called to mind Kant's abstract metaphysical 'Ideas', but careful readers knew it was, even then, merely 'a device of representation'. Compared to most other works in political philosophy of the time, it was bold, far-ranging, and ambitious; but it appealed, repeatedly, to our contemporary intuitive understandings and judgements to generate a confirming 'reflective equilibrium'. That the current 'political conception' is significantly different is

---

[44] Much depends on how we interpret 'adequate all-purpose means' in the definition of basic liberalism above. No doubt this is meant to be somewhere between what would be warranted by the difference principle and what Ronald Reagan's advisers would count as a 'safety net', but the further we move from the difference principle in economic justice, I suspect, the harder it is to justify, or get reasonable agreement, on the strict priority of liberties over economic issues.

[45] The current political conception, however, is more severely restricted to such ideas.

undeniable; but many exaggerated accounts of the change, I think, are due to misunderstandings of the original account.

Second, we should remember that the old, unmodified *A Theory of Justice* is still on the table, as it were. To alter the metaphor, copies may still be used in the philosophy classroom, even if not, any more, in Congress or the courts. My point is not the trivial one that we have a right, according to *Political Liberalism* as well as in fact, to reject Rawls's second book and believe in the first. (Political liberalism, of course, tolerates and seeks support from much more radically distinct comprehensive doctrines than that espoused in *A Theory of Justice*.) The point, rather, is that *Political Liberalism* does not deny, in any wholesale way, that the principles and arguments of *A Theory of Justice* are true, important, and better grounded than competing 'reasonable comprehensive' theories. There are, admittedly, some specific points in *A Theory of Justice* which Rawls now claims were unduly vague, needlessly ad hoc, and even inconsistent with its other claims.[46] Still, if, as Rawls says, that earlier work expresses a (partially) comprehensive doctrine, then surely it still counts, by his criteria, among the 'reasonable' ones, the truth or falsity of which Rawls's political liberalism refuses to judge. *Political Liberalism* does imply that, as with Catholicism and utilitarianism, the truth or superior rationality of justice as fairness as a comprehensive doctrine should not be presupposed (or, normally, even asserted) in public debates and official decisions about fundamental constitutional issues. Many will no doubt challenge this restriction, but it is important to see at least that Rawls's argument for this new restrictive proposal does not withdraw the claim that the old doctrine is supported by better reasons than are competing comprehensive theories of justice. Also Rawls is still committed to the view that the old doctrine may be more profoundly grounded, in a sense, than the new political conception.

[46] It is natural to suppose that anyone who accepts *Political Liberalism* must entirely reject p. III of *A Theory of Justice* as an argument for stability. However, with some changes, p. III can be seen as making a reasonable argument for the proposition that if a society adopted justice as fairness as its comprehensive doctrine, then there are reasons to suppose it would generate strong stabilizing forces tending to maintain the citizens' willing acceptance of its principles. This, I take it, is somewhat more modest than how Rawls now sees the initial project of p. III, for it leaves open the possibility that, as Rawls now believes likely, given the freedoms allowed in such a just society, moral and religious disagreements would (almost) inevitably develop. The modest thesis, then, does not resolve the problem that pluralism poses for the liberal, and so, from Rawls's perspective, the second book would still be required. This is compatible, however, with the view that *A Theory of Justice* gave good grounds for the more modest thesis and that this thesis is not an insignificant one.

In so far as *A Theory of Justice* proposed more comprehensive moral ideas, a kind a partial Kantian liberalism, it remains a competitor for allegiance, and inspiration for further development, in the philosophical project that each person may have of trying to find, for him- or herself, the most reasonable comprehensive moral/political theory. It may seem a bit odd, but it is consistent, to treat the old justice as fairness as a reasonable partially comprehensive moral doctrine that may, or may not, guide its advocates to join an overlapping consensus on justice as fairness as a restricted political idea.[47] If it does, they may come to see *Political Liberalism* not so much as rejecting or abandoning the old *A Theory of Justice* as partially cloning it, drawing from it the basic materials to build up a similar, but more modest and practical, counterpart to be used in a different forum.

[47] Rawls's reply at the APA meetings treated this point briefly, perhaps as obvious, saying that in principle the earlier book is still 'on the shelf' and might be a part of an overlapping consensus with other comprehensive doctrines, 'why not?'

10

Conscience and Authority

INTRODUCTION

My topic is conscience and its relation to authority. The problem is an old but persistent one. Some think the following is a truism, boringly obvious: *One should always follow one's conscience.* But that is too quick. What if conscience conflicts with the direct commands of those who have authority over us? Such conflicts occur dramatically in war, but also in business affairs and in mundane, everyday life: one's superior officer, one's boss, or the law of the land insists, 'Do it,' but conscience objects, 'Don't do it.' Which should take precedence? Maybe the answer is 'Sometimes conscience, and at other times, authority.' But then how can we reasonably decide *when* conscience should give way to authority, and when it should not?

In favour of conscience, some argue that we lack moral integrity if we violate our conscientious convictions just because someone told us to. But, again, the issue is not that simple. Those who have legitimate authority over us are not simply 'someone' who happened to tell us what to do. To acknowledge that they are authorities is to recognize that there are *good reasons* for them, rather than us, to have the right to make certain decisions. To ignore this crucial point can be disastrous, especially in times of crisis that call for immediate action. Even in the absence of crisis, when we have ample time to reflect, the need for authoritative decisions to coordinate group activities is a vitally important factor that our deliberations, and even consciences, should take into account. If we were to ignore the moral reasons for having authorities, choosing to guide our conduct instead entirely by promptings of individual conscience formed in ignorance of these reasons, chaos would be the result in both civilian and military contexts.

So, then, should we adopt the extreme opposite policy: *Always obey the orders of our lawful superiors*? Unfortunately, from a moral point of view, this solution is also too simplistic. For practical purposes, it is, of course, necessary for legal and military codes to insist on unquestioning obedience to authorities in all but a few extraordinary situations—for example, where to obey would plainly be a 'crime against humanity'. Virtually all moral traditions acknowledge that no secular authority is infallible or worthy of obedience in absolutely all possible circumstances. To be sure, even in the exceptional cases there are usually some good reasons to obey, but the reasons are not always decisive, not always sufficient grounds to override the moral repugnance of what has been ordered. My point here is not new or radical. It was affirmed in the Nuremberg trials, and it is presupposed by anyone who acknowledges that Germans in the early 1940s would have been justified in resisting Hitler's orders to exterminate European Jews.

In order to see the need to qualify a policy of always submitting to authority, we also should remember that such a policy would cover much more than the dramatic and dangerous cases that we typically see in films, where there is flagrant disobedience to direct orders (and even mutiny) in an emergency situation. (Think, for example, of *The Caine Mutiny*.) The unqualified policy would also dictate unquestioning conformity in less volatile situations, where there is ample time to reflect, minimum risk of harm, and a respectful alternative to outright defiance, for example, protest through recognized channels or resignation.

We face, then, a moral issue that is not amenable to simple solutions. We cannot hope to resolve it definitively here; but perhaps we can make some progress, at least in thinking more clearly about the problem. In philosophy the path to progress is typically to examine carefully the central ideas in a controversy. This is because ambiguities and misunderstandings often cloud the real issues. The key idea in our problem is *conscience*. Before we can say to what extent, and why, we should respect and follow our consciences, we need to examine the different sorts of thing that conscience has been thought to be.

For this purpose, it is helpful to distinguish between various *particular* 'conceptions' of conscience and a very *general* 'concept' of conscience. The several conceptions of conscience are specific interpretations, or more detailed understandings, of a general concept, or core idea, of conscience. This core idea which they have in common is, very roughly, the idea of a capacity, attributed to most human beings, that enables them to sense or immediately discern that their acts (or omissions) are morally wrong, bad, and worthy of disapproval.[1] The general

---

[1] Roughly, to say conscience is a capacity to 'sense or immediately discern' is to say that it is a way of coming to the relevant moral beliefs about one's acts by means of feeling, instinct, or personal judgement. Becoming convinced *by conscience* that one's conduct is immoral is supposed to be distinct from reaching that conclusion by explicit appeal to external authorities or by engaging in discussion with others, though perhaps

concept also includes the idea that their consciences tend to influence their conduct but rarely control it completely. Moreover, it is assumed that people tend to suffer mental discomfort and lower self-esteem when they act against their consciences. This general idea leaves open further questions about how conscience is acquired and developed, how it operates, what it purports to 'say', how trustworthy it is as a moral guide, whether it is universal or found only in certain cultures, and what purposes it serves for individuals and society. Particular conceptions of conscience fill in these details in different ways.

My plan here is to describe briefly three particular conceptions of conscience, which I call (1) the popular conception, (2) the cultural relativist conception, and (3) the Kantian conception.[2] More specifically, these conceptions are: first, a popular idea that conscience is an instinct, designed by God or Nature to signal us when our acts or intentions are wrong; second, a deflationary cultural relativism that regards conscience as nothing but our unreflective responses to whatever values we have picked up from our culture (or special subculture); and third, a familiar metaphor, described by Kant, that presents conscience as 'an inner judge' that condemns (or acquits) us of the charge that *we have not done our best* even to live up to our own judgements about what is right.

To preview my conclusions, I maintain that the last conception is the most plausible but that, no matter which conception you choose, conscience is not a foolproof, completely reliable guide to what is morally right. Conscience, then, cannot always trump authoritative commands. But neither do authoritative commands always trump conscience. In fact, from a moral point of view, both should be seen as ultimately subject to review in a process of informed, reasonable moral deliberation and discussion. This process cannot *guarantee* that our conclusions are correct, but it would be an illusion to think that either conscience or authority provides a more basic or reliable guide. In fact conscience presupposes willingness to engage in this process, *when time allows*, for without this we can never be confident even that we are doing our best to do what is right. Moral integrity is not achieved by blind obedience

most people would grant that public opinion and authoritative pronouncements tend to influence the development of consciences and so may indirectly affect what conscience 'says' on particular occasions.

[2] The three conceptions of conscience discussed here, along with another, are discussed more fully, with more extensive comparisons and citations, in my essay 'Four Conceptions of Conscience', in *Nomos XL: Integrity and Conscience* (New York: New York University Press, 1998), 13–52.

to either conscience or authority. It is found only in resolute adherence to *our best judgements* after taking into account, in the deliberative process, both the preliminary warnings of conscience and the grounds for respecting legitimate authorities. The proper time for such moral deliberation is not in the heat of battle, of course, but in advance, when we can stop to think without causing anyone harm.

THE POPULAR CONCEPTION

Let us begin with the popular conception: conscience as an instinctual access to moral truth, given to us by God or Nature. There are many variations, but, for contrast, I describe an extreme version. Here are the main themes.

1. Each human being is born with a latent conscience, which normally emerges into its full working capacity in youth or young adulthood. It is a capacity to identify, among our own acts and intentions, those which are morally wrong and those which are morally permissible. Conscience, however, does not identify acts and motives as morally admirable or praiseworthy. At best conscience is 'clear' or 'clean', not self-congratulating.

2. That certain acts, such as murder and adultery, are morally wrong is a matter of objective fact, independent of our consciences. That is, what makes such acts wrong is not just that conscience disapproves. Conscience merely alerts and warns us, like a gauge that indicates the presence of electrical problems but does not identify them specifically and is not itself the cause of trouble.

3. Conscience originates as a gift of God, or Nature, to human beings, a special access to moral truth that can work independently of church authority and rational reflection.[3] Appealing to conscience is not the same as using rational, reflective judgement to resolve moral questions. Conscience may be partly shaped and informed by such judgements, as well as by public debates, religious education, and so on; but it is not an intellectual moral adviser, only an instinctual inner 'voice' or sign that indicates a moral problem, warns us when tempted, and prods us to reform when guilty.[4] If the signal is correctly identified and

---

[3] It should be noted that the 'natural law' tradition in Western religious ethics, unlike the 'popular' religious conception, emphasizes individuals' *reason* as their mode of access to moral truth. This makes Aquinas's view more similar to Kant's, which is why, for starker contrast, I selected the 'popular' view.

[4] Typically one's conscience is pictured not as judging the moral quality of particular acts from first principles but rather as identifying a limited class of (one's own) wrong

heard, conscience is a reliable source of moral knowledge. However, to explain the fact that outrageous acts are often committed in the name of conscience, the popular view admits that conscience is not always identified, heard, and interpreted correctly.

4. God or Nature is supposed to have designed conscience as a personal guide, not for judging or goading others. Judging that an act is wrong for oneself entails that it is wrong for anyone unless there is a relevant difference between the cases, but others' cases may differ in so many ways that one has no practical licence to make extensive generalizations from what one 'learns' from one's own conscience.

If we accept this popular conception of conscience, what should our attitude be towards what our consciences seem to tell us? Since the popular conception regards conscience (once properly identified) as a generally reliable indicator of moral truth, we would have good (moral) reason for not 'dulling' our consciences, for 'listening' carefully for the signals of conscience, and for being cautiously guided by what it apparently tells us to do. Several factors, however, combine to recommend caution even to the firm believer in the popular conception. For example, though conscience is supposed to be a reliable signal of moral truth, it is not necessarily the only, or most direct, means of determining what we ought (and ought not) to do. When secular and religious authorities, together with the professed conscientious judgements of others, all stand opposed to what we initially took to be the voice of conscience, then these facts should raise doubts. Even assuming that 'genuine' pronouncements of conscience are reliable, *we* may not be reliably distinguishing these from our wishes, our fears, and the echoes in our heads from past lessons of parents and teachers. In effect, we need to check our supposed instinctual access to moral truth by reviewing evidence that is more directly relevant, for example, benefits and harms, promises fulfilled or broken, and the responsibilities of our social roles. To confirm that our instinctive response is a reflection of 'true conscience' rather than some morally irrelevant feeling, we would need to check its claims in some way, for example, by trying to determine whether the response coincides with reflective moral judgement, based on careful review of pertinent facts, in consultation with others. Without such a check, there is no way to be confident that the instinct

---

acts by the means of characteristic painful feelings aroused in contemplating them. This is a feature of several conceptions of conscience that fits well the metaphor of conscience as a warning, nagging, and reprimanding, Jiminy Cricket or a tiny angel that follows us through tempting times.

that we are about to rely on is really 'conscience' rather than some baser instinct.

By analogy, suppose we believe we have an intuitive sense that somehow signals dishonesty in job applicants with considerable regularity when this 'sense' is properly identified and used under ideal conditions. Although the suspicions we form by consulting this intuitive sense might provide useful warning signs, they would be no substitute for investigating candidates' records and seeking direct evidence of dishonest conduct. Only examination of the relevant facts could check whether what we take to be an accurate intuitive signal really is so.

Besides this practical problem, several considerations suggest that we would do well to look beyond the popular conception for a more adequate interpretation of conscience. For example, the popular conception draws major conclusions about ethics from assumptions about theology (or Nature) that are widely contested today. Many regard the alleged instinctual access to moral truth as unduly mysterious, scientifically unsupportable, and out of line with our best theories of moral development. Even among religious thinkers the popular view fails to muster strong support, for theologians are radically divided about how we come to know right and wrong and about the relative importance of conscience, reason, scripture, and church authority.

A deeper problem is that the popular view of conscience as an instinctual indicator of morality neglects the prior and indispensable roles of reason and judgement in determining what is morally right and wrong. Basic morality, I believe, is ultimately a matter of what free and reasonable people, with mutual respect and proper understanding of their condition, would agree to accept as a constraint on the pursuit of self-interest and other goals. That is not the sort of thing that anyone could plausibly claim to know directly 'by instinct'. Once we have a basic grasp of the *reasons* for moral principles, our respect for these principles may be signalled by unbidden 'pangs' and 'proddings' that feel like instinctual responses. But these count as signs of conscience only because they reflect our prior *judgements* about what morality reasonably requires of us.

THE CULTURAL RELATIVIST CONCEPTION

Some of those who cannot accept the popular conception of the origin and function of conscience adopt an extreme cultural relativist conception.[5] The term 'relativism', of course, is used loosely to refer to many different ideas, but let us stipulate here that the 'cultural relativist conception' is the view that the promptings of conscience are *nothing but* feelings that reflect the norms which one has internalized from one's culture. Such feelings are supposed to serve to promote social cohesion by disposing individuals towards conformity to group standards. This relativist conception replaces the theological story about the origin and function of conscience with a contemporary sociological hypothesis, but, more radically, it goes beyond this empirical hypothesis by claiming that conscience reflects 'nothing but' whatever cultural norms one has internalized. That is, this conception is actually a combination of two ideas: (1) a common *sociological* explanation of the genesis and social function of the feelings we attribute to 'conscience' and (2) a controversial *philosophical* thesis that the cultural norms which express themselves in what we call 'conscience' are inherently immune to objective moral assessment, i.e. none are morally better or more justifiable than any others.

The cultural relativist conception, then, is not merely a view about the origin and function of conscience, but also a view about its reliability as a moral guide. Regarding origin, the cultural relativist explains the 'conscientious' person's feelings of constraint as due to a learning process by which one inwardly accepts local cultural norms as one's standard of self-approval. Regarding function, the cultural relativist sees the development of conscience as a way by which social groups secure a measure of conformity to their local standards without relying entirely on external rewards and punishments. Regarding reliability, the cultural relativist holds that, although conscience rather accurately reveals the local norms that we have picked up from our environments, there is no objective standard by which we can ever determine that some cultural norms, but not others, are morally 'true' or 'justified'.

What are the implications of cultural relativism regarding the attitude we should take towards our consciences? If cultural relativism is true, in every culture people will tend to feel 'spontaneously' that certain acts are 'bad' and 'worthy of disapproval'. But how *should* informed and reflective persons regard these feelings and respond to them if they think

   [5] Types of relativism are usefully distinguished in Richard Brandt, *Ethical Theory* (Englewood Cliffs, NJ: Prentice-Hall, 1959), ch. 11; William Frankena, *Ethics* (Englewood Cliffs, NJ: Prentice-Hall, 1973), ch. 6, esp. 109–10; and James Rachels, *The Elements of Moral Philosophy* (New York: Random House, 1986), 12–24. See also John Ladd (ed.), *Relativism* (Belmont, Calif.: Wadsworth, 1973); David Wong, *Moral Relativity* (Los Angeles: University of California Press, 1984).

cultural relativism is true? Clearly, they should regard these feelings as just what they are (according to cultural relativism), namely, a fairly reliable sign that we are (have been, or soon will be) in violation of some cultural norm that we have internalized. Given this, we can expect that we are likely to experience further internal discomfort and to incur the disapproval of others if we continue to act as before (or as planned). These expectations give a prudent person *some* self-interested reason to 'heed conscience', and if the norms of that person's culture serve socially useful purposes, that person would have *some* altruistic reason to obey the promptings of 'conscience'.

But this is only one side of the picture. Those who accept cultural relativism also have reason to try to 'see through' and get rid of their feeling that acts against conscience are 'wrong', 'immoral', or 'unreasonable' by some objective, culturally independent standard. When the rewards of acting against conscience outweigh the unpleasantness of residual guilt feelings and predictable social disapproval, then the smart thing to do, assuming cultural relativism is true, would be to stifle conscience, or if need be, simply tolerate the discomfort it causes in order to gain the greater rewards to be had by violating it. In short, if we accept cultural relativism, we should not always follow conscience. Quite the contrary. Cultural relativists see the promptings of conscience as rather like beliefs that we can recognize as mere superstitions: we are tempted to accept them but we really think they have no objective foundation. Given this attitude, they should often suppress or ignore their consciences, just as they would a superstitious belief.

Some may conclude that these implications, by themselves, are enough to show that cultural relativism in untenable; but quite apart from this, there are ample reasons to doubt the cultural relativist conception. It seems strikingly at odds with the ordinary understanding of conscience, and its radical denial that moral judgements can be objective is not supported by its observations of cultural diversity.

Consider, first, the cultural relativist's empirical hypothesis that people tend, unconsciously and passively, to internalize the values of their culture from an early age. No doubt this is partly true, but it ignores the role of active, mature deliberation and social debate in shaping the moral convictions that inform our consciences. No doubt conscience reflects moral standards that we have internalized, but these standards need not have been adopted uncritically, without reason.

Second, the cultural relativist's insistence that cultural standards are not subject to objective moral criticism is a methodological assumption, not a valid conclusion drawn from empirical studies. It is in fact a radical moral scepticism reached only by a giant step beyond science into an area of perennial philosophical controversy. The empirical observations that cultural standards differ and that people tend to internalize their local standards do not, by themselves, prove anything about objectivity in morals or any other field. What is objectively true or reasonable to believe, whether in normative or descriptive matters, is not constituted simply by the fact that people agree about it; by the same token, objectivity is not necessarily undermined by the fact that people disagree. The issues are more complicated than that.

Third, in its effort to avoid being unduly judgemental, cultural relativism interprets 'conscience' as a morally neutral term, referring to internalized norms of *any* kind, no matter how cruel, oppressive, superstitious, or arbitrary these may be. Thus, for example, when Heinrich Himmler *felt disapproval* of himself for momentary feelings of pity for the Jews that he was gassing, the cultural relativist supposes this to be his 'conscience speaking' just as much as when a reformed slave trader first *felt a loathing* for his dirty business.[6] Value neutrality may have its uses in empirical studies, but the most common, and plausible, understandings of 'conscience' are not morally neutral. We presuppose that, even though they may be mistaken, anyone who has a conscience and follows it must understand and endorse at least the basic elements of a moral point of view. When Himmler, governed entirely by self-interest and Nazi ideology, *felt bad* about sympathizing with the innocent people that he helped to slaughter in the Holocaust, those 'bad feelings' should not be confused with pangs of *conscience*.

THE KANTIAN CONCEPTION

Let us turn now to Kant's metaphor of conscience as an inner judge.[7] The idea is that we experience conscience *as if* we were brought to trial, accused, scrutinized, and then either acquitted or found guilty. The pangs of conscience feel like a harsh but just sentence imposed by a judge who knows us all too well. A crucial part of the metaphor is that in the inner court of conscience we ourselves play all the roles: we are

---

[6] Himmler's attitude is evident in the quotations cited in Jonathan Bennett, 'The Conscience of Huckleberry Finn', in Christina Sommers and Fred Sommers (eds.), *Vice and Virtue in Everyday Life*, 3rd edn. (New York: Harcourt Brace Jovanovich, 1993), 25–39.

[7] Kant's ideas about conscience are most fully expressed in MM, 26–7 [233–5], 156 [394], and 188–91 [437–41] and in R, 173–4 [185–7].

not only the accused, but also the prosecution, the defence, and the judge who reaches a verdict and imposes sentence. A guilty verdict, in effect, is the painful realization that we have failed to live up to our own moral standards. These standards are moral judgements we have made previously, for example, in criticizing others. They become so deeply embedded in our personalities that we experience an immediate dissonance, or involuntary discomfort, when our conduct violates them.

One standard particularly important for conscience, Kant reminds us, is a 'duty of due care': that is, at times we need to scrutinize carefully the moral judgements that we normally take for granted in order to reassess whether these are really as reasonable as we have supposed. Especially when simply sticking by our previous moral assumptions would inflict serious harm on others, we need to rethink those assumptions carefully and honestly. Moral reason, not conscience, *imposes* this duty, but it is a standard that every reasonable person, presumably, has internalized. Conscience simply *alerts* us, painfully, when we are neglecting this duty of due care. Conscience, then, not only threatens to punish us for violating our previous standards of conduct; it also warns us against moral complacency, that is, against always taking for granted, despite evidence to the contrary, that our old standards are still reasonable ones. Kant's example was the Spanish Inquisitioners, who burned at the stake those they believed to be heretics. They may have acted according to their moral beliefs, Kant concedes, but they failed in their duty of due care, a duty to re-examine critically their moral assumption that burning heretics is right.

On the Kantian view, then, conscience has two important, but limited, tasks: (1) the general task of judging whether our conduct lives up to the moral standards that we have accepted and (2) the special task of prodding us not to neglect the duty to re-examine carefully our previous moral standards when there is some reason to question them. This idea has two striking advantages: first, it attributes to conscience a significant function that it can serve well; and, second, it does *not* assign to conscience a more ambitious function for which it is utterly unsuited. Let me explain.

The general function of conscience is to alert us when we are not doing our best to live up to our own moral standards. The pangs of conscience result from an implicit comparison of two things that each of us ordinarily knows well enough: the standards we accept for what we *should be doing* and our understanding of what we *are actually doing*. When there is a discrepancy between these, it is usually obvious. You do not have to be a genius or a moral expert to see that what you are doing (or about to do) is just what you have always believed to be wrong. This task of comparison, in fact, seems so easy and manageable that Kant remarked (with slight exaggeration) that there is no such thing as an erring conscience. His point was not that we always know what is *really* right, but merely that we can rather easily recognize when our acts violate what we *believe* is right.

The more ambitious task that Kant, quite rightly, does *not* ascribe to conscience is the difficult job of mustering all our best resources to find out what is really right—or, to put it more modestly, to make our most reasonable judgement about what is right. This is not the business of the 'inner judge' of conscience. That can only apply our previous moral opinions. Trying to determine, as best we can, what is really right is the role of practical reason, actively employed in reviewing the facts, the alternatives, and the various complex considerations that favour one moral conclusion or another. Such reasoning requires consultation with others and confrontation with opinions that differ sharply from our own. It is not a purely intellectual process, for it must give due weight to human feelings. Nor is it reasoning in a vacuum, for it takes place within a framework of constraints widely accepted as fundamental for any moral thinking. Kantians have a view about how to describe this framework, but others do as well; and so, except for a brief postscript, this must remain a topic for another occasion.

Now let us compare this Kantian conception of conscience with what I called the popular conception. Both acknowledge that the voice of conscience typically appears without an invitation: it warns, threatens, prods, and punishes us even when the last thing we want is to engage in serious moral self-appraisal. As Kant puts it, conscience is something we 'hear' even when we try to run away, a voice that 'speaks involuntarily and inevitably'. In this way, conscience is more like an instinct than a capacity for moral deliberation and reasoning. But, unlike the popular conception, the Kantian view does not treat conscience as a mysterious 'signal' implanted in us, inexplicably, as a guide to moral truth. Instead, the Kantian metaphor represents conscience as a familiar inner conflict experienced when we realize that what we are doing violates *our own internalized moral judgements*. This sort of inner conflict is not a mystery, but is in fact just what contemporary psychology would lead us to expect. Notice, too, that Kantian conscience is not a non-verbal signal, like a flashing light. The metaphor represents it as *speaking* to us, accusing, examining, and passing sentence, in a familiar moral vocabulary. The point is that we are judging ourselves by standards we understand and can articulate. Kantian conscience, moreover, is not a private line to moral truth, something that might substitute for serious moral reasoning with others. What it reveals is not an objective truth about what we ought to do, but only that our conduct is out of line with *what we have previously judged* that we ought to do.

Now consider how the Kantian conception compares and contrasts with the cultural relativist conception. These are similar in one respect: both can explain the promptings of conscience naturally as responses triggered by an awareness that we are deviating from internalized standards. Unlike the cultural relativist's, however, the Kantian conception of conscience is explicitly a *moral idea*, never meant to be *neutral*, say, between Hitler's cohorts and those who conscientiously opposed them. Also, unlike relativism, the Kantian view does not hold that cultural norms are immune to objective moral evaluation. Like most of us, Kant would not hesitate to say that the Holocaust was *really immoral*, even if it was once the policy of a Nazi culture. That is a judgement that is no doubt deeply embedded in our consciences, but the task of showing why such judgements are justified is the business, not of conscience, but of public reasoning from the fundamentals of a moral point of view.

The implications of the Kantian conception regarding our attitude towards our own consciences should now be clear. Conscience is no substitute for moral reasoning and judgement, but in fact presupposes these. A clear conscience is no guarantee that we have acted in an objectively right way, and so it is no ground for self-righteous pride or presumption that our moral judgement is superior to those who conscientiously disagree. However, in so far as the warnings and pangs of conscience reflect our recognition that our conduct falls short of our moral standards, they are reliable at least as a sign that we are not doing our best. Conformity to conscience is necessary, and perhaps even sufficient, to avoid being worthy of *moral blame* (even though conscience cannot assure us that our conduct is morally correct).[8]

Of course, our impartial moral judgements (about what *anyone* in various situations *should* do), even when correct, will not have an effect on our conduct unless they are *applied* to our own case, which is a function of conscience. Thus, as Kant says, conscience ought to be 'cultivated' and 'sharpened' as well as heeded. Again, conscience makes one *painfully* aware of one's misdeeds, and so it also helps motivate us to apologize, make restitution, and reform. In all these respects conscience is to be respected, even though its functions are limited.

[8] 'But when a man is aware of having acted according to his conscience, then as far as guilt or innocence is concerned, nothing more can be demanded': MM, 161 [401].

IMPLICATIONS FOR CONSCIENCE
AND AUTHORITY

Now let us return briefly to the initial problem of how conscience relates to authority. Admittedly, we have only examined three conceptions of conscience, and the moral grounds for respecting authorities have only been assumed, not discussed critically. None the less, my reflections here point towards certain tentative practical conclusions.

First, the most plausible conception of conscience, the Kantian one, gives us strong reasons to cultivate and respect our conscience but no reason to suppose that our consciences are infallible guides to morally justifiable conduct. It is a reliable guide as to whether we are living up to our own internalized moral standards, but it cannot *guarantee* that our standards are really justifiable as correct or reasonable.

But none of our conceptions of conscience guarantees that a conscientious decision is an objectively right one. The popular conception *says* that conscience, properly identified and used in ideal conditions, is a reliable sign of moral truth; but we have seen reasons to doubt this. Cultural relativism implies that we may be uncomfortable in acting against conscience; but it insists that this discomfort is purely subjective, having no firmer basis than early, unconscious internalization of local norms. The Kantian conception gives reason to believe that conscience should be respected, but it insists that conscience is fallible and must be checked by public, reason-governed, critical discussion of the standards that our consciences habitually rely upon.

The upshot is that, under any of our interpretations, conscience does not determine what it is objectively right to do. Under the best interpretation, it must be respected, for its judgements are reliable, within their limits. But, given this view, conscience is never sufficient by itself: only engaging in explicit moral reasoning, with others, enables us to live with a reasonable hope that our moral beliefs are justified. Ironically, assuming the 'duty of due care', we cannot even have a *clear* conscience unless we are willing to check the opinions that our consciences rely upon by engaging in this process of moral reasoning. If this is right, there are good reasons for ethics courses—and for continuing the moral dialogue long after the classes are over.

POSTSCRIPT

Regarding the conflict between conscience and authority, my theme has been a modest one: both should be respected, but neither is an infallible

moral guide; and if we cannot satisfy both, there is a need, time permitting, to look for a resolution in a process of moral reasoning. In this
process we survey the facts of the case, critically examine relevant arguments, and listen to diverse opinions, considering all this *from a moral
point of view*.

This last qualification is important, but you would be right to wonder
what features are inherent in a moral point of view. To ask this is to
raise some of the deepest issues in moral theory, issues that have been
debated for centuries. Obviously I cannot say much about them at this
late hour, but I will conclude my remarks by sketching some basic points
that I draw from Kant. There are four main points, corresponding
roughly to Kant's different formulations of the basic principle of
morality.[9]

First, in looking for *moral* policies we are not merely trying to find
policies that serve our own interests or the interests of our favourite
groups. Our policies must be such that we could reasonably choose them
for anyone in comparable circumstances to act on. What is good for the
goose must be good for the gander—at least when there are no morally
relevant differences between gooses and ganders.

Second, human beings are not mere expendable commodities,
tools or toys that can be used and discarded. Enemies, then, are not
merely enemies; we must grant to each person a basic respect as a
human being. No one's interests then can be arbitrarily discounted, and
when we think that the common good overrides an individual's
interests, this must in principle be morally justifiable even to that
individual.

Third, human beings are not mere animals or robots, to be manipu-
lated or compelled to behave as we wish. They can be held responsible
for their own conduct, responsible for controlling their passions and
appetites by reason, and responsible for constraining themselves by
moral principles, whether they feel inclined to or not. This is not simply
a matter of the attitude we should take towards *other* people. First and
foremost, morality requires each of us to hold *ourselves* responsible as
moral persons, without pretending that we are merely the instruments
or victims of others.

Fourth and finally, particular moral principles can be understood as
just those principles that reasonable, responsible, mutually respecting
persons could agree upon as a fair basis for reciprocal relations in a
moral community. Even if universal agreement cannot be found, we do

[9] Kant's formulations of his basic principle of morality, the Categorical Imperative,
are in G, 88–9 [421–2], 96 [429], 98–9 [431], and 100–2 [433–4].

our best if we live by the principles that, in honest deliberation and dialogue, we would recommend for universal agreement.

These ideas are far from a complete framework for moral deliberation, and they do not always yield quick and easy answers. Nevertheless, I believe that they are a crucial part of a reasonable framework for further thinking about moral problems.

BIBLIOGRAPHY

Adams, Robert M., 'Common Projects and Moral Virtue', *Midwest Studies in Philosophy*, 13 (1988), 297–307.

Allison, Henry, *Kant's Theory of Freedom* (Cambridge: Cambridge University Press, 1990).

Aristotle, *Nicomachean Ethics*, in Richard McKeon (ed.), *The Basic Works of Aristotle* (New York: Random House, 1941), 935–1112.

Arntzen, Sven, 'Kant's Denial of Absolute Sovereignty', *Pacific Philosophical Quarterly*, 76 (1995), 1–16.

Baron, Marcia, 'Kantian Ethics and Supererogation', *Journal of Philosophy*, 84 (1987), 237–62.

Bennett, Jonathan, 'The Conscience of Huckleberry Finn', in Christina Hoff Sommers and Fred Sommers (eds.), *Vice and Virtue in Everyday Life*, 3rd edn. (New York: Harcourt Brace Jovanovich, 1993), 25–39.

Bentham, Jeremy, *'A Fragment on Government' and 'An Introduction to the Principles of Morals and Legislation'*, ed. Wilfrid Harrison (Oxford: Blackwell Publishers, 1960).

Bittner, Rudiger, *What Reason Demands* (Cambridge: Cambridge University Press, 1989).

Brandt, Richard, *Ethical Theory* (Englewood Cliffs, NJ: Prentice-Hall, 1959).

——*A Theory of the Good and the Right* (Oxford: Clarendon Press, 1979).

——'Toward a Credible Form of Utilitarianism', in Hector-Neri Castañeda and George Nakhnikian (eds.), *Morality and the Language of Conduct* (Detroit: Wayne State University Press, 1965), 107–43.

Byrd, B. Sharon, 'Kant's Theory of Punishment: Deterrence in its Threat, Retribution in its Execution', *Law and Philosophy*, 8 (1980), 151–200.

Cummiskey, David, 'Kantian Consequentialism', *Ethics*, 100 (1990), 586–615.

——*Kantian Consequentialism* (New York: Oxford University Press, 1996).

Darwall, Stephen L., 'Two Concepts of Respect', *Ethics*, 88 (1977), 36–49.

Dean, Richard, 'What should we Treat as an End in Itself?', *Pacific Philosophical Quarterly*, 77 (1996), 268–88.

Donagan, Alan, *Choice: The Essential Element in Human Action* (London: Routledge and Kegan Paul, 1987).

——'Comments on Dan Brock and Terrence Reynolds', *Ethics*, 95 (1985), 874–86.

——'Consistency in Rationalist Moral Systems', *Journal of Philosophy*, 81 (1984), 291–309.

——'Moral Dilemmas, Genuine and Spurious: A Comparative Anatomy', *Ethics*, 104 (1993), 7–21.

Donagan, Alan, 'Moral Rationalism and Variable Social Institutions', *Midwest Studies in Philosophy*, 7 (1982), 3–10.

——'The Relation of Moral Theory to Moral Judgments: A Kantian Review', in Baruch Brody (ed.), *Moral Theory and Moral Judgments in Medical Ethics* (Dordrecht: Kluwer Academic Publishers, 1988), 171–92.

——'The Structure of Kant's *Metaphysics of Morals*', *Topoi*, 4 (1985), 61–72.

——*The Theory of Morality* (Chicago: University of Chicago Press, 1977).

Duncan, A. R. C., *Practical Reason and Morality* (Edinburgh: Nelson, 1957).

Feinberg, Joel, 'The Expressive Function of Punishment', in Joel Feinberg, *Doing and Deserving* (Princeton, NJ: Princeton University Press, 1971), 95–118.

Firth, Roderick, 'Ethical Absolutism and the Ideal Observer', *Philosophy and Phenomenological Research*, 12 (1952), 317–45.

Frankena, William K., *Ethics* (Englewood Cliffs, NJ: Prentice-Hall, 1973).

Hampton, Jean, 'The Moral Education Theory of Punishment', *Philosophy and Public Affairs*, 13 (1984), 208–38.

Hare, R. M., *Freedom and Reason* (Oxford: Oxford University Press, 1963).

——*Moral Thinking* (Oxford: Clarendon Press, 1981).

Hart, H. L. A., 'Prolegomenon to the Principles of Punishment', in H. L. A. Hart, *Punishment and Responsibility* (New York: Oxford University Press, 1968), 1–27.

——and Honoré, A. M., *Causation in the Law* (Oxford: Clarendon Press, 1959).

Herman, Barbara, *The Practice of Moral Judgment* (Cambridge, Mass.: Harvard University Press, 1993).

Hill, Thomas E., Jr., *Autonomy and Self-respect* (Cambridge: Cambridge University Press, 1991).

——*Dignity and Practical Reason in Kant's Moral Theory* (Ithaca, NY: Cornell University Press, 1992).

——'Four Conceptions of Conscience', *Nomos XL: Integrity and Conscience* (New York: New York University Press, 1998), 13–52.

——'Moral Dilemmas, Gaps, and Residues', in H. E. Mason (ed.), *Moral Dilemmas and Moral Theory* (Oxford: Oxford University Press, 1996), 167–98.

——'Reasonable Self-interest', *Social Philosophy and Policy*, 14 (1997), 52–85.

Hobbes, Thomas, *Leviathan*, ed. Michael Oakeshott (New York: Macmillan Publishing Co., 1962).

Holtman, Sarah, 'Toward Social Reform: Kant's Penal Theory Reinterpreted', *Utilitas*, 9 (1997), 3–21.

Hruschka, Joachim, 'Imputation', *Brigham Young University Law Review* (1986), 699–710.

Joerden, Jan C., 'Zwei Formeln in Kants Zurechnungslehre', *Archiv für Rechts- und Sozialphilosophie*, 77 (1991), 525–38.

Kant, Immanuel, *Anthropology from a Pragmatic Point of View*, tr. Mary Gregor (The Hague: Martinus Nijhoff, 1974).

——'The Contest of the Faculties', in Hans Reiss (ed.), *Kant: Political Writings* (Cambridge: Cambridge University Press, 1991), 176–90.

——*Critique of Judgment*, tr. Werner S. Pluhar (Indianapolis: Hackett Publishing Co., 1987).

——*Critique of Practical Reason*, 3rd edn., tr. Lewis White Beck (New York: Macmillan Publishing Co., 1993).

——*Kants gesammelte Schriften*, ed. under the auspices of the Königliche Preussische Akademie der Wissenschaften (Berlin: Walter de Gruyter, 1908–13).

——*Groundwork of the Metaphysics of Morals*, tr. H. J. Paton (New York: Harper and Row, 1964).

——'Idea for a Universal History with a Cosmopolitan Purpose', in Hans Reiss (ed.), *Kant: Political Writings* (Cambridge: Cambridge University Press, 1991), 41–53.

——*Kant's Philosophical Correspondence 1759–99*, ed. and tr. Arnulf Zweig (Chicago: University of Chicago Press, 1967).

——*Lectures on Ethics*, tr. Louis Infield (New York: Harper and Row, 1963).

——*The Metaphysics of Morals*, tr. Mary Gregor (Cambridge: Cambridge University Press, 1996).

——*Observations on the Feeling of the Beautiful and the Sublime*, tr. John T. Goldwait (Berkeley: University of California Press, 1960).

——'On a Supposed Right to Lie because of Philanthropic Concerns', in Immanuel Kant, *Grounding of the Metaphysic of Morals*, tr. James Ellington, 3rd edn. (Indianapolis: Hackett Publishing Co., 1993), 63–7.

——'Perpetual Peace', in Hans Reiss (ed.), *Kant: Political Writings* (Cambridge: Cambridge University Press, 1991), 93–130.

——*Religion within the Limits of Reason Alone*, tr. Theodore M. Green and Hoyt H. Hudson (New York: Harper and Row, 1960).

——'Theory and Practice', in Hans Reiss (ed.), *Kant: Political Writings* (Cambridge: Cambridge University Press, 1991), 61–92.

——'What is Enlightenment?', in Hans Reiss (ed.), *Kant: Political Writings* (Cambridge: Cambridge University Press, 1991), 54–60.

Korsgaard, Christine, *Creating the Kingdom of Ends* (Cambridge: Cambridge University Press, 1996).

Ladd, John (ed.), *Relativism* (Belmont, Calif.: Wadsworth, 1973).

Lyons, David, *Forms and Limits of Utilitarianism* (Oxford: Clarendon Press, 1965).

MacIntyre, Alasdair, *After Virtue*, 2nd edn. (Notre Dame, Ind.: University of Notre Dame Press, 1984).

Moore, G. E., *Ethics* (Oxford: Oxford University Press, 1912).

——*Principia Ethica* (Cambridge: Cambridge University Press, 1903).

Morris, Herbert, 'Persons and Punishment', *Monist*, 52 (1968), 475–501.

Murphy, Jeffrie G., 'Does Kant have a Theory of Punishment?', *Columbia Law Review*, 87 (1987), 509–12.

——*Kant: The Philosophy of Right* (London and New York: Macmillan, 1970).

Murphy, Jeffrie G., 'Kant's Theory of Criminal Punishment', in Jeffrie G. Murphy, *Retribution, Justice, and Therapy: Essays in the Philosophy of Law* (Dordrecht and Boston: D. Reidel Publishing Co., 1979), 82–92.

Nagel, Thomas, 'Sexual Perversion', *Journal of Philosophy*, 66 (1969), 5–17.

Nell [O'Neill], Onora, *Acting on Principle* (New York: Columbia University Press, 1975).

O'Neill, Onora, *Constructions of Reason* (Cambridge: Cambridge University Press, 1989).

Paton, H. J., *The Categorical Imperative* (London: Hutchison and Co., 1958).

Potter, Nelson T., and Timmons, Mark (eds.), *Morality and Universality: Essays on Ethical Universalizability* (New York: Atheneum, 1971).

Rachels, James, *Elements of Moral Philosophy* (New York: Random House, 1986).

Rawls, John, *Political Liberalism* (New York: Columbia University Press, 1993).

——'Themes in Kant's Moral Philosophy', in Eckhart Forster (ed.), *Kant's Transcendental Deductions* (Stanford, Calif.: Stanford University Press, 1989), 81–113.

——*A Theory of Justice* (Cambridge, Mass.: Harvard University Press, 1971).

——'Two Concepts of Rules', *Philosophical Review*, 64 (1955), 3–32.

Reath, Andrews, 'Kant's Principles for the Imputation of Consequences', *Jahrbuch für Recht und Ethik*, 2 (1994), 159–76.

Ross, W. D., *The Right and the Good* (Oxford: Clarendon Press, 1930).

Rousseau, Jean-Jacques, *The Social Contract*, tr. Donald Cress (Indianapolis: Hackett Publishing Co., 1988).

Scheid, Donald, 'Kant's Retributivism', *Ethics*, 93 (1983), 262–82.

Sherman, Nancy, 'The Virtues of Common Pursuits', *Philosophy and Phenomenological Research*, 53 (1993), 277–99.

Stocker, Michael, 'The Schizophrenia of Modern Moral Theories', *Journal of Philosophy*, 73 (1976), 453–66.

Williams, Bernard, 'Persons, Character, and Morality', in Amelie Oksenberg Rorty (ed.), *The Identities of Persons* (Berkeley: University of California Press, 1976), 197–216.

Williams, T. C., *The Concept of the Categorical Imperative* (Oxford: Clarendon Press, 1968).

Wong, David, *Moral Relativity* (Berkeley: University of California Press, 1984).

INDEX